THE
BEAUX-ARTS
and nineteenth-century French architecture

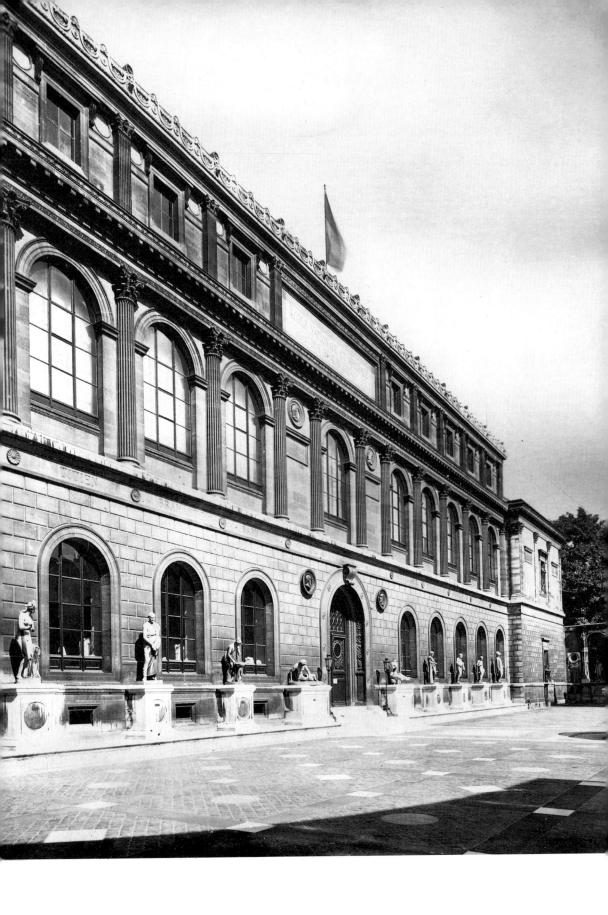

THE
BEAUX-ARTS

and nineteenth-century French architecture

Edited by

ROBIN MIDDLETON

The M I T Press

Cambridge, Massachusetts

1 (frontispiece)   F. Duban. Façade of the Palais
des Etudes, Ecole des Beaux-Arts, Paris, 1833–39.

First MIT Press edition, 1982

First published by Thames and Hudson, London
© 1982   R.D. Middleton   Joseph Rykwert   Werner Szambien
Georges Teyssot   Helene Lipstadt   Annie Jacques   Neil Levine
C. Marmoz   David Van Zanten   B. Bergdoll

Printed and bound in Great Britain

Library of Congress catalog card number: 81-82327

ISBN 0-262-13173-0

Contents

Introduction

R. D. Middleton

THE ARCHITECTURE OF 19th-century France has been but fitfully and inadequately studied. Until a few years ago the general account offered and accepted was not very different from that provided in 1889 by Lucien Magne in *L'architecture française du siècle*. The relevant chapters of André Michel's *Histoire de l'art* of 1926, and Henry-Russell Hitchcock's *Architecture: nineteenth and twentieth centuries* of 1958, are, equally, no more than variations and elaborations of that earlier framework. More information has been provided but no enhanced understanding. The publication of Louis Hautecoeur's *Histoire de l'architecture classique en France*, in particular the last two volumes, of 1955 and 1957, might have been expected to produce dramatic changes. And there was, indeed, a change. The sheer mass of information and detailed knowledge compacted into those books enlarged one's vision of building activity in 19th-century France as never before. But Hautecoeur's work, at best, can be regarded only as encyclopaedic. He was not concerned with ideas. He avoided as far as possible any discussion of architectural theory and was himself altogether averse to offering interpretations – for which we might, perhaps, be thankful. Any real grasp of the intricacies and complexity of architectural development during the period has remained a chimera. Simple facts alone have been adduced. And even these could not always be relied upon – slack proofreading as well as hasty research was to blame. Though far more unnerving was the evident failure to consult original documents, surviving drawings and family papers, even when these were available. Hautecoeur's history is built largely on the standard published sources; it is a useful resumé, no more. No inkling of the passionate adventure of spirit and emotion embodied in such buildings as Labrouste's Bibliothèque Ste-Geneviève, Duc's Palais de Justice or Garnier's Opéra is allowed to ruffle his pages. For any more personal or idiosyncratic interpretation anyone even marginally interested in French architecture of the period has had to rely on the scattered pages and paragraphs offered in Sigfried Giedion's *Space, Time and Architecture – the growth of a new tradition*, which appeared first in 1941 and then over and over again. Succeeding generations of architects have all too eagerly accepted and relied on his maverick interpretations. With the publication, in 1977, of *The Architecture of the Ecole des Beaux-Arts*, edited by Arthur Drexler – until then custodian of the orthodoxy of the Modern Movement at the Museum of Modern Art in New York – the sheer silliness of Giedion's account was laid bare.

There, Neil Levine's essay in particular, brilliantly unravelling the complex of aims and attitudes involved in the making of Labrouste's Bibliothèque Ste-Geneviève, underlined the inadequacies of Giedion's and all other interpretations, though even Levine's analysis I would judge as partial and constrained – I am thinking especially of his refusal to take proper account, not make mere acknowledgment, of utopian socialist thought in the evolution of Labrouste's conceptions. Moreover, Levine's obsessions have a madness of their own; but they are at once a challenge and liberation from all other banal and propagandist summaries. He, alone almost, has opened up the architecture of 19th-century France to speculation and enhanced understanding.

In France itself, in recent years, much speculation has been indulged in and much money provided for a range of extraordinary research projects. These have, on the whole, been of the inadequate kind. But it is in that country, ultimately, that the basic research will have to be done and is, indeed, now being undertaken. Viollet-le-Duc was exposed recently to public gaze in a whole series of exhibitions to mark the centenary of his death. Family papers passed then into public museums, local archives were filleted to establish the provenance and dates of his buildings, and much inquisitive zeal was aroused. We now know, reasonably well, what he did. But the springs of his activity have not been examined, nor have the notions and theories that are his greatest claim to fame. Viollet-le-Duc is only one of a whole range of dominant figures who urgently require investigation and assessment. If all the new activity has brought us only marginally closer to a real knowledge of his work, how murky must be our insight, how crude our perception of the endeavours of those other commanding figures? And what of that whole range of less spectacular architectural works and those organizations and institutions that conditioned the pattern and form of development in 19th-century France? There have been one or two attempts in the past few years to record the history of building in provincial towns – Auxerre and Rennes – but not enough exploration to make possible any comparative study or useful synthesis. The Conseil des Bâtiments Civils has stirred no historian, nor has the Service des Edifices Diocésains. The studies that have been done are far too tentative. Clearly this is not the time to expect anything of a useful or convincing general theoretical character. Historians will have to continue instead to establish the facts, and to make particular interpretations within circumscribed areas. The present collection of essays, all of a somewhat different and heterogeneous nature, is a part of such a programme. They emerged from a conference on the Ecole des Beaux-Arts and its influence held at the Architectural Association in London in May 1978, the outcome, in turn, of the interest aroused by an exhibition organized two and a half years earlier at the Museum of Modern Art. The information and occasional insights they offer will help, I hope, to change to just that degree our inner image of 19th-century France. In reading them it is important to bear in mind always that the cultural context of France was very different indeed from that of England, or for that matter the USA. Nineteenth-century architectural studies are well advanced in these two countries, in England especially; and all too readily are the phases of development and the criteria recognized there taken as the model for what happened in France. Some of the buildings might look similar,

but the contexts within which they were designed were totally unlike. In France an intellectual tradition was strong in architectural circles, which makes for a difference of approach. That tendency to centralize power and establish control in Paris, which is so much a feature of all French operations from the mid-17th century onwards, is of prime importance in the history of 19th-century architecture, starting with the teaching establishments such as the Ecole Polytechnique and the Ecole des Beaux-Arts, and continuing with those institutions which were the chief patrons of architecture – the Conseil des Bâtiments Civils, the Commission des Monuments Historiques, the Service des Edifices Diocésains and of course the State, in the form of Prefectures and other such bodies. The Académie served as the ultimate arbiter. Very few buildings of interest were commissioned by private individuals or firms. The plans that were inspected and passed by the committees of the great institutions were controlled, altogether effectively, by a very small number of men. However opposed their opinions might have been as individuals, together they established an extraordinary degree of architectural uniformity throughout France.

Those architects in whom leadership might be said to have been vested were institutionalized – or rather they worked within an institutional framework. They were restricted by law from undertaking more than one major commission at a time, which meant in effect that they devoted far more energy and care than their counterparts in England to each of their major works. Despite all institutional limitations, their buildings embody more of their individual sensibility and creative endeavour than the works of their foreign contemporaries. And this was a considered aim of the French system. The great public buildings were conceived of as paradigms. They should, rightly, command our attention. The myriad village churches, country houses, suburban residences and cottages which constitute the force of the architectural language in 19th-century England are not paralleled in France. The major architects there scarcely indulged in building of that sort, and, if they did, regarded it as subsidiary work. This, of course, should make research and analysis all the easier; instead it demands an even greater degree of precision in determining aims and assessing the extent of fulfilment.

2   P. Delaroche. Painting in the hemicycle (Salle des Prix) of the Ecole des Beaux-Arts, late 1830s, photographed in 1929.

I

The Ecole des Beaux-Arts and the classical tradition

Joseph Rykwert

THE CONCEPT OF TRADITION and the definition of classicism are both hazy enough to make you wonder whether the 'and' in my title implies a joining or a separation. You would almost be justified in asking whether there *can* be any necessary connection between the chimera of a classical tradition and that clearly defined institution, the Ecole des Beaux-Arts, which retreated, irrevocably, into history after 1968.

But look at it from another point of view: imagine yourself in the tribune of the hemicycle in the Ecole. This was its spiritual centre, and the speaker from that tribune had before him not only the body of students and his colleagues, but also the panorama of all the great artists of the past, painted in the smoothest and the dryest manner of Paul Delaroche, a pupil of Baron Gros and the master of Jacques-François Millet; smooth and dry the figures are, but also 'natural', disposed in relaxed attitudes and looking benevolently down on their putative successors. No wonder all Viollet-le-Duc's eloquence failed him in that setting and his lectures ended in fiasco.

Delaroche's programme, the choice of the great masters, imposed itself obviously: he could draw on Pliny's last few books for antiquity, and on Vasari for more recent times. Few exotic artists' names were generally known in the late 1830s when the painting was done; and few medieval ones, for that matter: Giotto, Duccio and Cimabue. And they fitted comfortably enough within what at that time could pass for classical. Though when W. M. Thackeray visited the school, and wrote with some disapproval that 'all was classical', he had in mind the exclusive dependence on ancient myth for the programmes in the painting school.

The visitor who approached the hemicycle through the Palais des Etudes had to pass through a room filled with plaster casts of ancient statuary and architecture. All this indicates a measure of agreement about what the incipient artist, whatever his skill, was to be presented with as exemplary.

Not that any reference to the Middle Ages was to be excluded from his attention. Delaroche painted many medieval subjects himself, mostly taken from French and Italian history; though you may remember also his pathetic picture of the two princes in the Tower awaiting their murderer.

Delaroche was sure in the possession of his cultural heritage. And in fact, by his time the word 'classic' had assumed the meaning that we now tend to give it. Its first comprehensive definition, which gave the word instant currency, was in the Diderot and D'Alembert *Encyclopédie*, in an article written by Chesneau du Marsais; it provided the obligatory reference to ancient grammarians, to naval affairs – since *classis* was a ship, and *classici* was a name for sailors – and to social or income classes. But Chesneau starts with a particular French usage: classics are authors who are taught in class, exemplary authors. This is the older usage sanctified by the Académie dictionary, which goes on to suggest (following Voltaire) that the name applies particularly to the best authors of the reign of Louis XIV. That is the sense of the word which Sainte-Beuve picks up in 1850, when he embarks on a closer approach to describing what makes a classic. There is little that is better in the many volumes of the *Lundis*. His only two exemplars are literary: Racine's *Athalie*, and Bossuet's *Discourse on Universal History*. Since, however, it is architectural classicism that I speak of, these examples must remain glosses. I quote them because in the Ecole the many difficulties which literary critics over the last century experienced in circumscribing this difficult word were easily avoided. In a lecture, for instance, which we must take as magisterial for the Ecole, since it was Julien Guadet's inaugural one – first given in November 1894 and reprinted in all subsequent editions of his *Cours* – he offers 'that basis of logic which can only be acquired by studying the classics' as the remedy against all the vagaries of unlicensed imagination. But even Guadet will not take the word for granted, since to him the beautiful title 'classic' is of course the definitive canonization of a work of art. This canonization, he goes on, is never decreed: it is self-evident, *il s'impose*. It is beyond any constraint of period or place. Or if you would prefer another of his aphorisms, it is all that remains victorious in the eternal battles of art and in possession of a universally declared admiration. His candidates for this canonization are Dante, Shakespeare and Sophocles. For us architects, he continues with a fine show of latitudinarianism, it is the Parthenon and the Roman baths and amphitheatres, but it is also Sancta Sophia and Notre-Dame, it is St Ouen at Rouen as well as St Peter's or the Palazzo Farnese in Rome and the Louvre in Paris. Such liberality and inclusiveness, he says, have always been the generous and philosophical conception of the Ecole; since – and here Guadet must have pointed to Delaroche's panorama above the students' heads with an inclusive wave of the hand – in this painting, which is the pantheon of art, the unquestioned masters of all art have been grouped to preside over the students' studies.

Such grandiloquent gestures usually evade pressing questions. The reputations of artists are not quite as gilt-edged as Guadet would have had his students believe: several of the brilliantly lit figures in that painting have retired from the first rank; other giants have emerged. That is not the point at issue, however. Let me suggest my first real difficulty. A universal past, free from any value except an abstract excellence, is chimerical. And Guadet's preferences, though implicit, are quite clear. I don't wish to bore you with figures, but I will cite as one example the first volume of his lectures, which has 541 numbered figures. Of these, 80 or thereabouts are explanatory diagrams, leaving 460 examples; about 20 of these are what you might call exotic: Byzantine, Turkish, Chinese; and 40 are medieval European ones. The rest are either antique – that is Greek

and Roman – or of the Renaissance and after. You will have to take it on trust that the same goes for the rest of the book; even when he discusses vaulted churches, when you might justifiably think that Guadet was *bound* to show many medieval examples, you will be surprised how he manages to avoid them. And then some only appear as negative instances: S. Michele in Lucca (which Guadet wrongly calls the cathedral) is only shown as an example of the lie in architecture. To be fair, he finds the same fault committed by Perrault in the great eastern façade of the Louvre, where the articulation by columns does not correspond to the interior articulation of the section. A lie, which, he tells his students, the ancients *never* committed.

Demonstrable and evident a falsehood as his account of the lie is, it is nonetheless interesting in itself. And of course, later, when discussing the orders of architecture, Guadet has to eat his words when he considers the Doric order, which, in spite of any special pleading, he describes in the conventional way, as a stone construction that perpetuates a repertory of wooden forms. Compare his peremptory and superficial treatment of the origin of the orders with the infinitely more thoughtful and sensitive treatment of the same material by Auguste Choisy, fifteen years before Guadet's lecture; and which Choisy summed up in a masterly way in his general history of architecture. Choisy was an uncompromising positivist; there was nothing so thoroughgoing about the soft-edged Guadet. For himself, he seems to have preferred other accounts of the origin of the orders, such as had been worked out by J.-B. Lesueur. Lesueur, one of Percier's pupils, whose virtuous republican parents had baptized him Jean-Baptiste as well as Cicero, attempted to derive a wholly stone Doric order from Egyptian precedent (a suggestion already made much earlier by Heinrich Hübsch, a pupil of F. Weinbrenner at Karlsruhe). Both Lesueur and Hübsch are better known as successful practitioners than as archaeological theorists: Lesueur as the rebuilder of the Hôtel de Ville in Paris, and Hübsch as the one who completed Karlsruhe and built Baden-Baden. It is, I think, a clear mark of the generation break that Hübsch and Lesueur still attempted detailed archaeological research, as did Cockerell and even Viollet-le-Duc. In Guadet's time the professor of architectural theory could dismiss such

3   J. Guadet. Alpine Hospice, Grand Prix exercise, 1864: elevation.

speculations, which he called archaeological, with contempt in the interest of a higher architectural truth.

Guadet, in his lectures, was offering a unified view of theory and practice, in which he spoke for the whole of the Ecole. His legislation was tyrannical and absolute. He had been teaching in his *atelier* as professor for over twenty years when the school council appointed him to the chair of theory. The four volumes of the *Cours* to which I have referred are a summary of his views, and it has remained in use since its first publication at the beginning of the century. If I may digress, personally, for a moment, I shall confess that in 1969, when the Ecole and all its works seemed quite overthrown, I asked a Paris bookseller if it were possible *now* to buy a copy of Guadet cheaply. On the contrary, he said, the four volumes had much risen in price since the May events; 'after all', he justified the change, 'theory is to be all the vogue again, and there is no other book on theory, is there?'

We must therefore reckon with Guadet's work, however unsympathetic we may find it, not only as a summary account which dominated the Ecole and therefore in a way all architectural discussion for three generations, but also as one which continues to work its influence even in our time. Its real force lies in an assertion which has not been seriously examined: it presents to the student as well as to the practitioner only that which is absolute

and beyond any doubt. No controversial material is included between its covers. That is Guadet's boast. He is a self-confessed enemy of speculation. With some pride he writes in his inaugural lecture of the part that he played as a young man in eliminating the influence of Hippolyte Taine from the Ecole; Taine, the most influential positivist philosopher, was appointed to the chair of theory and aesthetics after Viollet-le-Duc's withdrawal.

Urbanity and exactitude were the qualities which Taine saw as the hallmarks of a young classicism: the very words were coined when the Académie Française had been instituted at Richelieu's behest. But urbanity and exactitude were too finicky and too pedantic criteria for criticism such as Guadet's. And, in fact, all that Taine and Sainte-Beuve and their contemporaries exalted as classicism, which in literature reached its peak at the beginning of Louis XIV's majority, and may be taken to last until the death of Racine – all that is only a shadow to the men of the Ecole. They had really become separated from the intellectual life of Paris. Let me remind you, to restore the balance a little, that Guadet's Grand Prix exercise, the Alpine Hospice, was almost con- 3 temporary with Manet's *Olympia*. And when he gave his inaugural lecture, Van Gogh, Gauguin and Seurat were already dead, men of whom no sign will be found in anything that emanates from the Ecole.

I do not wish to be factious. But think of it:

in 1894, Richardson's work was done, as was the bulk of Sullivan's. Horta had built the Tassel house. And yet, unperturbably, Guadet imparted four volumes' full of the absolute to the eager students, who apparently regarded his teaching as being beyond the corrosive influence of doubt.

If I may look more closely at this operation; after some preliminary, and quite elementary, instructions, he proceeds to reprint his inaugural lecture. He goes on then to the main rules of composition: general proportions first and specific ones after; proportions of interiors follow, and the general principles of structure. Then simple elements: walls, and wall openings such as doors; column runs (and, therefore, colonnades and arcades); roofs and vaults, and what he calls secondary elements. Then, for two volumes, he describes building types, and ends with an inductive chapter, which turns out to be an account of circulation areas, vertical and horizontal. After this, there is a chapter on façades, and the whole book ends with an account of professional practice. But his rather loose structure does not allow us to account for the nature of Guadet's authority. I must, therefore, ask your indulgence to look at one symptomatic detail, and that is his treatment of columns. Of the seventy illustrations in that section, only five are of Gothic buildings, of which the first, the Doge's Palace in Venice, is only there to suggest that buttresses or piers at the corners would have been a more *logical* way of dealing with the lateral thrust in that building than the iron ties that run between its columns. Later in the book, he has words of praise for other details of the Doge's Palace. But the bulk of the section's many illustrations deal with the orders. The orders, he says, are the acme and the synthesis of the study of columns and colonnades. Why this should be so is not explained. May I remind you that we are dealing with absolute and incontrovertible assertion. When he comes to the Ionic order he dispenses his readers from considering the legendary origins of the Doric order in a male figure, and the Ionic in a female one. He allows that there may have been ethnic preferences for one order over the other which would account for the names; and even that there may be some association between strength in one and grace in the other. But the hoary Vitruvian myth he regards as unworthy of his serious attention.

Now this was not the view of the architects in the past, nor even of their public. Writing to his patron, Jean Fréart, Lord of Chantelou, Nicolas Poussin invites him to take in all beautiful things at his leisure: 'The pretty girls you will have seen in Nîmes will not have pleased you any less, I am sure, than the fine columns of the Maison Carrée, since these last are only ancient copies of the youthful first.' Poussin was never vague, and he was not just nudging his patron suggestively; on the contrary, he was referring to another passage in Vitruvius which derives the proportions of the Corinthian order from a graceful maiden. But such references are in fact separate instances of a major truth. Chantelou himself pays homage to it some twenty years later when he writes to his brother, the Lord of Chambray, about his mission to welcome the great Bernini on his journey to Paris. When the great man had left his litter for the coach, after the preliminary compliments, he made a little speech in which he assured Chantelou that the beauty of all things in the world, including architecture, lay in proportion; that it would even be right to maintain that it is a divine part, since it has its origin in Adam's body, which was not only made by God's hand, but modelled on his image and likeness; and that the variety of the different orders of architecture derived from the varieties in male and female bodies, 'and he added many things on this matter which we know well enough'. These rather casual remarks show what Poussin, and Bernini, and the two Fréart brothers took for granted, as did most of their contemporaries: that the orders, and all of architecture in fact, was guaranteed, sanctioned by a natural seal. Architecture was the shelter of the human body and was also its likeness. The ancients had stated it in detail, explicitly in the text of Vitruvius; and the text was borne out by the monuments. The natural proof was not enough however; not only in nature, but in the very making of buildings, the rightness of the antique models was demonstrated, since they bore in the details of the orders the marks of having been first made in a remote and golden past by venerable ancestors, whose first actions were guarantors of the designers' procedure as powerful as the example of nature.

Both arguments could be traced back to man's account of himself and of his origin, an account which all the men involved in building – from Alberti to Jacques-François Blondel – accepted with few, if notable, exceptions. One was the searing intelligence of Descartes, which left its mark on architecture, though he had little to say about it himself. In the generation which followed him, Claude Perrault overthrew the magnificent fabric of a harmony between the noble senses of hearing and of seeing; it was a harmony that was regarded as another, and equally powerful, guarantor of the rightness of antique example, since its discovery was credited both to the Greek mathematician-philosopher Pythagoras, and to the musical blacksmith of Scripture, Tubal-Cain. The orders, on Perrault's showing, could not be dispensed with, however; they were the nearest thing architecture could show to a *habitus*. They were the moral guarantee that the wilful fancy of man could be restrained, could be checked, by the reasonable exercise of a rational authority. The orders and the authority of Vitruvius were essential to the creation of an educated taste, since it was to taste, the irrational faculty in all of us, that the architect addressed himself. But the social aesthetic that he created, the philosophy of art which corresponded to the desire of the French for both a grandiose and a plain style of architecture – an architecture which would commemorate the glories of the greatest monarch on earth – did not outlast the climax of that reign. The radical questioning of Perrault was unacceptable to the majority of his successors, however much they admired the details of his achievement.

Within his lifetime a reply had come to some of his postulates: the great Newton himself revived the harmony between the noble senses when he proposed an exact correspondence between the seven colours of the spectrum and the seven notes of the octave. It became the justification of some later speculation on the orders; and, in fact, throughout the 18th century the newly recorded exotic architectures, as well as the domestic and apparently barbarous ones, could be rationalized, incorporated and renewed when treated in such terms.

Inevitably, I abbreviate and therefore caricature. Still, it is the most notable glorifier of Newton in the visual arts who shows how sturdy the old beliefs were. Etienne-Louis Boullée, writing about the time of the Revolution, suggests that the rational programme for teaching architecture would begin with inviting the student to draw the primitive hut described by Vitruvius, followed by plans and sections and structural details, thus demonstrating to the student that his art is firmly based in nature. Boullée's language still echoes the ideas of the previous ages, even in his deliberate and wilful misreading of Perrault's theoretical writings. But all this was to come to an end with Boullée's pupil, Jean-Nicolas-Louis Durand. There is, of course, something paradoxical in invoking him, since he taught not at the Ecole des Beaux-Arts or any of its predecessors but at the Ecole Polytechnique. There are good and important reasons why it was the Ecole Polytechnique, not the Ecole des Beaux-Arts, which welcomed the most radical architectural thinker. The new school of architecture under the Revolution, which survived the hard times the old academies experienced under the Convention, was led by David Leroy, who had visited Greece to produce the first reliable – more or less – survey of Greek architecture for the use of architects; and, for the younger men, by Charles Percier, who, with his partner Pierre-François-Léonard Fontaine, was to create that memorable new style for the Empire of Napoleon, with which Europe would echo for several decades. And Percier, who was a close acquaintance of Durand, may be taken to share some of his ideas, which would have percolated to students of architecture as well as to their teachers.

Since Durand's course of lectures on architecture, read before students in military uniform, was the most complete statement, perhaps the only complete statement, of an architectural theory at the crucial moment of historical change, it is almost too neat to find that his systematic teaching turns against the brief reflexions on the teaching of architecture which his master and friend, Boullée, had written only months previously.

The attack on the notion of the primitive hut occupies much of Durand's attention in the early part of his course. Having once disposed of the way in which the architect's operation is rooted in the past, he invites him to jettison the link with nature: the orders are in no way related to any concept of imitation. His dismissal of this link with nature is much more firm and much more explicit than Guadet's was to be. The orders were acceptable only because they had become a necessity through force of habit.

This is an echo of Perrault, of course, an

29

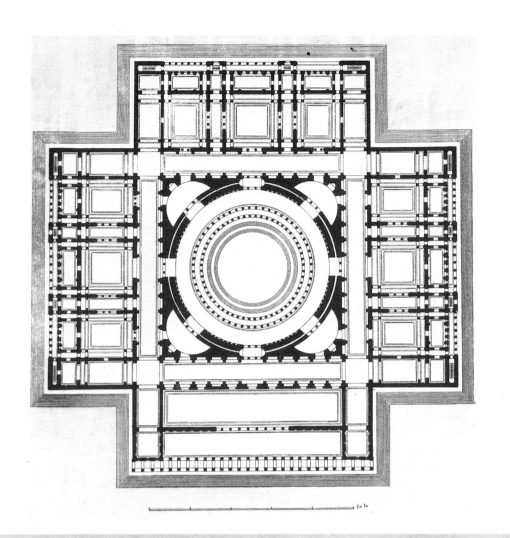

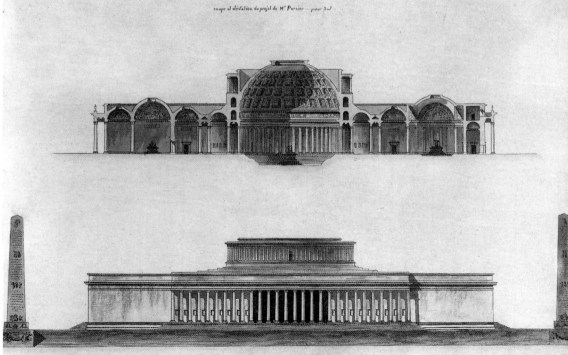

coupe et élévation du projet de Mr Percier — partie Sud.

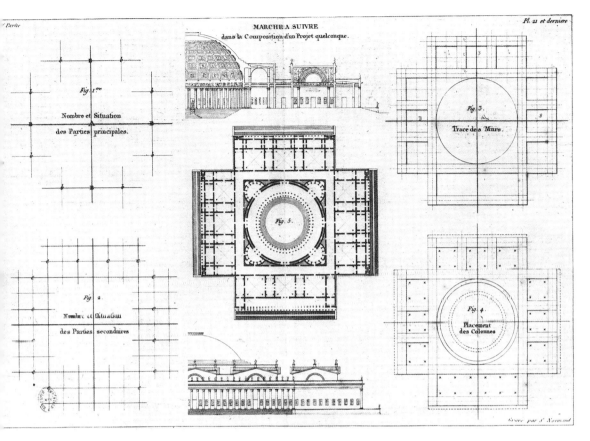

4, 5 (facing page)   C. Percier. Monument destiné à rassembler les différentes académies, 1786: plan, section and elevation.

6   J.-N.-L. Durand. Marche à suivre dans la composition d'un projet quelconque, from the *Nouveau Précis*, 1813 – a regularization of his already simplified version of Percier's project (see ill. 15 and pp. 21–23).

echo which you may still detect in Guadet's rather dismissive tone. But there is perhaps more to be said here. Guadet and Durand both justify the orders in the same way, as the most obvious and most acceptable method of making columns of different sizes and shapes. Guadet's eclectic asides and parentheses, the way in which his treatise is padded with comparative material about functional types (a section of his book which Durand had in fact half promised to supply), should not deflect our attention from the close parallel between him and Durand. Not only is the treatment of the orders close to its original, but right at the very outset of the book, when he is merely describing the elementary drawing procedures, Guadet introduces the notion of axial drawing, and warns the student that he is to learn much more about it. And the careful reader will notice that in this section he proposes a *méthode à suivre*, which echoes the title of Durand's most important plate, headed *Marche à suivre*; here, in an analysis of a Grand Prix project of Charles Percier suitably adjusted to Durand's own manner, his method of design by composing elements on grid sections directed and organized by axes is explicitly set out.

I am unable to comment in detail on this plate now. It seems to me, however, to announce a whole revolution in attitudes to design, for which there is no precedent. It had been only thirty years, after all, since Pierre Patte published Jacques-François Blondel's course of lectures on architecture, in which the academic doctrine was set out according to the latest lights, but the great analogical structure of ideas was confirmed and rejustified. Of axes there is not a word, and little of grids. Certainly there is no indication of the sort of method which Durand was to set out with ruthless clarity. All previous ideas of architecture are to be discarded by Durand since they are to do with the pleasure of sensations. Imitation, which is the chief justification of such ideas, must be wholly abandoned when we talk about architecture. The method by which thinking and teaching is to proceed is that architecture must be analyzed down to its simplest components, which are of three kinds. The first is based on the nature of the materials, the second on the past, that is, on the force of habit. Both of these are approximate. To them a third is to be preferred, since it is easiest to understand and therefore most economical (you will forgive me if I risk carica-

ture again), and this is the repertory of elementary geometrical forms – of which the circle and sphere must have our absolute preference.

These forms we may then compose in various ways according to a particular method. It is a method from which there is no appeal. Nor is it a method which can be improved, tinkered with, or discussed. The steps are so tightly argued, the postulates so explicit, that it is only if we are prepared to question them that the whole system begins to shake.

Between Guadet and Durand there is a century exactly. Yet for the two writers, in spite of the blurring of edges over the years, the organization of the architect's work remains very similar. Neither Henri Labrouste nor Viollet-le-Duc, and certainly not A.-C. Quatremère de Quincy before them, had succeeded in modifying the cage which Durand had erected. Only in the method of drawing, since Durand had professed a puritan contempt for the wash rendering, was there any essential change.

What I would wish to argue, therefore, is that Durand had made a break with the past, a break perhaps more radical than that which Brunelleschi and Alberti had made four hundred years earlier, though the results of their rethinking of the architectural process are more evident to the naked eye.

The break occurs almost precisely at the turn of the century. And from that time on, in spite of various exceptions, the attitude propounded by Durand dominates architectural thinking to the exclusion of all others, since it proposes a wholly unhistorical, wholly a-prioristic approach to design, in which the procedure of the architect is wholly autonomous, and the past a mere repository of conventions.

The fixity of the intellectual structure, and the reduction of the past, puts me in mind of an aphorism of T. S. Eliot's. Tradition, he says, can't simply be inherited, it must be laboured for. You can't approach it without a historical sense; and a historical sense means that you appreciate the *pastness* of the past as well as its presence.

Now, to Eliot, these two notions are essentially separate and complementary. If you make the past a repository you deny its presence. And if the repository is one of present convention, you deny its pastness. In that sense the Ecole des Beaux-Arts denied the possibility of tradition in architecture in that vital sense in which Eliot spoke of it. In so far as a tradition in architecture can be called classical, it must rest on two analogies: of the building as a body, and of the design as a re-enactment of some primitive or – if you would rather – of some archetypal action to which our procedure might refer. From Vitruvius to Boullée, the texts suggest something of the kind, always in different contexts, since such ideas do not contain, or even imply, the repertory of norms and procedures which the constant alteration of circumstances forces you to renew, to rethink and to alter. I suspect that those of you who have followed me so far will have deduced the answer to my original question. Insofar as we can isolate something which in architecture can be called a classical tradition, then the Ecole des Beaux-Arts had very little to do with it. In fact, its father, its spiritual progenitor, though he stood outside its organization, based his total system of an ahistorical architecture on a denial and an overthrow of that tradition, confident that after the zero point of the Revolution a wholly rational architecture could be erected on absolutely valid laws. And that, perhaps paradoxically to some, seems to me the most unclassical thing about the Ecole. We must understand, wrote Friedrich Nietzsche, 'that all classical taste contains a certain dose of lucidity, frigidity, hardness; above all, logic and felicitous intellectual life. . . . Artistic forms are not to be played with; life is to be recreated so that it will of necessity express itself as a pattern.'

Taken in that sense, the Ecole des Beaux-Arts has stood for a century and a half as an all-too solid monument to the classical tradition. But some of us think that if it were dismantled, the tomb might turn out to have been empty all the time.

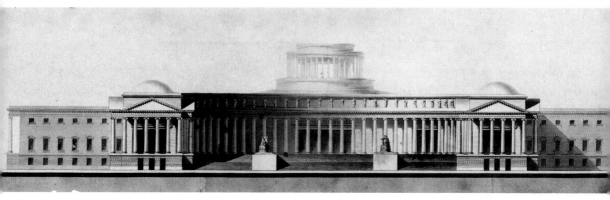

7   J.-N.-L. Durand. Museum, 1779: elevation. For the plan see ill. 10. (Beaux-Arts)

8, 9   M.-J. Peyre. Bâtiment qui contiendroit les académies, 1753, published in 1765: plan, and elevation of the central building.

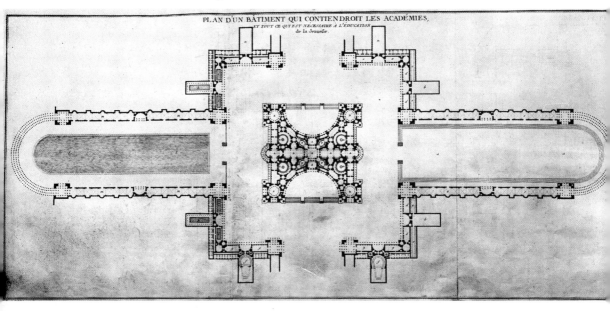

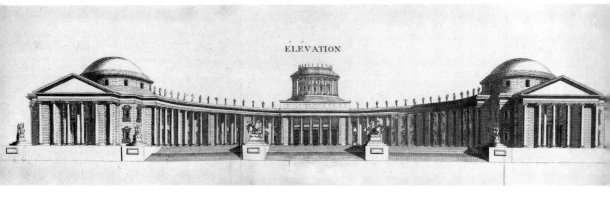

II

Durand and the continuity of tradition

Werner Szambien

IN STUDIES OF 18th- and 19th-century architecture, mention of Jean-Nicolas-Louis Durand (1760–1834)[1] is now almost obligatory, though to hail him as a new Vitruvius, as a critic has recently done, is something of an exaggeration.

Durand is usually thought to have broken the continuity of the classical tradition in architecture. I am not concerned here to isolate any such break. Breaks of this sort tend to be discerned when a more gradual process of transformation cannot be recognized, either because the true facts are not yet established, or because the subject is not closely enough studied. Adducing new information, I intend rather to review the question of rupture or continuity from a different point of view.

Durand began his career in the 1770s and was to finish it in the 1830s. Between his second Grand Prix, of 1779, and the construction of his country house at Thiais, in 1825,[2] Durand passed through several stages of development during which he rejected a range of traditional elements, while retaining others.

The complexity of his activity – and of his life – explains in part why Durand has been classified in so many different ways. He has been called a builder, a functionalist, a rationalist, a revolutionary architect, a utilitarian, and an architect of the rising bourgeoisie. He has been seen as the last exponent of classical architecture, as the begetter of modern functionalism; he has been set in the decline of the baroque tradition, and in the history of the rise of the engineer.[3]

Each of these descriptions contains a modicum of truth, but their multiplicity points to a certain confusion. This is because almost all information about him comes from his own publications[4] – as can be seen in the handful of articles[5] and the single chapter[6] that have been devoted to him. Most historians accept that Durand's influence was 'important'.

Durand should, of course, be assessed in relation to the teaching tradition of the 18th century, both at the Académie d'Architecture and at the Ecole des Ponts et Chaussées; his method should also be viewed in relation to the scientific instruction of Monge, Lagrange and Hassenfratz,[7] but here only an aspect of this architectural inheritance will be considered. In 1802, reviewing the *Précis*, Détournelle praised Durand as a man schooled in the good taste of J.-D. Leroy and M.-J. Peyre: 'The Ecole Polytechnique was thenceforward to become a kind of nursery, providing the necessary intellectual nourishment for those destined for greatness as engineers. They needed a leader, a man who, himself a pupil of the *bonne école*, could inspire in others that regenerating purity which David Leroy, Peyre and other architects of taste had brought to its full brilliance.'[8] Détournelle was, of course, citing Durand's mentors during his training at the Académie d'Architecture. The younger Rondelet, Durand's biographer, mentions only Boullée; neither Leroy nor Peyre is named.[9]

The first known project by Durand is a design for a Museum, a submission for the second Grand Prix, of 1779.[10] The front elevation is taken from M.-J. Peyre's 'Bâtiment qui contiendroit les académies', designed in Rome in 1753, but published only in 1765.[11] Durand copied the motif of the semicircular arrangement of Peyre's central building but added wings. The cross at the centre of Durand's plan – evident also in those of Gisors and Delannoy for the same competition[12] – might well have derived from Boullée's 'Bibliothèque publique',[13] if this was, indeed, done by that date.[14] If not, it might come from Vanvitelli's Caserta, built from 1752 on.[15]

The plan once formulated, Durand continued to use it for years – for the Museum illustrated in the *Précis*, for instance, which was used by

7, 10

9

10

11

12

13

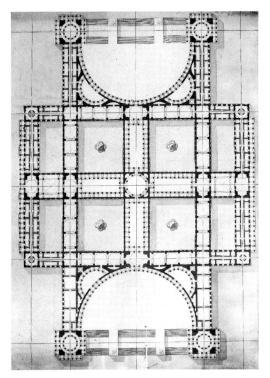

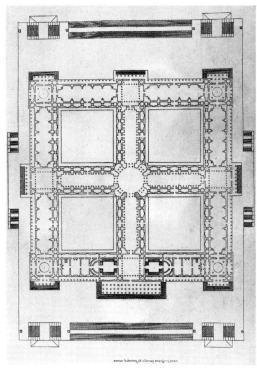

10 J.-N.-L. Durand. Museum, 1779: plan. For the elevation see ill. 7. (Beaux-Arts)

11 M.-A. Delannoy. Museum, 1779: plan.

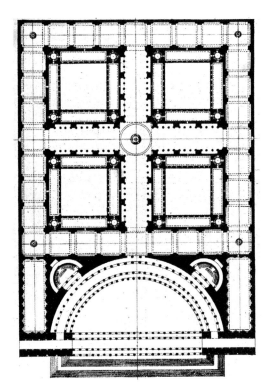

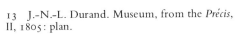

12 E.-L. Boullée. Bibliothèque publique: plan. (Bibliothèque Nationale)

13 J.-N.-L. Durand. Museum, from the *Précis*, II, 1805: plan.

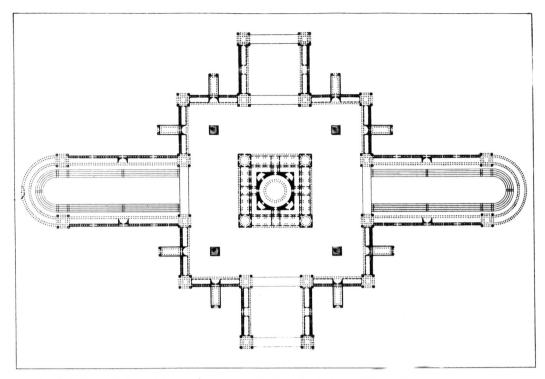

14   J.-N.-L. Durand. Ensemble formé par la combinaison de plusieurs édifices, from the *Partie graphique*, 1821: plan.

Klenze as the model for the Glyptothek in Munich, built between 1816 and 1830;[16] while Durand's favourite pupil, the German architect C. W. Coudray, was made to copy both Peyre's designs and those of his master during his apprenticeship in the early years of the 19th century,[17] indicating that they were still considered as valid formal solutions.

The influence of Peyre's design can be remarked many years after its conception. Twenty years later than the Coudray copies, Durand published an 'Ensemble formé par la combinaison de plusieurs édifices' in his *Partie graphique*. The detail of this might not correspond that closely with Peyre's project of 1753, but Durand's design can nonetheless be viewed as a corrected version of Peyre's, which survived thus for seventy years.

It was typical of Durand to adapt another's design. Throughout, he tailored traditional arrangements to accord with his own ideals, reducing all compositions to standardized, elementary forms, such as the circle or the square, made up of a repetitive pattern of basic units. Durand not only corrected originals, he reduced plans to abstract diagrams, failing often to note the source of his examples and even their function.[18]

One of the most famous academic designs of the late 18th century was subject to such a rearrangement: Percier's 'Monument destiné à rassembler les académies' of 1786.[19] The title, it should be noted, is a variant of Peyre's. Durand published Percier's project in 1805 as a prototype for an Institute, but it was subjected to change. Durand systematized the proportions of the plan. He left out the platform supporting the building, and the obelisks framing it. He extended the steps the full length of the wings. Instead of one large main entrance we find three smaller ones. The entrance hall is subdivided to mirror those of the other three wings. The corridors are aligned. The doorways are reduced in size. As for the front elevation, Durand added niches and Diocletian windows,[20] leaving out the colonnade around the dome.

In 1813, in the revised edition of his lecture course, the *Nouveau Précis*, this simplified project becomes the model for the 'Marche à suivre dans la composition d'un projet quelconque', where no specific function is designated. The whole is reduced to a didactic

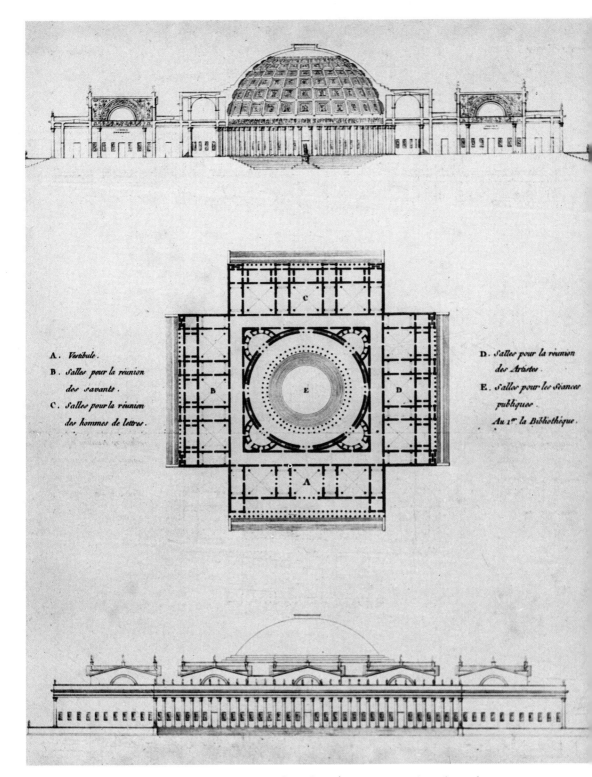

A . *Vestibule*.

B . *Salles pour la réunion des savants*.

C . *Salles pour la réunion des hommes de lettres*.

D . *Salles pour la réunion des Artistes*.

E . *Salles pour les séances publiques*.

Au 1er. la Bibliothèque.

15   J.-N.-L. Durand, after C. Percier. Institute, from the *Précis*, II, 1805: section, plan and elevation. For Percier's original project see ills. 4, 5.

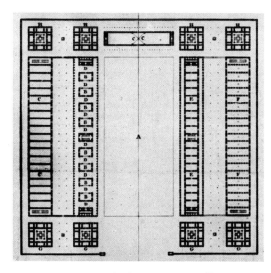

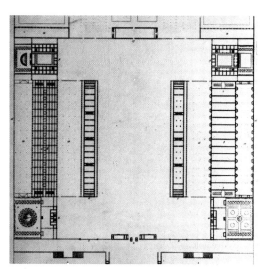

16 J.-.N.-L. Durand, after A. Detournelle. Barracks, from the *Précis*, II, 1805: plan.

17 A. Detournelle. Cavalry Barracks, 1799/1800: plan.

formula, copied by his pupils until the early 1830s.[21]

At times his contemporaries protested at his rearrangements. Though flattered to find his 'Cazernes de cavalerie', of Year VIII (1799/1800), illustrated in the *Précis* as a prime exemplar for a barracks, Détournelle repudiated the changes Durand had made and republished his original version.[22] If we compare Détournelle's original with Durand's adaptation it will be seen that no more than a general resemblance survives. Durand retained only the overall organization, with its great courtyard, serried rooms and stables and detached buildings, not unlike some of Ledoux's customs barriers for Paris. The proportion and detail were completely altered.

For the projects of some of his predecessors and even his contemporaries, Durand showed more respect, especially for those of Boullée. Durand was trained early, in Panseron's *atelier*, so that by the time he was employed by Boullée, in 1776, he may be assumed to have become an assistant.[23] Many of Boullée's drawings are executed in a manner similar to the few originals known by Durand. Some of Boullée's designs might well have been drawn up by Durand, who might even have contributed to them. Certainly many of the most typical features of Boullée's projects survive in the work of Durand.

An instance of such continuity is the project for a palace at St-Germain-en-Laye, designed by Boullée in 1785, and taken over by Durand for his *Précis*, with changes, as a 'Plan général d'un palais'. Both plans are based on a radially composed composition in a big park. Many other such comparisons might be drawn.[24] The most striking example is the theme of the domed circular building. In 1781, Boullée designed a circular Opera House, followed, in 1784, by the famous Cenotaph for Newton (the most popular of his designs, the prototype of a whole series of projects, by Delespine, Gay, Labadie, Lefèvre, Lequeu, Molinos, Moreau, Sobre and Vaudoyer).[25]

When drawing up the *Rudimenta Operis Magni et Disciplinae* between 1788 and 1793,[26] Durand conceived of several vast circular domed buildings in the Boullée manner, in particular Boullée's 'Temple à la Nature' (1793) and his 'Monument destiné aux hommages dûs à l'Etre Suprême' (*c.* 1793). Durand's conceptions, of which seven tiny sketches are preserved,[27] have the same encircling colonnades and porticoes, and in one instance the outlying monumental columns. These exhibit differing arrangements and proportions, but the basic organization in each case is the same.

During the darkest days of the Terror, in the Year II, 1793/94, a series of competitions was organized under David's patronage and

18　E.-L. Boullée. Project
for a Palace at St–
Germain-en-Laye, 1785:
plan. (Bibliothèque
Nationale)

19　J.-N.-L. Durand.
Plan général d'un palais,
from the *Précis*, II, 1805.

20   E.-L. Boullée. Opera House, 1781: elevation.
(Bibliothèque Nationale)

21   E.-L. Boullée. Monument destiné aux
hommages dûs à l'Etre Suprême, c. 1793:
elevation. (Bibliothèque Nationale)

22   J.-N.-L. Durand. Sketch of a circular
building, 1788–93. (Coll. Baderou, Rouen)

23 J.-N.-L. Durand and J.-T. Thibault. Temple décadaire I, 1794: elevation.

24 J.-N.-L. Durand and J.-T. Thibault. Temple décadaire II, 1794: elevation.

25 Casse. Temple de l'honneur et de la vertu, 1810, from *Choix*: elevation.

26 J.-N.-L. Durand. Corrected version of Ste-Geneviève, from the *Précis*, I, pt. 1, 1802: elevation.

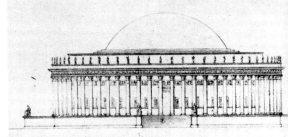

26

judged by the 'Jury des Arts'. Working with Thibault, Durand won most of the prizes.[28] Among the entries were two 'Temples décadaires', assigned to the *culte décadaire* decreed by the Revolutionary authorities. The temples provide two formal solutions. The first is well known; it shows a circular domed building with unbroken wall surfaces and long flights of stairs leading up to four porches. The second, dedicated to the 'Etre Suprême', is surrounded by a giant colonnade. The interior and exterior decoration of the dome, the main feature of both temples, is the same: a globe outside, a star-filled sky inside. Although Coudray was to copy the first,[29] Durand did not include the projects in his *Précis* – their political overtones were perhaps too blatant. He continued, however, to approve the formal arrangement. In 1802, in the very first plate of the *Précis*, the famous criticism of Soufflot's Ste-Geneviève (Panthéon), he offers as an alternative a tholos, close to the second 'temple décadaire'. Later, in 1810, Durand's pupil Casse designed a similar 'Temple de l'honneur et de la vertu,' set on a hill, exactly like some of its predecessors, related to a square forecourt at a lower level. Thus, from 1781, the date of Boullée's design for an Opera House, to 1810, when Casse's temple was engraved, the formula for the circular domed building remained unchanged, demonstrating even more clearly than in the instance of Peyre's Académies that Durand made no formal break between the architecture of Louis XVI and that of the First Empire.

It is more difficult to trace the influence of Durand's other master, J.-D. Leroy,[30] by comparing designs; for Leroy was more of an archaeologist and historian than an architect. Having travelled to Greece in 1754 and 1755 and having published his findings in 1758, even before Stuart and Revett, he was one of the foremost representatives of Greek taste and certainly one of the most influential.[31] He became J.-F. Blondel's successor as professor of architecture in 1773, having been his assistant since 1762. His Greek taste and his scepticism with regard to the orders influenced Durand's work, but his prime influence was felt on Durand's view of the history of architecture.

In his *Recueil et parallèle* of 1800, Durand arranged buildings, all drawn to the same scale, and grouped them together as building types. The buildings, copied from all kinds of publications by archaeologists, architects, and travellers, encompassed all periods and styles. The title of the work recalls Fréart de Chambray's and Dumont's *Parallèles*.[32] Durand, however, concentrated neither on the orders, like Fréart, nor on a single building type, like Dumont; he was interested in all architecture. Never before had so many buildings been shown on the same scale as in Durand's *Recueil*.

His model for thus recording an array of plans to a single scale on a single plate is a comparative table of the evolution of temple design included in the second edition of Leroy's *Ruines* of 1770.[33] This plate shows, in three parallel rows, the development from the primitive hut to Solomon's Temple and to the Temple of the Sun in Baalbek, and from the catacombs to St Peter's. This is Leroy's vision of the history of architecture, showing continuity of development and progress, from the simple to the complex, from ancient to modern.

Another architect to provide Durand with a model was Victor Louis, who set the plans of the principal theatres of Europe on a single plate in his *Salle de spectacle de Bordeaux*, in 1782.[34] After the publication of the *Recueil*, however, the method was widely adopted, as is evident in the works of Dubut, Normand and Bruyère.[35]

Perronet, also Durand's tutor at the Académie d'Architecture,[36] cannot be assigned a role as important as that of Leroy. Durand certainly admired Perronet's structural finesse – in particular his abilities as a bridge-builder and canal-maker[37] – but he had no particular interest in engineering, neither during his training nor later, when he himself was teaching engineering students the principles of architecture. However, his reduction of these principles to their barest essentials no doubt made them the more useful to engineers.

In order to judge the extent to which Durand reduced these principles, one must turn to the traditional core of architectural theory, the orders.

Leroy's influence was evident early in Durand's career. In the final project for the Delathuille house, of 1788, he indicates on the garden front that distinctive Doric order, with fluting only at the base and at the top, that Leroy had measured at the Temple of Apollo at Delos. When the project was published seventeen years later in the *Précis*, Durand omitted this feature – a leitmotif of the Greek Revival in France – and replaced it with simple unfluted Doric columns.

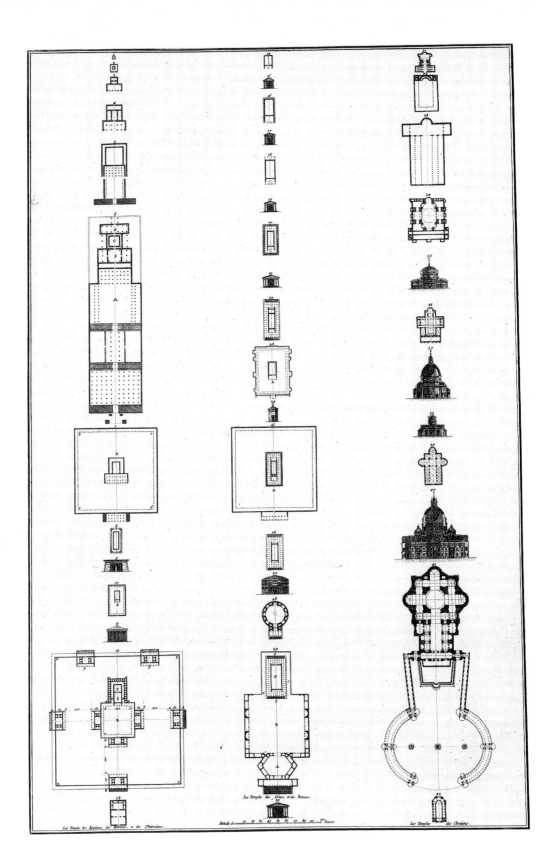

Les Temples des Égyptiens, des Hébreux, et des Phéniciens.

Les Temples des Grecs, et des Romains.

Les Temples des Chrétiens.

Echelle de

27 J.-D. Leroy. Comparative survey of temples and churches, from *Ruines des plus beaux monuments de la Grèce*, 2nd ed., 1770.

28 J.-D. Leroy. Doric order from the Temple of Apollo at Delos, from *Ruines*, 1770.

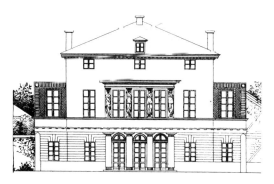

29 J.-N.-L. Durand. Project for the Delathuille house, Paris, 1788: elevation of the garden front, as published in J.-C. Krafft and N. Ransonette, *Plans, coupes, élévations des plus belles maisons ... à Paris*, 1801.

30 J.-N.-L. Durand. Project for the Delathuille house, Paris, 1788: elevation of the garden front, as published in the *Precis*, II, 1805.

This is in accord with a rule observed throughout the *Précis*: buildings should have either the Doric or the Corinthian order. Clearly, Durand's architectural ideas had changed by this date; Leroy's order was too idiosyncratic for didactic purposes. A comparative plate 31 of the five orders shows that Durand's aim was by then to teach the basic vocabulary of architecture, nothing more. The profiles are taken for the most part from Vignola;[38] but changes were made – Durand's profiles, for instance, are simplified in detail. More significant, the Composite order, as found in the treatises of Claude Perrault, Fréart de Chambray and François Blondel, is replaced by the Greek 32 Doric. This represents an acceptance, at least, of the Greek taste initiated by Leroy.

A few years later, in 1813, when the *Nouveau Précis* came out, important changes were made. The 1802 plate of the Ionic order was replaced by another, showing a new system for all the 33 orders. Durand simplified the Doric, Tuscan and Corinthian orders, left out the Ionic order and put in a pre-Corinthian early Greek capital instead. The names of the orders are also omitted; they are numbered from 1 to 5. This is more than an extension of Greek tastes. The orders are offered as standard accessories to architecture. Durand is applying here his principle that the orders belong to a category of forms which are not necessary, but are instead something to which we have become accustomed, through use: 'The familiarity of something can finally make it somehow indispensable; thus a need has been created within us for those forms and proportions that are associated with ancient buildings.'[39]

In his late works, it appears, Durand used only the two orders shown in the illustrations of the *Précis*. The Corinthian, he maintained, was to be used for large public buildings,[40] as in his monument for the Place de l'Etoile in 34 Paris, of 1807.[41] Doric was to serve for the lowest class of private buildings,[42] as in the pier capitals of his country house at Thiais.[43] 35

In the *Partie graphique*, Durand provided no specific rules for the indication of capitals, as he had done in 1802.[44] Ultimately, capitals were reduced to V-shapes to be filled as required. This was the graphic formula adopted by his pupils at the Ecole Polytechnique – often in conjunction with the famous square grid.[45] The authority of antiquity was thus spurned, though a customary indication does survive.

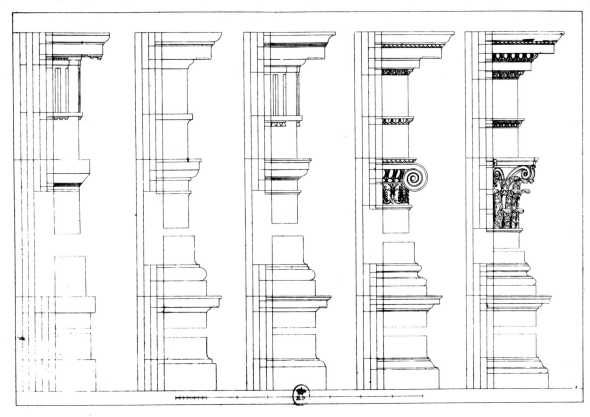

31   J.-N.-L. Durand. Details of the five orders, from the *Précis*, I, pt. 1, 1802.

32   François Blondel. The five orders, from the *Cours d'architecture*, 1698.

33   J.-N.-L. Durand. Details of the orders, from the *Nouveau Précis*, pt. 1, 1813.

34   J.-N.-L. Durand. Monument for the Place de l'Etoile, Paris, 1807: detail of the elevation. (Bibliothèque Nationale)

· A LA VICTOIRE ·

35 J.-N.-L. Durand. Country house at Thiais, 1825: Doric capital.

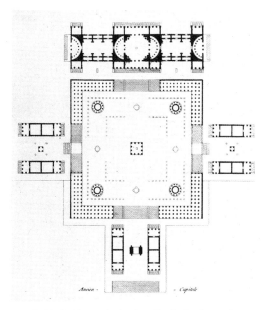

36 J.-N.-L. Durand. Ancien Capitole, from the *Recueil*, 1800: plan.

Durand, it is evident, modified the classical tradition, not only with regard to the orders but even in matters of composition. As early as 1800, in the *Recueil*, Durand showed Palladio's plans of the Roman baths alongside a rectified version – as, of course, Leroy had done for the Propylaea at Athens. Throughout the *Recueil* plans are thus 'improved'.

Durand's method is seen best in connection with the drawings of the Capitol in Rome, 36 supposedly based, in the first edition of the *Recueil*,[46] on Piranesi, though this borrowing from Piranesi is not altogether obvious.[47] Durand shows a multilevelled group of temples, colonnades and obelisks, arranged around a square. His pupils had to copy this in a rectified version, shown in a drawing by Fransoz.[48] In 1821, the Capitol reappears in the *Partie graphique* as an 'Ensemble formé par la com- 37 binaison de plusieurs édifices'. The focal building is transformed into a kind of theatre-temple. As usual, neither the original design nor the function of the building is mentioned. The original plan, after a series of transpositions, emerges here as an abstract, schematic demonstration of compositional rules and principles.

There are many similar examples: for instance the 'Nymphée de Néron'[49] or the Roman Arsenal.[50] Durand's method is applied to all kinds of designs and buildings, reducing them to exemplars of his compositional logic. Durand says, on the subject of elevations:

> The elevation of a building is, and can only be, no more than the natural and inevitable outcome of the ground plan and the section, and it is far easier to create it without referring to a model. On the whole, the less a model is slavishly copied, the closer one will be to an understanding of the real business of composition.[51]

Durand's relation to inherited tradition – that of classical Greek and Roman architecture, academic architecture, Louis XVI architecture and 'Revolutionary' architecture – is ambiguous. His work is in some ways closely connected to it; but in other respects he remodels it laboriously to accord with his own ideals, both theoretical and compositional, based on economy and convenience. The ultimate variant of a theme is usually preceded by several intermediate stages, in which the original features are slowly excised, regardless of historical truth or archaeological authenticity and sometimes regardless even of the building's function.

32

Paradoxically, such transformation led to historicism.[52]

I have ignored Durand's theory itself, for Durand's examples do not always accord with his theoretical expositions. He differs far more from his mentors in intent than is evident in his designs. In theory, he has little in common with Boullée, in particular regarding notions of *caractère* and expression in architecture.[53]

His drawings, however, reveal him as a simplifier and a popularizer; hence the polemic directed against him in the 1830 and 1840s. Gottfried Semper described him as a 'Schach-brettkanzler für mangelnde Ideen' ('Chancellor of the Exchequer [punning on chequerboard] of nonexistent ideas') and his plans as 'Assignaten' (worthless paper money).[54] César Daly dismissed Durand's 'système à carreaux'[55] as a means of simplifying current models.

In practice, Durand upheld inherited traditions. He broke with them only in his radical theories. Therein lies his originality.

37 J.-N.-L. Durand. Ensemble formé par la combinaison de plusieurs édifices, from the *Partie graphique*, 1821.

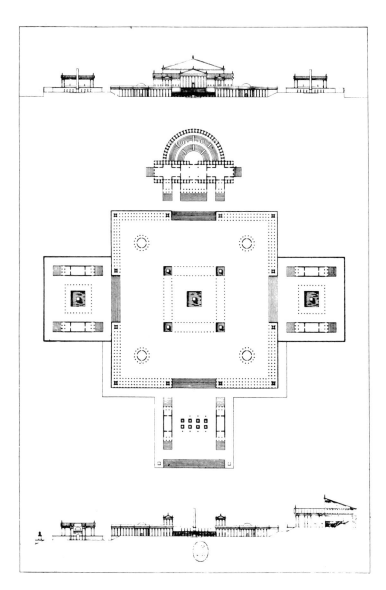

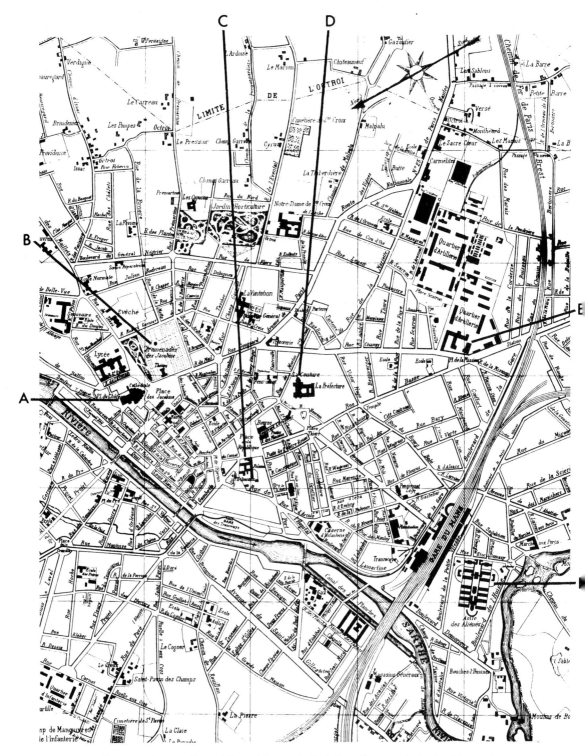

38   Map of Le Mans in 1891. From left to right: A, Cathedral; B, Promenade des Jacobins; C, law
courts and prison (former Visitandines convent); D, prefecture (former abbey of Notre-Dame de
la Couture); E, artillery barracks (former Mission hospital); F, lunatic asylum (see ill. 49; enlarged
to the south). The circular market was in the central square, north of the Visitandines (C).
(Archives Nationales)

III

Planning and building in towns: the system of the Bâtiments Civils in France, 1795–1848

Georges Teyssot

The *département*, aided by the state, is about to build a *palais de justice*. This new building will use Greek forms; but as it will consist of only a single storey it cannot be very imposing. The Conseil des Bâtiments Civils, faithful to its budget, the worst enemy of the beautiful (I am speaking of the budget), has deleted from the plans everything that is not directly useful, and I fear that the Bourges Palais de Justice will be a distinctly flat kind of edifice. They ought to have built in the Gothic style.

Stendhal, *Mémoires d'un touriste*

The Institut de France was founded on 25 October 1795, to further methodical study. Successor to the academies that had been abolished in 1793, it soon became a new focus of power, serving to establish the world of the intellect as a third force, equivalent in a way to that of the church and the state. Many of its members, however, were government officials. It was divided into three classes: physical science and mathematics; moral science and politics; and literature and the fine arts. Each class was divided into sections, four for the fine arts: painting, sculpture, architecture, and music and declamation. Each section had six members. The role of architects was thus greatly diminished in the new organization. The old Académie d'Architecture, as Louis Hautecoeur has pointed out,[1] was made up of a group of professionals concerned with professional matters, who, together with the king's three architects, formed the Conseil des Bâtiments, whereas the third section of the fine arts class of the new Institut was concerned with 'theory' and the award of the Prix de Rome. Architects of the Institut were no longer responsible for the control of public building, which was handed instead to the Conseil des Bâtiments Civils, an administration established on 27 April 1791, as a part of the Ministry of the Interior. The Ministry was to be responsible for public buildings, such as churches and presbyteries, law courts, all manner of detention centres, prisons, hospitals and charitable institutions.[2]

After the interlude of the Convention, the Conseil des Bâtiments Civils, re-established on 11 December 1795, took over the powers of the famous Commission des Artistes. This further concentration of power within a state institution reinforced a trend that had already been remarked at the end of the *ancien régime*; there was now not just a split between those who upheld taste and beauty (the high priests of art in the temple of the Institut) and those who dealt with practical problems in the role of technicians and administrators, but, with the clear demarcation created between the Beaux-Arts and the Bâtiments Civils, a final break between the world of individual creativity and that of the systematizers, so violently disliked by Quatremère de Quincy, among others.[3] Such systematization transformed the approach to design, providing standardized solutions for town and country planning, determined henceforth by criteria such as security, health and efficiency.

I hope, if possible, within the discontinuities of history, to isolate a recognizable period, characterized by a particular approach to urban planning as imposed by the Bâtiments Civils – a period that coincides with that of 'technology' as interpreted by J. Guillerme and J. Sebestik; 'technology', they have written, 'arises from a desire to codify technics, taking into account the means of production and social needs'.[4] Thus, between 1750 and 1770 it might be possible to discern the beginning of a specific attempt at rationalization (of the 'mechanical' machine, and thus of work), requiring the development of a universal symbolism of machines and their products. For J. Beckmann, the founder of technology at the university of Göttingen, technology was to be identified with *Entwurf*, just as architecture in the age of Enlightenment was to be identified with the project – architecture was not built, it was described, projected like the plans of John Gwynn and Pierre Patte, for London and Paris. From Diderot to Babbage one notes a constant attempt to produce a code of signs; from the unification of meaning sought for in the *Encyclopédie*, to the attempt to typify the aims of production and classify the mechanical processes conceived by Beckmann, and thus to Babbage's calculating machine.[5]

The revolution in drawing, prompted by the teachings of Gaspard Monge, the revolution in architectural design, instigated by J.-N.-L. Durand, and the system of representation provided for drawing by the Baron de Gérando,[6] are all aspects of the desire to give meaning to a process of rational planning. This historical episode corresponds to an extended age of the Enlightenment, 1750 to 1840, identified by D. Richet.[7] Further research might be directed at isolating the moment of its demise, to discover whether the Utopian vision in Enlightenment architecture fades at the same time as the rationalist Utopia of technology, overtaken by thermodynamics, the physical sciences and chemistry in the third decade of the 19th century.[8]

If my hypothesis is tenable, it will help to reveal the beginnings of contemporary architecture in France; it will show a basic continuity in architectural practice from J.-F. Blondel to Durand and on to E.-J. Gilbert, architect of the Charenton asylum, of the Hôtel Dieu and the Mazas prison, all in Paris. Such a continuity would begin with the unity of approach shared by those early leaders of fashion, M.-J. Peyre, C. de Wailly and others, and the application of their methods to all planning in France. The change they wrought was achieved by two distinct means: first by a change in methods of design, the system of the Beaux-Arts, second by the bureaucraticization of professional practice between 1795 and 1845, achieved largely by the Service des Bâtiments Civils – though not without difficulty, as we shall see.

Viollet-le-Duc's retrospective assessment of the situation is accepted as correct by many, even up to the present:

Administrative centralization removed not only the schools from the provinces, but with them the competent students, all of whom were absorbed by Paris or two or three large centres . . . . For proof one need only glance at the churches, town halls, markets, hospitals, etc. built between 1815 and 1835 . . . . Nine-tenths of these buildings (and I am not concerned here with matters of style) reveal a dreadful ignorance of the most elementary principles of building.[9]

The organization of the Bâtiments Civils

The Bâtiments Civils was an executive body, composed of a Council, an administrative organization and a handful of inspectors and architects. Lucien Bonaparte, when Minister of the Interior, formed a Council of three members, J.-B. Rondelet, A.-F. Peyre and J.-F.-T. Chalgrin. They inspected all projects, controlled costs, payments, arbitration etc. They were assisted by a secretary, Mermet, and an office of draughtsmen. Three inspectors were appointed to inspect building work, produce reports and certify payments; Mouchelet, Bonnet and L.-C.-F. Petit-Radel were the first of these, to be joined later by J.-A. Raymond and J.-F. Heurtier. Finally, an unspecified number of architects were commissioned to take charge of the building and repair work.[10] In Year IX, no more than thirteen architects were employed.[11] The whole organization was reformed in 1812 by the Minister, Montalivet: the Council was then made up of five to seven inspectors-general (Heurtier, Peyre, Rondelet, Garrez, Norry, Guy de Gisors and Cellerier), a group of honorary members and a secretary.

The procedure for assessing projects was adopted from the Conseil des Ponts et Chaussées: a member of the Council was nominated to report on any particular business (a design, an estimate, a certificate of payment, a dispute, etc.), the report was then read to the Council which, as a rule, endorsed the recommendations offered. These were transcribed as the minutes of the meetings. Inevitably members specialized in particular areas; Pierre Baltard, for instance, became expert in prison design, Guy de Gisors concerned himself with inspections in the western provinces, etc. The model for what was to become the body of architects of the Bâtiments Civils was provided by the organization of the engineering corps of the Ponts et Chaussées.[12] Though the Bâtiments Civils, it is worth noting, was never able to marshall a corps of 477 qualified members as could the Ponts et Chaussées, which, by a decree of 7 fructidor Year XII, was to establish an almost military discipline.[13] With the Bâtiments Civils, too, it was necessary to establish a programme of teaching, for David Leroy's Ecole Spéciale d'Architecture could not provide enough graduates.[14]

There were not enough architects, nor were they sufficiently able. All available personnel were employed. Napoleon appointed an engineer of the Ponts et Chaussées as director of the Travaux de Paris. By a decree of 11 January 1811, the post was given to Louis Bruyère as 'Maître des requêtes'. He was to stand in for the Minister and to preside over the meetings of the Conseil des Bâtiments Civils. Two days later, the archaeologist, Alexandre de Laborde, *auditeur* on the Council of State and a count of the Empire, was made director of the Ponts et Chaussées for the Département de la Seine.[15] These two functionaries were intended to control the development of the capital. The Minister of the Interior, according to a biography of the period, 'regretted that the instruction of architects had, until then, been directed to the art of drawing rather than to any proper consideration of the visual impact a building might have on its surroundings, the use to which it was to be put, the needs it should satisfy and those processes of construction which should ensure the long life of a building and a reduction in cost'.[16]

Following a plan conceived by Rondelet, this administrative takeover of public building by engineers could, or indeed should, have involved the transformation of the Ecole d'Architecture into the Ecole des Bâtiments Civils, a proposal made on 10 April 1819, by Alexandre de Laborde.[17] He was appalled, he noted, 'that most of the projects for buildings sent from the different towns of France need to be corrected and often redrawn completely in Paris by the Conseil des Bâtiments Civils before being built,' and he regretted that 'the architects involved formed neither a proper body nor a corporation'. He defined the range of knowledge he considered necessary for the efficient government architect – law, administration, physics, chemistry and calculus were among the subjects included in his programme. His reforms were based on two series of proposals, administrative and educational.

Firstly, a director-general of the Bâtiments Civils was to be appointed within the Ministry of the Interior – he would take over the functions of the director of the Travaux de Paris (a post retained by the engineer Bruyère until 1820, when he was replaced by Hely d'Oissel), though his authority would extend throughout France. He would, however, be subordinate to the Direction des Départements et des Communes. Laborde was thus, even at this early stage, proposing a director of planning who, while reinforcing control over Paris, would have extended control over the planning of the whole country. His proposal, in effect, was for a chief architect to be attached to the prefecture of each *département*.

Secondly, the jury of the Ecole Royale d'Architecture was to be nominated by the director-general of the Ministry of the Interior, and the director of the Bâtiments Civils would be president.

In Laborde's proposal, pupils were to be selected for the posts of *inspecteur* within the Bâtiments Civils by monthly competitions (*médailles de mois*) and by an annual competition (*le grand prix*);[18] the programmes for the monthly competitions were to be written by the members of the jury, the role of the Beaux-Arts section of the Institut thus being reduced to the writing of the programme of the Grand Prix, which it was still to award.

These proposals encouraged the development of 'administrative architects'. A few months later however, on 4 August 1819, they were rejected in favour of the establishment of the Ecole Royale des Beaux-Arts (the internal regulations of which were finalized only in 1823). A decision of political expediency had been made. Architectural education remained under the control of the Institut, thus favouring the development of a liberal profession.

Yet architecture and planning in the first third of the 19th century were dominated by the system imposed by the Bâtiments Civils – a chapter in itself in the history of state control. This organization, flexible and in a state of continual evolution, aimed at something midway between its original model, the engineering corps of the Ponts et Chaussées, and the practices of a liberal architectural profession. With the creation of the Ecole, these practices were soon to be codified as the Beaux-Arts system. Debate on administrative matters and on professional qualification was highly active in the years between 1820 and 1840, as is evident in the critical articles of the architect Picolet on the routine nature of architectural education, or those of the editor Jeannin in the *Journal du génie civil*.[19] The state of balance that had been achieved was broken, and the importance of the Bâtiments Civils organization, based on the employment of state functionaries, declined progressively, until it was no more than a faint memory in the French administrative system. In 1896, the Direction des Bâtiments Civils was dissolved, its role subsumed by that of the Beaux-Arts.[20]

It is not easy to give a clear picture of the activity of the Service des Bâtiments Civils in the early years of the century. One must step back to get some notion of the overall strategy and at the same time pinpoint the methods of the new surgery being performed on the urban tissue of the country, which served as the basis of the urban pathology that was to change the towns of France during the first half of the 19th century. Something of this sort has been the aim of my research, incomplete as it might be. The statistical analysis offered of the architecture of the Bâtiments Civils, however straightforward it might seem, represents an attempt to provide an overall view of its aims and activities; certainly any such assessment needs to be revised and refined in relating the figures to other factors – wealth per capita, the population of each *département*, etc. It is also possible to take a single town as an example of the change in planning strategy in the 19th century, as has been done by a group of researchers for Bourges.[21] One might also analyze each stage in the realization of a project in detail in an attempt to grasp the strictly architectural problems involved, which is what we have done in trying to formulate the complex history of the building of the prison and tribunal at Le Mans, in the Sarthe.

The Le Mans prison and tribunal

One might ask, why Le Mans? Because it was to that town that the young Louis Bruyère, fresh from the Ecole des Ponts et Chaussées, was appointed sub-engineer (*sous-ingénieur*) on 1 April 1786. He was later to make his reputation with a plan to bring the waters of the river Ourcq to Paris, in order to increase the supply of drinking water (1802), and soon after with a design for the port of Comacchio on the Adriatic (1805). He was eventually appointed secretary of the general assembly of the Ponts et Chaussées and director of the Travaux de Paris (1811–20).

In 1789, Bruyère took over the works at Le Mans, a small town of 18,000 inhabitants. His opportunity was provided by the opening of vast work-houses by the Treasury in the face of a dangerous rise in unemployment.[22] Up to 4,000 workers were to be employed at a time, making up the roads of the *département* and working on the construction sites on the outskirts of the town. In this connection, Bruyère submitted plans to the municipality and the regional authorities for using the confiscated buildings and sites of the old religious communities. Among these plans was a project for a market-place on the site of the Minimes convent, which was to be demolished. Included also on the site for the market was the convent of the Visitation. On 12 September 1792 the authorities of the *département* informed the chief engineer that this last, whose chapel of 1737 lay on the east of the proposed square, was to be transformed and used by the new state administration.[23] In the time remaining to him in Le Mans, Bruyère was unable to realize his proposals for the market-place, being occupied with the laying out of the Promenade du Greffier and with the Place des Jacobins, which extended beyond the walls of the old town behind the apse of the cathedral.

The Jacobins and Cordeliers convents became national property in May 1791.[24] Bruyère proposed a grand layout, involving the destruction of all extant buildings and the formation of an open site, on which he placed a cattle market and walks planted in quincunx around a parade-ground intended for public festivals and the manoeuvres of the local garrison. It was a typical engineer's approach; the cleared area, modelled discretely by axes, terraces, banks and quincunxes, allowed the whole to remain open for army use. A dual potential was offered: on the one hand the provision of normal building sites on the perimeter, and on the other unlimited possibilities by way of buildings, temporary or permanent, in the central area. The sale of the building sites was to pay for the works. The municipality provided the design for the uniform façades to be built around the edge.[25] The structures proposed for the main area were numerous, among them 'a mound in the style of an English rock garden topped with an architectural feature'[26] – a project typical of the Revolutionary period.

38,

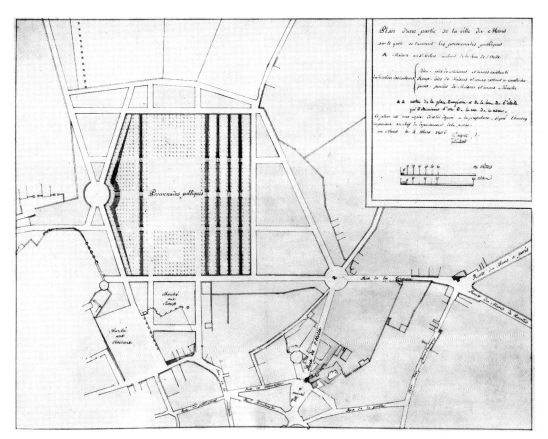

39   R.-F. Chaubry. Plan of the area of the Promenade des Jacobins and cattle market, Le Mans, dated 4 March 1806. (Archives Nationales)

Delarue was later to build the municipal theatre on the edge of this esplanade.[27]

In January 1793, in the face of mounting revolutionary activity, Bruyère resigned to set up as an architect in Paris.[28] He was replaced by the engineer in ordinary, J.-B. Béchet-Deshourmeaux who, when the fuss was over, was requested by the Conseil des Bâtiments Civils to suggest the most suitable site for a prison. Having ruled out an earlier proposal to use the old archbishop's palace for the purpose, the Conseil enjoined him to 'reconcile the sacred rights of humanity with the restrictions required in the maintenance of public order'.[29]

The great phase of transformation of the state and the town had begun. The first stage in this attempt at spatial control was the establishment of the carceral system (prisons), the judicial system (law courts) and a repressive system (police). In 1801, Chaptal had initiated an enquiry throughout the *départements* to establish what sites and buildings were available. In the small town of Le Mans, his plan was imposed, first by rendering obsolete the uses to which many spaces had previously been put and then by providing substitutes. The convents – the Cordeliers, Jacobins, Ursulines, Minimes, etc. – were suppressed, as was the general hospital, and the sites and buildings were assigned to new institutions in a process of architectural regularization and redistribution. The prison and law courts were installed in the convent of the Visitation; in 1812 the 41, 42 prefecture of the Sarthe was installed in the abbey of Couture, which had already served as 38 a dedicatory temple and as a police barracks;[30] the old Mission hospital sheltered prisoners during the Revolution, before being transformed first into a work-house by the architect, Guyot, in 1811, then into a cavalry barracks, in 1815, and finally, in 1871, into an artillery 38 barracks; the college of the Oratory became a school, temporarily, in 1814, permanently,

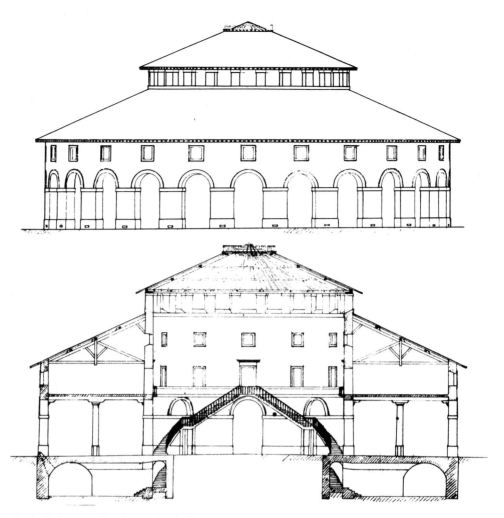

40   L.-A.-D. Lusson. Circular market hall, Le Mans, 1819: elevation and section.

in 1851; the abbey of St Vincent was to contain the seminary, then a home for the aged, and so forth.[31] The final stage in the process of renewal involved the development of new building types and the erection of new buildings. This phase began slowly, but activity increased greatly towards the second half of the 19th century. Under the First Empire a small abattoir and a police barracks were built. In 1819, a circular market hall, built by the architect Lusson with the help of Bruyère, prompted much correspondence on account of its unusual shape. The architect Delarue built the asylum (1828–34), the theatre on the Promenade des Jacobins (1838–42) and the new archbishop's palace (1845–47), while the architect L'Hommond provided plans for the new cloth market and the new abattoir in 1842.[32]

As already noted, in July 1797 a decision was made to install the legal institutions in the Maison des Visitandines, the convent of the Visitation, adjoining the market square, the commercial centre of the town.[33] The Minister demanded a degree of prudence. In February 1801, Chaptal wrote to the authorities of the *département*, 'I request that architects should suggest to the Bâtiments Civils only those works that are absolutely necessary. They should avoid in their designs all superfluous arrangements and decoration which might, needlessly, destroy the original character of the buildings .... They ought, in adapting buildings to new uses, to consult with the administrators of the institution concerned, who are also to sign the plans sent to me.'[34]

After much discussion between the chief engineer, René-Ferdinand Chaubry, assisted by Béchet-Deshourmeaux, and the Minister concerning the plans and estimates,[35] the project was accepted at the beginning of 1803.[36] In April 1805, work was stopped because the estimate had been exceeded.[37] This situation was resolved by the Conseil in November 1807, despite the fact that the cost of rebuilding had by then risen to 120,000 francs, largely because of the laying down of a boundary road.[38] The building was to be transformed for two uses: a prison on the ground floor, law courts on the first. Accepting as far as possible the position of existing walls, the new plan allowed for the separation of men from women and of those already condemned from those accused or under arrest.[39] The entrance to the prison was through an opening formed in the apse of the chapel. Beyond this, arranged around the entrance court, were the guard house and hospital. Isolation cells were built into the cellars of the convent, under the cloisters. The cellars had no windows, and opened only through doorways into the central court, which, when fully excavated, was to be at basement level. A new stair within a square cage was to be built to provide public access to the civil and criminal courts, the offices and the archives situated above the prison. The works were finished in 1808. The chief engineer, Philippe Vallée, described the installation then as 'a sound construction' and extolled 'the dignity of the government that commissioned it, the enlightened humanity of the magistrate who conceived it, and the zeal and knowledge of the engineers who planned and executed it'. He added: 'in the placing of openings to ensure the free circulation of air, in the adequate supply of water and the use of ventilators, this establishment – bars and grilles apart – appears to be a hospital rather than a place of detention'.[40]

The *département's* prison was an expression of the new standards of punishment imposed by French society, an instrument of egalitarian justice, a manifestation of the autonomy and uniformity of the judicial system.[41] Even if its methods were still rough, the 'form' of the prison, the planning, the organization and the subdivisions, was intended to serve as a technical instrument that would 'reform' the individual. The engineers who conceived the arrangement thought, naturally enough, to render it qualitatively similar to that of the other institutions – some less gloomy – that

were being built for a modern society. The 'white' hospital and the 'black' prison are based on a common rationale and disciplinary aim; expressions of a single ideal, they have the same institutional status. The two establishments reform, respectively, the body and the soul; they both provide for a free circulation of air and of water; they reconcile the 'rights of humanity' with the needs of security.[42]

Parallel to the dictates of security and control, another limitation was imposed on the design. This took two forms; firstly an ever more rigorous use of space through detailed allocation of areas and even volume, and more careful programming of requirements and patterns of circulation; secondly administrative control through increasingly refined directives as to the estimates of cost. A concern for estimates gave to the designers and surveyors of the projects a new mastery of understanding of sizes and costs. Quantity surveying, measurements and figures imposed new disciplines. The practice of architecture itself was transformed, a cause, no doubt, of the new simplicity, clarity and purity of form characteristic of the neoclassicism of the period. This dual standard – the allocation of space through programming and the careful calculation of needs and of costs – could lead to contrary results, for the extreme simplicity of architectural forms does not necessarily lead to efficiency in planning. During the Empire and Restoration there was neither the knowledge nor a profession capable of providing a solution to the new exigencies of architecture. There was, thus, in the early years of the century, a reorganization of roles, a new division of labour. One sees this reflected in the work of the architects at Le Mans.

In 1809, in a memorandum to the Minister, the prefect proposed Antoine-Pierre Guyot as architect to the *département* 'because engineers are, as a rule, unaware of the new modes of architecture'.[43] Whether he meant mode or style, the prefect was clearly thinking in terms of a manipulator of form. Guyot was employed. In 1810, he provided the plans for the rebuilding of the archbishop's palace and seminary. In 1811 he designed the installation of the workhouse in the old Mission convent, and the new police barracks. Finally, in 1814, he restored the school.[44] These projects cannot be analyzed here; it is enough to cite the smug comments of the engineers quoted in the prefect's report on the architect: he was judged to be 'a good decorator and an excellent draughtsman', but in 'no way fitted to discuss or analyze a project of the importance of that in question'. The prefect, discussing the work-house,[45] continued: 'he restricted himself to the drawing up of plans, sections and elevations and the organization of the interior. As for the rest, that is for the central concerns, such as the quantities and costs, the measuring and fixing of prices, which go to make up the total expenditure, these were outside his range of knowledge, or rather beyond his understanding.' He accused him of making mistakes and handing over this aspect of the work to a 'specialist'.[46]

One should not conclude from this dispute that engineers were the more suitable agents for urban development; they were certainly key agents, but the end of the story suggests that the confrontation was not of so clear-cut and professional a nature.

New codes (passed between 1808 and 1810) called for a rearrangement within the prison. In 1814, the chief engineer Jean-Antoine Daudin and the engineer Béchet-Deshourmeaux pre-
42 sented a more complicated plan incorporating the new government requirements: as before, men and women were to be segregated, but new divisions were demanded within the arrangement of the cells – for those under arrest, for those under interrogation, for those already sentenced and for those in local police custody (in all, accommodation for 128 men, 85 women). Also included was a keeper's house and a military prison (for 19 men).[47] This complex arrangement of segregated areas, set within an old building, was unacceptable; the chapel was partially taken over, the bays of the cloister were transformed into rooms 'without air or light', arbitrary partitions were erected, etc.

The problem was still unresolved in 1816, when Jules Pasquier, prefect of the Sarthe, announced that modifications had been made to the design at the request of the engineer, the mayor and a committee of enquiry.[48] The engineer, Béchet-Deshourmeaux's successor, Pierre-Bernard Cherrier, strongly supported by the council of the *département*, accused his predecessors of having sacrificed all salubrity in the division and subdivision of the prison according to sex, age and category of crime,[49]
43 and proposed instead to put up a new building on an adjacent site. The Conseil des Bâtiments Civils was unwilling to accept this proposal.

A year later, justifying the project for a new building, the engineer of the Ponts et Chaussées of the Sarthe noted that 'the prisoners' cells having now been reduced to simple rooms, none too high, built against existing walls, the cost will be no more than that of the first design'.[50] From this remark one may judge the engineer's simplistic approach: the main walls, either existing or yet to be built, were to be arranged as a series of courts, each serving a different category of prisoner, and the cells were to be built *against* these walls. The faults in the plan, from a purely functional point of view, are readily enumerated: there was no easy communication between one part and another or between different floors; areas allocated to different uses were disproportionate (the sick-bays, for instance, were extensive enough to make a whole hospital); no allowance was made for the prisoners to work together; cells were ventilated and lit only through grilles in the doors, etc. The simplification of the architecture was the result of no more than an apparent rationalization, and the dull repetition of courts and cells was a return to the system of camp and barracks design. The prefect, pressed by his own council, asked the advice of the Conseil des Bâtiments Civils. Heurtier, its president, dispatched the architect Guy de Gisors to investigate. He provided a more elegant solution,[51] proposing that the main 44 cloister of the old convent be divided into four courts to serve men and women being questioned and under arrest, with the sick-bay and the administrative offices between these courts and a new punishment block set on an open site alongside.

This project was also rejected by the council of the *département*, determined to erect a new building, independent of the law courts.

In December 1817, Gisors suggested that another architect be consulted. At the same time he defined the limits of his role as a state architect: 'Though it might be my duty to provide sketches to indicate how a plan might be altered or rectified, I would be exceeding my role in providing a design to be taken over by someone else'.[52] Gisors thus affirmed his *liberal* conception of the profession; an attitude, as we have seen, consolidated at the Ecole des Beaux-Arts in the face of all attempts to train architects as administrators.

A month later Cherrier's design was rejected by the Conseil des Bâtiments Civils, and the

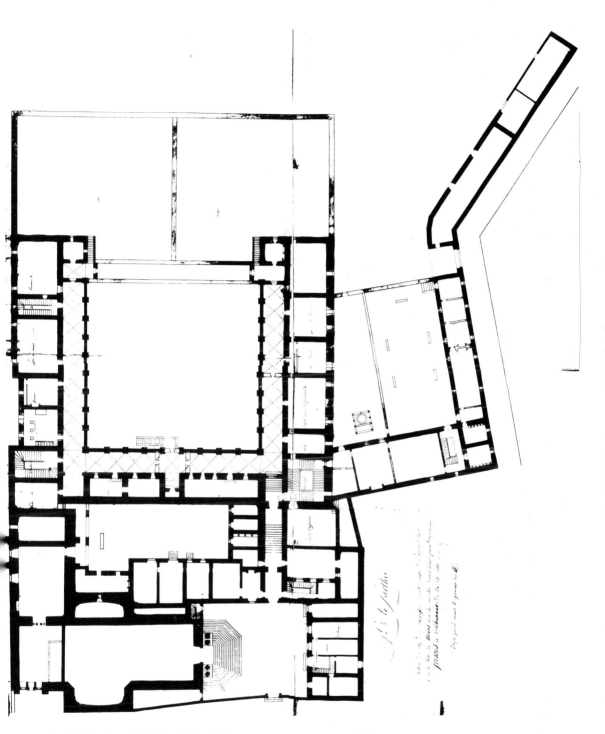

41   R.-F. Chaubry with J.-B. Béchet-Deshourmeaux. Conversion of the Visitandines, Le Mans,
into law courts and prison: ground-floor plan, dated pluviose Year XI (January 1803). Here, as in
the succeeding plans (ills. 42–48), south is at the top.
   The chapel is at the bottom left, the infirmary and concierge's lodgings in the lower right.
Centre right is the square stairwell leading up to the courts; beyond that, on the right of the
cloister, the prisons for women and men under sentence; on the left, those for women and men on
remand. (Archives Nationales)

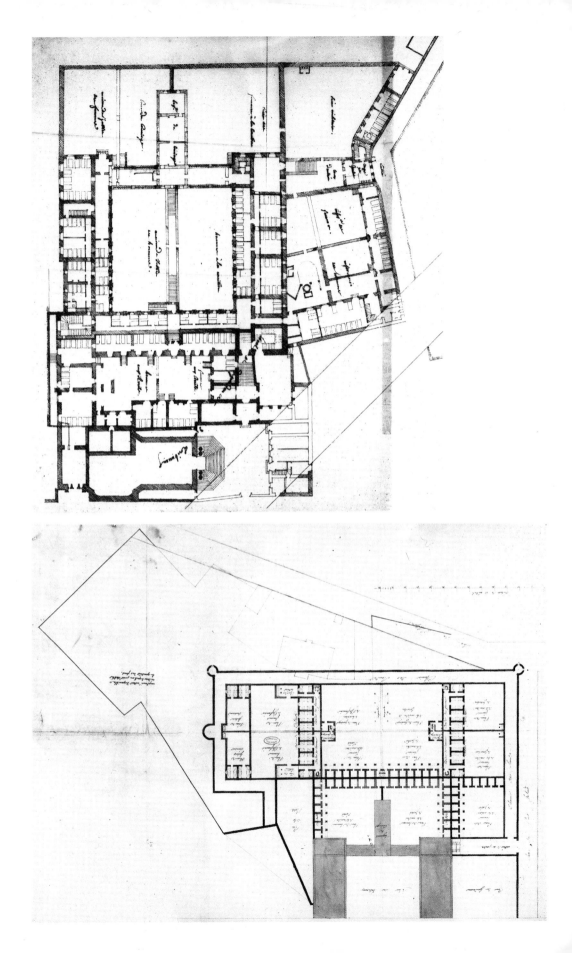

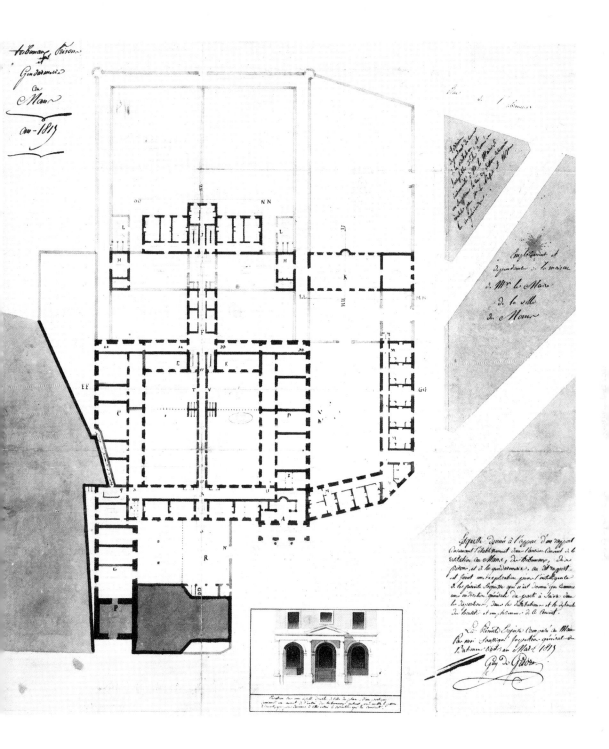

◁ 42   J.-A. Daudin and J.-B. Béchet-Deshourmeaux. The prison at the Visitandines altered and enlarged: ground-floor plan, dated June 1814. Chief additions are the concierge's house, in axis with the centre of the cloister, and a military prison, top right. (Archives Nationales)

◁ 43   P.-B. Cherrier. Plan for a new prison on a site to the south of the Visitandines, 1816–17. The existing cloister and concierge's house are shaded at the bottom. (Archives Nationales)

44   G. de Gisors. Plan for rationalization and enlargement of the prison and courts, March 1817. The inset elevation shows a new entrance to the courts (at A, above). (Archives Nationales)

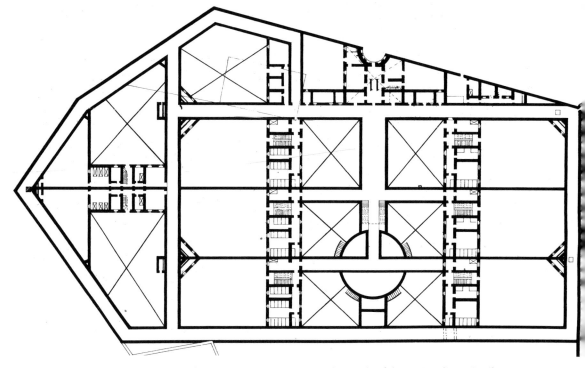

45–47 J.-A. Alavoine. Project for a new prison on a site to the south of the Visitandines, April 1818. (Redrawn from originals in the Archives Nationales)
  Above: ground plan. The entrance is at the top, flanked by cells for prisoners in transit, and a guardroom. A central axis leads from the entrance to the chapel. To the right of it is accommodation for women (detention on the outer edge, recreation space flanking the axis); to the left, in mirror image, accommodation for men. The wedge shape at the far left contains the infirmary. (Open spaces are marked by diagonal crosses.)

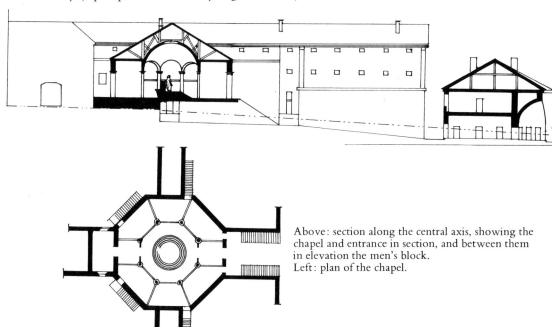

Above: section along the central axis, showing the chapel and entrance in section, and between them in elevation the men's block.
Left: plan of the chapel.

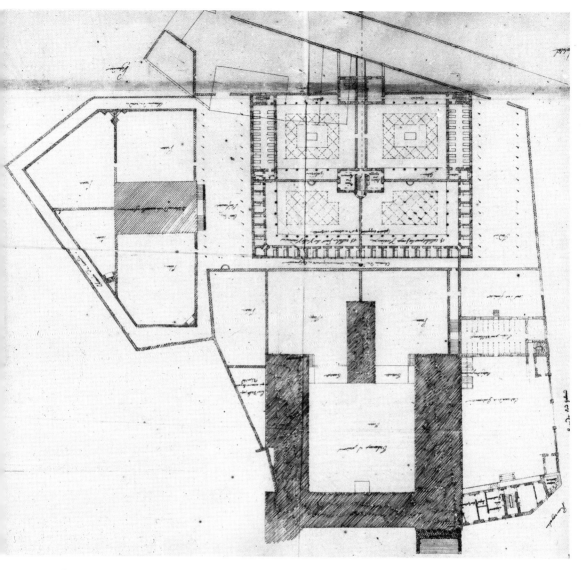

48 Delarue. Project for an asylum and barracks on the land of the Visitandines, March 1825. The cloister and concierge's house are shaded at the bottom. (Archives Nationales)

dead Cellerier's partner, the architect Alavoine, was sent to investigate. Following the request of the council of the *département*, Alavoine submitted two proposals in the spring of 1818, both uninspired.[53] The second consists of two groups of buildings, one for men and one for women, each divided into three areas (questioning, arrest and punishment) together with a guard house, a military prison and an infirmary. At the centre is a circular chapel to provide an element of variety in the all-too-insistent grid. Then, in March 1825, Delarue (chief architect of the *département* from 1828 to 1864) proposed

-47

that the site of the convent of the Visitation be used for an asylum and a barracks.[54] In the end, the prison remained below the law courts – and has remained there right up to the present – and an asylum was built to Delarue's design outside the town, on the banks of the Huisne, near the abattoir.

48

49, 50
38

What is one to conclude from this study? In France, at the beginning of the 19th century, it would seem there was a change in the intellectual approach to design. A clarity of aim and a logic of process were imposed on built form through the formation of programmes

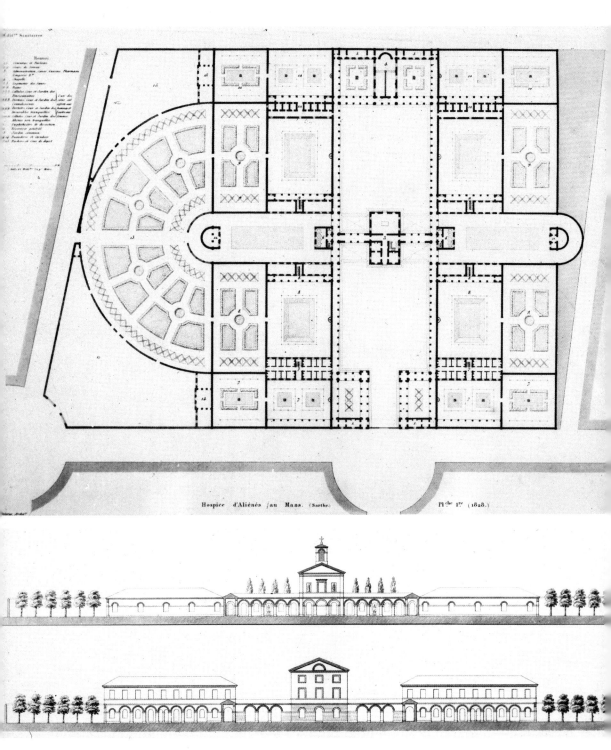

49, 50　Delarue. Lunatic asylum, Le Mans, 1828–34: plan, and sections across the first courtyard (bottom), showing the central administration and services building flanked by wards for convalescent patients, and across the second courtyard, showing the chapel flanked by cells for violent women patients. (From Gourlier, Biet, Grillon and Tardieu, *Choix d'édifices publics projetés et construits en France depuis le commencement du XIXe siècle*, I, 1824–36)

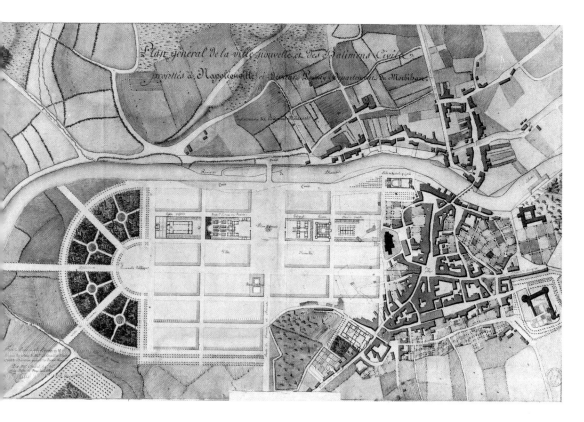

51 Layout of the new town of Napoléonville (formerly Pontivy), dated 25 pluviose Year XIII (February 1805). (Archives Nationales)

and rules and the deliberate changing of religious buildings into state institutions, demanding a novel approach to composition. Building became part of the 'democratic' approach to overall planning, reflecting general aims and regularizing the contradictory demands of society. A new understanding of the town was evolved, based on three premises: a uniform method of selecting and designating sites; a set approach to the determining of programmes related to needs, organizational requirements and methods of construction; and, lastly, a calculated balance between open and usefully built-up areas.[55] The building of these programmed areas, symbols of modern institutionalism and discipline, set within towns like so many 'heterotopies' (special places), was the calculated aim of the new town planning.[56]

There was planning, but not an overall plan; the old towns were transformed piecemeal, at their centres and in their outskirts. At Le Mans,

as elsewhere, there was no attempt to impose visual control in the form of boulevards, squares, etc., although new towns founded under the Empire are often cited as examples of such an approach – Napoléon-Vendée (on the site of La Roche-sur-Yon), Napoléonville (at Pontivy, in the Morbihan), or Comacchio in Italy.[57] But the layout at Pontivy, designed between 1803 and 1805 by engineers such as Chabrol and Pichot and by architects such as Guy de Gisors (he made his counter-proposals in 1808), cannot be regarded as an alternative approach applicable to towns such as Le Mans. Even if, as at Pontivy, the resulting plan might be reduced to the simplest of forms, with a checkerboard of plots and squares, the open sites of the new town and the built-up areas of the old were ultimately determined with equal vigour by the working methods of a state administration, providing a regularity of procedures, of function and of form.

Chemins, Canaux Ponts, et Chaussée.
Dun état bien dirrigé,
Font la prosperité.

52   Frontispiece of the *Recueil polytechnique des ponts et chaussées*. (Bibliothèque Nationale)

IV

Early architectural periodicals

Helene Lipstadt

DURING THE CONSULATE and early Empire, a period of almost no building activity in France,[1] there was one type of architectural boom: a boom in architectural publications. Contemporaries even remarked on the paradox. In 1804, it was reported in the *Journal des bâtiments civils*:

> Books published in parts, with engravings, increased enormously in number: twelve, at least, issued during the past six years, have had considerable success … which leads to the fond hope that when peace comes, we will have the architects able to design the most beautiful buildings. Nothing of note has yet been done; it is all still in the portfolios.[2]

The books included *recueils* by Percier and Fontaine (1798, 1801, 1809), Krafft and Ransonette (1801, 1805, 1812), Dubut (1803) and Clochar (1809); treatises by Durand (1800, 1802–05) and Rondelet (1802); a collection of Grand Prix drawings (1806) and the first part of C.-N. Ledoux's great work *L'Architecture considérée sous le rapport de l'art, des moeurs et de la législation* (1804). But of almost equal significance was the appearance of the first architectural magazine, the *Journal des bâtiments civils*, later to be known as the *Journal des bâtiments, des monuments et des arts*, and still later as the *Annales de l'architecture*. Founded by a group of contractors, it was to survive for ten years.[3] Also dating from this period was the first art journal, *Nouvelles des arts*,[4] started in 1802 by the painter C.-P. Landon, editor also of the *Annales du musée*, and the first engineering journal, *Recueil polytechnique des ponts et chaussées*, begun in 1803.[5]

The appearance of these publications is to be accounted for by the abolition of the royal *privilèges*, which had amounted to a form of censorship, the post-revolutionary habit of free expression and, linked to it, the inactivity of most architects – and Ledoux is only the most obvious example. But such factors do not explain the success of the books and the journals. Indeed, there were important inhibiting factors.

When, in October 1800, François Camille, a building contractor – traditional enemy of the architect – sent out one thousand copies of the *Journal des bâtiments* free to artists and architects, he had to confront the newly instituted censorship of Napoleon Bonaparte, First Consul, who nine months earlier had closed down sixty of the seventy-three Parisian papers and had since submitted the press to the most stringent of controls.

At first he had spared scientific, philosophical, literary and artistic periodicals from control. But his critics at once took advantage to make covert attacks in these papers. A spate of new ones were started. Soon censorship was extended to these too.[6] The *Journal des bâtiments*, it is worth remembering, expressed itself more freely than most in its criticism of Napoleon's public works.[7] In thermidor Year X (July 1802) it launched into an attack on the continued use of pre-revolutionary systems of measurement and terminology in the port of Brest, the most important of French naval establishments: 'It is scarcely surprising that in the port of Brest they are unfamiliar with the new measures, for, despite the onslaught of the Revolution that has shaken Europe, not to say the world, nothing there has changed in name or effect.'[8] The *préfet maritime* at Brest was duly offended and the police were compelled to reprimand the editors. This was not the last time that official scrutiny was to be directed at the magazine. In 1808 a reader commented: 'The 18th century produced fewer fine buildings than the 17th, and it is likely that the present one will likewise be inferior to that preceding it.' This was at once taken up by the police, who noted in their daily report to the Minister of the Interior: 'The editors reject the opinion, but why then did they publish the letter?'[9] During the Empire, especially, criticism and comment were watched for political overtones. The press was even advised not to describe the bas-relief or quote the inscription on the façade of Bernard Poyet's portico for the *Corps législatif* – a refacing of the old Palais Bourbon – 'only the quality of the artist's work', it was warned, 'may be the object of discussion and criticism'.[10]

Caution prompted Camille from the start. To the police he sent a printed prospectus that seems never to have been distributed to the public. Therein he expressed an intention to replace 'the lines of communication that the Revolution has broken', because 'contractors and workmen have no central focus for communication'. As to any wider aims, he was quite specific. 'We will leave politics to its ten or twelve controllers, the *fine arts* to the *fine artists*, and the sciences to *our masters*.'[11] In the first issue he asserted the most mundane of hopes. 'What we hope to deal with is the day-to-day price of the raw materials used by contractors.'[12]

And so he began, twice weekly listing the cost of building materials. One hundred and forty pages appeared each month, amounting to four octavo volumes a year. But with the publication of the third issue he started a transformation, to be completed within three weeks; the lists and accompanying advertisements were relegated to the back pages, and in their place were professional announcements, critical comment on current architecture and architectural practice, history, theory and, above all, debate. The *beaux-arts* he had advised the police that he intended to disregard were presided over by none other than A.-C. Quatremère de Quincy – his contributions signed 'Q***'. Alongside attacks on the newly instituted academies were expressions of Quatremère de Quincy's academic classicism, with its emphasis on 'la manière d'imiter la bonne architecture grecque'.[13] Such divergence of opinion was important, for, if his journal was to survive, it must attract as wide a range of readers as possible. Though Camille had taken his title from the state building agency, the Conseil des Bâtiments Civils, he received no official support or even encouragement.[14] Like the editors of most architectural journals to follow – and notably César Daly – he felt obliged to offer his readers 'an open forum'. The audience he

aimed at was even wider than might be expected. A number of architectural courses had been initiated after the Revolution by the *sociétés savantes*, replacements as it were to the academies of the *ancien régime*, where philosophers, scientists, architects and other men of learning gathered together for instruction and discussion in what Jules Michelet was later to characterize as an atmosphere of 'friendly sociability'.[15] The proceedings of such societies served, indeed, as the model for Camille's revised journal.

His aim, he claimed more than once, was to advance the aesthetic goals of the school of contemporary French architecture, by which he meant that of Paris, for he was much concerned to correct the backward state of building in the provinces. 'Of all the means one might use to this end, a periodical publication is at once the most convenient, the quickest and the cheapest.'[16] In a letter to the Minister of the Interior, Jean-Antoine Chaptal, he made clear his aesthetic preferences:

> Severity and purity, these are our rules. They are, if I may say so, our measures for praise and blame. They serve as the standards when judging those flights of imagination, and that richness of ornamentation masking poverty of invention, which frivolousness, a taste for unfettered individuality, and a lack of serious application have for some time produced in the French School.[17]

It is difficult to judge Camille's taste, for he illustrated and upheld for admiration only one example of contemporary architecture – a morgue designed by J.-B. Guignet. This Piranesian project was described as 'simple, solid and severe', but in no sense 'repellent'.[18] He limited his aesthetic preferences no doubt because most of the plates were probably paid for by contributors. There are a few examples of contemporary design, such as the decorations of public fêtes, but most of the plates illustrate new systems or inventions, such as a mechanical flute player or a method of building cellars devised in Holland. When the *Journal* became the *Annales de l'architecture* the number of plates increased, but the editorial policy remained much the same. There were illustrations of a new roofing system, new lamps and a lightning-conductor for a powder magazine, the design of a military engineer. The competitions and the few buildings that were undertaken at the period were illustrated, rather, in Landon's *Annales du musée*. Camille could offer no more than the forum for discussion that he had promised in his prospectus:

A periodical provides a range of knowledge at little cost; its clear and simple style can be understood by all. Changes in art may be followed day by day and, so to speak, step by step. It provides a *free forum* for discussion, for those for and against, in which a talented man who is too modest or too busy to write a book can make himself known to the enlightened public. It is a constant education.[19]

His contributors were for the most part anonymous, but they included architects such as C.-T. de Lussault, J. Thierry and C.-F. Viel. The only important figure in the field of architecture to appear was Quatremère de Quincy, who allowed extracts from his writings to be reprinted and contributed letters and even a review of J.-N.-L. Durand's *Précis des leçons d'architecture*. Therein he judged Durand a man of talent, his institution 'without equal in Europe', but considered that architecture could be learned only on the building site, not in books or schools.[20] Rondelet once wrote a reply to a reader who complained about a rise in the price of his book, but he cannot be considered a contributor. Nor indeed can Ledoux, whose *Architecture* could be ordered through the editorial office. Ledoux and Durand emerge as the favourite architects of the readers.

Whatever the practical nature of the *Journal*, implicit throughout was a belief in the artistic basis of architecture. This was a traditional attitude, inherent in the accepted image of the architect, cultivated in the system of education offered and in the organization of the profession. But already, with the bulk of building under the control of the state or in the impersonal hands of speculators or developers, the architect was more dependent on the client than was the artist. Architects, however, were not prepared to recognize any other kinship, not even with the rapidly rising engineer.

Engineers had become crucial to the state, not only in military exploitation, but in the centralization of control and the organization of public works throughout the new Republic and its conquered territories – in Italy, Germany and Holland. During the Consulate and Empire, the engineers of the Corps des Ponts et Chaussées gradually replaced architects as the instruments

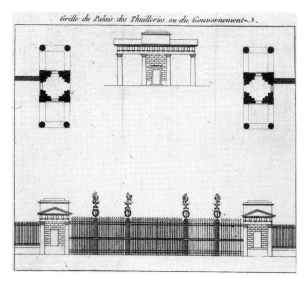

53 Grille du Palais des Thuilleries ou du Gouvernement, from the *Journal des bâtiments*, XI

of state control of building.[21] Organized in a para-military manner, well educated, disciplined, resourceful and ruthless, engineers were assigned to the *préfectures* and soon enough – though often not without conflict – replaced the provincial architects. Opposition on their part was fruitless, particularly after 1811, when the engineer Louis Bruyère was appointed to the control of the public works of Paris, a post that carried with it the presidency of the Conseil des Bâtiments Civils.

Engineers, not surprisingly, had no need of a periodical as a focus of identity. Yet attempts were made to provide one, as documents newly discovered in the archives of the Ecole des Ponts et Chaussées reveal.[22] A building contractor called Houard asked in December 1802 for permission to edit a periodical for the Conseil des Ponts et Chaussées. He was rudely dispatched and all chief engineers were stringently prohibited from co-operating with him: 'the proposal put forward is not only of no benefit to the public or the members of the Ponts et Chaussées, but implies no editorial control and might thus compromise the institution and lead designers astray'.[23] Houard determined, nonetheless, to proceed, and at least one engineer, Piou, disregarded the instructions he had received and subscribed to the new magazine, the *Recueil polytechnique des ponts et chaussées*. His name appears on the list of 223 subscribers, together with those of 150

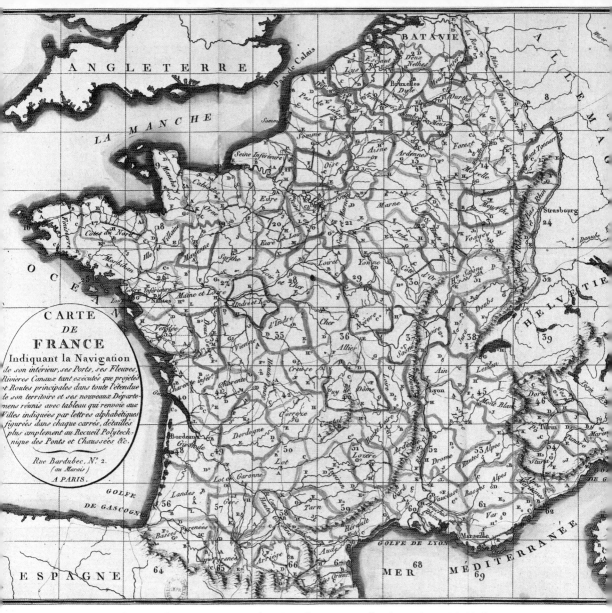

54   Map of France showing existing and projected waterways, by the engineer M.-H. Devert, from the *Recueil polytechnique des ponts et chaussées*, I, Year XII [1803]

other engineers, the Ecole des Ponts et Chaussées itself, 13 architects and several notable personalities of the period: Julie Récamier's husband, a banker; Josephine Beauharnais-Bonaparte's son; the First Consul's librarian; and the Minister of the Interior.[24] The magazine seems to have been issued under the protection of Herbert d'Hauteclair, administrator of the Corps des Ponts et Chaussées under the *ancien régime*, Directeur du Pavé de la Ville de Paris in 1789, and Lebrun, an Inspecteur in the Corps.[25] Despite this protection however the review was short-lived. Two volumes only appeared, one in 1803, another in 1807.

Architects were addressed in the subtitle, but the focus of attention was on engineers and engineering:

Our aim is to uphold the views of the government and its invincible head in all matters of internal and maritime navigation; the making and maintenance of roads, public building and civic constructions of all kinds; the draining of marshes to improve sanitation; the planting of woods and forests; in short, anything relating to the Ponts et Chaussées, that profession which is one of the most honourable and useful to society.[26]

Readers of the *Recueil* were offered no discussion of aesthetic theory or building technique, but rather plans for regional and even national development: the term *territoire*, denoting the area of government control, appears again and again. Political implications, absent in the architectural *Journal*, are at once apparent. The frontispiece alone of the *Recueil* proclaims the engineers' concerns and aims:

> Chemins, Canaux, Ponts, et Chaussée,
> D'un état bien dirrigé,
> Font la prosperité.

The *Journal*, in contrast, cautioned against all such larger ambition: 'Soyez plutôt maçon', it proclaimed. The editor, Camille, outspoken for once, enlarged on his intentions: '"Be a builder rather" is our motto, because that's what we can do. . . . If architects do not themselves debase the respect usually accorded to their estate by becoming contractors, or associating with them, and if builders stop wanting to call themselves architects, so as to take over businesses and exploit them to the ruin of their owners, then, one might wager, things will improve.'[27]

The engineers were challenged to enlarge the prosperity of France by driving new roads and channels of communication through the country and even beyond – canals, in particular, were a subject of constant study in the *Recueil*, and on one occasion those already built and all those projected were drawn on a map to show how the country might best be served and controlled. The architects of the *Journal* on the other hand were subjected to the frustrations of unbuilt competition entries, diatribe and futile debate. The competition for a *Colonne nationale*, won by Moreau, prompted no less than thirty-five letters, attacks and counter-proposals, including one from no less a man than Louis-Pierre Baltard.[28] Even built works stirred the rage of the inactive architects. The Pont des Arts, the first iron bridge in Paris, was denounced as unpleasing and undemocratic. It would have been better had it been built in stone, on a different spot, and designed by an architect. One detractor, it is scarcely surprising to find, was Charles-François Viel, inveterate hater of all elegant and economical construction. The bridge, he declared, was 'Gothic in its lack of substance, both in plan and in elevation, with piers no more than two metres wide, allowing for no wearing with time'.[29]

Engineers, though they contributed often enough to the *Journal*, did not deign to respond to such attacks. There was no need. Indeed, throughout the century they were to find that the best response to architects' criticism was silence. Engineers engaged in debate with other engineers only, and not unless the stakes were high. One such occasion was provided by the building of the Ourcq canal, about sixty-five miles long, an early and extraordinarily ambitious attempt to indulge in regional planning. The administrative battle stirred by this project involved a struggle between Girard, a young engineer, protégé of Bonaparte, and the Conseil des Ponts et Chaussées itself for control of the Corps des Ponts et Chaussées. An article appeared in the *Recueil* on the subject, but no lively debate was offered, only a plea for tolerance and patience. Whichever side won, Houard intended to survive.[30]

The editors of the *Journal* and the *Recueil* had more in common than might be expected. Both, for a start, masked their identities. François Camille was in fact Maurice-François-Camille Le Bars, a joinery contractor (*entrepreneur en menuiserie*). He was not only a joinery contractor but, as Le Bars, a speculator in real estate. His true identity and the range of his capitalist enterprise is revealed in the police archives, in the records of the Conseil des Bâtiments Civils among his lawyer's papers and in the attacks of a rival editor.[31] He applied to the police for permission to start his magazine under the name of Le Bars, but in the role of editor he identified himself always as Camille, carrying on a correspondence under that name, for instance, with Emiland Gauthey, Inspecteur des Ponts et Chaussées. On one occasion, as 'F.C.L.B.', he addressed a letter to his alter ego, Camille, requesting that it be published.[32] Houard, as editor of the *Recueil*, used only his initials, M.B.A.H. His identity is revealed in a contract between himself and the owner of the review, Louis Baratin. Houard was the son of a contractor (*maître terrassier*). Between 1788 and 1809 he steadily enhanced his standing, signing official documents under the *ancien régime* as a *maître terrassier*, later, in a letter to the Conseil des Bâtiments Civils, as *employé et entrepreneur des ponts et chaussées*, then as *artiste des bâtiments et ponts et chaussées* and, finally, throughout the remainder of the Consulate and Empire, as *architecte*. He claimed also to have worked on the gardens of Versailles, a claim reinforced by his inclusion in the *Almanach des Bastimens* of 1790, as 'entrepreneur de plantations et jardins à l'anglaise'.

Houard and his father had worked in the region between Chartres and Le Mans, in which his 'intimate friend' and apparently patron, Herbert d'Hauteclair, had large estates. Moving to Paris, he continued his trade, but dabbled, like Camille, in property. He certainly had interests in the Filles de Calvaire *quartier*, for which he drew up a plan. Together with Soulavie, a diplomat, he also drew up and published a plan of Paris, which he maintained was subscribed for by thousands and ran into at least six editions during the course of the century. In his speculative and building activities, in particular in the provision of plans, *devis et marches*, he was aided by François-Marie Courtépée, who tactfully signed himself 'aussi architecte' on their contract. In drawing up his large-scale maps he was helped by a certain Devert, with whom he has been confused and compounded, a fictional character, Benoît-André-Houard Devert being evolved.[33]

During the Revolution, Houard claimed, he founded the Point Central des Arts et Métiers, one of the more active *sociétés savantes* concerned with architecture, and he was, he said, responsible for drawing up the programme for its journal. But his name does not appear in any of the surviving issues of the journal nor is he listed among the society's members. Several of these, it should be remarked, contributed to the *Journal des bâtiments*, whose editor Camille is likewise not recorded as a member of any *société savante*.[34]

Camille and Houard rose from similar social backgrounds to become editors and property speculators, and their activities might be judged together to have been of the opportunistic kind and thus readily dismissed, but there was more to their ambition than money making. In taking for their editorial model the *sociétés savantes*, they were both aiming at intellectual enterprise of a new kind, effacing themselves, throwing open discussion to their contributors. In the *Journal des bâtiments*, as has already been stressed, this is particularly evident. Readers provided the copy and it was mainly of the critical sort; they debated endlessly – discussions on Quatremère de Quincy's concept of 'character' in architecture ran into hundreds of pages of print – but the most urgent issue of all, it seems, was that of architectural identity. Like the editor,

the readers aspired to be architects and were determined to define that profession. In ventôse Year X (March 1802) a mason wrote to the *Journal des bâtiments* to carp at the looseness of the definition of the term. There were, he said, at least seven different types of architect:

les architectes compositeurs et constructeurs
les architectes censeurs
les architectes dessinateurs
les architectes éditeurs
les architectes jurés-experts
les architectes entrepreneurs
les architectes ENTREPRENANTS[35]

Soon readers had identified twenty-seven categories of architect, ranging from the traditional naval, military and hydraulic architects (as described in the treatises of Vitruvius and Belidor) to newly evolved types such as the landscape architect, the rural architect (exemplified by that proponent of *pisé de terre*, François Cointereaux) or the architect of fireworks (Ruggieri, who had designed the *fêtes* of the Revolution). Clearly, putative architects were seeking desperately to define their cultural boundary. Self-assured engineers had no need for such debate. There is nothing in the pages of the *Recueil* to tell of any unease. Not surprisingly, Camille advised his readers to look to the engineering profession as a model:

Architects have a disability from which difficulties arise for themselves and to the detriment of their art: they are not organized as a body related to the government, like the engineers . . . it might well be that they should form such a body, with all the advantages enjoyed by engineers; there would be less dissension among themselves and more respect for one another. They could then be appointed to departmental positions, according to merit, and enjoy the confidence of the government.[36]

Though architects might cast envious eyes on the engineer's lot, there was in no sense active opposition between the two groups. Engineers, indeed, if one is to judge from contributions made to the *Recueil*, were heedless of any disparity either in activity or status. Yet there were real differences. Engineers were trained in a disciplined manner to acquire precise, useful knowledge, and all who graduated were assured of proper, active employment, albeit in the provinces for the most part. Architects were trained as a rule at the Ecole des Beaux-Arts, but, though this institution might seem to hold the keys to the profession, anyone who could pay for the patent, costing one hundred francs, could call himself an architect. Nor was he even then certain of employment. The top jobs, the key government commissions, went invariably to the winners of the Grand Prix, and though the students were educated in *ateliers* loosely attached to the Ecole, the Grand Prix was awarded not by the professors of the Ecole but by the entire Académie des Beaux-Arts, where architects were in a minority. In theory, any student, even an engineer, could win the coveted prize. But only one student each year could thus achieve high professional status. Obsolescence was built into the system of architectural education. Most students were expendable.

Edouard Charton, the educational reformer, author of the *Dictionnaire des professions ou guide pour le choix d'un état*, published first in 1840, commented wryly: 'there are few professions in which it is easier for mediocrity to win out over merit ... it is one of the pleasantest and most respected careers for a young man, especially if he has means and does not need to work.'[37]

It is no wonder that the engineers refrained from comment when architects battled in the pages of the *Journal*. The endless exchanges and polemics in the 19th-century architectural press – architect against building contractor, architect against engineer, 'true architects' against 'false architects', who paid for the patent but did not merit the title – are skirmishes in a war of definition that can be called the 'dialectic of distinction'. The position and very existence of each professional group and of its members, bound to each other by relations of dependence and competition, are described by these polemical diatribes. This quest for distinction is a political and cultural struggle for survival in which there are enemies and allies. The most fundamental and debilitating contests occur, however, when the closest neighbours confront each other. It is a paradox of social conflict that those with the most in common will be the bitterest enemies,

for they have the most to gain by victory. The enemy of the architect in 19th-century France is the architect.

The simplistic view of an indivisible corps of engineers united by a conscious desire to supplant the architect is a myth, present in the 19th century but made universally familiar by Sigfried Giedion in *Space, Time and Architecture*. The engineers respond to the attacks of the architects with silence, the privilege of those in power. The polemic waged by architects against engineers in the 19th century failed to engage the attention of their supposed rivals; it served only to obscure the more fundamental conflict between architects and architects.

By harbouring, propagating and even, in the case of the *Journal des bâtiments*, insidiously inspiring polemic, the editors of architectural magazines proferred their help in this battle of distinction. Publication in the magazine of original texts and descriptions of projects gave architects publicity, and more. The architects who contributed regularly to the *Journal* were minor municipal architects like Vicl and Lussault, little-known writers and administrators like Guillaumot. Excluded from the newly refounded Institut's Section des Beaux-Arts and from imperial patronage, threatened by the arrival of a new generation, that of Percier and Fontaine, architects turned first to the unofficial academies, the *sociétés savantes* and the magazines for confirmation of their social existence as architects. Lussault even acknowledged the role of the *Journal* in enabling him to call himself an artist:

Citoyen, upon receiving the letter you were so kind as to send me on 9 nivose last, I was not a little surprised to find myself addressed (on what foundation I know not) as a distinguished artist; I, who imagined that my isolation, or rather the obscurity to which the nature of my work during the past five years has confined me, would scarce allow me to consider myself even as an artist.[38]

Pont sur un chemin
de fer

Huillard
Elève de Mr Balla

55   C.-G. Huillard. Railway Bridge, Prix d'Emulation, first class, 1852. (Beaux-Arts)

V

The programmes of the architectural section of the Ecole des Beaux-Arts, 1819–1914

Annie Jacques

ONE ASPECT OF THE TEACHING of architecture at the Ecole des Beaux-Arts that has been little studied is the monthly architectural competition, both in the form of sketch designs (*esquisses*) and rendered projects (*projets rendus*), together with other related competitions, such as the Rougevin prize, starting in 1857, to be followed by the Achille Leclère, Chaudesaignes, Godeboeuf, American Architects and others.

Submission for the Prix de Rome – in the architectural section at any rate – was a rarified affair, with regard to both the programmes and the style of drawing and composition (see Chapter VI). The day-to-day activity in the Ecole was reflected more faithfully by the monthly competitions (Concours Mensuels d'Emulation), judged by a jury made up by teachers within the Ecole, and not by members of the Académie des Beaux-Arts within the Institut, as with the Prix de Rome, which was judged by very different criteria.

Every pupil, in the first and the second class, was required to enter at least two of these competitions every academic year, under threat of expulsion from the architectural section and the necessity of reapplying for admission.

Whatever the aspiration of the pupils for the prestigious Prix de Rome competition, it was the monthly competitions that were most representative of the teaching of the thousands of architects, French and foreign, who passed through the Ecole des Beaux-Arts during the 19th century – imperative for the foreign students, who were not eligible for the Prix de Rome. In all, 6,500 pupils were admitted between 1819 and 1914, a period in which only 100 were to win the Grand Prix.

The programmes for the Grand Prix, drawn up by the Académie, were notably different from those for the monthly competitions, written by the professor of architectural theory

at the Ecole. David Van Zanten, in his contribution to *The Architecture of the Ecole des Beaux-Arts*, has already noted that 'the Concours d'Emulation projects seem practical and relevant, whereas the Grand Prix projects seem impossible and megalomaniac' (p. 232). Some study of the programmes for the Concours d'Emulation, therefore, seems to be required. Certain themes remain constant, others emerge fitfully, while some appear not at all. Certain subjects were set for particular years. Technological innovations were taken up on occasion, though many inventions were ignored.

Long-term projects, drawn up in the *ateliers*, conforming to the sketches done first *en loge* (booths within the Ecole), alternated with short-term projects, drawn up in twelve hours *en loge*, on demi-Grand-Aigle (Elephant) sheets, about 35cm × 51cm.

The subjects were set by the professor of architectural theory, hence their significance, for it is easier to direct study by setting a programme than by delivering lectures on theory, which students may or may not attend. The men who held this position through successive years from 1819 to 1914 were Baltard, Blouet, Lesueur, Guillaume, Guadet and Blavette.

Louis-Pierre Baltard (1764–1846), succeeding Dufourny, occupied the chair from 1819, when the Ecole des Beaux-Arts was formally re-established, to his death in 1846. Trained in the *atelier* of the younger Peyre, he first became known for his drawings; indeed it was as a painter that he was sent to Rome by a patron, in 1786, for he was never to win the Grand Prix.[1] Nonetheless, in Rome he mixed with the *pensionnaires* of the Villa Medici. With the founding of the Ecole Polytechnique in 1794, he began to teach the course on civic architecture. From 1813 onwards he served also as architect to the Panthéon. In 1819, at the age of 55, he became professor at the Ecole des Beaux-Arts. For twenty-seven years he retained this position. During the last four years, from 1842 to 1846 (when he was between his 78th and 82nd year) he was helped by his son, Victor, officially appointed as his assistant. Baltard hoped that his son would succeed him, but it was not the professors who made such appointments.

Abel Blouet (1795–1853) was elected in his place. He was of humble origin, the son of an artisan, who had entered the Ecole des Beaux-Arts and eventually won the Grand Prix, in 1821. He stayed in Italy for five years and then extended his classical education with an official archaeological expedition to the Morea (the Peloponnese), from 1828 to 1831. But his interests were to be directed rather to contemporary matters: he travelled to the United States of America with the magistrate Demetz to study penitentiaries, a journey that resulted in several publications, one of particular note, that written with Hector Horeau. Blouet had by then taken up a position on the Conseil des Bâtiments Civils. In 1846 he became professor at the Ecole. His last official appointment was as architect to the château of Fontainebleau. He died, relatively young, in 1853.

He was replaced by Jean-Baptiste-Cicéron Lesueur, a man of Blouet's generation, indeed a man born one year earlier than Blouet, in 1794. Lesueur had also won the Grand Prix earlier, in 1819. His chief activity, some private houses apart, was the reconstruction of the Paris Hôtel de Ville, begun in 1835. Elected professor in 1853, he maintained his position for thirty years. Even the reforms of 1863 scarcely disrupted the continuity of his teaching – 'I will hold them still with my programmes', André reports him as saying – for on 11 March 1864 he was appointed by the Minister to take charge of the architectural competitions, and when on 15 January 1873 the chair of architectural theory was re-established, Lesueur was appointed to it. In this particular field, it must be clear, the reforms of 1863 had little effect. Lesueur continued active to his death in 1883.

Edmond-Jean-Baptiste Guillaume took over from him. Born in 1826, Guillaume was also a Grand Prix winner, in 1856, who followed a traditional career, designing both private and public buildings, acting, most notably, as architect to the Louvre and the Tuileries. His professorship was, indeed, somewhat subordinate to his architectural career. He died in 1898, but Julien Guadet had been called in four years earlier to act as his assistant, at least in the writing of programmes for the Concours.

Julien Guadet, born in 1834, is perhaps best known of the professors of theory at the Ecole, his reputation established by his *Eléments et théorie de l'architecture* (see Chapter I), and, to a lesser extent, by his role in the events of 1863. Like his predecessors, he was a product of the Ecole, winner of the Grand Prix in 1864, Inspecteur for the Bâtiments Civils and the Théâtre-Français. He was, however, more closely linked to the teaching of the Ecole than Guillaume and Lesueur, for in 1871 he succeeded Constant-Dufeux as tutor in one of the official *ateliers*.

The last professor one can consider as belonging to the 19th-century succession was Victor-Auguste Blavette, appointed in 1908, on Guadet's death. Born in 1850, Grand Prix winner in 1879, Blavette worked also for the Bâtiments Civils, and was architect to the international exhibitions of 1889 and 1900.

These six men chose all the subjects considered by several generations of architects. The professors set about twenty subjects a year, ten for each class, alternating long and short programmes (sketches and rendered projects). Over a period of almost a hundred years, from 1819 to 1914, there were more than five hundred different programmes – a total of some significance, for in theory no programme should have been repeated more than four times during the period. In practice, matters were otherwise, for certain subjects were repeated far more often then others, while some were set only once.

Several subjects were repeated throughout the century; baths, in particular, emerge as a favourite theme, appearing no less than fifty-one times in a range of guises: bath houses, private baths, steam baths, thermal baths, seaside baths and bathing centres.[2]

Another favourite subject was the school, which was set on sixty-three occasions, to cover the whole range of French education: primary schools, village schools, secondary schools, lycées and all schools of higher and university education, schools of arts and crafts, naval and military schools, art and architectural schools, schools of music, botany, medicine, chemistry, veterinary science, schools of engi-

89–92

63

neering and more. All branches of the sciences and the arts were thus represented, showing how faithfully the Ecole reflected the contemporary concern with education.

A third notable category was the monument. There are no less than seventy-one: commemorative and allegorical monuments, monuments dedicated to Virtue and Peace, to the artistic fraternity and to a series of great men, Poussin, Homer, Napoleon, Louis XIV, or simply 'great Frenchmen', whether under a monarchy, an empire or a republic.

In contrast, certain subjects were rarely set. One, the greenhouse, which might be thought characteristic of the 19th century, appears only occasionally. Baltard alone set this subject, first in 1824 (when it was associated with an orangery), then in 1825 and 1835 (for the first class), as a winter garden. Iron and glass building was regarded always as a secondary type of architecture.[3] With the exception of the extremes – subjects set more than fifty times or no more than once or twice – most of the programmes were repeated six or seven times in the course of the century, reappearing at about twelve-year intervals. Although the range of subjects is varied, it gives a distorted view of the architectural activity of the period.

One can classify the subjects according to their suitability and unsuitability to the times. There is a comparatively limited range of themes of classical inspiration, nymphea, grottoes, dairies, Roman houses, triumphal arches, naumachia, etc. Dairies, for instance, which seem to derive also from 18th-century garden architecture, were set on eleven occasions between 1819 and 1860, principally by Baltard. Blouet took up the subject in 1850, for the second class. Nymphea, which might also be seen as garden structures, were set by almost all the professors as sketch designs for the first class, in 1836, 1846, 1852, 1859, 1864, 1873, 1880 and 1890. Guadet and Blavette alone rejected the theme.

Another subject with little relation to reality, serving as an exercise in pure composition, was the House for Four Brothers, set in 1853, and repeated in 1860 and 1871 by Lesueur, on all three occasions as a rendered study for the second class. The programme was regarded always as the essence of a pure compositional study, and was repeated much later between the two World Wars. A similar programme was the House for Three Artists set as a rendered project for the first class in 1876.

56 F.-A. Duquesney. Telegraph Building, Prix d'Emulation, 1816. (Beaux-Arts)

Of another kind were those programmes closely linked to contemporary events and technology. A Telegraph Building was, surprisingly, set in 1816 by Dufourny, Baltard's predecessor, when the telegraph network was still in an experimental state. The younger Baltard returned to the subject in 1844, as did Blouet in 1851. By then, however, the programme had little point, for in 1844 visible telegraphic communication was superseded by the electric telegraph. Railway architecture (stations, signal boxes, tunnels etc.) also appeared early; in 1842 a Railway Station was the subject of a sketch design for the second class. The younger Baltard, who probably set the programme, was clearly something of an innovator, for the inauguration of the first railway in France, between Paris and Orléans, took place only in the following year. The subject was repeated in 1852 and 1858, and then, much expanded, in 1891 for the Prix de Rome. A design for the Metro was proposed only in 1904, four years after the opening of the first Paris lines with station entrances by Guimard.

57   F.-L. Boulanger. Théâtre forain, Prix d'Emulation, 1833. (Beaux-Arts)

Industrial architecture was not the concern of the Ecole. The word 'factory' (*usine*) does not appear in any of the programmes. Yet, in 1879, 1888 and 1893, there was a Tapestry and Porcelain Manufactory and in 1896 a Trading Post in Alaska. Commercial buildings provoked little interest, even in that century of banks and great department stores. A Bank was set on only three occasions between 1875 and 1899 – with the notable addition of the Grand Prix programme for 1889, won by Tony Garnier. As for the department store, it appeared only in its old guise as a Bazaar in 1831, 1833 and 1840, to be overlooked during the Second Empire, and to emerge once more in 1889. The individual shop was more popular; there are confectioners, jewellers and other shops, including even one for a butcher, set by Blouet in 1848.

Another subject reflecting the real life of the 19th century was that of the international exhibition, appearing first in 1853, two years after the 1851 exhibition in London, to be repeated, regularly, every six or seven years, in the first class.

The greater part of the programmes set for the students at the Ecole can be divided, roughly, into three categories:

Public buildings or buildings to be used by the public: schools, which have already been mentioned, are included in this group, as are administrative and other service buildings such as prefectural offices, town halls, municipal buildings, law courts, exchanges, museums, libraries, post offices, hospitals, almshouses, markets, theatres, cafés, fountains, 57, etc.

Ecclesiastical buildings: from the private chapel to the cathedral, including all variety of churches, their furnishings in detail and ancillary structures, together with related buildings such as bishops' palaces, convents etc. With ecumenical tact, Protestant churches, mosques and synagogues were included, but only towards the end of the century.

Private buildings: this includes a whole range of programmes, from town houses to country mansions, from the houses of great collectors to hunting lodges, all of the luxurious kind. Housing as such was dealt with only in the second class and then in the form of a middle-class house or an apartment block.

58   E. Brune. Café in a Public Park, Prix d'Emulation, 1862. (Beaux-Arts)

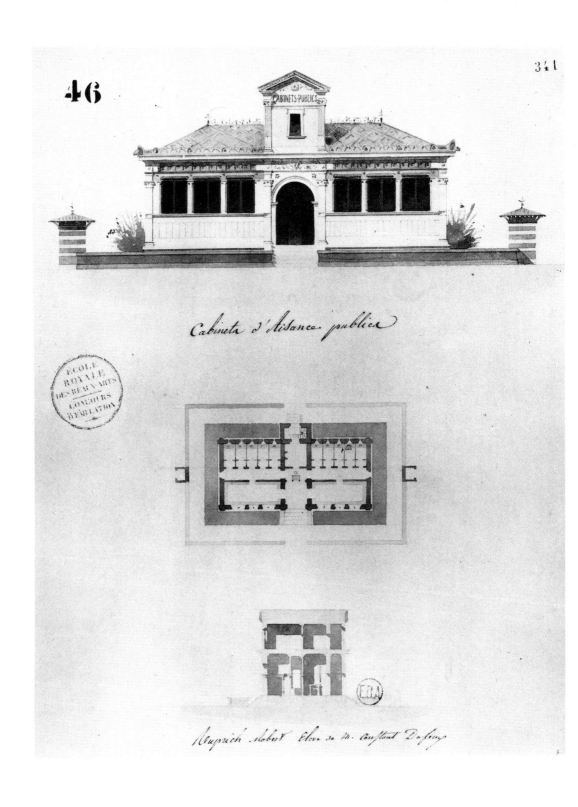

Cabinets d'Aisance publics

Ruprich Robert Elève de M. Constant Dufeux

59   G. Ruprich-Robert. Public Lavatory, Prix d'Emulation, first class, 1847. (Beaux-Arts)

Town planning was hardly tackled at all, providing no more than the setting for an individual building, in the form of a public square. But in that form it appears often enough.

Having summarily reviewed the programmes, it remains to distinguish the contribution of each of the professors.

During the twenty-six years of his professorship Louis-Pierre Baltard introduced many new themes, greatly increasing the range, hitherto extremely limited. His son, Victor, serving as his assistant during his last four years, was no doubt responsible for the introduction of a further range of odd and altogether adventurous themes: a Railway Station in 1842, and the only monument to be dedicated to men of science, Papin and Watt. He was also concerned with social issues and hygiene; in 1844 he set as a subject for the second class a Public Swimming Pool, and noted in the programme that 'workers might benefit from swimming'. Another unusual programme, set likewise for the second class, was a Cow-shed with Sick-bay; this however had already been proposed by Victor's father, in 1820, as a Sanitary Cow-shed. It was then thought that the proximity of cows might cure chest complaints.

Abel Blouet continued in this experimental tradition, especially in the second class, setting his students new subjects of a practical and commonplace kind: Post-inn; Butcher's Shop; Public Letter Writer's Stall; Steam-ship Booking Office; Communal Bakehouse; Park Café; Bandstand; Public Lavatory, etc.

Lesueur and Guillaume were less imaginative and certainly less innovative. They took their themes from the stock established by their predecessors, and not only the themes but often the texts of the programmes, which are repeated word for word, from ten or twenty years before. And their contemporaries were well aware of the situation. André, writing Lesueur's obituary in 1885, noted: 'During his last years his programmes might perhaps have been lacking in variety and appeared out of date, for the professor showed insufficient concern for contemporary social and industrial conditions which might have changed the study of architecture to some extent'.

Julien Guadet, in contrast, wished to invigorate the programmes: 'he made his students aware of the most pressing realities, the concerns of the moment, the most up to date concepts' – so, at any rate, wrote Pascal in his obituary. In fact, what Guadet did was to eliminate the more anachronistic subjects, such as the House for Four Brothers, and put the emphasis on those of a more contemporary nature, without introducing anything new.

One last point remains in considering the programmes, their differentiation according to class. Clearly, those for the Grand Prix and those for the monthly competitions, which were more practical, more commonplace, formed a hierarchy. There was also a distinction between those for the first and second class submissions. For the second class, the subjects were simpler: primary schools, small town halls and libraries, or provincial theatres. First class subjects were related always to larger towns or provincial capitals, while the Grand Prix projects were connected with the capital city or some national enterprise.

Each of these levels seems to have related to a stage in a possible career; it would be of interest to analyze the careers of architects who emerged from the Ecole, to see if they did reflect their level of attainment at the school.

What emerges from this short resumé is the variety and the novelty of the programmes during the first half of the century – the basis, perhaps, of the early success of the school and its ability to attract foreign students – while the less enterprising and routine nature of the programmes in the second half of the century might be held accountable for the failure of the school in the early 20th century.

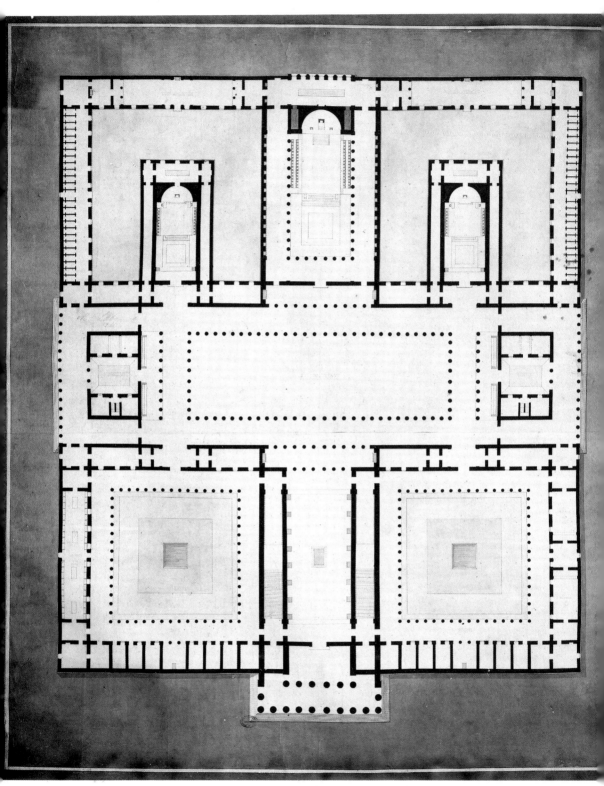

60   H. Labrouste. Cour de Cassation, 1824: rendered plan. (Beaux-Arts)

VI

The competition for the Grand Prix in 1824: a case study in architectural education at the Ecole des Beaux-Arts

Neil Levine

THE COMPETITION FOR THE GRAND PRIX, or Prix de Rome, was the final hurdle in the education of a 19th-century French architect.[1] The award was the highest possible achievement for a student at the Ecole des Beaux-Arts and virtually ensured a prestigious career. It is therefore quite natural that the prize-winning drawings submitted in the annual competition should be the best known examples of Beaux-Arts design and the basis for analysis and discussion of the methods taught at the Ecole.[2] Surprisingly, very little has been written about the competition itself: how it worked, what students took part in it, who judged it, how and why decisions were made.[3] One would like to know, for instance, what the average age of the winner was and if he should be thought of as a student or a young professional; whether the judges were the old fogies they are usually depicted as being; whether the competition was really anonymous; whether the programmes were as unrealistic as they are assumed to have been; what the relationship was between the Académie des Beaux-Arts and the Ecole in this one instance where their paths formally crossed. It is hoped that, by investigating one year in particular, answers to these as well as to the more fundamental questions of criteria of judgment may be suggested.

To understand how these school projects relate to the overall development of 19th-century French architecture one must determine to what extent the prize was awarded simply on merit and, ultimately, what constituted merit in the eyes of the jury.

Until quite recently, most modern architects and historians scoffed at the abstract composition, pompous decoration and virtuoso drawing of these apparently vapid 'paper plans'. Grand Prix designs were the symbol of the Ecole's academic devotion to the classical style and its

expression through drawing. The current rehabilitation of the Beaux-Arts has, therefore, stressed other aspects of the method. While the structural rationalism of some teachers and students of the Ecole has been pointed out, an apposite case has also been made for the role of elemental planning or composition in Beaux-Arts design.[4] However, in using winning Grand Prix projects as examples, it has been assumed (1) that the jury of the Académie chose in each case what it considered to be the best project, and (2) that it chose that project on the basis of its composition or plan. This flies in the face of the century-old modernist critique, which held that the Beaux-Arts was simply about drawing columns and pilasters and pediments and triumphal arches.

The revisionist approach predates by at least fifteen years the exhibition of 'The Architecture of the Ecole des Beaux-Arts' at the Museum of Modern Art in New York in 1975.[5] Before that, the study of Grand Prix designs was usually based on published documents. The premiated projects of the late 18th and early 19th centuries were available in the form of engravings, and the 19th-century winners, from 1823 on, were even more easily available in the photographic reproductions published by Guérinet.[6] But the earlier engravings reduce all the lusciously washed renderings to thin abstract lines on folio-sized paper, and the later, smaller, mass-produced photographic images give even less idea of the scale, clarity and punch of the originals.

It was extremely large wash drawings that the jury of the Académie looked at when it made its decision to send one architectural student each year to Rome to continue his studies for five years more. These drawings were worked on by the student for about four months in an effort to inspire the jury with enough confidence in his conscientiousness, as much as in his talent, to warrant the five-year investment in him. Each of the eight students usually submitted a minimum of five renderings, most of which measured over a metre wide, both their number and size increasing throughout the century. The total number hanging on the walls of the annual public exhibition was therefore at least forty or fifty. To get a better idea of what this must have looked like, it should be noted that this represents about one-third of all the student drawings in the show at the Museum of Modern Art, yet that exhibition covered more than a century.[7] Furthermore, no complete set of winning drawings was exhibited and, as is also true of the earlier publications referred to, only premiated projects were included.

One would naturally like to know all the losing projects as well as the winning ones in order to understand the Académie's decisions. Unfortunately, there has never been a publication, periodical or otherwise, containing all the drawings by all the competitors in any one year.[8] The Ecole kept only the winning renderings and *esquisses*, or preliminary sketch designs, on which those renderings were based.[9] Through a series of fortuitous circumstances I have been able to locate the eight designs for 1824, and have therefore chosen that year as a case study.[10] It was, luckily, a particularly noteworthy year since the winner, Henri Labrouste, was to become one of the leading figures in the development of modern architecture. The Second Grand Prix (second place) went to Louis Lepreux; and a Deuxième Second Grand Prix (third place) was awarded to Léon Vaudoyer.

The competition: structure and programme

The study of architecture at the Ecole des Beaux-Arts did not consist of a series of courses eventually leading to a degree. Rather, it was based almost entirely on monthly competitions, mainly in design, that provided the student with the knowledge and experience he would need to win the Grand Prix. As Richard Chafee has pointed out in his comprehensive discussion of the curriculum, the student moved at his own pace and could spend anywhere up to fifteen years at the Ecole.[11]

Normally, right after secondary school, the student began in what was called the second, or lower, class and, after winning a certain number of competitions, was promoted to the first, or upper, class.[12] Here the design competitions were more exacting and medals were given out to the winners. Each medal was worth a certain number of *valeurs*, or points, depending on whether the project was a sketch or a rendering. These determined his ranking in the class and, in turn, his eligibility to compete for the Grand Prix. Any success whatsoever in that competition further increased his standing. Every year the top student was awarded a prize called the Prix Départemental, which acted as a kind of incentive.[13] The winner was thenceforth excluded from Ecole competitions and could devote all his efforts to winning the Grand Prix.

The competition for the Grand Prix was held in the buildings of the Ecole des Beaux-Arts but was administered by the Académie des Beaux-Arts. The structure of the *concours* remained constant throughout the first half of the century. The rules set forth by the Académie and approved by the Minister of the Interior, Montalivet, in 1810 were the basis for the printed regulations published in 1822, 1835 and 1846.[14] The first major changes were made in 1855 followed by a series of revisions from the 1860s on.[15] This discussion will, therefore, be concerned primarily with the first half of the century.

Until 1864, the competition was a two-stage affair. On the basis of an *esquisse*, or sketch design, the original number of thirty competitors was reduced to eight finalists. They then produced large-scale renderings of their sketches, and it was based on these that the final judgment was made.[16] While the competition was nominally open to any French architectural student under thirty years of age, it was effectively reserved for students in the first, or upper, class of the Ecole des Beaux-Arts in Paris and, in fact, until 1835 was restricted to those approximately fifty upperclassmen.[17]

Any student in the first class who had previously been a finalist or had won a medal for a rendered project in one of the school's monthly competitions was eligible. He simply had to notify the authorities of his intention a fortnight prior to the scheduled event and his name was placed on a list according to his ranking. The top thirty were automatically admitted. Usually fewer than thirty signed up, and then a *concours d'essai*, or tryout, was held one week prior to the *concours définitif*, or competition proper, to fill the remaining places. The 1824 competition was one of only three times during the Restoration when this was not necessary. The yearly average of students who were admitted in this way was between five and six. They, too, were almost always members of the first class.[18]

The *concours d'essai* consisted of an *esquisse* based on a programme written by the professor of architectural theory of the Ecole. It was judged, however, by the members of the architectural section of the Académie. During the 1820s it usually took place on the first or second Friday in May. The student was given twelve hours, and the jury was held the following day. The programme usually called for a small building, such as a gymnasium (1825) or an oratory for a cemetery (1826), or simply part of a building, such as the main entrance to a church (1814, 1818) or the central courtyard of a palace (1822).[19]

The first stage of the competition proper began the following Friday morning shortly after 8:00 o'clock. The Académie supplied the programme. At 7:00 am the architectural section of the Académie met at the Ecole. Each of the eight members was supposed to have prepared at least one subject. In 1824, nine were submitted, a little above the average of seven to eight for the years 1817 to 1827.[20] A vote was taken to reduce this to three; but the final choice was made by lot.

The programme for the Grand Prix invariably called for a large governmental, institutional or representational building or complex located in a major city. The city was more often than not Paris. Since the indications regarding both site and function could be quite minimal, this built-in familiarity was a great aid to the students. Between 1817 and 1827, eight out of the eleven programmes called either explicitly or implicitly for buildings in Paris.

The programme selected in 1824 was for a Cour de Cassation (Supreme Court of Appeal), obviously located in Paris. The eight other proposals were an Auberge dans les Alpes (Inn in the Alps), an Hôtel des Ambassadeurs Etrangers (Foreign Embassy), a Musée des Beaux-Arts (Museum of Fine Arts), an Académie de France à Rome (French Academy in Rome), a Maison de Campagne pour un Prince (Country House for a Prince), an Edifice pour l'Industrie (Building for Industry), an Edifice pour l'Exposition des Beaux-Arts

(Fine Arts Exhibition Building) and an Athénée (Athenaeum). The Académie de France à Rome and the Maison de Campagne pour un Prince were the runners-up.[21]

Aside from the Cour de Cassation and the Auberge dans les Alpes, the subjects were typical. The Hôtel des Ambassadeurs had been proposed in 1819 and 1823; the Edifice pour l'Industrie in 1819, 1820, 1822 and 1823; the Athénée in 1822 and 1823; and the Edifice pour l'Exposition des Beaux-Arts in 1822 and 1823. The latter was proposed again in 1825, along with the Athénée; the Maison de Campagne pour un Prince in 1825, 1826 and 1827; the Musée des Beaux-Arts in 1827; and the Académie de France à Rome in 1826, when it 101, was selected. Other programmes proposed 102 often between 1817 and 1827 were a Chambre des Pairs (House of Lords, 5 times); a Maison d'Arrêt ou Correction (Gaol or Penitentiary, 5 times); an Ecole des Arts et Métiers (School of Arts and Trades, 4 times); a Trésorerie (Treasury, 4 times); a Sépulture Royale (Royal Sepulchre, 3 times); a Cimetière (Cemetery, 3 times); a Palais de Justice (Courthouse, 3 times); 88–96 and a Bibliothèque Publique (Public Library, 65 3 times).

While it was only by chance that the Cour de Cassation was chosen its first time around in 1824, it was selected once again in 1859, 80 just prior to the actual rebuilding of the Cour de Cassation, planned by Louis Lenormand 62 in the late 1850s and carried out by Louis Duc beginning in 1862. It should therefore come as no surprise that, despite the grandiose sounding titles of the buildings, the programmes for the Grand Prix were quite often directly related to current events. This was as true of the Restoration period as it had been of the Empire. The programme of 1819 for a vast Cimetière ou Champ de Repos (Cemetery or Resting Place), on a flat site 'like the Montrouge plain, or a sloping [one] like the cemetery of Père Lachaise',[22] was contemporary with E.-H. Godde's realization of Frochot's earlier plans for the cemeteries of Montmartre and Montparnasse in 1818–24. The programme of 1820 for an Ecole de Médecine (Medical School) 'accompanied by a Botanical garden'[23] coincided with the projected expansion of the Paris Medical School in the south-east corner of the Jardin du Luxembourg during the early 1820s. A botanical garden was in fact created there for it at the time.

61   C. Jacquemin-Belisle. Palais de Justice, Tours, 1840–51. Compare the elevation with Lepreux's project, ill. 67.

The relationship between the Grand Prix programme and contemporary building could also be of a more general order. In 1821, the 88–96 subject was a Palais de Justice pour le Chef-lieu d'un Département (Courthouse for the Capital of a *Département*), one of the rare specifically non-Parisian subjects. This building type was one of the major preoccupations of architects working in provincial capitals during the Restoration, with the courthouses built at Marseille, Périgueux, Angoulême, St-Etienne, St-Lô, Valognes, Valence, Aix, Orléans, and 61 Tours being among the most prominent.[24] On the other hand, no programme could have been more directly inspired by a specific 73–77 event than the one of 1822 for a new Paris Opera House. This was first proposed the previous year after it was decided to demolish Victor Louis's theatre on the square Louvois following the assassination there of the Duc de Berry on 13 February 1820. A temporary opera house had been built by François Debret in 1820–21 between the rue Le Peletier and the rue Drouot. Similarly, the death of Louis XVIII in September 1824 inspired the proposal of a Sépulture Royale for the Grand Prix of 1825.

Both the programme chosen in 1825 for an Hôtel de Ville pour Paris (City Hall for Paris) 97– and that of 1827 for a Muséum d'Histoire Naturelle (Museum of Natural History) heralded the extensive rebuilding and expansion of those two buildings in the following decade. While the idea of enlarging the Hôtel de Ville dated back to the closing years of the Empire, it was only carried out by Godde and Lesueur beginning in 1837. The major expansion of the Museum at the Jardin des Plantes was begun in 1833 under the direction of Charles Rohault de Fleury. Similarly, the proposal of a Chambre des Députés (Chamber of Deputies) in 1822 preceded the campaign to complete that building undertaken by Jules de Joly in 1828. The subject of a Bibliothèque Publique pour la Capitale du Royaume (Public Library for the Capital of the Kingdom), proposed in 1825, 1826, 1827 and 1828, was of such contemporary interest that it was a runner-up in the two years preceding its selection in 1828. This coincided with the increasing possibility that the Bibliothèque Nationale would be rebuilt. Plans were presented by Jacques-François Delannoy from 1824 to 1827 and then, from 1829 on, by Louis Visconti, following his appointment

62 L. Duc, E.-T. Dommey and L. Lenormand. Cour de Cassation, Palais de Justice, Paris, projected 1857–58, begun 1862. (From F. Narjoux, *Paris: Monuments elevés par la ville, 1850–80. Edifices judiciaires*, 1880)

as architect.[25] It was Delannoy's son Antoine who won the prize in 1828.

The programme of 1824 for a Cour de Cassation was no less a product of circumstances. The Cour de Cassation occupied the former quarters of the Parlement de Paris in the north-west corner of the Palais de Justice on the Ile de la Cité. The lack of space and need for replanning that entire complex were acutely felt throughout the first half of the century. In 1847, the architect Félix Pigeory noted in his *Monuments de Paris* that 'of all the public buildings in Paris, the Palais de Justice is unquestionably the most broken up, the most besmirched by confusion, irregularities and incongruities'.[26]

The Cour de Cassation was already in the early 1820s apparently the most vocal in making its demands heard. It was particularly hard-pressed for space since its three separate courts – the Chambre Civile, Chambre Criminelle and Chambre des Requêtes – had to share the two courtrooms inherited from the former Parlement: the Grand' Chambre and the Chambre de la Tournelle. The government responded in 1826 by commissioning a series of studies for the enlargement of the Palais, although nothing

definite was approved until the end of the following decade, nor did any significant rebuilding get under way until the 1840s.[27] Before that, however, certain palliative measures were taken. In 1817, Antoine-Marie Peyre reinforced the supporting structure of the Grand' Salle, or Salle des Pas Perdus, after weaknesses in Salomon de Brosse's work had been discovered. From then, through the 1820s, Peyre continued to remodel parts of the building, including the Conciergerie and the entrances from the Cour de Mai and the quai de l'Horloge. In 1833–34 Alphonse de Gisors, who had competed for the Grand Prix in 1824, began the restoration of the Cour de Cassation and rebuilt the 15th-century Galerie St-Louis to serve as its lobby. Finally, in Jean-Nicolas Huyot's project of 1837 for the total rebuilding of the Palais de Justice, approved in 1840, and in the one carried out by Louis Duc, 62 E.-T. Dommey and Louis Lenormand in the 1840s, '50s, and '60s, the Cour de Cassation was greatly increased in size but preserved in its traditional location.[28] It was, however, set off from the hubbub of the rest of the Palais and, befitting its exalted role, was given a monumental façade on the quai de l'Horloge.

The Cour de Cassation is the highest court in the French judicial system. It has the power to quash (*casser*) any judgment made by a lower court of last resort. It was established by the Revolutionary government in 1790 in order to ensure the exact and uniform application of the law throughout France.[29] Its area of concern is limited to questions of law rather than to questions of fact. It can set aside the judgment of a lower court only when there has been a violation of the law, that is to say, when the law has either been misapplied or misinterpreted. Once a decision is annulled, the case is referred to an appellate court other than the one that rendered the judgment in question.

The idea of the Cour de Cassation originated in the *ancien régime*'s Conseil des Parties, which grew out of the medieval Conseil du Roi. The rules of procedure governing a petition for review of judgment date back in essence to the regulations adopted for the Conseil des Parties in 1738. Naturally, these were considerably revised in 1790. At the time of its creation, the Cour de Cassation, then called a Tribunal, was divided into two sections, the Bureau des Requêtes, a screening body, and the Section de Cassation. In 1795, the Section de Cassation was split in half and the triple division of the court into a Chambre des Requêtes, Chambre Civile and Chambre Criminelle was instituted.[30] During the succeeding thirty years continuous revisions and additions to the rules of procedure resulted in such confusion that Charles X turned his attention to systematizing the court's operations soon after acceding to the throne in 1824. In January 1826, he enacted an order that codified, streamlined and, in some instances, revamped the procedures of the Supreme Court of France.[31]

The imminent structural reorganization, combined with the need for a third courtroom to correspond with the physical reorganization of 1795, made the programme of a Cour de Cassation an extraordinarily relevant one in 1824. But, unlike most other Grand Prix subjects, it was unusual in being for so special a function and for one so far removed from the daily experience of a young architectural student. While he may never have visited an inn in the Alps or an atheneum or even the Chambre des Députés, he would have had a general idea of the character appropriate to such buildings. But how could he begin to differentiate a Cour de Cassation from a Palais de Justice? This was not a generic distinction, such as a church versus a museum, nor simply a hierarchical one, such as a parish church versus a cathedral, but rather the delimitation of a unique subspecies. In fact, the subject proposed had no independently existing prototype. The programme for 1824 is, therefore, particularly interesting because it forced the members of the Académie to define what they wanted more clearly than usual. Some programmes, such as the one of 1822 for an Opera House, contained an unusually long list of functional requirements, but no programme in the 1820s had as elaborate a discussion of character as the one in 1824.

The programme, which in the 1820s was between one and two pages long, ordinarily consisted of three sections: a short introductory paragraph, referred to as the *chapeau* by students; the main text outlining the building's requirements; and, finally, the dimensions of the building or site and the number and scale of drawings required.[32] Most programmes took it for granted that the student knew what the building should be like and therefore began by simply indicating its general nature, size, and location. In 1817, for instance, the programme began like this: 'A Conservatory or School of Music and Declamation in which the Government will house and train under the direction of skilled masters fifty students of both sexes'.[33] The *chapeau* was usually no more than a sentence or two.

The building's requirements were set forth in terms of the elements of its plan, starting with the main rooms or spaces and ending with the subsidiary ones. Sometimes a final sentence or two might be added to remind the student of the character of the institution. In 1817 the Académie noted that a Conservatoire de Musique should be recognizable by a 'simple yet grand and fluent progression in its general layout and the elegant purity of its architecture',[34] a sort of *basso continuo* underlying the melodic line of a soprano. In 1821, the programme for a Palais de Justice added that the 'distinctive character of this building is a noble simplicity';[35] and in 1826, for an Académie de France à Rome, it noted that the decoration 'should exhibit the effects of the influence of the beauties of the monuments of Rome ... and in its style should respond to the royal munificence that will erect it'.[36] Sometimes, though not often, the remarks about character or style

81–
88–
101
102

could be proscriptive, as in the programme of 1819 for a Cemetery. To ensure the desired 'character of solemn simplicity', the student was advised that the 'general arrangement of the place ... does not permit the use of picturesque methods that caprice and vanity could give rise to'.[37]

The programme for 1824 began on a note of caution. Since seventeen of the thirty students had taken part in the competition just three years before on the subject of a Palais de Justice, and one of them, Henri Labrouste, had come second, the Académie straightaway warned them that a Cour de Cassation is an 'institution which must be distinct from a Palais de Justice'. If the 'distinctive character' of a typical courthouse was 'a noble simplicity', the particular character of the 'supreme tribunal' should be 'nobility' combined with 'severity'. The Académie felt the special character of a Cour de Cassation could only be expressed by a truly 'antique' solution.[38]

To give the students a better idea of what they had in mind, they cited the 'tribunals of Athens and Rome', claiming that their function had in no way changed and the same courtrooms, waiting rooms, reception rooms and offices found in those classical buildings 'are still being used in modern times'. For that reason, a Cour de Cassation 'is, unquestionably, one of those buildings that can be treated in an antique style, without deviating from our own practices'. The extraordinarily explicit *chapeau* concluded with the equally unusual injunction that, because of the nature of the subject, 'the competitors must employ in the composition of this building a genre of architecture that responds to the noble and severe character of a tribunal of such importance'.[39]

The outline of functional requirements forming the main part of the programme proceeded in typical fashion from the general to the specific and thus established an abstract hierarchical pattern in the student's mind. He was told that a Cour de Cassation is divided into three sections, or branches, each needing a courtroom, a council room and at least two offices, one for the president and the other for the vice-president. He was not, however, given the names of the three branches, nor were their specific functions described. He was told that one of the courtrooms, though not which one, had to be bigger than the others in order to hold plenary sessions. It had to seat sixty

and have a throne for the king as well as several large reception rooms 'near by'. The other major element to be included was a 'hall or covered *atrium*' that should connect 'directly or indirectly to the various parts of the building according to their importance'.[40] Those various other parts of the building were then listed as follows:

1. a *parquet*, or ministerial staff quarters, including a waiting room, several offices for the Attorney General and offices for six advocates-general
2. a *vestiaire*, or robing rooms, for forty-eight judges plus two larger ones for the president and the vice-president
3. a *greffe*, or office of the court clerk, composed of six rooms plus its own depository and archives, divided into four sections each having a small office
4. a two- or three-room *bureau d'enregistrement*, or registry office
5. a library and archives
6. a refreshment bar with a waiting room; and lodgings for the concierge

The students were advised that they could place the library and archives on a second floor but in that case they would have to provide a separate plan. Otherwise, the building was to be a single storey high, as were almost all Grand Prix projects, and 'completely isolated'.[41] It was to be contained within a rectangle no longer than 180 metres on a side. The overall size of just under 35,000 square metres was average for a single building throughout the entire 19th century. Buildings with extensive landscape gardening, such as an Ecole de Médecine (1820) or an Académie de France à Rome (1826), might occupy a site ranging anywhere from 90,000 to 200,000 square metres; while large urbanistic complexes, such as a Promenade Publique (1818), a Cimetière (1819) or a Muséum d'Histoire Naturelle (1827), could cover up to 500,000 square metres.

The students were required to present for the first stage of the competition a sketch plan at a scale of .001m/m and a section and an elevation at twice that scale. A plan, section and elevation were always required for the *esquisse*. Sometimes a site plan was added. If the building or site was unusually large, as in 1818, 1819 and 1827, the scale of the sketch site plan was generally .0005m/m. A scale of .001m/m for the building plan with double that, or .002m/m, for the elevation and section

101, 102

was normal. The resulting sketches, which could be done either on one sheet of paper or several pasted together, would then measure about .40 metres wide by .50 metres high.

For the final stage, the scale of the rendered plan was ordinarily doubled or quadrupled while that of the elevation and section could be increased anywhere from fivefold to tenfold. In 1824, however, the scale was quintupled for each, so that the rendered plan would be approximately 1 square metre and the elevation and section each 2 metres long. In addition to the amplified scale, the number of renderings was also often increased by one or two. In 1824, a large detail drawing of the order of the façade, at a scale of .05m/column diameter, was required along with a section 'showing the decoration' of the largest courtroom to be drawn at the same scale.[42] The obvious purpose of this was to highlight the student's understanding of the elements of classical architecture as well as his skill as a draughtsman.

The importance the Académie attached to the questions of proportion and decoration is more than hinted at by the comparative scale of the drawings required. The choice and delineation of the appropriate classical order ultimately carried the burden of proof of the student's talent and skill. The programme for 1824 was more explicit than usual in impressing this upon the competitors, for the Académie apparently saw the order as a major factor in making a Cour de Cassation differ from a Palais de Justice. So that the student should be left in no doubt as to the pre-eminence of this element, the Académie made one final stipulation regarding the precision they wanted in the indication of the order in the sketch: 'Since it is assumed that the main façade of such a building must be decorated with an architectural order, it is to be indicated clearly enough in the sketch so that its character can in no way be changed in the rendering'.[43] This extraordinary statement raises the question of the relationship between the two stages of the competition for the Grand Prix. The distinction between sketch and rendering has never been brought to bear on the analysis of the subject and may well provide the key to unlocking many of the mysteries.

The finalists

The programme was given to the students in 1824 shortly after 8:00 o'clock on Friday morning, 14 May. The thirty were, in order of ranking (with year of birth followed by year of admission to the Ecole):[44]

1. Henri Labrouste (1801/1819)
2. Léon Vaudoyer (1803/1819)
3. Jules Bouchet (1799/1817)
4. Narcisse Gilbert (1797/1816)
5. Théodore Labrouste (1799/1817)
6. Alphonse-Eugène Hubert (1797/1817)
7. Louis Durand (1801/1819)
8. Etienne-Théodore Dommey (1801/1818)
9. Louis Lepreux (1795/1818)
10. Alphonse de Gisors (1796/1814)
11. Antoine Tavernier (1796/1815)
12. Louis Duc (1802/1821)
13. Achille Normand (1802/1817)
14. Charles-Edouard Isabelle (1800/1818)
15. Joseph-Frédéric Debacq (1800/1818)
16. Joseph-Léon Chabrier (1798/1820)
17. Jean-Louis-Victor Grisart (1797/1818)
18. Antoine Delannoy (1800/1819)
19. Philarète Goujon (1794/1821)
20. Félix Fries (1800/1820)
21. Charles-Pierre Lebarbu (1796/1815)
22. Hilaire Garlin (1796/1817)
23. André Arthaud (1796/1812)
24. François-Alexis Cendrier (1803/1820)
25. Pierre-Camille Piron (1797/1816)
26. Pierre-Léonard Laurécisque (1797/1820)
27. Alfred Pommier (1802/1819)
28. Raphael Lignière (1803/1820)
29. Louis-Henri-Victor Leplus (1798/1819)
30. Achille Poirot (1797/1816)

Each student had just a little under twenty-four hours to complete his sketch. During this time he was not allowed to leave the school building nor have any contact with anyone outside the building.[45] Since the student's entire career could depend on this one sketch, the competition was as mentally devastating as it was physically gruelling. In 1827, Théodore Labrouste, who was approaching his thirtieth birthday and had already been unsuccessful a number of times (including 1824), became so violently ill in the night that he barely finished. He reported to his brother Henri afterwards that, unable to eat, 'I did nothing but vomit throughout the night.... They had to take me out of the room to let me breathe the fresh air.... I had several times given up ... doing the sketch.' Feeling better by dawn, however, 'I took courage again ... but I did not have time to add wash to my sketch.'[46]

The sketches had to be done in ink and could not be on tracing paper. Normally, the drawing was finished with light washes of grey, pink, green or brown. The project had to be turned in by 7:00 o'clock the following morning. In 1824, only Gisors and Grisart failed to turn theirs in. Twenty-eight completions out of thirty was average for the 1820s. The sketches were collected and endorsed by the professor of architectural theory of the Ecole, who from 1818 to 1846 was Pierre Baltard. Since, for the avowed purpose of anonymity, the students did not sign their drawings, Baltard placed an identifying number or letter on the back of each one. In 1824, as apparently throughout the 1820s at least, that number was the same as the student's ranking, a circumstance that clearly compromised any possible anonymity.[47]

The sketches, along with the programme, were placed on exhibition at the Ecole on Saturday morning 15 May at 9:00 o'clock. The order in which they were hung was apparently also determined by class standing as a result of a decision made at a general faculty meeting the previous month.[48] At 1:00 pm the jury met to select the eight *logistes*, or finalists. This jury was composed of the eight members of the architectural section of the Académie plus the president, vice-president and *secrétaire perpétuel*. The president in 1824 was the painter Etienne-Barthélemy Garnier (1759–1849); the vice-president was the architect Charles Percier (1764–1838); and the *secrétaire perpétuel* from 1816 to 1839 was A.-C. Quatremère de Quincy (1755–1849). Out of a possible ten, only five members of the jury showed up in 1824. That was the smallest group during the 1820s, the average being eight to nine. The architectural section was in fact short one man, since Maximilien Hurtault (1765–1824) had died on 2 May and was not replaced by Jules Delespine (1756–1825) until 26 June.

The five members of the jury for the first stage of the *concours* were Percier, J.-N. Huyot (1780–1840), J.-T. Thibault (1757–1826), A.-L.-T. Vaudoyer (1756–1846) and Quatremère.[49] All four architects were closely connected with the Ecole. Vaudoyer, Percier and Huyot had won the Grand Prix – in 1786, 1783 and 1807 respectively – and all three taught *ateliers*. Thibault taught the course in perspective at the Ecole while Vaudoyer was also the school's *secrétaire-archiviste*. The average

age of the five was sixty-one. Two of the members of the architectural section who did not attend were the oldest: Bernard Poyet (1742–1824), winner of the Second Grand Prix in 1764; and Jean Rondelet (1743–1829), professor of construction at the Ecole. Pierre Fontaine (1762–1853), Percier's former partner and winner of the Second Grand Prix in 1785, was the third absentee.

The voting took place by secret ballot and could hardly have been impartial. While thirteen *ateliers* were represented by the competitors, the largest contingents were from those run by Académiciens. In fact, more than half the students came from *ateliers* taught by members of the jury. Percier and Huyot each had four taking part and Vaudoyer a total of nine.[50] Furthermore, it was Vaudoyer who, as Secretary of the Ecole, was responsible for preparing the ranked list of students by which the sketches were identified. And, naturally, many of the best students already had a distinctive manner or approach to design which would have been quite obvious to someone as close as one's father, as in the case of Léon Vaudoyer, or one's teacher of almost seven years, as in the case of Théodore Labrouste.

The eight finalists were selected in order of preference.[51] An absolute majority was necessary and three or four ballots were often cast for each place.[52] The order of selection was therefore significant and was referred to as the *ordre de réception en loge*. (A *loge* was the small room in which the finalists, called *logistes*, would complete their renderings.) The eight chosen in 1824 were selected in the following order (with their class ranking in parentheses):[53]

1 Louis Lepreux (9)
2 Félix Fries (20)
3 François-Alexis Cendrier (24)
4 Louis Duc (12)
5 Léon Vaudoyer (2)
6 Raphael Lignière (28)
7 Théodore Labrouste (5)
8 Henri Labrouste (1)

Six of the finalists had previously competed for the Grand Prix, and three had been *logistes* at least once before.[54] They ranged in age from $20\frac{1}{2}$ to $28\frac{1}{2}$ years old. Their average age of $23\frac{1}{4}$ was the youngest for the decade, when the average was $24\frac{3}{4}$, and in marked contrast to the 1830s and '40s when the average age of the finalist reached $25\frac{1}{2}$. The group repre-

63   L. Vaudoyer. Bains d'Eau Minérale (Spa), 1824: rendered plan. (Beaux-Arts)

64   L. Vaudoyer. Cour ▷ de Cassation, 1824: sketch elevation, plan and section. (Beaux-Arts)

sented a cross-section of the first class of the Ecole. Half of them were in the top third of the class, one in the middle third and the remaining three in the bottom third. The order in which they were selected did not in the least correspond with their class ranking; that would have been most unusual, and in fact never occurred during the 1820s. During those ten years the top-ranked finalist was chosen first three times but he was also chosen eighth three times; and the one ranked eighth of the group was chosen third twice, fourth twice and even first once.

Louis Lepreux, who was ranked first out of the eight, was by far the oldest and was in fact the second oldest of the entire group of thirty. He was born on 18 October 1795, in Paris, where he lived at 16, rue Serpente, in the heart of medieval Paris near the Place St André

des Arts.[55] He was admitted to the Ecole des Beaux-Arts on 13 February 1818, as a student of Antoine-Marie Peyre, who was then remodelling the Palais de Justice. With the advantage of being more than four years older than most entering students, Lepreux did extraordinarily well in the architectural composition *concours* of the second class. Within less than ten months he was promoted to the first class, on 30 November 1818, by which time he had joined the Vaudoyer-Lebas *atelier*. The average time it took the seven others to be promoted was just under a year and a half, which was quite a bit better than the two to three years it took the average student in the 1820s.

As a member of the first class, Lepreux continued to do outstandingly, yet never won the Grand Prix. In six years he won six medals in composition and an honourable mention

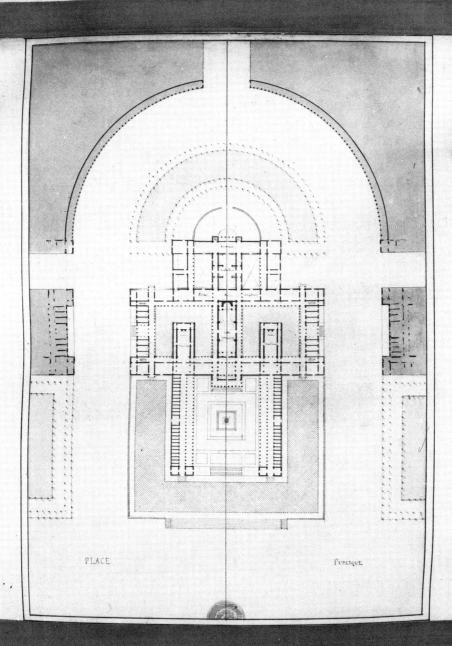

PLACE   PUBLIQUE

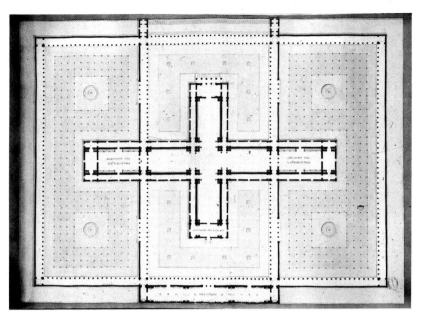

65   T. Labrouste. Public
Library, 1821: rendered plan.
(Beaux-Arts)

66   T. Labrouste. Cour de
Cassation, 1824: sketch
elevation, section and plan.
(Beaux-Arts)

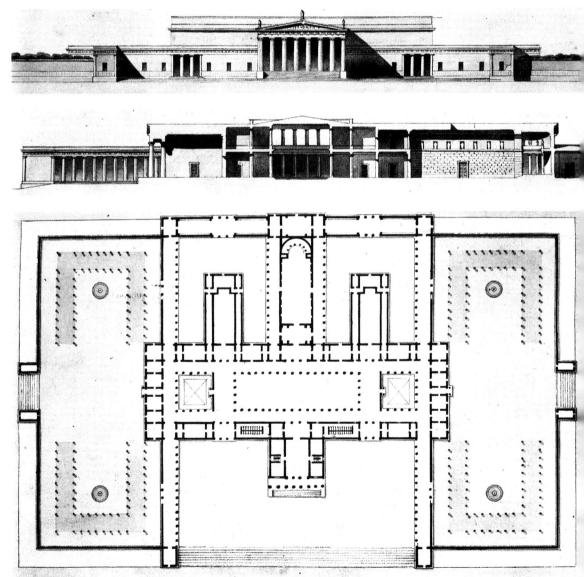

in mathematics despite the fact that he never pushed himself very hard. Between 1821 and 1824 he entered only half the monthly competitions. He took part in the *concours d'essai* for the Grand Prix in 1820 and competed in the competition proper each year from 1820 to 1825. He was a *logiste* twice, the first time in 1822 when he was chosen fifth, and then in 1824. By that time he stood ninth in the class and at the end of 1824 was second runner-up for the Prix Départemental. With two more medals the following year, Lepreux won the Prix Départemental in 1825. That signalled the end of his school career, for he turned thirty before the Grand Prix competition of 1826. Lepreux went on to conduct a modest practice in Paris combining private and governmental work. He succeeded Paul Letarouilly as architect of the Collège de France in 1858 and Théodore Labrouste at the Bibliothèque de l'Arsenal in 1880. He died in 1881.

Félix Fries had a much less remarkable student career. He was the only non-Parisian of the finalists, having been born in Strasbourg on 7 October 1800. While at the Ecole he lived at 19, rue des Marais, near the Place de la République.[56] He entered the Ecole on 25 October 1820, over a year and a half after Lepreux, beginning as a student of Hurtault but soon switching over to Huyot's *atelier*. Fries progressed very slowly and was not promoted to the first class until 16 January 1823, more than two years after he entered. He was the last of the eight finalists to be promoted, and spent by far the longest of all of them in the lower class.

Fries was not terribly assiduous. He entered only three-quarters of the Ecole competitions in 1823 and 1824 and completed just two-thirds of them. Although he won only one first-class medal, he was considered a very tough competitor by the other students. He competed twice for the Grand Prix and was a finalist both times, being selected second in 1824 and first in 1825. When Henri Labrouste heard of the results in 1825, he wrote to his friend Dommey, who was chosen second, saying that it would not be easy to overcome Fries: 'I appreciate Fritz's talent greatly and ... I consider him a very formidable competitor'.[57] Fries won the Second Grand Prix that year (and Dommey an honourable mention) and apparently left the Ecole soon thereafter to begin a prolific, if undistinguished, career.

He returned to his birthplace to collaborate with his former Ecole classmate J.-G. Stoltz on the building of the workers' housing for the Société Industrielle de Mulhouse (1826–28), one of the first planned *cités industrielles*. In 1844, he was appointed City Architect of Strasbourg and in that capacity built numerous markets, schools and churches before his death in 1859.

François-Alexis Cendrier was ranked twenty-fourth out of thirty when his sketch was voted third best in 1824. He was born in Paris on 12 February 1803, and thus was just over twenty-one years old at the time. He lived at 51, rue des Gravilliers, in the working-class third *arrondissement*, just south of the Conservatoire des Arts et Métiers.[58] He entered the Ecole on 6 March 1820, as a student of Vaudoyer and Lebas and, like Fries, took longer than usual to be promoted. He entered the first class after almost eighteen months on 30 November 1821.

Cendrier progressed slowly but eventually became one of the top students. It took him over two years to win his first medal in composition. This was not for lack of trying. In 1823 and 1824 he entered every monthly competition, completing half of them in 1823 and a third in 1824. In the next four years, however, he won six medals and was awarded the Prix Départemental in 1828 with the second highest number of points for the 1820s.

Cendrier competed for the Grand Prix six years running, beginning in 1824. Although he was a finalist in both 1826 (chosen first) and 1827 (chosen seventh), he never managed to win the top award, and went to Italy on his own in 1830. He later became a specialist in railway stations, working for the Compagnie du Chemin de Fer d'Orléans and then for the Compagnie du Chemin de Fer de Paris à Lyon. His involvement with large spans and iron was also reflected in the project he did for the Palais de l'Industrie in 1853–55 in collaboration with his former *atelier*-mate J.-M.-V. Viel. Cendrier died in 1892 at the age of eighty-nine.

Louis Duc's architecture was of a much more 'artistic' nature. This was presaged by his swift progress and great success at the Ecole. Duc was born on 25 October 1802 in Paris and lived at 251, rue St Honoré on the elegant right bank.[59] He was a member of the Châtillon *atelier*, having entered the Ecole on 11 June

1821. Duc's drawing immediately showed a marvellously deft touch. He won six competitions, four of which were for sketch compositions, in his first year and was promoted to the first class on 8 October 1822.

In his first year in the upper class, Duc entered all eleven competitions, finished seven of them and won four medals. In 1824, he took part in seven of the ten, completed four of them and won a final medal. He competed unsuccessfully for the Grand Prix in 1823, but was a finalist in both 1824 and 1825, when he was fifth *en loge* and won the Grand Prix. Duc became one of the leading architects of France. His two major works are the Bastille Column (1834–40) and the restoration and enlargement of the Palais de Justice (begun 1840), which won Napoleon III's Prix de 100,000 Francs in 1869 as the greatest artistic achievement of the Second Empire. Duc became a member of the Académie in 1866 and died in 1879, the most esteemed representative of the French classical school.

Léon Vaudoyer was the son of A.-L.-T. Vaudoyer, the Secretary of the Ecole. The elder Vaudoyer, who became a member of the Académie in 1823, ran the most important *atelier* of the period and clearly destined his son to follow in his footsteps. Léon was born in Paris on 7 June 1803 and, because of his father's position, lived in the buildings of the Institut de France on the quai de Conti.[60] He entered the Ecole on 10 October 1819, at the age of $16\frac{1}{2}$. Despite his youth (and perhaps because of his father), he was promoted to the first class within less than a year, on 29 September 1820. He had just turned seventeen.

Vaudoyer's student projects were generally quite competent but never brilliant; he was particularly effective in using his time efficiently. In 1821 he entered every monthly competition, in 1822 eleven of the twelve and in 1823 nine of the eleven, but he never completed more than half. In 1822 he finished just two of the eleven, yet won medals in both. He seems to have had the highest average of medals per competition completed. In all, he won eight medals and was awarded the Prix Départemental in 1823.

Vaudoyer competed for the Grand Prix six times and made it as a finalist five of the six. This was extraordinary for the period and could only be matched by Abel Blouet, who was a finalist five years in a row from 1817 to

1821. Except for 1826, when his sketch was placed second, Vaudoyer was usually in the lower half of the group (fifth in 1821; eighth in 1823; fifth in 1824). In 1822, when he was placed fourth, he won an honourable mention. Of the eight finalists in 1824, Vaudoyer was also the youngest when first received *en loge*. In 1821 he was not yet eighteen. The average age of the seven others as first-time finalists was $22\frac{1}{2}$. The average for all first-time finalists in the 1820s was just under $24\frac{1}{2}$.

Vaudoyer finally won the Grand Prix in 1826 and, after five years in Italy, began a career of teaching, writing, travelling and designing that would, like Duc, carry him to the top of the architectural profession. His best-known works are the restoration and enlargement of the Conservatoire des Arts et Métiers in Paris (begun 1838) and the Cathedral of Marseille (begun 1856). Vaudoyer was elected to the Académie in 1868, two years after Duc, and died four years after that in 1872.

Raphael Lignière was the least successful of the group both at the Ecole and after. Significantly, he was the only one to have been a finalist just once. He was born in Paris on 6 July 1803, and was therefore the youngest of the eight (Vaudoyer was one month older). Lignière lived in the aristocratic seventh *arrondissement* at 33, rue de Varenne.[61] He was admitted to the Ecole as a student of Vaudoyer and Lebas on 21 June 1820, and showed such promise that he was promoted to the first class within thirteen months, on 31 August 1821.

Lignière did not win a medal in the first class, however, for over two years despite the fact that he was a dogged competitor. He entered every competition in 1822 and completed three-quarters of them. In 1823 he again entered every one and completed seven of the eleven, finally winning his first medal. He took part in the *concours d'essai* for the Grand Prix in 1822 but was not selected as a finalist in the competition proper. In 1823 he gained the final slot for the competition through the *concours d'essai* but did not make it to the final stage. After 1824 Lignière competed eight more times until he was disqualified by his age. After leaving school he went into private practice but almost nothing is known of what he did. He is the only one of the eight finalists of 1824 who passed into total oblivion.

The final two places were filled by the

Labrouste brothers. Both were born in Paris and lived in the sixth *arrondissement*, near the Ecole, at 39, rue de Seine. Théodore Labrouste, the older of the two, was born on 11 March 1799, and was the first of the eight to enter the Ecole.[62] He was admitted on 20 October 1817, as a member of the Vaudoyer-Lebas *atelier*. Although he won nothing in his first year and a half, he became a member of the original first class on 28 May 1819, when the two-class system was instituted and a sketch competition for non-medallists was held to complete the class of fifty.

Théodore Labrouste was an incredibly zealous student. He took part in almost every monthly competition from 1819 to 1826 and usually completed at least half and sometimes more than three-quarters of them. His work, solid but never stunning, was always overshadowed by his brother's. He did not win his first medal until April 1821, and although he competed for the Grand Prix in 1821, 1822 and 1823, he did not make it as a finalist.

Théodore Labrouste's luck changed perceptibly soon after his brother won the Prix Départemental in 1822 and withdrew from Ecole competition. Between 1823 and 1826 he won ten medals and the Prix Départemental for 1826. After having competed unsuccessfully for the Grand Prix in both 1825 and 1826, his sketch was selected second in 1827 and, at the age of twenty-eight, he finally won the prize that year. Upon returning to Paris from Italy, he worked for the government, first under his friend Charles Rohault de Fleury at the Jardin des Plantes and then on his own, beginning in 1841, at the Bibliothèque de l'Arsenal. His most important work started in 1845, when he became chief architect of Paris hospitals. In this capacity he designed and built a number of large medical institutions in Paris and the nearby suburbs, including the Maison Dubois and the Hospice des Incurables at Ivry. Théodore outlived his brother Henri, and died in 1885.

Henri Labrouste was born on 11 May 1801, and showed an interest and talent in art from the outset.[63] Following in his older brother's footsteps, he joined the Vaudoyer-Lebas *atelier* and was admitted to the newly formed second class of the Ecole on 22 July 1819. He was promoted to the first class within ten months, on 30 May 1820, just after his nineteenth birthday. Of the eight, only Lepreux managed

to be promoted faster (by about three weeks), but he was five years older than Labrouste at the time.

Henri Labrouste won three medals in his first eight attempts as a member of the first class and was ranked sixth at the time of the Grand Prix competition in 1821. He was placed third *en loge*, just behind Abel Blouet and Emile Gilbert, and won the Second Grand Prix at the age of twenty. He won two more medals that year and entered all twelve competitions in 1822, completing eight, winning a sixth medal and, with that, capturing the Prix Départemental for 1822. He had amassed fourteen points in just over two years and, at $21\frac{1}{2}$, was four years younger than the average Prix Départemental winner during the 1820s.[64]

In 1822 and 1823 Labrouste tried for the Grand Prix but failed to make it as a finalist both times. Since he could no longer take part in Ecole competition, he got a job working for the architect Godde on the construction of the Church of St Pierre du Gros-Caillou, begun in 1822. It was quite usual for students at the Ecole to gain a practical knowledge of building in this way. Théodore Labrouste worked for the Department of Public Works throughout the latter part of his school career; and Félix Duban worked for his brother-in-law Debret on the construction of the new building for the Ecole des Beaux-Arts from 1820 to 1823.

Henri Labrouste finally won the Grand Prix on his fourth try, in 1824. After five years in Italy, he returned to Paris and opened what would soon become one of the most important teaching *ateliers*. His first major building was the Bibliothèque Ste-Geneviève (1838–50), 122 located next to the Panthéon. This was followed by the Seminary of Rennes and the Bibliothèque Nationale, both begun in the 1850s and occupying him until his death in 1875. Labrouste's radical use of iron and astringent sense of form heralded to most younger architects in both France and elsewhere the birth of a modern architecture. He was elected to the Académie in 1867, one year after Duc and one year before Vaudoyer.

It is quite clear that those who took part in the competition for the Grand Prix were the *crème de la crème*. Three of the eight finalists in 1824 went on to win the Grand Prix in the following three years, and three of them later became members of the Académie.[65] Most of the others had more than respectable careers.

More than half eventually worked for the government and eleven of the original group of thirty were awarded the Legion of Honour, six of those rising to the rank of Officier and one to Commandeur.[66] They all came from similar backgrounds and formed an elite group. According to another student, the architect was the most well prepared of all the students at the Ecole and invariably came from an upper middle-class family.[67] Twenty-two of the thirty were born in Paris, as were seven of the eight finalists. Three of those, Henri Labrouste, Théodore Labrouste and Léon Vaudoyer, went to the same private secondary school, the Collège Ste-Barbe. Six of the eight were members of one *atelier*, the one run by A.-L.-T. Vaudoyer and his nephew Hippolyte Lebas. The elder Vaudoyer was both a member of the jury and governing board of the Ecole and a member of the Académie, which might explain why his son Léon was the most successful Grand Prix competitor in the 1820s.

Charges of favouritism and even nepotism were often made. According to Pierre Baltard, the professor of theory, the source of unfairness lay in the fact that the prize culminating study at the Ecole was awarded by the Académie, an independent but by no means unprejudiced body (of which he was not a member!). In 1822 he published a brochure describing the problem and calling for certain reforms. He noted that when the Académie was composed of forty members under the *ancien régime* 'the most encouraging form of protection was assured the students by the Académiciens themselves, who ... divided it up among an equal number of students'. But the number of students had increased tremendously, while the number of Académiciens had been reduced to eight. Consequently, 'the same feelings of interest and dependence have ceased to exist, while as a result of the concentration of the means of protection in the eight architects who are members of the Institut, the adoption of a small number of favourites must necessarily take place ...'.[68]

Baltard had a point. Many of the Académiciens conducted *ateliers* and their students predominated in the competition for the Grand Prix. From 1800 to 1820 Percier's *atelier* filled the *loges*. Between 1817 and 1820 half the places were taken by students of his. In 1819 the number reached five out of eight. During those twenty years thirteen Grand Prix winners came from his *atelier*, with his students winning every single year from 1808 through 1816! After Percier began to withdraw from teaching, the Vaudoyer-Lebas *atelier* flourished, especially after Vaudoyer was elected to the Académie in 1823, followed by Lebas in 1825. In 1821 two of their students were selected as finalists, in 1822 three, in 1823 two again, then six in 1824, two in 1825, five in both 1826 and 1827, four in 1828 and three in both 1829 and 1830. During that ten-year period the *atelier* produced five Grand Prix winners, eight Seconds Grands Prix and two honourable mentions. After Vaudoyer retired, Huyot's *atelier* took over, producing two finalists in 1834, then four in both 1835 and 1838 and three in 1836. In that decade Huyot's *atelier* produced four Grands Prix.

Baltard recommended broadening the jury to include the non-Académiciens who were members of the jury of Ecole competitions. He suggested that the Grand Prix be awarded only every other year with the Prix Départemental replacing it in alternate years.[69] He felt that students who proved themselves at the Ecole were often bypassed by the Académie. This point seems less well founded. More than half the winners of the Prix Départemental in the 1820s went on to win the Grand Prix, namely Blouet, Gilbert, Henri Labrouste, Léon Vaudoyer, Théodore Labrouste and P.-J. Garrez. Three of the others, Bouchet, Lepreux and Cendrier, all won the Second Grand Prix; and the fourth, Dommey, was twice awarded an honourable mention. On the other hand, both Alexandre Villain, who won the Grand Prix in 1820, and Duban, who won the Grand Prix in 1823, were runners-up for the Prix Départemental in the previous years; and Delannoy, Grand Prix in 1828, was the second runner-up for the Prix Départemental in 1827.[70]

In general, there was a much greater correlation between success at the Ecole and success in the Grand Prix competition than Baltard admitted. When we compare the eight finalists in 1824 to the twenty-two who did not qualify, we find, as in most years, that those eliminated either made it to the final stage in other years or were mainly in the bottom half of the class. Bouchet won the Second Grand Prix in 1822; Grisart won the Second Grand Prix in 1823; Gisors, a finalist twice, won a Deuxième Second Grand Prix in 1823; Durand was a finalist four times; Dommey, a finalist three times, won honourable mentions twice; and Delannoy, a finalist four times, won the Grand Prix in 1828. Of the sixteen others, Isabelle was the only one to go on to a distinguished career without having been recognized in Grand Prix competition. Two-thirds of the remaining fifteen stood below the middle of the class.

It is further interesting to note that the finalists were quite a bit younger than the others. The average age of those eliminated was almost twenty-five, whereas that of the eight finalists was just over twenty-three. Pierre Baltard considered this another nefarious consequence of the system. He claimed that a jury viewing just one sketch was easily swayed by the project of a young and 'immature' student and that the Académie generally favoured 'the least advanced . . . and promising talent to the detriment of established talent and experience'.[71] But the order of the Académie's choice of sketches in 1824 specifically denies that. The top four students were decidedly older than the bottom four, and the descending order from first to sixth position went from oldest to youngest. The relationship between age and position is in fact so striking that one is rather inclined to give credence, based on this instance alone, to the much more commonplace charge that the Académie generally gave preference to the older student. The jury would have had no difficulty in identifying the authors of the sketches, and, since the award was in effect a travelling fellowship, such practice should hardly strike one as unusual in the academic world.

The factor of age, however, can only partially explain the great discrepancy between the order in which the finalists were chosen and their relative ranking in the class, since the order was almost completely reversed by the Académie's final decision. Henri Labrouste had a brilliant record at the Ecole and was ranked first in his class yet just barely made it as the eighth finalist in May 1824. Nevertheless, he was awarded the Grand Prix four months later. This suggests, first of all, that the juries for the Ecole competitions and the Grand Prix did represent different institutions and often different purposes, as Baltard maintained, but also, and perhaps more significant, that the Académie may have been looking for different things at different stages in the competition. Any consideration of that must begin

with an analysis of the sketches and conclude with a comparison of the renderings.

The sketch

The twenty-four hour sketch tested the student's intelligence in analyzing the programme and his clarity of purpose in defining a general solution. The problem was to distinguish the significant elements, decide on a *parti*, or scheme of organization, and then compose the elements into an appropriate form. While certain rules or conventions governing composition were almost always adhered to, there was also quite a large area for individual choice and variation.

In 1824 the programme called primarily for three courtrooms to be combined with a fourth element referred to as a 'hall or covered *atrium*'. An odd number of major spaces having the same function normally meant that one was to be bigger than the others and located on the central axis.[72] The courtroom containing the king's throne would obviously be the main one with the two others subordinate to it. But the relation of the primary to the secondary courtrooms was left up to the student. It depended to a great degree on the form and placement of the atrium. How he interpreted the atrium was perhaps the most crucial decision the student had to make, and here his ability to read between the lines of the programme was particularly at issue.

A 'hall or covered *atrium*' was less defined as a shape than a courtroom, which, according to Beaux-Arts precedent, was oblong and terminated in a hemicycle. As Quatremère de Quincy noted in his dictionary of architectural terms, the meaning of the word atrium was exceedingly 'ambiguous' regarding both its function and location. According to Vitruvius it was a 'kind of covered portico', but Quatremère also pointed out that Vitruvius used the term interchangeably with *cavaedium*. Throughout Roman times the atrium was often 'confused' with the *vestibulum*, or vestibule, and thus Quatremère acknowledged that 'it must be even more difficult nowadays to adduce the true meaning of *atrium* and decide on its placement and function'.[73]

The programme left much to the imagination. It simply stated that the 'hall or covered *atrium*' should 'connect directly or indirectly' with the 'various parts' of the building 'according to their importance'. But the 'various parts'

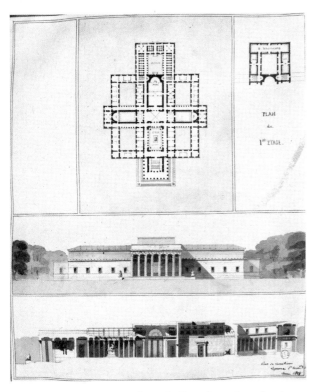

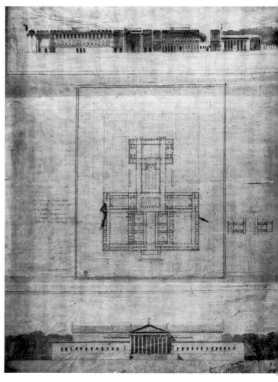

67 L. Lepreux. Cour de Cassation, 1824: sketch plan, elevation and section. (Beaux-Arts)

68 F. Fries. Cour de Cassation, 1824: sketch section, plan and elevation. (Tracing; Académie d'Architecture, Paris)

in question were specifically defined as being everything except the three courtrooms. Was the student then to assume that the courtrooms were not to be joined to the atrium? Nothing was said about the relative size of the four major elements. Should the atrium be the largest space; should it be equal to the largest courtroom; or should it be smaller? Since it was to be a point of connection and distribution, how should it relate to the vestibule? Should it be an extension of it; should it replace it; or should the two remain separate?

One clue regarding size was that the atrium was the last of the major spaces mentioned in the programme. The order in which the elements were listed was almost always an indication of the relative importance the Académie attached to them.[74] In referring to antique precedent, the *chapeau* not only made that order clear but also hinted at the correct placement of the atrium by distinguishing it from the porticoed courtyard, or peristyle,

that might serve as the main waiting room:

> Athens and Rome had their tribunals composed of vast rooms where justice was administered; of an atrium and of porticoes to wait for the moment of hearing, of reception rooms, of judges' chambers, of archives and of an infinite number of rooms that are still being used in modern times.[75]

Lepreux responded to the programme with a sketch that is nearly biaxially symmetrical. He interpreted the atrium as a self-contained introductory space. It mirrors the main courtroom and together they form the longitudinal arm of a Greek cross laid over a square. The lateral arm, half as wide, is composed of the two smaller courtrooms set at right angles to the main one. The four re-entrant angles are closed to make courtyards. At the central crossing is a groin-vaulted hall wider than it is deep.

The atrium is set between an open vestibule containing the main stairs and a central hall serving as a waiting room for the three court-rooms. The atrium is a glassed-over court in the middle of which is a figure of Justice seated on a high base. The proportion of its width to its length is 2:3, which follows one of the three ratios recommended by Vitruvius. The four inset corner columns relate it to his description of the tetrastyle atrium and thus reinforce its 'antique' character.[76]

The four courtyards, the main courtroom and the atrium are all the same size. The ministerial staff quarters, the office of the court clerk and the registry office are grouped around the open courts but are not related to the atrium in any particular way. The robing rooms surround another court appended to the rear, with the library and archives placed on a second floor above them. The rear court, with its understated entrance, projects from the block and mirrors the six-column-deep octastyle Roman Doric portico on the front. This is topped by a flat attic inscribed with the name of the building. The roof of the central hall and main courtroom rises above, while the council rooms and offices of the two smaller courtrooms form one-storey projections to the left and right.

Each element in Lepreux's project is clearly articulated and expressed both in plan and in elevation. The parts are evenly distributed; the whole is well balanced; and more than in any of the other projects the plan reads at a glance as a simple, coherent figure. The lines of the plan are carefully graded in thickness to give relief to the prominent spaces; and the rich texture of washes makes the elevation and section the most highly finished of the eight, with the resulting plasticity and sense of atmosphere giving the project all the more presence. Above all, two things stand out: the clarity of the extremely conventional Greek cross plan and the severity of the unpedimented portico.[77]

Fries chose a *parti* that is essentially the same as Lepreux's in its general disposition. The three courtrooms and atrium again form the arms of a Greek cross at the centre of which is a main waiting hall. But only the two front re-entrant angles have been closed in to make courtyards so that the overall shape of the plan is a stubby, inverted T. The central axis is defined by a highly ornate, pedimented, deca-style Corinthian portico raised above a base-ment. A shallow vestibule created by two screens of columns precedes the skylit atrium. The atrium is long, high and narrow and, with its upper-storey colonnade above a blank wall, it seems to be more like an entrance hall than an atrium court.[78] Openings off to the left and right lead to the offices of the ministerial staff and court clerk, respectively. These, along with the judges' chambers, are organized around the two deep courtyards. The library and archives are located on an upper level to each side of the atrium behind the raised colonnades.

A glassed-over central hall set perpendicular to the main axis is the focal point of the plan. This porticoed court, or peristyle, is a double cube surrounded by wide passages connecting the three courtrooms. The smaller courtrooms to the left and right, like the main one straight ahead, have a central nave with side aisles separated by two-storeyed colonnades. Passages on each side of the main courtroom lead from the central hall to a rear court containing the council and reception rooms. The bifurcation of the longitudinal axis at the centre of the building gives the plan a directionality along the lines of a tuning fork.

Fries's plan is much less decisive and contained than Lepreux's. It is uneven in treatment and bottom-heavy. The complexity of the functional organization of the lower part, especially, reduces the impact of the orthogonal relationship of the primary elements. The rich *poché*, characteristic of Fries's planning in general, has an 18th-century quality that is entirely consistent with his development of an extremely varied sequence of interior spaces and vistas. The bombastic Hellenistic portico, much more noble than severe, adds a final baroque note.

Cendrier placed the three courtrooms at right angles to one another, as did Lepreux and Fries, but did not make them contiguous. The two smaller ones are shifted forward along a deep longitudinal atrium that doubles as a central waiting hall. The continuous space going from front to rear with laterally appended courtrooms recalls the juror Thibault's project for a Palais de Justice of the 1790s, published by Durand in his *Précis des leçons d'architecture* (1805) and ultimately the source for both the first and second prize-winning designs in the competition of 1821.[79] Cendrier turned the central vaulted space into a skylit peristyle and placed a deep open porch

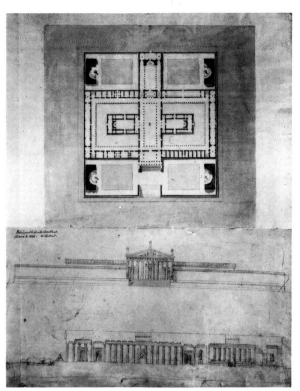

69   F.-A. Cendrier. Cour de Cassation, 1824:
sketch plan, elevation and section. (Tracing;
Académie d'Architecture, Paris)

This approach was new at the Ecole in the 1820s. As also seen in a project of 1821 for a Public Library by Théodore Labrouste, it tended to produce a lateral or horizontal treatment, more like a landscape and less like a figure.[80] Both the elevation and section of Cendrier's sketch emphasize the continuity of horizontal lines with an expression of Doric calmness and breadth. The portico is stretched to ten columns above the uninterrupted roof-line of the lateral courtrooms and the low blank wall extending the entire width of the site. Even the atrium and central courtroom, which are the tallest volumes, are only one storey high. The height of the entablature of the Doric order is continuous from entrance portico to rear tribune, thus accentuating the severity of the conception.

Duc's project spreads out laterally like 70 Cendrier's but is contained within a rectangle occupying the rear half of its square precinct. It can be thought of as either a truncated version of Lepreux's scheme or a synthesis 67 of Lepreux's and Cendrier's ideas. The two 69 smaller courtrooms face each other across a central atrium and together form a broad lateral axis across the front of the building. The atrium, which is a combined entrance hall and waiting room, leads directly along the shallow longitudinal axis to the central court-room. The other parts of the building join the ends of the three courtrooms in two L's, enclosing courtyards. The building is extremely compact yet each of the three courtrooms is expressed on the exterior by a projecting portico or pavilion. Since the only evidence we have of Duc's project is the small block plan recorded by Henri Labrouste, it is impossible to comment on more than the clear and straightforward relationship of the building to the site and its directness of expression.

Léon Vaudoyer's project differs markedly 64 from the four previous ones in its arrangement of the major elements and its relationship to the site. The three courtrooms are set parallel to one another, and each is preceded by its own vestibule and outside entrance. The main building faces a public square and is developed as part of a large urban complex. Two wings project to enclose a deep forecourt, which serves as a background for a central fountain. Side wings bordering the square are continued in flanking buildings on the left and right whose

between it and the pedimented decastyle Greek Doric portico. The main courtroom, replacing the hemicycle and prison in Thibault's plan, is directly in line with it but raised up a few steps.

The two smaller courtrooms are treated less grandly than the central one. They establish a secondary lateral axis marked at the middle of the atrium by a seated figure of Justice. The two axes describe an attenuated Greek cross that divides the walled precinct into four equal parts. The main rectangular block of two square courtyards fills half the site and seems to have been drawn down in place along the expansive central axis. The three sides of each porticoed courtyard contain the various daily functions of the Cour de Cassation and are reached from the corners of the atrium.

Cendrier's plan is more schematic than the first two and appears by contrast both static and unfocused. The parts are less differentiated and, rather than forming a clear figure, they seem to result from subdivisions of the site.

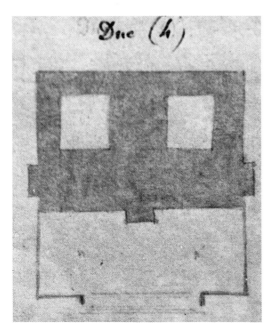

70 L. Duc. Cour de Cassation, 1824: sketch
block plan. (Drawn by H. Labrouste; Académie
d'Architecture, Paris)

central vestibule serving the main courtroom.
Porticoes surround the flanking courtyards and
link the standardized offices of the ministerial
staff and court clerk to the reception rooms
behind the main courtroom. A smaller block
at the rear houses the library and archives all
on the same floor. The library is a direct extension of the main courtroom; the side wings of
the rear block continue the axis of the forecourt
wings after a short hiatus. The gap creates a
tension between the two major overlapped
rectangles of the plan and gives what might
otherwise be a stable open-ended Greek cross
a directional pull.

The most striking quality of Vaudoyer's
design is its urban development. Vaudoyer
was particularly noted as a student for his
skill in designing elaborate environmental set-
tings for his buildings,[81] and his was the only
plan in 1824 to include the *entourage*, as it
was called. The sketch is light and elegant with
an airiness that matches the openness of the
design. The plan itself, though somewhat
diagrammatic, is dynamic and the major elements, though strung out, read at a glance.

Lignière's plan is an inverted T, articulated 71
almost exactly like the top half of Fries's, but 68
its synthesis of atrium and main waiting hall
relates it directly to Duc's. The courtrooms 70
stem from three sides of a central nine-square
block, the fourth side of which serves as the
main entrance. The deep diastyle hexastyle
portico precedes a vestibule containing a flight
of stairs that leads up to a centrally domed
space. This 'atrium' opens out laterally into a
Roman thermal hall, three bays wide, connecting the two smaller courtrooms. The main
axis leading to the largest courtroom is emphasized by the slightly deeper central bay. An
anteroom preceding the courtroom mirrors
the stairwell opposite it.

The circulation pattern forms a Greek cross
of five squares, with the remaining four corner
squares of the central block set off to contain
the concierge's lodging, refreshment bar and
registry office. The other parts of the building
tie in to the pseudo-atrium at its corners. The
offices of the court clerk and ministerial staff
ring the two lateral courtrooms; the robing
rooms, library and archives surround and
isolate the long, single-nave main courtroom.
The three arms are lengthened by the inter
position of a square court behind each courtroom.

lateral façades echo the side entrances of the
court building. The rear opens out onto a
semicircular space that is ringed with concentric
rows of trees and bounded by a portico.

The main courtroom, indicated as an 'assembly room', is the focal point of the plan and
the geometric centre of the site. The three-bay
skylit room divides the main rectangular block
into two nearly square courts. The two smaller
courtrooms project into those courts parallel
to the main courtroom, and all three are linked
together across their entrances by the front
wing of the block. Both smaller courtrooms
have their own tetrastyle vestibules, or waiting
rooms, entered from the projecting wings
that contain the judges' robing rooms and
terminate in small entrance pavilions.

The central courtroom is entered at the base
of the forecourt through a pedimented, deca-
style, Roman Doric portico. Directly behind
is a small, totally covered atrium five intercolumniations wide by three deep. While
the proportion is one recommended by Vitruvius, he stipulated that the longer dimension
be the depth. Vaudoyer's atrium is linked to
the two other vestibules through screened
intermediate spaces, but the connections are
tenuous and the atrium reads simply as a

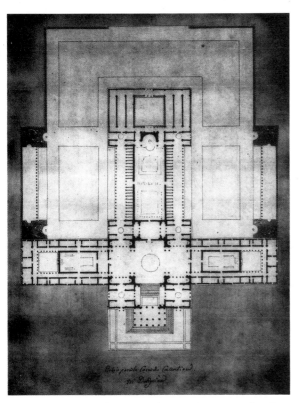

71 R. Lignière. Cour de Cassation, 1824: sketch plan. (Tracing; Académie d'Architecture, Paris)

71 Lignière's plan presents a strong figure but is highly unbalanced. The most important elements are overshadowed by secondary ones. Some areas, such as the main waiting hall, are aggressively characterized at the expense of others, such as the two smaller courtrooms, that are made so insignificant as to lack even the conventional apsidal tribune. Yet the powerful interlocking geometry and structural system give the project a certain panache.

66 Théodore Labrouste's composition is closest
64 to Vaudoyer's in its arrangement of major
69 spaces but also recalls Cendrier's in the geometry of its site planning. The central courtroom divides the rear third of the building into two courtyards, with the two smaller courtrooms projecting into them parallel to the central one. The front third of the building is left open to the street to form a broad shallow forecourt bounded by colonnades. The central axis is marked by a pedimented octastyle Doric portico which, like Cendrier's, is Greek rather than Roman. The portico is silhouetted against an attic that masks the upper-floor library and archives and is set off by contrast with the two flanking entrances to the smaller courtrooms. The deep central porch contains a vestibule with stairs to the library and archives that overlook the central atrium. The atrium is treated as a two-storey basilica: it is entirely covered and receives daylight at either end through the colonnaded gallery.

Théodore Labrouste's atrium is almost exactly the same proportions as Cendrier's but is set athwart the central axis and thus corresponds to the peristyle rather than to the atrium in Vitruvius's description of the Roman house.[82] It establishes a major cross-axis right after the entrance and links the three courtrooms along its far side, thus becoming the central waiting hall. Its floor is sunk a few steps below the level of the surrounding two-storeyed colonnades. The wider passages on the short sides serve as corridors to the two smaller courtrooms. Spur walls along the far side of these passages separate the atrium from two square courts that extend the space laterally out to walled gardens. Broad side entrances terminate this bisectional axis. A suite of rooms, overlapped by the courtrooms and main entrance and overlapping the garden wall, surrounds the central space. On the extreme left and right, looking onto the gardens, are the offices for the ministerial staff and court clerk. The two suites of judges' robing rooms are located to the left and right of the main entrance with the registry office and refreshment bar just beyond. The council and reception rooms continue the side colonnades around the rear and overlap the wall of the precinct like the Gallery of Antiquities in his earlier project for a Library.

Théodore Labrouste's sketch for the Cour de Cassation is a fleshed-out version of the Library. The lateral stress in the plan derives 65 from a subdivisional approach to the site, but the resulting relationship of the main elements to one another is less schematic than in Cendrier's project. The major spaces are clearly differentiated and boldly scaled, though perhaps somewhat disproportionately so. The composition is tight and drawn with a dry and sure touch that gives it a solemn, dutiful character.

Henri Labrouste evolved the same scheme 72 as his brother but pulled out the main entrance and closed in the forecourt to make the building

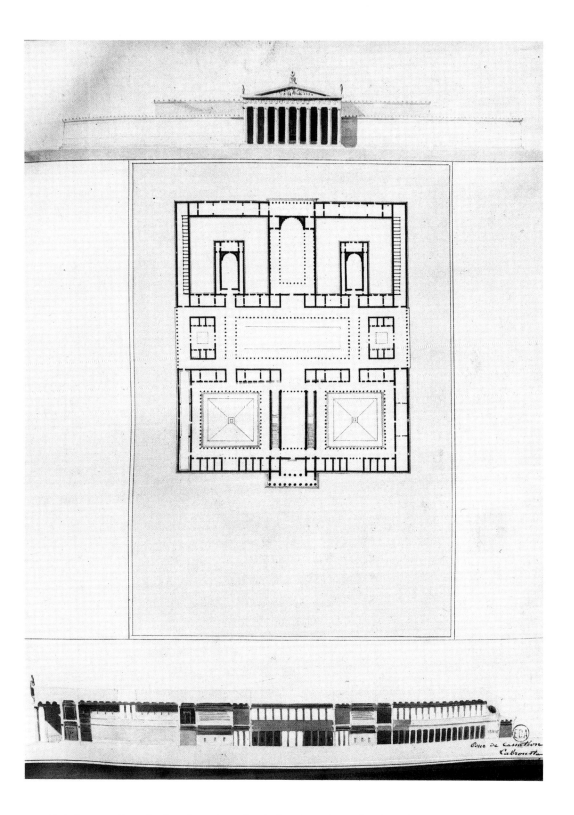

72   H. Labrouste. Cour de Cassation, 1824: sketch elevation, plan and section. (Beaux-Arts)

entirely self-contained. Aside from the porticoes in the centre of each façade, the exterior is totally blind and recalls Cendrier's elevation. A low blank wall defines the perimeter of the block with the upper part of the atrium rising above. A decastyle Greek Doric portico, with a low pediment like Théodore's, announces the main entrance.[83]

A central atrium *cum* waiting hall runs perpendicular to the main axis and divides the building in half.[84] The front, or lower, part is composed of two courts lying on each side of a main entrance hall, which is a long, narrow, skylit, two-storeyed volume similar to Fries's atrium in form and function. Its doubled walls isolate the offices of the court clerk and ministerial staff, which surround the open courts, and also contain stairs leading to the upper-floor archives and library, which overlook the atrium as in Théodore's project.

The atrium is here also in effect a peristyle composed of two-storeyed colonnades. It is skylit and proportionately less narrow than Théodore's. An extra row of columns, inserted at either end, marks the axis of the two smaller courtrooms while at the same time providing support for the outer clerestory wall of the atrium. The doubled passages create stoa-like extensions of the central space, which screen off the registry office and refreshment bar, each organized around a small court in a seemingly freestanding block.[85]

The double courtyard block at the rear is divided in half by the main courtroom, with the two smaller ones parallel to it and projecting into the courts. The judges' robing rooms are placed along the outside wings while the rear is for the council and reception rooms. The central courtroom, composed of a nave and side aisles, has a gallery providing clerestory 68 lighting as in Fries's project; but whereas Fries treated his secondary courtrooms in the same way, Labrouste gave them a simple, one-storey nave. On the other hand, Fries gave his atrium, his central hall and his main courtroom each a different elevation, while Labrouste rigorously maintained throughout the entire length of the building the horizontal division between the two storeys. He concentrated on varying the amount of openness and closure to develop the section as a sequence of light and dark.

Henri Labrouste's sketch is the most abstract and unemphatic of the group. The various elements tend to read as discrete units only tenuously held together. The atrium, which in Théodore's design gives focus and coherence 66 to the main horizontal block, here becomes an open-ended void separating the building into front and rear halves. Those two sections are more or less equally weighted, with the entrance hall matching the main courtroom and the two courtyards above mirroring those below. The result is a nearly biaxially symmetrical plan that describes, like Lepreux's, a Greek 67 cross in a frame. But the figure-ground relationship is reversed. In Lepreux's sketch, the figure of the cross stands out defining the four significant elements, while in Labrouste's the cross recedes and the open ground of the courts takes prominence. The diffusiveness of the image is reinforced by the flat, pale, atonal quality of the drawing. The exterior is more ethereal than severe while the interior is disturbingly lifeless and still.

On first analysis, the subtle variations in personal expression and interpretation among the eight sketches seem outweighed by the more pronounced similarities in form and composition. The plans of Lepreux and Fries, or Duc and Lignière, essentially differ on the basis of whether the rear courtyards are closed in; and the projects of Henri and Théodore Labrouste would look practically identical were it not for the different treatment of the front courtyard. The atrium is the same, while the parallel arrangement of the courtrooms is also shared by their friend and *atelier*-mate Vaudoyer. The Académie's general attitude towards student originality, reflected in the way in which the competition was conducted, helps explain this uniformity and also provides a clue to understanding its method of discrimination.

The room in which the twenty-four-hour sketch was done, called the *lieu* or *salle du concours*, was apparently the same or similar to the one used for the school's monthly competitions.[86] A central corridor divided two rows of cubicles formed by partitions spaced about two metres apart. These cubicles were open on the side facing the corridor although they could be screened off by curtains. During the regular monthly competitions, students conversed and ate lunch in the central space.[87] They were free to enter each other's cubicles and could use the opportunity, as a student remarked at the time, 'to try and pick up a

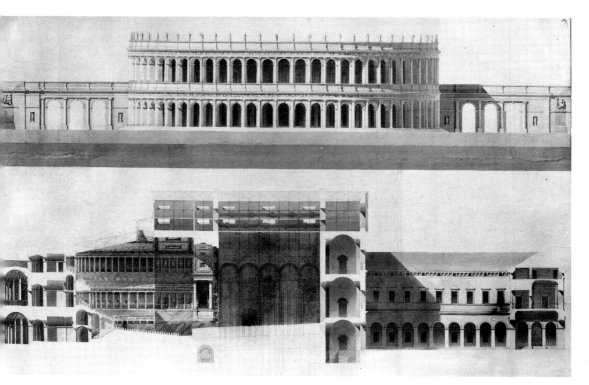

73 E. Gilbert. Opera House, 1822: rendered elevation and section. (Beaux-Arts)

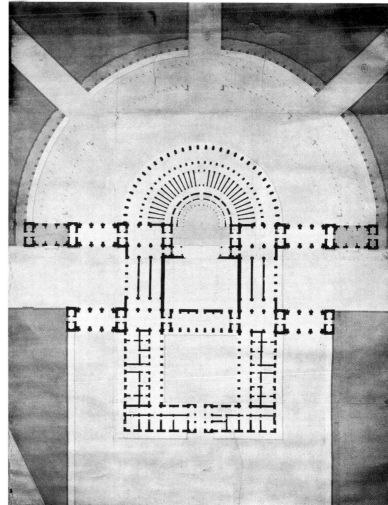

74 E. Gilbert. Opera House, 1822: rendered plan. (Tracing by H. Labrouste; Beaux-Arts)

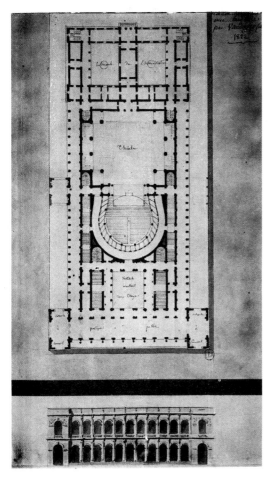

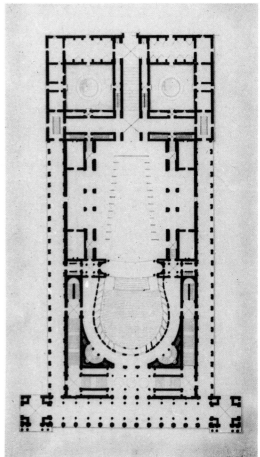

75 L. Vaudoyer. Opera House, 1822: sketch plan and elevation. (Beaux-Arts)

76, 77 H. Labrouste. Opera House, 1822: sketch plan and elevation – below. (Académie d'Architecture, Paris)

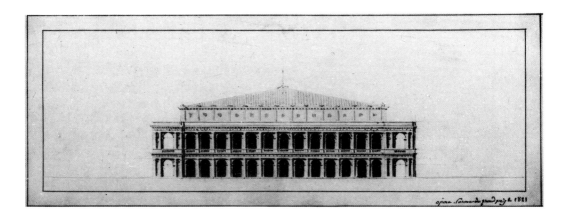

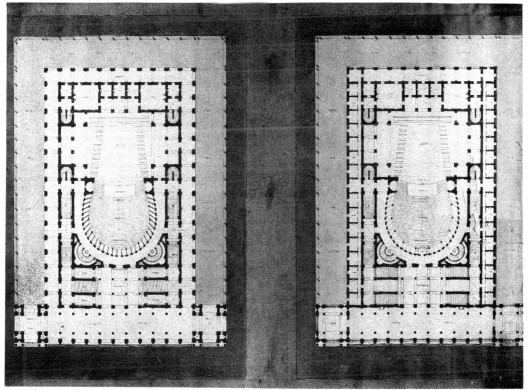

78   A. Blouet. Théâtre pour l'Académie Royale de Musique, 1820: rendered elevation and plans. (Beaux-Arts)

good idea or two'.[88] Nothing in the Académie's rules specifically enjoined those competing for the Grand Prix from having contact with one another during the twenty-four hours, nor is there any indication of other differences in procedure.[89] We can therefore be fairly certain that students as close as the Labrouste brothers and Vaudoyer did discuss and show each other their projects, but it is highly unlikely that this resulted in any major changes. The integral and premeditated quality of their designs rather points to the fact that any effective interaction took place before the morning of the competition. The teachers and jurors were well aware of this; serious projects, said Baltard, 'cannot be improvised'.[90]

The students had a fairly good idea of what the programme might be a year in advance. The subjects that came in second and third stood the best chance of being selected in the following years; and they did not remain secret for long, since success in Grand Prix competition redounded almost as much to the teacher as to the student. After describing to his brother, a day or two after the competition, the subject chosen in 1827, Théodore Labrouste added that 'reportedly M. Lebas proposed a military school and M. Debret a library'.[91] These were in fact the two runners-up. Students who intended to compete the next year would have been foolish not to devote their time to working on those subjects. Debret's Bibliothèque Publique was chosen in 1828, and Lebas's Ecole Militaire finally came up in 1833. It was unusual for the programme to be selected on its initial proposal as in 1824. But since it had to be prepared well in advance, a totally new subject would in all likelihood have been bruited about and even tried out by the teacher who was formulating it.

The jury and students alike showed only a modicum of concern for originality in the choice of *parti* and the general composition of a project. The Grand Prix of 1822 was awarded
73, 74 to Emile Gilbert for an Opera House, modelled on the Roman Theatre of Marcellus, that was almost an exact duplicate of one for which he won a medal in an Ecole competition in 1820. The Académie lauded his design of 1822 for 'recalling' the 'forms of antique theatres' and 'applying them felicitously to our modern uses'.[92] In the same Grand Prix competition,
75–77 Léon Vaudoyer and Henri Labrouste chose a different *parti* and offered almost identical

designs based directly on another project that won a medal in that Ecole competition of 1820. Abel Blouet's design of a Théâtre pour 78 l'Académie Royale de Musique (Theatre for the Royal Academy of Music), modelled on the 18th-century theatre of Bordeaux and the Odéon in Paris,[93] was in fact chosen first by the school's jury in 1820; however, they felt that Gilbert's design deserved to be judged on its own merits because it represented the application of a different 'type', and so he was awarded a deuxième, or second-place, medal specifically on the basis of his *parti*.

Within the limits of Beaux-Arts conventions, there were usually only two or at most three possible *partis* for any given programme.[95] An instance when there were more can be seen in a very rough sketch on an unidentified 79 subject by Henri Labrouste where he is trying to visualize the four possibilities. Following this preliminary analysis, the student would have to decide fairly quickly on the one he thought best and then stick with it, for normally there would not be time to change.[96] It appears that the jury often had a preconceived idea about which was the best and thus *a priori* considered one type of scheme more appropriate. In explaining its choice of Gilbert for the Grand Prix in 1822, the Académie pointed out that 'first of all' his project had 'the advantage' of the antique model.[97]

Gilbert's sketch had been selected first, so they were being entirely consistent. Vaudoyer's 'modern French' scheme had been selected 75 fourth, after the two more classical, or at least Italianate, designs of Jules Bouchet and Fontaine's nephew Pierre-François-Louis. The younger Fontaine was awarded the Second Grand Prix, Bouchet a Deuxième Second, and Vaudoyer was given an honourable mention. Labrouste, whose sketch as we saw resembled Vaudoyer's so closely, was not even selected as a finalist. This had nothing to do with his choice of *parti* nor its dependence on Blouet's earlier design. Rather, Vaudoyer's is better proportioned and in that respect follows Blouet's example more faithfully. Labrouste's building looks lean and skimpy; he 77 stretched out Blouet's façade two extra bays and made the entrance hall uncomfortably shallow. The Académie acknowledged that Vaudoyer's plan was especially generous in its public spaces and would thereby create 'a handsome impression'.[98]

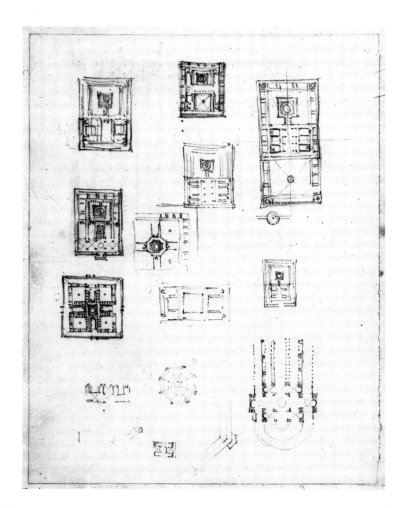

79 H. Labrouste. Sketch plans on an unidentified subject, *c*.1824. (Académie d'Architecture, Paris)

It also seems quite certain that the Académie made its decisions on a strictly comparative basis by weighing the compositional variations on a few standard types of *parti*.[99] The choice of finalists in 1824 specifically suggests that the jury first divided the projects into groups by type and then chose the best version of the most promising variations of each. The eight sketches exhibit two different *partis*, and the order of selection unmistakably reveals which one the Académie preferred. All four top projects have the main courtroom set perpendicular to the two smaller ones, which establish a cross-axis. Three of the other four have the courtrooms lined up parallel to one another on discrete longitudinal axes. Each represents a distinctly different interpretation of its type, and the order of selection here again reveals a significant aspect of the Académie's point of view.

A cross-axial scheme lent itself most readily to the expression of variety within unity and the balance of major and minor elements that the Académie usually sought.[100] In its ideal form of the Greek cross, it was the plan-type preferred perhaps above all others for representational buildings of a lofty and didactic character. Amant-Parfait Prieur and Pierre-Louis Van Cléemputte chose Jacques-Pierre de Gisors' adaptation of it to the programme of a Museum in 1779 as the first plate in their original publication of the Grands Prix (begun 1787).[101] In succeeding years it was the *parti* that won the top prize for Louis-Guy Combes in 1781, Percier in 1786, Vallot in 1800, André Châtillon in 1809, Auguste Caristie in 1813, both Louis-Nicolas Destouches and Charles-Henry Landon in 1814 and Van Cléemputte's younger son Lucien in 1816.[102] Three of these were for an Academy or Institute, two for a Cathedral, and one each for a Library-Museum complex and a Town Hall.

The Académie obviously felt that the perfect
67 Greek cross of Lepreux's design was the most
appropriate form for the Supreme Court of
France since twenty-five years later, when the
programme of a Cour de Cassation came up
again in 1859, it awarded the Grand Prix to
80 François-Philippe Boitte for a revised version
of Lepreux's scheme.[103] With its four major
elements, the programme was tailor-made for
a Greek cross, but only if you interpreted the
atrium as the Académie intended. Lepreux
recognized the Vitruvian distinction between
an atrium and a peristyle alluded to in the
programme and correctly interpreted the atrium
as an introductory court serving the entire
complex and not just the three courtrooms.
Set longitudinally on the main axis, it defines
the formal approach to the courtrooms; and,
placed in the lower part of the plan, it is equal
in size to the main courtroom without appearing
to dominate it. By contrast, a parallel placement
of the courtrooms would either leave the size and
shape of the atrium indeterminate or necessitate
an inordinate lateral atrium-peristyle contradict-
ing the main axial approach.[104]

Lepreux's sketch, as we have seen, had much
to recommend it in terms of proportion,
articulation and finish. Its façade, though somewhat finicky in scale, is as 'foursquare' as Ledoux
said a building symbolizing justice should be.[105]
The Académie appreciated its 'severe character
and suitability in terms of style', but, as the
jury later explained, it was 'above all' the
arrangement of 'the *atrium* corresponding to
the three courtrooms' that made them prefer
Lepreux's design.[106] Lepreux's choice of so
simple and perfect a figure as the Greek cross
must have been seen as a sign of his maturity,
and his project set the standard against which
the others were judged.

The sketches of both Fries and Cendrier
are less complete realizations of the cross-axial
parti and lack the evenness and balance of
68 Lepreux's. Fries interpreted the atrium correctly
in terms of placement but not form. It is
the starting point for a dramatic spatial sequence
leading to the central courtroom; and, in an
almost too literal interpretation of the programme, it serves to connect the various
offices rather than just the courtrooms. But
its functional aspect and corridor-like narrow-
ness allow the central waiting hall to vie with
it in importance. The grouping of rooms
around the atrium makes that part of the

building seem congested and awkward and
almost an afterthought, since the lines of
structure and circulation are discontinuous
with the rest of the plan, and the roofline
of the upper-floor library and archives interrupts
the elevation. But Fries's really serious mistake
was to use the Corinthian order to express
'nobility' combined with 'severity'. It is the
only design that is not Doric. Since he could not
change it, and therefore had no chance of
winning, the selection of his sketch in second
place simply emphasizes the importance the
Académie attached at this stage to his having
chosen the right *parti*.

Cendrier's scheme stresses more explicitly 69
than Fries's the orthogonal relationship of the
major elements but does so at the expense of
differentiation. The atrium is correctly placed
along the longitudinal axis but is hardly
distinguishable from the central courtroom,
another indication of how important the jury
considered its placement. Modelling his atrium
on the waiting hall of Thibault's earlier Court- 87
house enabled Cendrier to increase its size by
doubling its function and thus produce an
elegantly simplified variation of the cross-axial
parti. If Lepreux's plan represents the ideal
expression of the cross-axial scheme in a
Greek cross inscribed on a square, then the
deviations from it in the designs of Cendrier
and Fries may best be understood as the result
of attenuation and condensation. Whereas Fries
focused attention on functional distinctions
in eliminating the rear half of the square while
preserving the cross intact, Cendrier stressed
the processional axis by abbreviating both the
lateral arms of the cross and the depth of the
square itself.

The two versions of the cross-axial *parti*
chosen last are both truncated Greek crosses
lacking the lower or introductory arm entirely.
While Duc preserved the upper half of the 70
square enclosure, Lignière eliminated that too. 71
Without the lower arm of the cross, there
was no possibility of a separate and deep
atrium. Since the apparent reason for the
Académie's preference for the cross-axial *parti*
lay in its provision for such a grand formal
approach, it is no wonder these two variations
were chosen last. The exceedingly compact
quality of Duc's sketch provides little room for
any hierarchical distinction among the four
major elements and virtually no room at all
for a waiting hall to supplement the atrium.

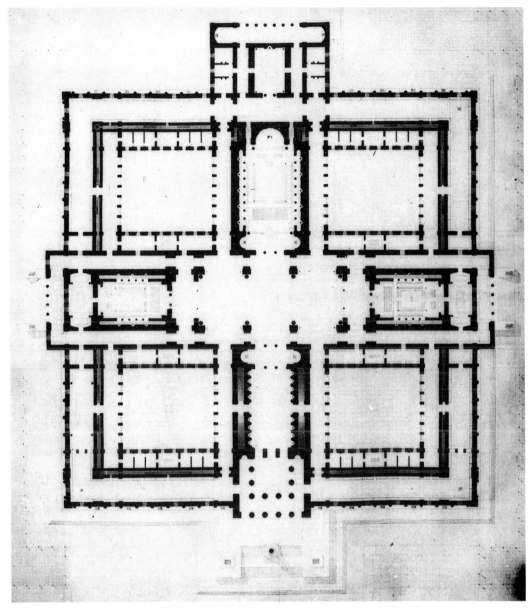

80   F.-P. Boitte. Cour de Cassation, 1859: rendered plan. (From Ecole Nationale des Beaux-Arts, *Les Grands Prix de Rome d'Architecture de 1850 à 1900*, pub. A. Guérinet, n.d.)

Overburdened as it may be, the atrium gives a proper directional emphasis and coherence to the scheme. By contrast, the indecisiveness of Lignière's atrium allows for a loose, lateral spread that is reflected in the general shapelessness of the main rooms and the ill-conceived emphasis on the connection between the two minor courtrooms. The undue prominence given to the library-archives area and the choice of a vaulted Roman system of con- struction are completely out of character, and show a lack of judgment. Lignière's sketch was selected only after the Académie picked out what it considered the best example of the less appropriate *parti*.

The placement of the courtrooms on three parallel axes immediately indicated the proto- type of the 16th- and 17th-century palace, with its tripartite division of the main block into pavilions and its enclosure of a forecourt by projecting wings.[107] In France, the traditional placement of the block *entre cour et jardin* gave an inherent directionality and circumambiency to the scheme.[108] Of the three who chose this

64   approach, Vaudoyer developed the implications of the extended courtyard-block *parti* most fully. His mixture of Italian and French precedents gives the design a pragmatically rather than an ideally suitable character and necessarily emphasizes the courtrooms and their auxiliary spaces rather than the atrium. It was virtually impossible to provide an enclosed approach on axis without denying the nature of the *parti*, so Vaudoyer made a trade-off. He gave up a true atrium for a large open courtyard. An atrium-shaped space was set lengthwise behind the main portico, but, as just one of three vestibules, it hardly asserts itself as the fourth major element. Vaudoyer also found it necessary to disregard the requirement that the building be 'entirely isolated'. The jury was apparently willing to forgive this too, since the 'appropriately noble and impressive elevation'[109] that resulted was entirely consistent with the *parti* chosen.

66   Théodore Labrouste's project is a more contained variation on the courtyard-block *parti*. The three parallel courtrooms occupy the rear rather than the centre of the plan. The low wings are just barely extended to make a shallow forecourt and provide a base for the massive central block. In contrast to Vaudoyer's ultimate refusal to deal with the issue of the atrium, Théodore Labrouste gave it pre-eminence and thereby sacrificed much else to it. While it unifies the whole design and endows it with a much more 'antique' character, its lateral disposition contradicts both the main axial approach and the expression on the façade of the tripartite division within. The long axis ends in spur walls through which the central space leaks into smaller courtyards; the distended lateral block itself creates a large horizontal division, which fills up so much of the forecourt that the project finally appears unbalanced and incomplete.

72   Henri Labrouste restored a sense of balance and completeness to his brother's scheme by closing in the forecourt but thereby compromised the very idea of the *parti*. The directionality and circumambiency implied by the parallel placement of the courtrooms is contradicted by the overlaid cross-axial scheme defined by the entrance hall, atrium and central

courtroom. The increased size and complete envelopment of the atrium exacerbate its shortcomings. It is almost triple the size of the main courtroom, and the smaller courtrooms have no separate means of access nor any external expression. The extra row of columns at each end of the atrium simply points up the inadequacy of the connection to the main pattern of circulation.

Henri Labrouste's synthesis of two different *partis* diluted the clarity of each and resulted in a number of seriously unresolved areas. The definition of the secondary axes of the two smaller courtrooms is adventitious, ending below in a cul-de-sac.[110] The major cross-axis of the atrium, likewise, appears to lead nowhere. Logically, it should have terminated in the two smaller courtrooms rather than in the minor refreshment bar and registry office. This obviously unintelligent solution cast into sharpest relief the indecisiveness of his approach.

Based on the order of selection of sketches in 1824, it can be concluded that the Académie looked for clarity and decisiveness of intellectual perception in distinguishing the best examples of each *parti*. The first version of each is the purest and clearest representation of its type. The four cross-axial projects chosen after Lepreux's progressively depart from the ideal centrality of his scheme and distort its near biaxial symmetry. The final one by Lignière shares the lateral emphasis of the projects of Vaudoyer and the Labroustes. Of these three, Vaudoyer's is the most straightforward and uncompromising expression of the extended courtyard-block idea. Théodore Labrouste's version de-emphasizes its circumambiency and directionality. The containment and centralization of Henri Labrouste's, resulting from the superimposition of a Greek cross like Lepreux's, blurs the distinction between the two *partis*. Not surprisingly, the ultimate compromise was chosen last.

The jury disregarded two faults in Henri Labrouste's sketch that might well have disqualified him. The lateral porticoes of the front courtyards are seventeen columns deep, an anomaly only barely tolerated when the odd column was not lined up with an opening as it is here. More obvious is the fact that the section does not exactly correspond to the plan and was not drawn to the proper scale. Labrouste may have been tired, or nervous or just terribly rushed at the end. He was out of practice, for he had not been competing at the Ecole for over a year and a half. It was said that the only reason he was not awarded the Grand Prix in 1821 was that he was too young and that Blouet was overdue for it.[111] Perhaps the Académie was trying to make sure that the 'promising talent'[112] they had recognized three years earlier was given another chance before it was too late. It was easy to correct the mistakes in the sketch, but there was no way of altering the composition. A large question therefore remains to be answered. How, only four months later, could the Académie award Labrouste the Grand Prix for exactly the same design? Since the Académie was not a fickle body, something other than composition must have helped determine its final choice.

The rendering

If the twenty-four-hour sketch can be considered an exam, then the effort involved in the final rendering can be likened to today's thesis project. Although the two stages were inextricably linked until the 1860s, students at the Ecole always thought of them quite separately. 'The order of receptions [en loge] means nothing,' wrote Théodore Labrouste to his brother in 1827, hardly having to point out to him, as he said, that even someone with a last-place sketch could win 'if he knows how to study'.[113] Henri Labrouste stressed the overriding importance of the renderings to encourage his friend Dommey on hearing of his sketch being chosen second in 1825:

[The Prix de] Rome is not impossible if you work with zeal. I am not saying you should take me as an example, but just remember that I was received last; so work hard but don't tire yourself out or neglect yourself; work coolly and without counting on the prize. Don't believe the other competitors are invincible.[114]

The fundamental difference between the two stages of the competition was eventually recognized by the Académie. Beginning in 1845, the eight sketches were chosen by elimination rather than preference and were therefore no longer ranked.[115] Finally, in 1864, the twenty-four-hour sketch became an entirely separate competition just to select the finalists, who then developed their renderings on another programme altogether.[116]

Throughout the entire century, the students were usually given four months to prepare the final drawings. In 1824, the projects were due on 21 September, so they had about 125 days. Two or three days after the finalists were chosen, they gathered in a room at the Ecole to make tracings of their sketches on which the renderings had to be based. The originals were kept under lock and key until the day of judging, so the jury could verify there were no essential changes in composition. The students were then each assigned a separate loge, or small locked room.[117] Whereas the sketch that supposedly expressed their individual response to the programme was done in a communal setting, the renderings were to be done in total seclusion. Nobody except the school's concierge or the professor of architectural theory, Baltard, was allowed into the loges, and the students were expressly forbidden from entering each other's. All drawings, including studies for the final renderings, had to be done en loge. Every sheet of paper brought into the building had to be stamped and countersigned by Baltard to certify that it was absolutely blank.[118] (The stories one hears of drawings smuggled in or out usually date from later in the century.)

In 1824, however, the architects did not begin working in their loges until mid-July, because the building, which was designed by François Debret, the architect of the Ecole, to provide adequate space for students competing concurrently for the Grands Prix in painting, sculpture, architecture and engraving, was not completed until 1825–26. The preparatory studies were done in rooms provided by their teachers, generally in the buildings of the Institut.[119] Whether or not the student was confined to his loge from the outset, he was obviously free to discuss his project with anyone. But silence and secrecy were apparently the rule. Labrouste strongly cautioned Dommey in 1825 not to let anyone but his own teacher know what he was doing and not to seek help from anyone but him. 'Above all else, don't communicate with anyone,' he wrote from Rome, 'don't confuse yourself with too much advice, and draw your own conclusions on everything.'[120] Normally, the student immediately went to his own teacher for guidance, and that is exactly what Henri Labrouste told Dommey to do: 'You will begin by studying your project as conscientiously and as carefully as possible; you will study it under the eyes of M. Lebas.' The advice of one's teacher was considered paramount. 'You should rely on M. Lebas' advice for everything,' wrote Labrouste, 'follow it exactly: it is better than any other you can get.'[121]

The finalist actually had very little latitude in developing his design. While the rules for the Grand Prix merely stipulated that the renderings had to 'conform to their sketches',[122] they closely followed the guidelines established for Ecole competitions. The final plan had to maintain 'the disposition and the distribution of the main buildings set down in the sketch'.[123] In particular, it was forbidden to change the position of stairways, the number of bays or openings or the specific number of columns or arches. The decision in 1828 to allow the number of freestanding columns or pedestals, or doors or windows, to be increased or decreased by two 'for every ten on the same façade' legitimized what had for long been condoned.[124] But 'in no case' was the substitution of an arcade for a colonnade ever tolerated.[125] The programme of 1824 was even more restrictive than usual in specifying that the order had to be indicated precisely enough in the sketch so that it, too, could not be changed.

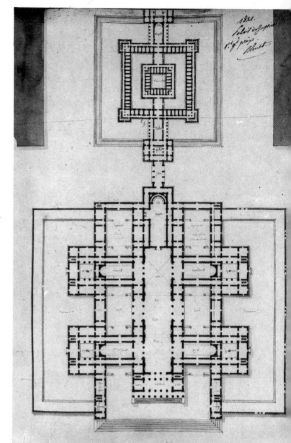

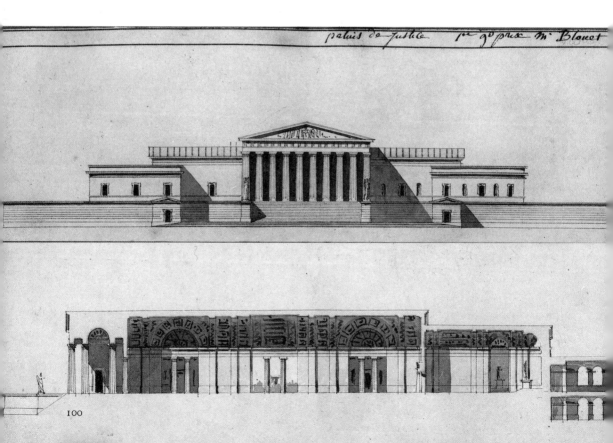

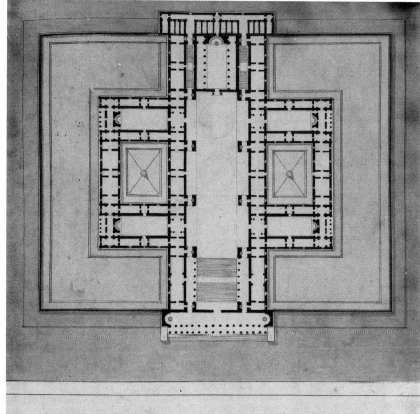

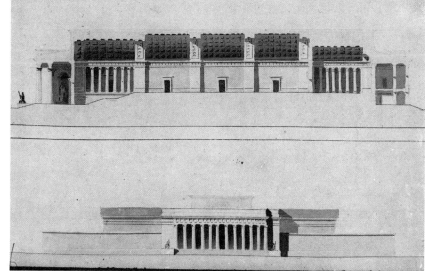

There were ways of getting around some of these prohibitions. The student might prudently leave certain areas in his sketch vague or incomplete, or he might even cavalierly indicate alternative solutions. For example, 81 the chapel in Abel Blouet's sketch for a Palais de Justice, which was placed first in 1821, has a transept only on the left. Since the one on the right was erased, it could be said he had not finished. Similarly, his elevation has niches alternating with windows on the right 82 but not on the left, which gave him the option to do either in the rendering. In Henri Labrouste's sketch, which was placed third that 83 year, the plan of the central waiting hall shows a ceiling with three domes while the section indicates a barrel vault; and the roof of the main hall is drawn in pencil so tentatively that Labrouste did not commit himself to any specific shape.

The sketches in 1824 show none of this. The
72 discrepancies in Henri Labrouste's section are
simply mistakes. The missing roof in his
elevation was a conventional trick for giving
the building a more imposing effect and was
even permitted by the Académie in the final
73 rendering, as can be seen in Gilbert's Grand
Prix of 1822. Perhaps the provision in 1824
about the order was understood as a sign of
the jury's intention to be particularly strict
regarding the necessary conformity of sketch
and rendering.

The four months of work was divided into
two phases: first, an extended period of
étude, or studying the project; second, the
meticulous process of rendering *per se*. Studying
the project meant reviewing it part by part
and working each out in detail. Quatremère
defined this 'study of the parts and the execution
of details' as the prerequisite for the correct
and final adjustment of part to whole.[126]
3 Julien Guadet, who won the Grand Prix in
1864 and went on to become professor of
architectural theory at the Ecole later in the
century, defined 'study' as synonymous with
'proportions' and considered it the second, or
decorative, part of architecture, the first being
the compositional and the third being the
constructional.[127] When, in 1855, the twenty-
four-hour sketch was temporarily increased to
ten days, the acknowledged purpose was to
give the student enough time to develop his
composition so that the process of 'studying
would not involve any changes other than
proportions or the introduction of details [of
decoration] not comprised in the sketch'.[128]

The object of studying the project was to add
character and coherence to the original scheme
without making any significant compositional
changes. This entailed mainly the refinement
of proportions, the clarification of relations
and, finally, the elaboration of character through
decoration.[129] To get just the right proportions
for a room or to give just the right depth to a
moulding could be painstaking work. Alfred
Pommier, one of the twenty-two eliminated
in 1824, described it as an incredibly fastidious
process of 'making study after study, tracing
upon tracing merely to lower or raise a line a
hairbreadth'.[130] There was much greater freedom in developing the decoration since the
sketch barely defined its parameters, but the
question of appropriateness could be just as
constraining.

The advice of the teacher was most important
in the earliest stages of studying the project.
He could point out how closing off a passageway
or increasing the depth of a room might add
significantly to the visual unity of the plan;
he might describe how to enrich the decorative
treatment of an important area; or he might
simply tell the student what examples or models
to look at. While reliance on such advice
caused some critics to claim that 'the details
of the final projects are much more the work
of the teachers than the students',[131] the student
had to work out most of the problems on his
own. He could follow up his teacher's suggestions by checking through such authorities
as Vitruvius, Palladio or Vignola in the school
library. For a detail of decoration or proportion
relating to antique precedent, he would probably consult the standard works of David
Leroy, Stuart and Revett, Delagardette, Mazois
or the recent publications of the Society of
Dilettanti. From there, he would go to the
special collection of drawings of antique buildings done by the former Grand Prix winners
while they were at the Académie de France in
Rome and kept for just this purpose at the
Ecole in Paris.[132] On specific issues of planning
or character, the previous Grand Prix designs
were models of convention. Over the years,
a student such as Labrouste had studied them
quite closely and copied most of them in his
sketchbooks. But for the detailed information
he would want at this stage, about how best
to render the foliage in a garden or highlight
an important decorative element, only the
original drawings would do. These, along with
the drawings of antique monuments done by
the students in Rome, were kept in the archives
of the Ecole and were normally available for
consultation on Mondays and Thursdays between 10:00 am and 2:00 pm. It is surely
an indication of how much they were referred
to by students working on their renderings that
during the three months 1 July – 1 October the
archives were open only to *logistes*![133]

Once the student had decided on all aspects
of his project, he began the final drawings.
They were in India ink and wash and were
always done entirely on his own *en loge*. The
meaning of the word rendering connotes both
accuracy and clarity. Labrouste felt the purpose
of rendering was 'to elucidate one's project'.[134]
As Boutard's dictionary of artistic terms explained in 1826, the drawings had to express

the composition fully and clearly in order 'to render it intelligible'.[135] The renderings demanded, as Quatremère noted in his dictionary the year before, an absolute degree of 'precision and finish in their execution'.[136] He defined rendering as 'synonymous with *finished, completed*' and added that while 'the finish or the *rendering* of drawings surely does not constitute the intrinsic value of the work, . . . it is an indication of experience and of the care that the artist has brought to all parts of his work'.[137]

The students worried a great deal about the visual effect of their renderings and sought to impress the jury with elaborate drawings often in excess of those demanded by the programme. This became so prevalent that in 1825 the Académie had to make a rule forbidding the submission of extra drawings.[138] Labrouste warned Dommey, who was not a particularly gifted draughtsman anyway, against 'giving too many unrequired drawings' for the psychological reason that 'one should not try to overwhelm the others nor give the impression of having done more than them'. However, Labrouste told him 'to add a roof plan', since 'that is a drawing which should always be required', and also to 'add some portions of the section or the ceiling in outline, but above all without pretension'. Labrouste told Dommey to avoid overworking his drawings or giving any appearance of 'ostentation'. The qualities sought for in the renderings were clarity, vibrancy and presence, and Labrouste told Dommey: 'the key to rendering with washes to elucidate one's project is to go fast'.[139]

The renderings of all premiated projects were normally retained by the Académie and preserved at the Ecole. Unfortunately, only Henri Labrouste's project has survived from 1824. But since the important remaining question is why Labrouste's renderings won over the jury despite the shortcomings of his sketch, a careful analysis of these drawings in comparison with his sketch is what is called for in any event. The generalizations that follow can be supported by visual evidence from other years.

Labrouste submitted one more than the six 86 required drawings. That was a roof plan, as he later suggested to Dommey. Most of the 60 renderings are quite large. The plan is approximately 1 metre square, and the elevation and 84 longitudinal section are each about 2 metres wide. The most striking impression is made by the large-scale details of the portico and cross-section of the main courtroom, the former 85 measuring 1.30 metres wide by .80 metres high, and the latter 1 metre wide by .65 metres high. As Labrouste also recommended to Dommey, he drew on the same sheet as the main elevation, to the right and just in outline, a five-bay 84 section of the main courtroom; and, on the same sheet as the portico, a section through the door and another through the portico itself, the latter showing, with a plan of the shaft below, the exact degree of inclination of the columns. The ceiling and roof structure is indicated throughout both sections. Though by no means unusual, this was not normal, and in 1828 the Académie made it a requirement.[140]

As part of the finish demanded in the renderings, the plan shows the added '*mosaïque*', 60 or indication of the floor and ceiling patterns and placement of furniture, while the other drawings are enriched by the addition of decorative sculpture and lettering along with the delineation of mouldings and stonework. Aside from the differences due to size and finish, the renderings look practically identical to the sketch. The actual changes in the plan are 72 subtle and superficially slight. All structural supports remain where they were, and the circulation pattern is unaltered. Some partition walls are shifted; doors and windows are added or relocated; and some load-bearing walls are replaced by columns, while the columns of the entrance hall are replaced by ceiling beams spanning the space. The few lines moved a 'hairbreadth' up or down or replaced by a row of dots graphically increase the unity of the design through the refinement of proportions, the clarification of spatial relations and the strengthened pattern of lights and darks.

The two areas most visibly affected by the changes are the atrium and the entrance hall. The most disjunctive factor in the sketch was the divisive atrium, and it is reduced in width by almost 10 per cent. Two columns from each side portico are eliminated, leaving the atrium just marginally wider than the central axis. An increased sense of continuity and directionality results from the substitution of walls with doorways for the open passages into the side porches at the ends of the atrium and between the entrance hall and the lower courtyards.

The changes in the lower part of the plan

begin with the portico. Labrouste gave it greater depth and relief by making it pseudo-dipteral, with the pronaos, as in the Parthenon, becoming hexastyle prostyle. The entrance hall is lengthened by the removal of the screens of columns that closed it off at either end and, at the same time, is isolated from the two flanking courtyards by the continuation of the side walls across the formerly connecting passages. A strong directional focus is produced by the screened passage that opens out from six to ten columns so that the entrance hall expands into the atrium. This arrangement mirrors the main portico at a reduced scale, thereby making a dynamic pattern out of the sequence of spaces.

The screened passage at the end of the entrance hall is also echoed across the atrium in the vestibule preceding the main courtroom. The ten columns of each screen are repeated in equal number in the end colonnades of the atrium, but again the central axis is subtly reinforced by the fact that the middle nine intercolumniations of the long sides of the atrium are wider than the rest. This refinement of proportions is reflected in all aspects of the atrium. Where it was twelve columns by thirty-two, it is now regularized to ten by thirty. With the wider intercolumniations of the central nine bays, the proportion of width to length of the open space is just over $1:3$, instead of the previous $13:37$, and the height is two-thirds rather than one-half the width. In a similar fashion, the proportions of the main courtroom are regularized and its diagrammatic relation to the lower hall and atrium thereby clarified. Based on the double-square composition of Palladio's design of an Ancient Basilica, the proportion of width to length of the nave is reduced from $7:15$ to $7:14$, which allows for a neat division of the chamber into two equal areas.[141] The overall proportion of the room is correspondingly broadened from $3:5$ to $2:3$.

The central importance and unifying power of the atrium is further emphasized by the increased width of its aisles in relation to the surrounding ring of space formed by the vestibule of the main courtroom, the passage from the entrance hall and the outer aisles at the ends of the atrium. This hierarchical distinction clarifies the atrium's relation to the rest of the building and makes it seem to pulsate at the core. The walls drawn from the two

smaller courtrooms down across the blocks containing the registry office and refreshment bar effectively delimit the central space. This turns the side entrances into true porches, but, more importantly, it helps to reinforce the secondary axes of the smaller courtrooms.

In the rendered plan the two smaller courtrooms are clearly linked to the lower courtyards. The extra wall just inside the courtrooms is eliminated to allow for a more ample vestibule opening directly from the atrium. This pattern is repeated on the opposite side in the vestibules that lead into the courtyards containing the offices of the court clerk and ministerial staff. The lower courtyards are squared up, having sixteen columns on a side, and, with the passages leading to the entrance hall now closed by doors, these courtyards manifestly become dependants of the functionally related smaller courtrooms.

Each area of the building is given an appropriate decorative character. The columns in the front courtyards are scaled down in size from those of the atrium to suit the particular character of their setting. Similarly, the central courtroom is given a more elaborate decorative treatment than either the atrium or the entrance hall, befitting its more elevated function. The upper colonnade, as revealed in the section. is Ionic, and the frieze of the intervening entablature is punctuated by paterae. The choice and proportions of the superimposed orders were undoubtedly based on the recent reconstructions of the Forum at Pompeii by François Mazois and Félix Callet, the latter having begun his drawings while a student in Rome in 1822 and completed them in Paris in early 1824.[142] The role of the central courtroom as the culminating element of the design is also greatly amplified in plan. The vestibule opens it out broadly to the atrium, and the aisles now continue uninterruptedly around into a council room behind. The window wall of this room replaces a portico, thereby closing the rear and decisively capping the plan.

The elimination of the rear opening and the de-emphasis of the cross-axis give a directionality and a sense of conclusion lacking in the sketch. The continuous outline of the major elements presents a strong figure. The space of the entrance hall forms a base that funnels into the atrium and central courtroom and then branches out into the two smaller ones like a candelabra. The image suggests an orans figure, an appropriately hieratic form for a 'supreme tribunal'. An ecclesiastical reference is unmistakable throughout Labrouste's reworking of the composition and gives the project a coherent framework. The early Romanesque church, with its narrow nave, broad transept and three apses *en échelon*, provided a plan-type that could smooth away the contradictions of the original scheme and allow it to sing out with renewed clarity and vigour. How much Labrouste's teacher, Lebas, had to do with this is hard to know. It seems highly likely though that Labrouste's skillful play on the historical source of the form of the early church in the Roman law courts must owe something to his teacher, who was just beginning the church of Notre-Dame de Lorette (1823–36), based on the Early Christian basilica of S. Maria Maggiore in Rome.

2, 84   The changes in the elevation add majesty and presence. The reversal of the pattern of light and shadow makes a dark foil for the columns of the portico, and highlights the sculpture in the pediment. The overall proportions of the façade are enhanced by the extension of the upper wall of the atrium beyond the middle of the wall below. (The end clerestories are now supported by the new end walls of the atrium rather than by the intermediate spine of columns.) The free-standing statues of the pediment are eliminated, and the lower cornice is lined up with that of the upper storey, giving the portico greater breadth. The portico itself is raised on a higher stylobate, while the height of the columns is reduced to about 6.7 lower diameters. The Doric order, seen close up in the large-scale drawing, is similar to that of the 4th-century Greek Temple of Zeus at Nemea and the Triangular Forum at Pompeii, where, as Baltard told his students, 'the proportions are more perfectly in harmony with the art of building and with the rules of good taste' than the earlier Doric and 'better related to and more consistent with our modern uses'.[143] Labrouste's choice of a Doric order halfway between the 5th-century Greek and the later, more slender Roman gives a perfect balance of nobility and severity and shows the kind of understanding of the continual progress and applicability of classical architecture that would have impressed the Académie.

The renderings of the elevation and section illustrate a complete scheme of decoration

hardly even hinted at in the sketch. The sculpture in the pediment relates to its triangular shape and announces the iconographical theme of the building. In the centre is a female figure seated on a throne, holding a table of laws in her left hand and pointing to it with her right. To each side are genii carrying lighted torches, while the rear of the throne forms an aureole or nimbus behind her. The other figures holding tablets and scrolls move toward the centre away from representations of blindness and darkness, seen on the left and right, and into the light shed by the law.

The central figure combines the composition of Raphael's painting of *Philosophy*, in the Stanza della Segnatura, with the attributes of Moses to produce a quasi-religious symbol. Significantly, Labrouste did not choose Raphael's representation of *Jurisprudence*, with her conventional attributes of balance and sword. His choice reflects the fact that the Cour de Cassation is not so much where justice is daily administered as where the law itself is affirmed and upheld. The reference to Mosaic law was particularly relevant in the context of post-Revolutionary France, where the nation's written, or statute, law had just received its ultimate textual form in the promulgation of the Napoleonic Codes.

The interior decoration of the building derives mainly from a combination of sculpture and the written word with the play of light and shadow. The seated female figure in the entrance hall holds a page in her left hand pressed against the side of the throne, while her right hand is extended out in a gesture of charity or clemency. Along the wall is a row of eight male and female figures in antique dress. The composition is framed by the sharp light, which picks out an inscription on the frieze just below the three windows. The text is a contraction of the fourth and eleventh articles of the Constitutional Charter of 1814, setting forth the fundamental principles of French law derived from the Declaration of the Rights of Man and of the Citizen of the Constitution of 1791: 'The individual liberty of Frenchmen is guaranteed; no one can be prosecuted or arrested save in the cases provided by law and in the form which it prescribes. All investigations of opinions are forbidden.'[144] The text is set between the dates 1701 and 1804, the latter being the year of the promulgation of the Civil Code, the first of Napoleon's

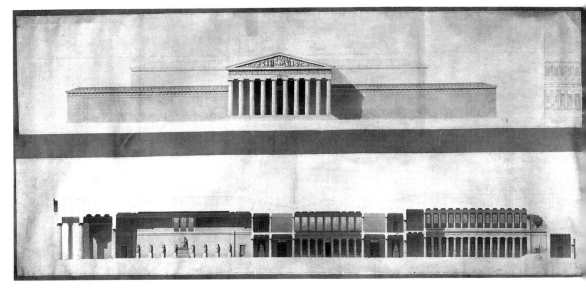

84, 85   H. Labrouste. Cour de Cassation, 1824: rendered elevation and longitudinal section (above), and rendered cross-section of main courtroom. (Beaux-Arts)

Codes and the one to which his name has become attached. The clarity of the entrance hall calls to mind Marie-Joseph Chénier's description of a modern secular religion of Reason, 'having neither secrets nor mysteries, with equality as its sole dogma and with laws for orators and magistrates for priests'.[145]

The atrium is more dimly lit. The inscriptions on the backs of the benches, partially obscured by the columns, are the only decoration. On the one on the left is the fifty-eighth article of the Charter of 1814, ensuring the independence of the judiciary: 'The ju[dges] appointed b[y] the king ar[e irremo]vable.' And on the one on the right is the sixty-second article, ensuring the individual the right to trial by peers: 'No one c[a]n be [de]prived of the [jurisdiction of his n]atural judges.'[146] The atrium is treated as a place to pause and contemplate the more quotidian effects of law before entering the central courtroom, where a soft and spiritual light leads the eye to the apse decorated with the legal codes themselves. The king's throne, based on Pompeian motifs, is set behind a balustrade on a high platform where the ascensional movement through the section culminates, an idea Labrouste probably picked up from Fries and Cendrier. In the dramatic cross-section, the empty throne directs attention to the curved surface, on which are inscribed in tabular form the five Napoleonic Codes. Labrouste chose to depict the Civil Code of 1804, the Criminal Code of 1808–11 and the Procedural Code of 1806, the three that specifically characterize the divisions of the Cour de Cassation.[147] On the frieze above, tying them together, is the first article of the Charter of 1814: 'Frenchmen are equal before the law, whatever may b[e their titles and ranks].'[148]

Labrouste's decoration presents a coherent image of the meaning and purpose of the French Supreme Court. In a sequence of light and dark spaces, the scheme develops from a generalized sculptural embodiment of the sacredness of written law to the textual reproduction of the laws governing France. The inscriptions taken from Louis XVIII's Charter properly show the legitimist continuation of Revolutionary principles;[149] and the quasi-religious character of the rendered project seems to fulfil Quatremère de Quincy's idea that 'a feeling of respect resembling the religious feeling of temples should inspire introspection

86 H. Labrouste. Cour de Cassation, 1824: rendered roof plan. (Beaux-Arts)

in approaching the sanctuary of justice'.[150] Through graphic and decorative changes, Labrouste's renderings gave an extraordinary sense of plastic reality to the belief in the interconnection between law and religion, both as institutions and as forms of building. Before the empty throne in the apse, one could almost hear the former Girondist and later Royalist Maximin Isnard declare: 'The law is my God and I know of no other gods.'[151]

The judgment: sketch versus rendering

A public exhibition of the final projects was always held on the three days prior to the judging. It was a well-publicized event and was usually reviewed in the daily press by such critics as Delécluze, who wrote for the *Journal des débats*. In 1824, the exhibition opened on 22 September, just six days after the death of Louis XVIII. The king's funeral took place on 23 September and may be one of the reasons why the exhibition does not appear to have been reviewed that year. Besides, it could in no way compete with the Salon of 1824, which was being held concurrently: with

Constable's *Hay Wain*, Delacroix's *Massacre at Chios* and Ingres' *Vow of Louis XIII*, that was the major artistic event of the season.

The exhibition was held in the main hall of the Ecole, and the projects were hung in the order in which the sketches were selected.[152] Although they were not otherwise identified for the general public, there was no pretence of anonymity when it came to the jury. On the morning of 25 September, when the judging was to take place, the gallery was closed to the public and, according to a decision of the Académie on the previous 10 July, 'above the work of each competitor was to be written his name, his age, whether he had previously won a Second Prix or an honourable mention, and the name of his teacher'.[153] This procedure, which was adopted by the Ecole the following year for all its competitions,[154] was maintained until 1846 but was observed only intermittently during the second half of the century.[155] Before 1824, the renderings were identified by a letter or number that ordinarily corresponded with the ranking of the student's sketch.

The judging took place in two stages. There was a preliminary session in the morning attended only by members of the architecture section and the officers of the Académie. Their 'preparatory judgment' was submitted to the entire Académie in the afternoon, at which time the final decision was made. The architects and officers met in the exhibition room on 25 September at 11:00 am. There were eight present. Although their names are not recorded, they probably included the five who judged the sketches – Percier, Thibault, Huyot, Vaudoyer and Quatremère – plus Delespine, Fontaine and the President of the Académie, Garnier. Their average age would have been $62\frac{3}{4}$. After the programme was read aloud, the first order of business was a comparison of the renderings with the sketches. The original sketches were brought out of safe-keeping (beginning in 1835 they were displayed alongside the renderings in the public exhibition), and two of the architects, in this case Thibault and Delespine, were appointed to report on the 'conformity' of the renderings to the sketches and their 'fidelity' to the programme.[156] They concluded that despite several 'slight changes' no project should be excluded.[157] It was almost unheard of for a project to be eliminated at this stage; although the jury

was probably fairly lenient, the students seem to have abided closely by the rules.

After 'discussing the strengths and weaknesses of each'[158] project, the vote was taken. As with the selection of sketches, it was by secret ballot and an absolute majority was needed to win. In 1824, Léon Vaudoyer defeated Henri Labrouste on the first ballot by a vote of five to three.[159] Another vote was then taken for the Second Grand Prix. Since Labrouste had previously won it (in 1821), he was ineligible. The section chose Lepreux's project also by a majority. A proposal was made to award an honourable mention, probably to Fries or Duc, but a majority voted against the idea. The vote in 1824 was quite typical. Although only two of the ten winners during the 1820s were chosen unanimously, the decision was often made on the first ballot and usually posed no problems.[160] There was only one deadlock, in 1825, when the section was unable to give any candidate an absolute majority, an unusual occurrence for that century.[161] The fact that both contenders for the top prize in 1824 had sketches ranked in the bottom half of the group was extraordinary, although, as we shall see, it was by no means unusual for the winner to redeem a passable sketch by a top-notch rendering.

Since the architects were nominally acting in an advisory capacity to the entire Académie, they always completed their deliberations in the morning with a statement of the reasons for their choices. These explanations generally amounted to no more than a sentence or two for each project. First there was a comment on the plan and then something about the character, style or decoration of the elevation. The plan was most often cited for the 'simplicity', 'unity', 'grandeur' or 'clarity' of its overall appearance along with the 'judiciousness', 'ingeniousness' or 'ease' with which it fulfilled the programme.[162] Sometimes the spatial development, or *marche* as it was called, was pointed out; and other times, though not often, an important requirement of the programme might be reflected in the comments, as in 1822 when the 'felicitous and easy exits' of Gilbert's project for an Opera House were praised for the 'rapid evacuation of the hall they would effect'.[163]

The qualities the Académie most often noted in the best elevations were similar: a 'simplicity', 'nobility', 'unity' or 'beauty' of appearance

73

combined with a 'judiciousness' and 'suitability' of character in style and decoration. These remarks were usually confined to the façade, although sometimes mention was made of the development of the decoration throughout the section. Beyond the particular appropriateness of the decoration to its subject, the Académie might praise the winning designs for 'correctness', 'good taste', 'fine proportions' and 'purity of style', based on well-chosen models, careful study and close attention to detail.[164]

In 1824, the architecture section singled out Vaudoyer's project for the 'felicitous disposition' and 'good distribution of the principal parts' of its plan in obvious reference to its broad, open layout. The 'noble and impressive elevation' was felt to be entirely 'appropriate to the character of the building as well as to its use'.[165] Lepreux's plan was particularly commended for the placement of its atrium. The jury felt that its generally 'good disposition' was remarkable 'above all [for] the way in which the *atrium* relates to the three courtrooms'. The 'severe character and suitability in terms of style' of Lepreux's façade were noted in a much less enthusiastic way than the qualities of Vaudoyer's façade.[166] Indeed, without taking such nuances into account, it is almost impossible to appreciate the full significance of the jury's conventional and elliptical phrases and, in particular, what they saw in the renderings that was not already manifest in the sketch. Forgetting the contradictory evidence of the order of the sketches, one might be left with the impression that the final decisions were equally based on composition alone.

The jury's comments in the 1820s do not often refer specifically to the degree of study or quality of execution evident in the renderings. This only became more common in the following decades and even then was usually treated as an added justification. In 1817, however, the section cited the young Blouet's design of a Conservatory of Music for the 'excellence in its details and study that gives promise'; and in 1826 Vaudoyer's design for an Académie de France in Rome was commended for an 'excellent study of dispositions and proportions learned from the great masters'.[167] Théodore Labrouste's renderings of a Museum of Natural History in 1827 were developed from a most cursory sketch that was just barely finished, as may be recalled. In choosing his project

for the Grand Prix, the section naturally acknowledged the extent to which the final drawings figured in their decision. They praised the 'beautiful style' of the façade for having been 'carefully studied both in relation to the general ordering of the whole and in its choice of forms and details', and concluded that the amount of work reflected in the project gave proof of 'a talent formed by the best studies'.[168] This was the highest possible praise the jury could offer, because the student who had shown himself to be 'educated in the sound principles of art' could, as they explained in 1819, be expected 'to profit greatly from his studies in Rome'.[169] For reasons that may well derive from the nature of the two-tiered system of judging, the section usually stopped short of such encomiums, thus leaving the final decision to the Académie as a whole.

The members of all five sections of the Académie des Beaux-Arts were supposed to meet in the exhibition room of the Ecole soon after the morning session was over. Of those forty-one, including the *secrétaire perpétuel*, Quatremère, only twenty showed up in 1824, which was about seven below average.[170] Of the fourteen painters, the five present were Garnier, Baron Gros (1771–1835), Guillon Le Thière (1760–1832), Charles Meynier (1768–1832) and Nicolas-Antoine Taunay (1755–1830); of the eight sculptors, the four present were François Bosio (1768–1845), Jean-Antoine Houdon (1741–1828), Claude Ramey (1754–1838) and Pierre Cartellier (1757–1831). The four engravers all came: Alexandre Tardieu 1756–1844), Boucher Desnoyers (1779–1857), André Galle (1761–1844) and Romain-Vincent Jeuffroy (1749–1826). None of the six musicians was there. Only five of the six architects who were at the morning session stayed through the entire afternoon. They were Delespine, Huyot, Percier, Thibault and Vaudoyer. The sixth. probably Fontaine, apparently remained for just a brief time. The average age of those present was just over $63\frac{1}{2}$. This was 3 years younger than those who were absent, among whom were Gérard, Girodet, Guérin, Carle Vernet, Vivant Denon and Cherubini.[171]

The meeting convened as usual at 1:00 pm. First Quatremère read the programme and then the minutes of the morning session. After hearing the architects' decisions and reasons, the Académie as a whole followed the same procedure as the section. They appointed two architects, this time Percier and Delespine, to 'confirm that the 8 projects are within the limits of the site and requirements of the programme [and] in conformity with their sketches'.[172] After an affirmative report, the vote by secret ballot was taken, with only eighteen jurors present at the beginning. The two projects that contested the prize in the morning came out on top again, but this time Léon Vaudoyer and Henri Labrouste each received nine votes.[173] Labrouste had picked up six to Vaudoyer's four. The vote was extremely close compared to the other three recorded in the 1820s, which were all decided on the first ballot. Usually three or four projects received votes, and the spread between first and second places was anywhere from eight to fifteen votes.[174] The second ballot again ended in a tie, nine votes for Vaudoyer and nine for Labrouste. On the third ballot, a deciding vote was cast in favour of Labrouste, giving him ten to Vaudoyer's nine. Apparently, after presenting the report with Delespine, Charles Percier left the room and did not return until the third ballot, at which time he 'quickly' cast the vote breaking the tie and reversing the section's earlier decision.[175]

Such a reversal was highly unusual. While the Académie as a whole awarded an additional third-place prize twice in the twenties and rescinded one on another occasion, it only rejected the section's first-place choice one other time between 1817 and 1836. In 1825 Duc was awarded the Grand Prix after having been the section's choice for the Second Grand Prix. Both disagreements occurred in the two years following the elder Vaudoyer's election to the Académie and may, therefore, indicate a realignment of forces in the Académie. (A similar situation probably explains the next major reversal which took place in 1854, the year after three new members of the architecture section were elected.)[176] The curious outcome of the vote for the Second Grand Prix in 1824 may also be explained in this way. On the first ballot, Lepreux received nine votes, Léon Vaudoyer seven, Duc three and Fries one. Two more ballots proved necessary. In the first run-off between the two top candidates, Lepreux and Vaudoyer each received nine votes. In the final run-off, Vaudoyer defeated Lepreux eleven votes to eight. Without any explanation, however, the Académie awarded the Second Grand Prix to Lepreux

and, following another vote of which no record survives, a Deuxième Second Grand Prix was awarded to Vaudoyer.

It may be that the decision to give Lepreux the higher prize was prompted by his age (he was one month short of twenty-nine while Vaudoyer had just turned twenty-one), but politics were also undoubtedly involved. The two-tiered system of judging left the door wide open for pressure to be exerted by the architects on their colleagues in other fields: 'One can imagine the confusion and uncertainty that must be felt by ... the painters, sculptors, engravers and musicians at the sight of a plan',[177] wrote Baltard in 1822, in his call for reform. He decried the fact that, 'when they have to form an opinion on the suitability of a project, on the necessary relations of the parts in a plan' or 'on the connection that should exist between plans, sections and elevations', the non-architects 'must rely' on the opinions of the architects who, 'in groups of two or three', then use their influence to promote their favourites.[178]

The more positive value of the two-tiered system of judging is perhaps only clearly brought to light by the unusual manifestation of the Académie's power as a whole in 1824. The Académie existed to maintain certain artistic standards that transcended any one art form or another. The design chosen for the Grand Prix was expected to demonstrate a full understanding of the principles of classical art, and therefore its quality was to be appreciated by anyone having the proper education and taste. If the vote of the section gave the stamp of approval of the specialist in matters of planning and appropriateness, then the decision of the Académie as a whole tacitly acknowledged the ultimate significance of those qualities of visual form and meaning that painters, sculptors, engravers and even musicians were just as capable of discerning, if not, in many cases, more so.

Although the Académie did not articulate it, the students at the Ecole were completely aware of the importance of diligent study, careful and thoughtful detailing and exquisite execution and finish in the renderings. A perfect illustration of this is the review that Henri Labrouste later wrote of the competition for the Grand Prix in 1840, which appeared in the first volume of César Daly's *Revue générale de l'architecture*. Labrouste based his own judgments almost entirely on the quality of the renderings. He noted first of all that second-place finalist Alexis Paccard's design for a Chambre des Pairs (House of Lords) was 'quite skilfully studied'.[179] In particular, his 'façade was remarkable for a monumental character that evinced quite serious studies', but the drawings were not completely finished, due to an illness, and so there was no way he could be considered for the prize. Labrouste thought that third-place finalist Antoine-Julien Hénard's 'plan was concise' and 'perhaps the best disposed', and if it were not for his 'weak façade' he might have won. However, it was fourth-place finalist Théodore Ballu's project that 'arrested everyone's attention', according to Labrouste. He explained that it 'was drawn and rendered with talent' and that Ballu 'seemed to be the one who worked the hardest'. He assumed Ballu would win the Grand Prix, and he did. The 'perfectly drawn' project Labrouste thought would win the Second Grand Prix was that of seventh-place finalist Auguste Titeux, and it did, even though 'the author seemed to have used the occasion to show off his talent as a draughtsman rather than the serious study of proportions and architectural forms'. Labrouste did not say a word about any other plan but Hénard's, and that was only to emphasize why he lost.

In 1840, as in 1824, the Grand Prix was not won by the student with the first-place sketch. In 1841 it was won by the second-place finalist and in the following year by the student whose sketch had come in fifth. This situation occurred often enough for César Daly to remark in his review of the competition of 1845, the first following the decision not to rank the sketches, that 'in effect, it is not always the best sketches that turn into the best *renderings*'.[180] He added that 'one must conclude that the visual effect of the drawing exercises an immense power over the judges of the competition'.[181] The statistics available for the twenty-eight years from 1817 to 1845 bolster the points made by Daly and Labrouste. Twenty-nine Grands Prix were awarded during that period. (There was none in 1818 but two each in 1819 and 1836.) Of those, fifteen were won by the student with the first-place sketch, which means that he had only a little better than a fifty per cent chance of winning. The second-place finalist won it seven times, while those lower down the list came out on top seven times.

More than half the winners of the Grand Prix began by winning a Second Grand Prix; but the winners of the Second Grand Prix show an even greater percentage of lower-place sketches. The first-place finalist won the Second Grand Prix only four times between 1817 and 1844, but it was won seven times by the third-place finalist, six times by the fifth-place finalist and five times by the one whose sketch had placed seventh. The Second Grand Prix might be given to an older student like Lepreux as the final recognition of many years of study, but more often it went to a younger student as a form of incentive. In order to see what separated a promising second-place project from a fully developed winning one, there is no better example to show the relation between composition, study, execution and experience than the competition of 1821, when Henri Labrouste came in second to Blouet.

It should be recalled that 1821 was Henri Labrouste's first try for the Grand Prix. His sketch was placed third, behind Blouet's and Gilbert's. He had been at the Ecole less than two years and had just turned 20 a week before. Blouet, who won the Grand Prix that year, was $25\frac{1}{2}$ years old and had been at the Ecole over six and a half years. It was his sixth try for the prize. He was a finalist the previous four times and won the Second Grand Prix in 1817 at the age of 21, with a second-place sketch his first time as a finalist. Although Labrouste eventually won the Grand Prix in less time than Blouet, their school careers were remarkably similar. The Académie recognized their talent early and allowed it to develop before sending them off to Rome.

The programme of a Palais de Justice, which had been proposed in 1820 and was a runner-up in 1819, called for four courtrooms and a chapel to be grouped around a central waiting hall.[182] The building was to be set between a large public square in front and a smaller one behind containing a prison connected by a gallery or bridge. The overall arrangement only had to be shown in the site plan, which Blouet did for the sketch, whereas Labrouste drew just the plan of the building.

Blouet's and Labrouste's projects are both based on the same *parti*, already established as a type in Thibault's earlier design. The courtrooms are set in pairs off a three-bay waiting hall occupying the central axis, which terminates in a chapel. The abstract clarity and geometric

83
81, 82

87

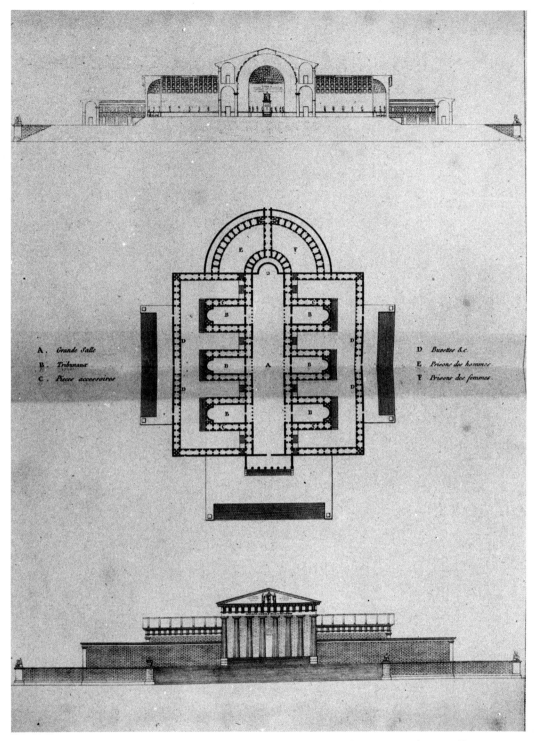

A . Grande Salle
B . Tribunaux
C . Pièces accessoires

D . Buvettes &c.
E . Prisons des hommes
F . Prisons des femmes

87 J.-T. Thibault. Palais de Justice, *c.*1795: section, plan and elevation. (From Durand, *Precis*, II, 1805)

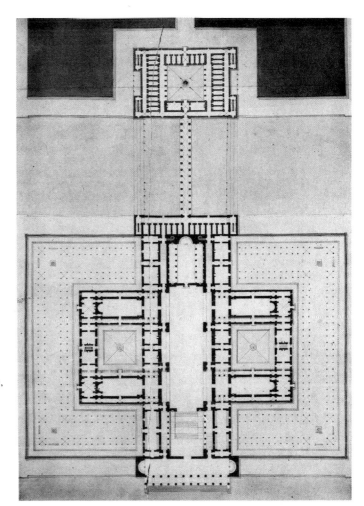

88 H. Labrouste. Palais de Justice,
1821: rendered site plan, central
section. (Beaux-Arts)

rigour of Labrouse's plan are extraordinary for
his age. The bold structural articulation of the
waiting hall defines the main volume within a
frame of circulation that is continuous from
the front of the building to the rear. The
elements in Blouet's plan are more particularized
and are interwoven in a more complex way,
making Labrouse's plan look simplistic by
comparison. The loose, sketchy quality of
Blouet's elevation and section is also livelier
and much more assured. Despite the scale and
integrity of Labrouse's section, the hesitant
quality of his elevation reveals a fundamental
weakness. While the differences between
Blouet's and Labrouse's projects at the sketch
stage are apparent, they are relatively insignificant in view of the similarity in composition.
Blouet's great advantage in experience and skill
would only be clearly demonstrated in the
renderings.

Neither Blouet nor Labrouse made nearly as
many changes in plan as Labrouse did in
1824. Labrouse, who made more, reduced his 88
portico by four columns; squared up the two
enclosed courtyards; and placed an arch at the
top of the stairs to delimit the central hall.
Blouet appears to have concentrated on thinking
about the relationship of the building to its
site and how to render that in as striking a
manner as possible. Since Labrouse had not
even included the prison in his sketch, he had
to develop the *entourage* from scratch. He
centred the rectangular block of the Courthouse
on the sheet between a large forecourt, based
on the Forum of Trajan, and a skimpy square
containing the prison. The exedrae bounding
the open space in front contrast in shape and
scale with the building without tying it into
the site.

While the arrangement of Labrouse's site

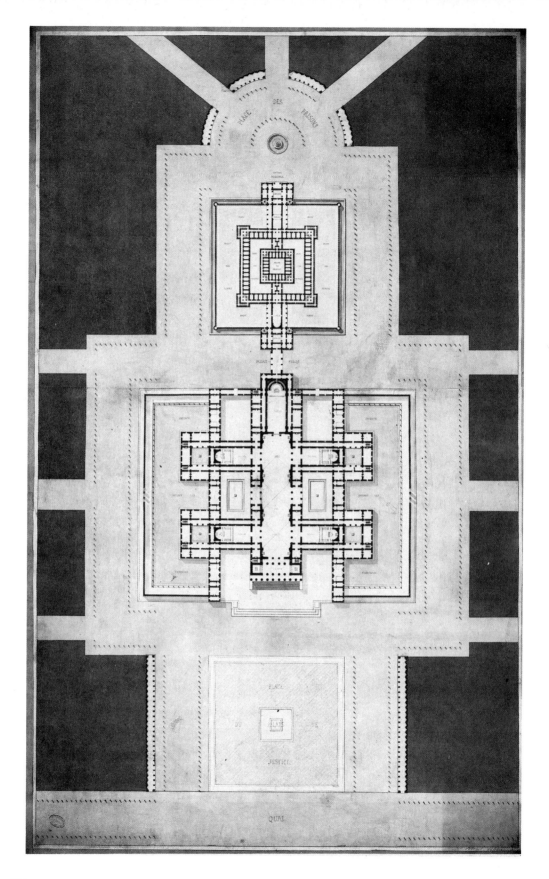

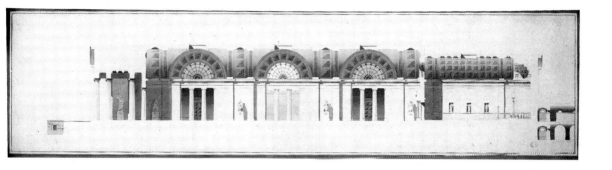

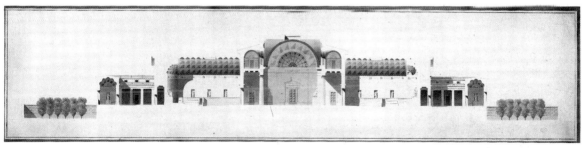

89–92　A. Blouet. Palais de Justice, 1821: rendered site plan, elevation, longitudinal section, and cross-section. (Beaux-Arts)

plan tends to diminish the impact of his building, making it appear cramped and static, Blouet's design causes his to expand and breathe with a presence that is distinctly anthropomorphic. The Courthouse itself is placed slightly below centre as an integral part of a generous sequence of public spaces flowing around the building and prison and out into a network of streets that extend the building's axes beyond the edges of the sheet. The main building appears to buckle the lateral belt of streets around what is best described as the waist of the plan. The Courthouse thus becomes the torso, while the streets radiating from the hemicycle above form a crown on the head of the prison.[183]

Part of the reason for the greater clarity and coherence of Blouet's design is simply his superior technical skill. His rendering is done with a much greater variety of wash tones, a more precise gradation of values and a more consistent use of cast shadow. The main elements of his Courthouse are outlined in a rich black against the lighter grey of the auxiliary rooms. This is set off by the slightly paler green of the walled gardens and the still paler grey of the ground. The various layers of depth give the appearance of a map in relief, and the prominent surfaces glint and dance in the light, accentuating the rhythmic movement of the plan itself.

89

Blouet's renderings of the elevations and sections are suffused with atmosphere and light and seem to grow directly out of the ground. The portico is a majestic frontispiece. It is richly modelled, with a finesse in the lettering and sculpture, and is brilliantly highlighted against the façade. The decorative scheme of the interiors is elaborate and coherent, judiciously balancing the secular and religious in both iconography and style. Like the elevation, the sections are drawn with a nervous line that gives precision and elegance to the design. Labrouste's elevation and sections look crude and naïve by comparison. While his longitudinal section has a severity from a distance, it disintegrates on closer inspection. In all his renderings, the drawing is limp and the modelling unsure, the forms wooden and inexpressive. The general level of quality is also inconsistent, and the more delicate transverse section appears almost to have been drawn by another hand. But the façade, more

than anything else, betrays Labrouste's inexperience. He had hesitated in the sketch and never resolved the problem of character. It looks more like a stock exchange or a market hall than a sanctuary of justice. The proportions and detailing of the gabled roof are simply awful and show none of the refinement and adjustment that was supposed to result from studying the problem.

The reasons the architecture section gave for awarding the Grand Prix to Blouet and a Second Grand Prix to Labrouste are unusually revealing. Blouet's project was singled out for its consistency and appropriateness. The jury felt it 'answered the demands of the programme with the most suitable character', that its 'plan has the greatest unity, and that the elevation and section partake of the same unity of style and character'.[186] The jury explained its selection of Labrouste's project on the basis of composition alone. It had, they reasoned, 'a plan of a beautiful simplicity [and] grand

93–96 H. Labrouste. Palais de Justice, 1821: rendered elevation, cross-section, detail of longitudinal section, and detail of elevation. (Beaux-Arts)

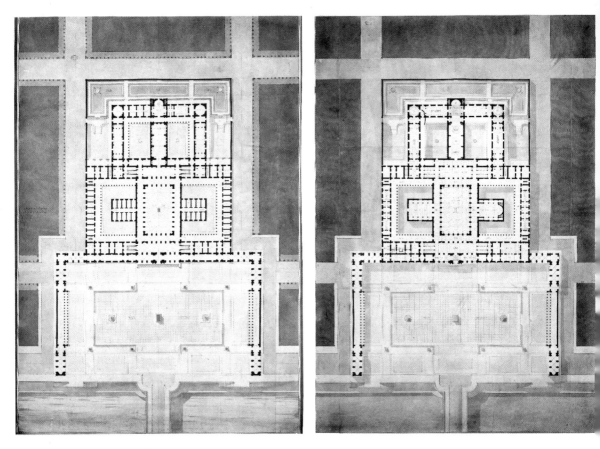

97–99   L. Duc. Hôtel de Ville pour Paris, 1825: rendered ground-floor and upper-floor plans, and rendered elevation and section. (Beaux-Arts)

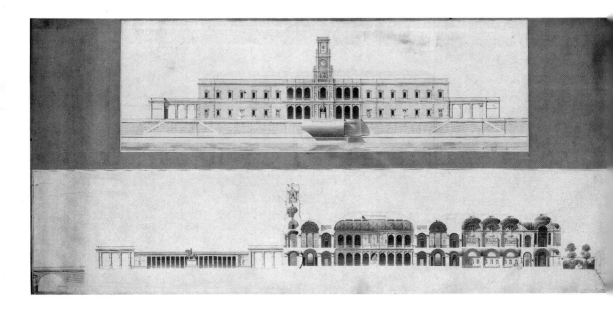

and ingenious disposition'.[185] They said nothing about style or character and did not even refer to the elevation. They added, however, that the plan 'showed promise of a talent who henceforth will know better how to bring together all the parts of architecture'.[186]

A project could win the Second Grand Prix for an outstanding quality such as composition; but the Grand Prix demanded a unified conception and treatment showing a mastery of 'all the parts of architecture', as the Académie put it. The renderings provided the evidence the sketch could not. The expression of character could only be mooted in the sketch. Proportions and decoration only began to be considered seriously in studying the project; and the individual's power of expression was inevitably judged in the execution and finish of the renderings themselves. Without the final projects of Vaudoyer and Lepreux, however, it is impossible to demonstrate conclusively that Labrouste won the Grand Prix in 1824 on the basis of his renderings. There was undoubtedly less difference in quality between his drawings and Vaudoyer's than between his and Blouet's three years before. Indeed, that is reflected in the closeness of the vote. (In 1821 Labrouste was not even considered in the balloting for the top prize.)[187] But Labrouste himself explained to Dommey his recovery from an eighth-place sketch by the work he put into his project in the four months before it was finally due; and the drawings themselves show all the characteristic signs that distinguish the other Grand Prix winners in the 1820s from those that finished second or third, providing visible proof that the student had mastered 'all the parts of architecture'.

Based on a comparison of the renderings submitted in 1821, 1822, 1823, 1825 and 1826, where in each case at least two or three projects have been preserved, it can be said that the overall plan of the winning project always presented the strongest visual image in terms of graphic design.[188] Blouet's plan of 1821 is characteristic in the way it fills and holds the page in an evenly valued pattern of lights and darks. The critic Delécluze described the desired effect as 'tapestry-like',[189] and, later in the century, the term 'mosaic' was extended from the plan of the building to include the entire sheet. The precisely balanced transitions in value gave the pattern the requisite effect of brilliance, which a student at the Ecole in the 1820s called 'illumination'.[190] If Blouet's plan of 1821 seems to radiate light, then Gilbert's plan of an Opera House in 1822 glows like a gilded crown. Neither Bouchet, nor Fontaine, nor Vaudoyer had anything near that quality in their designs of 1822. In 1825, Duc resorted to a form of trickery in order to create a stronger visual impression than his fellow competitors. He included the one-storey, extended forecourt wings and *entourage* of his City Hall on the upper-floor plan as well as that of the ground level! This allowed him both to increase the size of the drawing and to enliven the surface by a finer gradation of lights and shadows.[191]

The plan of Labrouste's Cour de Cassation is more hermetic, and its vibrancy and brilliance derive from the animation of line and surface. By contrast with the volumetric expansion of Blouet's design, the linear network outlining the hieratic figure in Labrouste's plan produces a mesmerizing pattern. Beginning at the portico, the outer walls of the entrance hall go up and around the two lower courtyards, turning first into the inner walls of the entrance hall, and then continuing around the courtyards again and across the entrance itself. The pattern branches out into the atrium and around the courtrooms, creating a maze that still rivets one's attention as it must have the jury's in 1824.

The graphic power of the plan made manifest the overall unity of the design, but the qualities of refined proportions, decorative imagination, thematic coherence and elegant finish were best seen in the elevation and sections. If it can be assumed that at least three-quarters of the time spent on the sketch was devoted to the plan, it is even more reasonable to assume that the major portion of the effort in the renderings went into exterior and interior design. The façade had to express the character of the subject, and all the projects that won did that by concentrating everything on one appropriate motif. In Duc's City Hall it was the loggia and tower denoting civic pride; in Gilbert's Opera House, it was the splendour of a Roman amphitheatre; in Duban's Custom House of 1823, it was the grand yet utilitarian-looking triumphal arch of the entrance, with a gable supported by a corbel table as in Labrouste's Courthouse of 1821, highlighted against the brick arcades on each side; and in Vaudoyer's Academie de France à Rome of 1826, it was the central block of an Italian villa

74

97, 98

60

84, 85

98

73

100

96

101, 102

100   F. Duban. Custom House and Toll House, 1823 : rendered elevation facing the city. (Beaux-Arts)

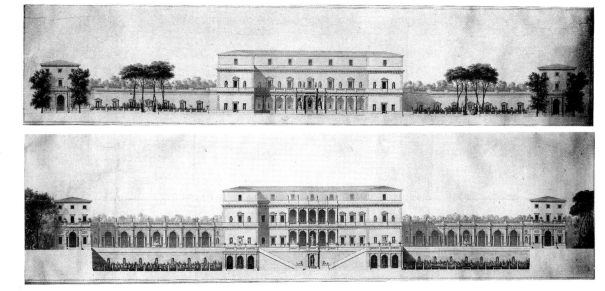

101, 102   L. Vaudoyer. Académie de France à Rome, 1826: rendered elevations of entrance side and garden side. (Beaux-Arts)

102 amid cascading terraces and gardens; more often, it was a temple front. In 1824, Labrouste proportioned his Doric order in such a way as to satisfy the combined demands for 'severity' and 'nobility'. He learned a lesson from Blouet by raising the portico on a high stylobate to increase its majesty. It is modelled with stunning clarity and relief and decorated with imagination and resourcefulness.

The interior decoration had to develop the design with consistency and drama. The stark and restrained decoration of Labrouste's Cour 85 de Cassation is as expressive of the subject of law as Duc's richly elegant and urbane decoration for a City Hall for Paris is of that 99 city's municipal pride. In Duc's City Hall, 102 as in Vaudoyer's Académie de France, the

iconographical theme is carried through every detail with more consistency and imagination than the projects that came in second and third. Whereas Dommey and Delannoy, in their designs for an Académie de France, simply included lots of decorative painting and sculpture, Vaudoyer organized his on the theme of the Académie's origin and placed at the entrance 101 a copy of Girardon's equestrian statue of Louis XIV. Labrouste, as we saw, concentrated on the singular importance of written law in modern France. The interior decoration is almost entirely restricted to a few carefully chosen phrases from the Constitutional Charter of 1814, which form a preamble, so to speak, to the drama of the Napoleonic Codes in the apse. The iconography thus unfolds in a clear and precise sequence of spaces that allows the meaning of modern French law to emerge as a stunning form of spiritual revelation.

In academic theory composition was considered a faculty similar to imagination or intelligence. 'Composition cannot be taught', wrote Julien Guadet in the four-volume compendium of his course in theory at the Ecole des Beaux-Arts.[192] He described composition as 'utterly personal, and owing a great deal to luck: he who hits upon a very fortunate composition for a given programme one day might not hit upon anything the day before or the day after'.[193] 'And, as for the *parti*, the lucky find', that, Guadet concluded, 'is a mysterious working of the intelligence'. It is a matter of 'inspiration' and therefore 'cannot be fruitful unless it is served by knowledge'.[194] What the student could learn was the vocabulary, the method, and the taste needed to study and refine the composition and execute it with care. If the sketch was an indication of innate ability, then the execution of the renderings took on a specifically moral value because they showed learning and work.

There is nothing new in defining execution and finish as qualities academic artists recognized as pre-eminent. In his review of the Grand Prix competition of 1845, Daly quoted Diderot writing about the Salon of 1767: 'A good sketch can be the work of a young man full of life and inspiration. . . . A beautiful painting is never anything but the work of a master who has reflected, meditated and worked a great deal.'[195] While the distinction between the sketch and rendering was characteristic of academic thought in general, it had a particular relevance for the study of architecture and, indeed, had its longest-lasting effect in that field. 'Those who wish to pursue the career of architecture', wrote Quatremère in 1825, can be judged mainly on 'the manner in which they render those sorts of projects' given in school competitions.[196] The student's renderings 'reveal the degree of intelligence and imagination he will later bring to the buildings that will be entrusted to him', for they are 'an indication of experience and of the care that the artist has given to all the parts of his work'.[197]

The sustained effort of studying a project was the true test of professional promise and reliability, and the renderings provided con-clusive proof of the individual's power of expression. 'Everybody can come up with projects, for better or for worse', wrote Boutard in 1826, 'but only the skilful architect can produce a well-studied project' that 'reveals his learning and adequacy' for the job.[198] The renderings required for the Grand Prix were at a large enough scale so that one could judge, in the minutest detail, how fully and convincingly the organizing idea and character of the project were expressed. They were similar in style and purpose to contemporary presentation drawings and contract drawings.[199] Indeed, the twenty-four-hour sketch designs were drawn in the same manner and at the same scale as the normal *avant-projet*, or preliminary plan, that architects presented for government approval before developing the final presentation drawings.

Whereas the sketch came more and more to dominate painting and sculpture as the ultimate expression of the artist's thought, almost the opposite was true of architecture.[200] This had to do with the increasing specialization of the building trades in the 19th century and the final severing of the connection between the professional architect and the craftsman. 'Formerly the architect's drawing was but the sketch of his building', wrote Quatremère in 1798, and 'that was so because the architect was the executor of his sketch.'[201] However, he continued, 'from the moment art became divided in actual fact and practice into invention and execution, from the moment there are men who invent or compose without knowing how to build, and others who build for them without knowing how to invent, it clearly becomes necessary to render drawings more fully, to make them more fastidious and more finished'.[202]

The triple division of labour required in the competition for the Grand Prix was modelled directly on the division of labour in actual practice. 'The architect conceives, then studies, then constructs', wrote Guadet.[203] First he composes or sketches out a general solution; then he refines and reworks it in detail; but, since he is no longer the 'master builder', most of his professional time is given over to preparing the precise working drawings that allow his plans to be built by others.[204] Guadet defined the education offered at the Ecole as a theoretical preparation for practice. One did not learn how to build; rather, one learned

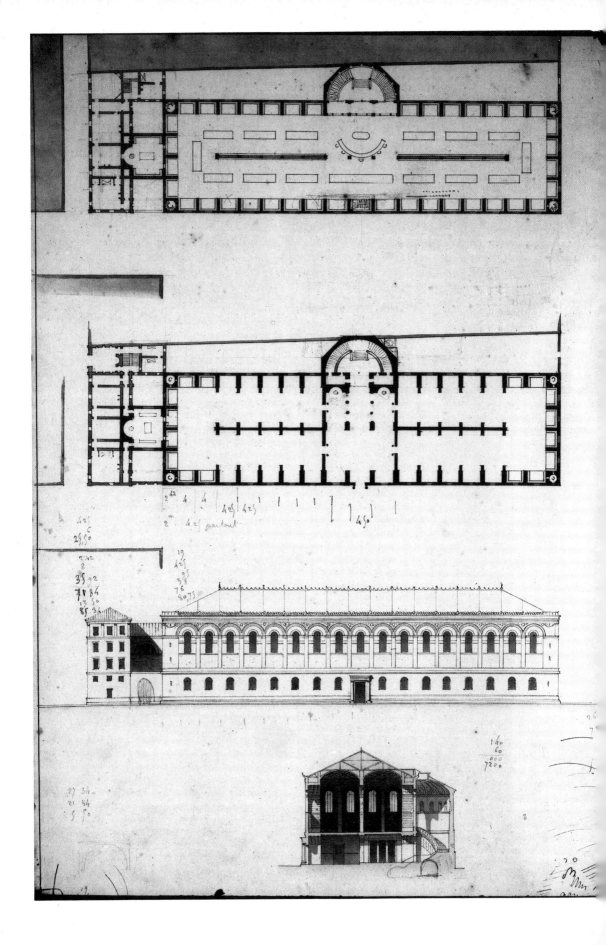

2⁴² 4 4 |4²⁵|4²⁵¹ | | | | |7 |4⁵⁰| |
m. 2. 4.25 partout

4.25
6
29,50

2.42
8
35.92
71.84
13.56
85.34

19
4.25
9.5
3.8
7.6
30.75

140
60
000
7200

96
7

27 3/4
21 84
5 50

to design in relation to what is 'buildable'.[205] The rendered project thus stood in relation to the working drawing as Guadet's notion of 'buildability' does to building.

The Ecole des Beaux-Arts was the most important school of architecture in the 19th century because it provided a professional education related to contemporary practice. It replaced the training of apprentices in the craft traditions with an approach geared almost entirely to design. The first duty of the architect, Guadet told his students, was to the client and the programme, not to the materials or methods of construction.[206] The Ecole taught the student how to interpret a programme, for his purpose was to serve the client's needs. The competition for the Grand Prix was a scenario for a successful career. The members of the Académie who wrote the programme were like an institutional client. The young architect first presented his schematic design for approval. Once that was accepted, he devoted the major part of his energies to careful design development using conventional, standardized details.[207] It is no wonder that the Ecole system became the model not only for the first schools of architecture in the United States but also for the standard office practice of the earliest large firms, such as those of H. H. Richardson, D. H. Burnham and Company and McKim, Mead and White.[208]

But above all else, the Ecole des Beaux-Arts was the training ground for France's architectural civil service, and the winners of the Grand Prix were primed to fill the top bureaucratic positions. Throughout most of the century, they averaged between $25\frac{1}{2}$ and 27 years of age.[209] After five years of further study in Italy, under the guidance of the Académie, they returned to Paris to begin careers in government service. Most of the professors at the Ecole and most of the teachers of important *ateliers* were drawn from their ranks. Most important buildings in Paris or the provinces were entrusted to this elite corps of designers, as, for example, were the Paris Opéra, the Central Markets (les Halles), the Bibliothèque Nationale, the Palais de Justice, La Trinité, the Petit Palais, the Sorbonne, as well as the Galerie des Machines. The Grand Prix programmes were preparation for the design of such large commissions, if not always for their structural solution. The designs produced in the Grand Prix competition were neither visionary nor unrealistic. They grew out of contemporary architecture and became models for later buildings, especially in provincial cities and foreign countries.

The competition for the Grand Prix presents the Ecole's elitism and concern for pure design in the most glaring light. These were the two points on which the Ecole was most often criticized by proponents of more liberal methods of education and by those who either wanted to return to the medieval craft traditions or to create an architecture more in tune with modern technology. The Ecole and the Grand Prix were subjects for criticism because they worked so well. They provided a solution to the problem of education in an age in transition between the death of craft techniques and the birth of modern technology and in the process made 'Beaux-Arts' architecture an international style and Paris a model city until well into the 20th century.

103

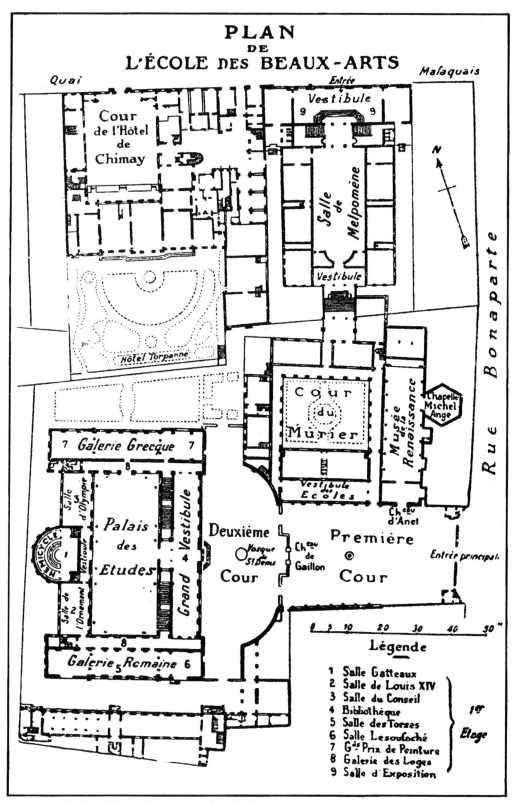

104   General plan of the Ecole des Beaux-Arts, Paris.

VII

The building of the Ecole des Beaux-Arts
C. Marmoz

THE BUILDINGS OF THE Ecole des Beaux-Arts were classified as Historical Monuments on 31 January 1972, yet they are still little appreciated in France, though Richard Chafee and David Van Zanten have written relatively recently about them.[1]

The Ecole was not built all at once. Situated on the site of the Couvent des Petits Augustins,[2] which became in time the Musée des Monuments Français,[3] it was built up around a core of older buildings.

On 6 April 1807, it was decreed that students of fine arts and architecture, who had long been established in *ateliers* in the Louvre, should be installed instead in Le Vau's Palais des Quatre Nations, opposite. A.-L.-T. Vaudoyer was appointed to liaise with the professors and to prepare a design for a Palais des Beaux-Arts. Several projects were presented,[4] but the location was settled by royal decree only on 18 December 1816 (following decrees of 15 September 1815 and 25 April 1816):

Louis, by the grace of God, King of France and Navarre, to all those who read this, greetings.
In accordance with the report of our minister, Secretary of State in the Department of the Interior, we have commanded and command all that follows:
1 The building of the Dépôt des Monuments left empty as a result of our injunction of 24 April last, is and remains at the disposal of the Ecole Royale et Spéciale des Beaux-Arts de Paris.
2 To this effect an overall plan will be drawn up which will be implemented in accordance with resources and needs.
3 Monsieur Lenoir, at present in charge of the monuments and Dépôt at the Petits Augustins will take up the same post at the royal church of St-Denis from

1 January 1817 and will continue to receive a salary of five thousand francs deductable from the funds available for the upkeep of the building.
4 Our minister, Secretary of State to the Interior, is charged with the execution of the present decree. Given in our château of the Tuileries, 18 December, the year of grace 1816, the twenty-second of our reign.
Signed Louis.[5]

Soon after this, Léonor Mérimée set up a committee to supervise the transfer of the Ecole to its new site.[6] Alexandre Lenoir's Musée des Monuments Français had been installed after the Revolution in the Couvent des Petits Augustins founded by Queen Margot, Henri IV's first wife, the decaying conventual buildings being adapted as a museum without any noteworthy structural alteration. Antoine Vaudoyer, who in 1804 had installed *ateliers* at the Palais des Quatre Nations, and who, from 1810 onwards, had been architect to the Musée des Monuments Français, was commissioned to dismantle the museum.[7] He saw to it that most of the exhibits were restored to their original sites,[8] though many remained where they were,[9] and he repaired the walls.[10] In 1819 new work was soon to transform the Petits Augustins radically, so that little of the original today remains. In September of that year, François Debret took over, 'charged, under the direction of the members of the Ecole des Beaux-Arts, with the preparation of plans, drawings and all works necessary for the transfer of this establishment to the Petits Augustins.'[11] This appointment was made under vigorous protest from Vaudoyer, who considered himself the logical choice.[12] But already, by 5 October 1819, Debret's plan for

105

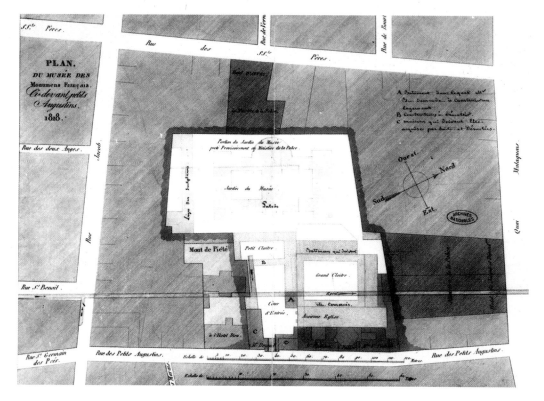

105   Site plan in 1818 of the former Musée des Monuments Français in the Petits Augustins, prior to the construction of the Ecole des Beaux-Arts. The convent buildings, at the bottom right, were to be preserved; other buildings (B, C) were to be demolished. The projected Loges appear at the top left, and the Palais des Etudes is shown in outline in the centre of the garden. The large shaded area at the far right would later be acquired. (Archives Nationales)

the Loges had been approved.[13] On 16 October 1819, Debret presented his design for the Palais des Etudes.[14]

Under a law prohibiting the accumulation of official commissions Debret was eventually compelled to relinquish work at the Ecole des Beaux-Arts, in order to concentrate on the restoration of the abbey church of St-Denis, which he had begun earlier. In January 1832, just before giving up the Ecole, which was taken over by his brother-in-law, Félix Duban, he reported on the works there:

On 3 May, 1820, the foundation stone of the Ecole des Beaux-Arts was laid in the gardens of the Petits Augustins; the works, estimated to cost 1,500,000 francs, were sustained by no more than 60,000 to 80,000 francs a year, sums which had also to cover the cost of the temporary installation of studios in the dilapidated buildings of the convent and the old church. To give some indication of the state of these buildings we would recall that, founded in 1685 by Queen Marguerite de Valois, first wife of Henri IV, they survived at all only because of the props put there when the Dépôt des Monuments was formed and which today still support most of the floors and even the main fabric. The foundations of the whole of the new building, in the form of a rectangle, are now laid, and the left wing is complete. The fine collection of architectural fragments left by M. Sue is already installed on the ground floor.

In the first floor rooms the results of the competitions instigated by the government for paintings for the Chambre des Députés and sculpture for the Colonne Vendôme have been displayed.

The right-hand wing and the building range at the rear have reached first-floor level.

The building, built without luxury, though in a monumental manner, will suffer greatly and will soon be in the same state as the Palais d'Orsay if annual funds are not to be allocated to it. Two to three million francs should be spent annually, until completion, not counting the work of maintenance and installation in the old buildings and also the building already complete and in use, called the Bâtiment des Loges.[15]

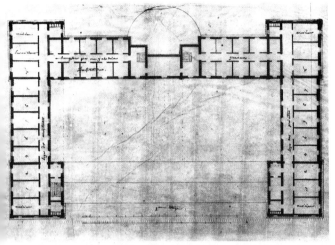

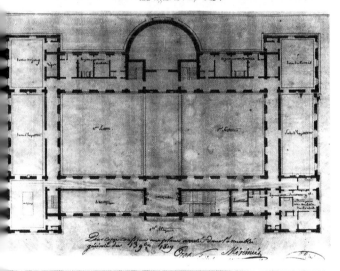

106–110   F. Debret. Approved
design for the Palais des Études,
13 November 1819: elevation, cross-
section, and plans of the second, first,
and ground floors. (Archives
Nationales)

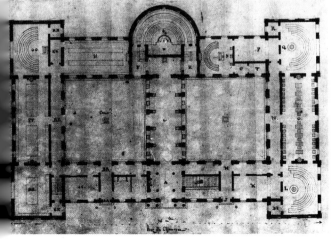

127

The existence of Debret's Loges, and of his Palais des Etudes complete on the south and up to first-floor level in the west and north wings, must have constituted such a limitation on Duban's freedom that one may seriously question the extent to which he should be considered the architect of the Ecole des Beaux-Arts.

Duban had been *sous-inspecteur* (under-inspector) of the works from the beginning.[16] In October 1819, Debret had put him forward as *directeur* of the works but his nomination was rejected by Decazes.[17] In 1823 Duban won the Grand Prix and went to Rome. Fresnel held the post of *inspecteur* during his absence, but soon after his return, in May 1829,[18] he took over from Fresnel, though the latter continued to accept the major responsibilities of that role.[19] Then, on 31 July 1832, Duban was named as architect by Count d'Argout.[20] He had officially replaced Debret.

Duban was to be assisted by Henri Labrouste, as *inspecteur*. H. Lebas and Deligny were to act respectively as site architect and *inspecteur* for maintenance work. Duban's first concern was to ensure that the work continued without interruption, and the contractors employed by Debret were retained.[21] He also took up Debret's proposal to use the funds available for 1832, which were inadequate to complete the north wing, to build the west wing,[22] but he held back work on the section that adjoined the completed south wing. To ensure that there would be no rising damp, he proposed a series of cellars under the buildings.[23] The creation of such a basement under one of the galleries had already been considered and approved by Mérimée, Caristie and the professors of the Ecole. However, on 25 January 1833, the Conseil des Bâtiments Civils suggested other changes, neither accepting nor rejecting the cellar project.[24]

Shortly after this, Duban presented a plan for a much more radical remodelling of the Ecole, superseding the designs of Debret. He had asked earlier for a programme of the actual requirements of the Ecole, and on 22 January 1833, Mérimée had sent him a 'list of the areas essential for the different departments of the Ecole'.[25] There were to be classrooms and studios for everyday teaching, exhibition areas for the Concours d'Emulation and the Grand Prix, and storage space for works sent from Rome. Mérimée also stipulated areas for 'the Musée des Etudes, the library, the exhibition

rooms, an assembly hall'.[26] On 5 April 1833, Duban submitted his proposal – five drawings and two written reports – *Rapport à M. le Ministre du commerce et des travaux publics sur les bâtiments de l'Ecole Royale des Beaux-Arts*.[27] and *Enoncé descriptif des distributions nouvelles pour le bâtiment principal de l'Ecole*.[28] The drawings have not yet come to light, but his intentions are clear from the surviving texts. He had acted swiftly, formulating his new design in no more than four months after Mérimée delivered his programme. After dismissing Debret's design with vitriolic comments,[29] Duban proceeded to present his own project tactfully and ably. Changes, he declared, are necessary,[30] not merely to provide facilities left out in Debret's building, which had in any case already been altered, but also to enhance the stature of the Ecole. He proposed that the different activities of the school should be separated, as had been demanded since 1817 by the director and professors. The Loges, as before, should be used for competition work while the main building or 'Palais des Beaux-Arts' should serve for exhibitions, an amphitheatre and official functions. For the library he proposed to add an attic storey.

According to Duban's scheme, teaching would take place in the new building rather than the cloister of the Petits Augustins. Those parts of the Palais already built were to be retained, except for the foundations of a gallery connecting the main block, on the east, to the amphitheatre on the west, cutting the courtyard in two (this gallery he had introduced in his plan for the cellars of 1832). The ground floor was to be used for the exhibition of sculpture and the works of the *pensionnaires*. Debret's monumental stair would be replaced by two flights of stairs giving direct access to the painting section and to the architectural section. As far as the decoration was concerned he proposed Corinthian and Ionic orders for the façade, with a richer treatment for the amphitheatre.[31]

At its meetings of 18 and 25 June 1833, at which Cortot, Ingres, Mérimée and Vinit were present, the Conseil des Bâtiments Civils asked for certain decorative details to be modified and strongly opposed the construction of the attic storey. It demanded, in addition, that the Arc de Gaillon be moved to face the façade of the chapel, as Debret had planned.

Privately, the *directeur* of the Conseil assured

Duban that the attic would be built. On a letter from Duban of 3 November 1833 he noted in the margin: 'I replied that he should indicate only the building already fixed and agreed; later, permission might be given'.[32] This assurance was, no doubt, verbal. Duban prepared a design without an attic storey, recently published by David Van Zanten.[33] But on 25 September 1834, when the Minister visited the site, permission was given for the construction of the attic. This was no more than eighteen months after Duban's first project had been set aside. That initial design, it seems, was, after all, the basis of all that was to be built – a supposition reinforced by a document in the Archives Nationales signed Morey and dated 1842, which shows the 'part built between 1820 and 1833' and two views of the courtyard.[34]

Duban was in all things obstinate and self-willed. In these drawings the part left by Debret in 1832 is included, but the attic appears as we know it today. It is thus not unreasonable to assume that the drawings represent Duban's initial project, set aside for diplomatic reasons but later taken up and built – a hypothesis confirmed, partly, by the fact that the screens flanking the Arc de Gaillon, and the façade of the chapel, which by 1842 must have been more or less as we know them, are not shown in their final form.

Though Duban might, for a time, have appeared to have agreed to the elimination of the attic storey, he was violently opposed to the recommendation of the Conseil des Bâtiments Civils that the Arc de Gaillon should be placed facing the chapel as proposed by Debret. He read a letter and addressed a report to the Conseil to this effect in June 1833. The arch, he stressed, was set on the axis of the Palais, its removal would be disastrous; it was his intention to keep both the Arc de Gaillon and Portique d'Anet[35] in their established positions as monuments to Lenoir's museum, the dispersion of which he regretted. With this intention in mind, he proposed that additional property be acquired to arrange a proper setting in the form of a larger courtyard between the eastern façade of the Palais and the Arc de Gaillon. One design already indicates both the semicircular court and the main courtyard. He proposed also to use other remains from Lenoir's museum on the walls. The main building itself was to be on a stylobate supporting copies of antique statues. It seems that his

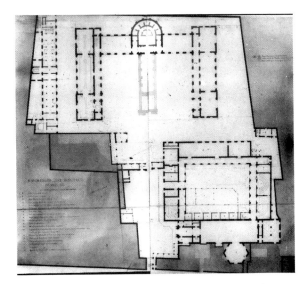

111 Plan of the Beaux-Arts in March 1833, before Duban's new proposals. Note the wing across the centre of the courtyard of the Palais des Etudes.

'notice des localités indispensables aux differents services de l'Ecole des Beaux-Arts',[36] together with the report of 5 April, in which he enumerated the rooms required for day to day teaching, had been accepted. On 18 June 1833, he delivered his 'project for the complete rebuilding of the buildings of Etudes Quotidiennes [everyday studies] . . . a description and estimate for the full restoration and reinstatement of the old convent church'.[37]

The Minister and the Conseil des Bâtiments Civils thus came to an agreement on this part of the scheme. In a letter dated 8 June 1834, Duban asserted his independence of the professors of the Ecole. There is no evidence, moreover, that he was influenced by his *inspecteur*, Henri Labrouste, soon to emerge as a strong architectural personality. But we have little surviving evidence of Duban's architectural activity at this time. A few accounts of the work in progress survive, several reports and a sketch of the cloister, before it was torn down, in axonometric section;[38] that is all.

Building proceeded without particular incident; the Minister approved the programme submitted on 1 October 1833, and on 21 October Duban was notified that building might start.[39] On 4 August 1834 'the base of the first-floor order of the main façade is being

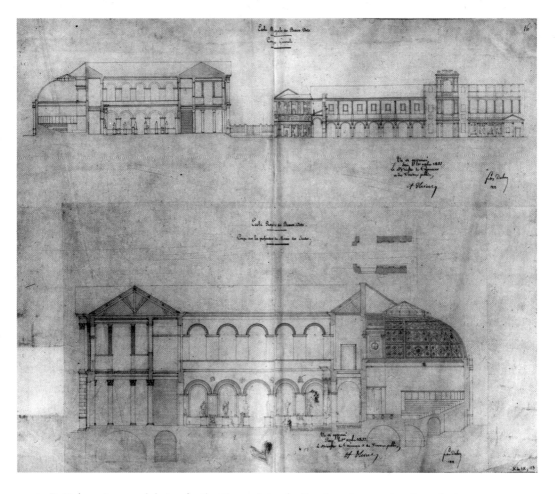

112   F. Duban. Approved design for the Beaux-Arts of 1 October 1833: section through the
centre of the site (above) showing cross-section of the Palais des Etudes and elevation of the range
with the Anet frontispiece; and a detailed cross-section of the Palais indicating decoration of the
hemicycle vault. (Archives Nationales)

completed. The opposite wall facing the court
is up to the level of the impost of the first-
floor windows; work proceeds also on the
surfacing of the interior of the right-hand wing,
and on the floor of its gallery at first-floor level
. . . the iron scaffolding is being assembled'.[40] By
then, Duban had decided not to use the columns
from Anet, which were in bad condition, and
replaced them instead with engaged columns.[41]
Additional sites in the rue Bonaparte, Nos.
14–16, had to be purchased in order to open up
the view from the street. Duban designed a
gate, which he later refused to entrust to the
firm that had won the contract, so important
did he consider the quality of the craftsmanship
necessary to give force to his details. The
porters' lodges were built in 1837, later to be
enlarged.[42] The final touches were the position-
ing of the copy of Michelangelo's *Last Judgment*

by Sigalon,[43] and the erection of a column
in the courtyard.[44]

By June 1839, 'the building works at the
Ecole des Beaux-Arts are complete. It is
required that they be formally handed over,
in the presence of the architect, to a committee
to which the following are designated: Rohault,
Caristie, inspectors general of the Bâtiments
Civils, and Gourlier, inspector of accounts.'[45]

The main work was complete, but Duban was
not yet finished; an anatomy theatre was
proposed but the sum allocated was insufficient:
the money was spent instead on the erection
of the white marble fireplace, crowned with
alabaster figures by Germain Pilon.[46] Funds
allocated in subsequent years permitted only
minor works, such as the dismantling and
erection of fragments from the Hôtel du
Faur in the garden.[47]

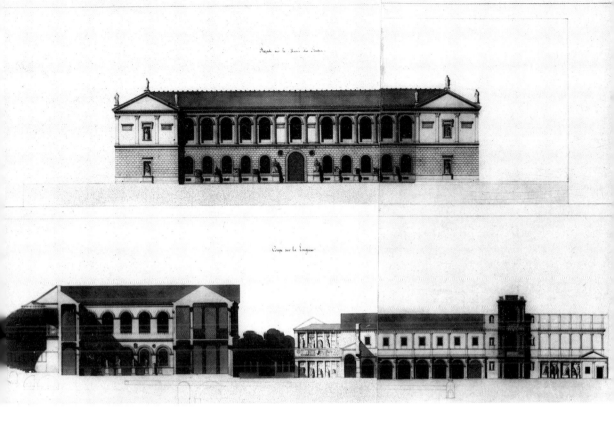

113 F. Duban. Rendered design for the Palais des Etudes without an attic storey, 1833: elevation, and section through the site (as opposite, above). (Archives Nationales)

More significant decorative projects should be noted: in 1843, Duban proposed to set up copies of Raphael's paintings in the north and south galleries on the first floor of the Palais courtyard. These had been commissioned by the professors of the Ecole, but Duban took on the task with zeal: 'although the professors do not appear to have wanted more than a direct copy of the *loggie*, I thought to reinforce their wishes in submitting a design that suggested the Vatican itself – something that would be both an addition to the Palais and a setting more worthy of the *loggie*'.[48] In 1852, supporting ledges and timber frames to support the painted panels were set up, though painting alone is mentioned in the accounts of that year.[49]

In spite of the fact that Duban was on bad terms with the Emperor because of disputes over his work at the Louvre, he was able to

undertake one major building for the Ecole. In 1844, the professors had suggested that a site on the quai Malaquais next to the Ecole be bought for a great Royal Library. No response was given.[50] Then on 13 November 1850, they addressed a letter to the minister 'asking him to purchase the site for sale on the *quai* adjoining the Ecole';[51] they wished that the site might be used for the Ecole. On 13 July 1855, the Conseil d'Administration, 'having learned that the site intended for the building of the Caisse des Dépôts et des Consignations was not to be used for that purpose, renews the request already made by the Ecole for an extension there'.[52]

But on 16 December 1855, a fire broke out in the amphitheatre causing much damage. The professors turned their attention to the restoration of Delaroche's paintings. Duban, 2

114 Decoration in one of the first-floor galleries round the courtyard of the Palais des Etudes, based on Raphael's *loggie*, projected by Duban in 1843 and executed in 1852.

however, had been active on his own account. In August he had written to the Minister on the subject of the empty site. A correspondence followed. Duban proposed at first that the site be used for private housing,[53] and obtained permission to build a luxury apartment block. But he was soon designing an extension to the Ecole des Beaux-Arts and an Ecole du Génie Maritime.[54] He allocated the better part of the proposed building to the Ecole des Beaux-Arts, which may have deterred the Ministre de la Marine from installing the Ecole du Génie Maritime there, though the decision might equally have been made by the Emperor himself, when he visited the Ecole des Beaux- on 28 April 1857. On this occasion, 'a design for an extension to the Ecole on an adjoining site on the quai Malaquais was shown to the Emperor who listened to Duban's explanation'.[55] Duban was paid fees for his two projects,

but they were not to be carried out. Instead, he was put in charge of the new extension to the Ecole des Beaux-Arts. On 6 January 1858, the Ministre de Finance wrote to the Ministre de l'Etat: 'the two plots on the quai Malaquais adjoining that of the Ecole should not be transferred, as already mentioned in a note of 29 May .... They should, on the contrary, be reserved for buildings that your department might be called upon to build at a future date.'[56] In February 1858, a committee was formed at the request of the Conseil d'Administration to consider such a building.[57]

On 3 April, Duban sent 'the first part of the estimate, which concerned the foundations, for the buildings to be erected on the quai Malaquais'.[58] The new plans showed 'first, a main building on the *quai* containing on the ground floor an entrance hall or exhibition room for the Grands Prix and painters' submissions from Rome; secondly, behind this building and linking it by a covered stair to the old buildings of the Ecole, a large hall for the storage of casts; thirdly, six studios.'[59]

Duban and the Commission d'Administration submitted revised plans. The new buildings were to occupy less space, since the library could be housed in the old buildings.[60] Their report was approved on 16 May 1860, providing for new buildings on the *quai* as well as for the installation of the museum of plaster-casts.[61] The first accounts for the year show that masonry work alone was paid for; but by the end of the year, Pyanet had made the model for an *oeil de boeuf* window and capitals with varying rosette patterns. Duban invited other well-known sculptors, such as Perrin,[62] and A. Beray, to submit designs for the sculpture of the three *oeil de boeuf* openings and the group 116 of six allegorical figures representing Painting, Sculpture and Architecture.[63]

Finally, in 1863, with the completion of the rear rooms and the stairway leading down to the Cour du Mûrier, the works were finished. The Cour du Mûrier itself had been de- 120 corated with murals, paintings, mosaic paving and casts of the Parthenon frieze and antique statues. In the centre, a fountain had been erected. The whole was of Pompeian inspiration.[64]

After many proposals and provisional installations the Conseil d'Administration decided finally that the library should be set up in the front room on the first floor of the Palais des

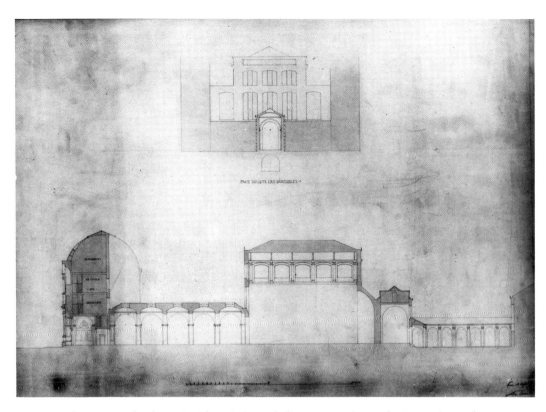

115 F. Duban. Design for the quai Malaquais site including an extension to the Beaux-Arts and apartments, September 1856: elevation of the apartment-block side, and section, showing the Beaux-Arts extension on the river front at the left. (Archives Nationales)

116 F. Duban. Quai Malaquais façade of the Ecole des Beaux-Arts, completed by 1863.

Etudes. In January 1864, A. Lenoir and César Daly announced that it was open to the public.[65]

The court of the Palais des Beaux-Arts was 117 to be open to the sky. On 9 March 1861 the committee charged with the arrangement of the new building proposed that it be glassed over. Duban took up the idea: it was the basis of his last major work at the Ecole. Though he had up to then used new materials, and metal in particular, but sparingly – largely for floor beams, especially in the quai Malaquais buildings – he took up metal and glass without hesitation as the proper solution to the pro-
118 gramme: 'eight Corinthian columns, 6.5 metres high, six Doric columns, 6.75 metres high, and cross-braces; four trusses and rafters of iron, lead to hold in position the panes of glass. The lights of double-polished glass to be ordered from merchants'.[66]

Metal was thus to be adapted to the classical orders. The final account, 'for covering the inner courtyard of the Palace',[67] shows that the new work was completed by 26 August 1867. Duban's work was done, but he continued to fuss with decorative elements. In 1866, Lenoir's bust by Dumont was erected, and, just before his death, on 4 August 1870, still fretting over details, Duban recommended a new gardener for the Ecole.

E. Coquart, who succeeded Duban, painted the walls of the glass-roofed court. He also put forward an ambitious project covering the whole of the site on the corner of the quai Malaquais and the rue Bonaparte; this was not built, though the sectional elevations are of interest in that they show Duban's buildings as they were shortly after his death.[68] Though Coquart added nothing of his own, he supervised the acquisition and adaption of new buildings: the house at 17, quai Malaquais, where Anatole France had lived, and the Hôtel de Chimay.[69] Mansart's interiors here have gone, but the 18th-century façade to the garden is still fine, as are the Empire salons on the first floor.

The Ecole des Beaux-Arts as it stands today is thus the product of more than one mind and more than one purpose.[70] It is, nevertheless, essentially Duban's masterpiece. How should we characterize it stylistically and architecturally?

Duban was inspired always by the past, and we have seen that to form the taste of his pupils he exhibited features from Lenoir's museum on the walls of the *cour d'honneur* and the court between the Arc de Gaillon and the Palais. But the sources of his own inspiration were more varied.[71] In designing the façade of the Palais des Etudes he acknowledged the influence of the Arc de Gaillon: 'the façade had been conceived, basically, not to be masked but to be preceded by this elegant portico, this 119 mark (if I dare say it) of the establishment'.[72]

But his façade is marked rather by the Italian Renaissance than by the French. Debret's design was of the chaste and dull classical kind; Duban enriched it with quattrocento and cinquecento detail, a style he was the first in France to take up. A new monumentalism appeared in his second project, where the main façade dominates the composition for the first time. The forceful character is accentuated by the introduction of an attic storey. The articulation of the first floor derives from the Vatican *loggie*, that of the ground floor from the Palazzo della Cancelleria. It is difficult to suggest any palazzo model for the court. There 117 are, throughout, affinities with Wren's library at Trinity College, Cambridge, and Klenze's Alte Pinakothek in Munich; but one cannot be sure that Duban was aware of Wren's work or had seen Klenze's drawings. Certainly, the detailing derives from Italian Renaissance models. Duban chose only the Renaissance elements from Lenoir's museum for display: the Arc de Gaillon, of the early French Renaissance, which is perhaps in part the work of an Italian sculptor, and items from Philibert de l'Orme's Anet, against the façade of the church. Sadly, he made no attempt to save the great cloister of the Petits Augustins in its entirety, difficult though this would have been. Of the old convent, he kept only the church and chapel, 104 whose Italian-style cupola was, together with that of the Couvent des Carmes Dechaussées, among the first to be seen in Paris. This he made into a museum of casts of Italian sculptures, still *in situ*. During the Second Empire, Duban's Italianate tastes were further developed in the building on the quai Malaquais. A more 116 audacious use of metal elements allowed an audacious arrangement of wide rooms. The style of the façade, which at first glance seems 1, 1 so novel, is in fact directly inspired by the façade of the Petite Galerie du Louvre, on the opposite bank of the Seine, a façade that Duban had himself partially restored with scant respect for Le Vau's early 17th-century work. For

117   F. Duban. Courtyard of the Palais des Etudes as originally built. (Musée Carnavalet, Paris)

118   F. Duban. Courtyard of the Palais des Etudes covered by an iron-and-glass roof, completed in 1867.

119 Façade of the Palais des Etudes, with the Arc de Gaillon in the axial position that Duban fought for in 1833.

120 The Cour du Mûrier, decorated and given a fountain by Duban before 1863.

the quai Malaquais he used Le Vau's wide, two-storey bays with, above, an expanded version of the *oeil de boeuf* openings that he had restored at the Louvre.[73] The influence of antiquity is strongest in the interior, with casts of the Parthenon friezes in the entrance hall, two Corinthian columns at the top of the steps that delineate the pronaos in front of the sanctuary of Melpomene, a great apse containing a statue of the muse of Tragedy. There are other traces of antique influence – on the ceiling of a second-floor room are representations of seated women holding a vase, a column and a bust, allegories of Painting, Architecture and Sculpture, all inspired from Greek vases of the sort Duban had seen in Etruscan tombs or in the Campana collection, now acquired by the state.

At this same period, Duban transformed the Cour du Mûrier, which he had first modelled on the old cloister, into a Pompeian atrium, reflecting not only the enthusiasm of his Italian sojourn but also a current Parisian vogue, inspired by Rougevin's and Alfred Normand's house for Prince Napoleon.[74]

The wide range of Duban's sources, together with his surprisingly bold, if not altogether successful, use of contemporary industrial materials for roofing the court of the Palais des Etudes, has led to his being labelled an eclectic, but his eclecticism is particularly selective. There is no hint of medievalism in his work. His tastes were of the classical sort. Yet he is not a classical architect. Hypersensitive, nervous to the point of breakdown, he evolved a style which is composite, lyrical and highly personal.

After Duban's death Daly remarked that any visitor to his work was inevitably bewildered.[75] Yet out of a condemned convent and Debret's dull building, he had created a complex urban tissue, a wholly successful series of spaces that evokes the architecture of Le Vau and also, much more strongly, Italy.

VIII

The book and the building: Hugo's theory of architecture and Labrouste's Bibliothèque Ste-Geneviève

Neil Levine

THE INVESTIGATION OF THE RELATIONSHIP between architecture and literature in the 19th century is of crucial importance. No other architecture has been so maligned for being 'literary', yet no other architecture has been as systematically dissociated from its contemporary literature as Romantic architecture.[1] The development of Romanticism in French architecture and its ultimate dissolution of neoclassicism began almost imperceptibly during the reign of Charles X and then continued without any apparent theoretical underpinning during Louis-Philippe's July Monarchy. The leaders of the Romantic movement, later called *Néo-Grecs*, were Henri Labrouste, Félix Duban, Louis Duc and Léon Vaudoyer. Between 1824 and 1827 they all went to Rome as *pensionnaires* of the French Académie after having won the Grand Prix at the Ecole des Beaux-Arts. By 1832 they had all returned to Paris. Both Duban and Labrouste had opened *ateliers* and had been involved in an abortive attempt to reorganize the teaching at the Ecole des Beaux-Arts, before being appointed by the government to complete the building of the Ecole itself.[2]

It was during those same years, 1824–32, that Victor Hugo, born a year after Labrouste in 1802, published his most original and influential writings about architecture. Since these generally deal with French medieval architecture and are ostensibly devoted to the need for its preservation and restoration, they have not been related to the *Néo-Grec* work of Labrouste and his contemporaries. Instead, their influence on the later medieval revivalists such as Lassus and Viollet-le-Duc has often been pointed out.[3]

There is no doubt that Hugo's thought had a great impact on the student generation of the

1830s, but their understanding of it was selective and hence only partial. While Hugo did say in October 1832 that to instil in the hearts of Frenchmen 'l'amour de l'architecture nationale' was not only 'one of the chief aims' of his novel *Notre-Dame de Paris* but also 'one of the chief aims of his life',[4] he prefaced that remark by making a clear distinction between preservation and contemporary architecture: 'In any case, whatever the future of architecture and however our young architects may one day settle the question of their art, while we wait for new monuments we must conserve the old.'[5]

Hugo did not prescribe the use of the Gothic style for new buildings. In the 1840s, Lassus and Viollet-le-Duc would propose that, by picking up where the Gothic architect left off, the 19th century could regenerate architecture.[6] A decade earlier, however, Hugo had come to the conclusion that the process of degeneration that began in the Renaissance had reached the point of no return. Architecture was 'dead, dead beyond recall'.[7] Buildings had forever lost the power to express human thought and had relinquished that power to the printed word. Hugo expressed this devastating opinion in the 'eighth edition' of *Notre-Dame de Paris*, published in December 1832. It implied that nothing so minor as the revival of one style or another could be considered an adequate response to the situation.

Hugo seems to have arrived at this view of architecture after giving the matter a great deal of thought during the preceding few years, so that by 1832 he could speak of it as 'a view, unhappily, deeply rooted in him and deeply pondered'.[8] Some early essays, republished in 1834 in *Littérature et philosophie mêlées*, show the shift in his thought from an optimism about the future of architecture to a decisive

121   H. Labrouste. Bibliothèque Ste-Geneviève, Paris, 1838–50: Reading Room, looking west from the east end, with the term representing Night in the foreground.

pessimism. This development brackets the publication of *Notre-Dame de Paris*. In July 1824, in the introduction to 'Idées au hasard', Hugo wrote that although architecture had not yet been reinvigorated by the Romantic movement, he firmly believed that would soon happen. The artistic 'revolution', which began in poetry, had already affected both music and painting; 'and before long it will surely revive sculpture and architecture, which died long ago, as do all arts in the grip of an *académie*'.[9] Architects simply had to reject the 'false taste' and 'conventions' of an academic classicism that had hindered the arts since the beginning of the 16th century. Hugo based his conclusion on a theory of progressive decadence culminating in the 18th century but did not as yet distinguish between the arts in this regard.

In the following year, 1825, Hugo wrote a short piece vehemently attacking those who were abetting the destruction of France's medieval monuments. He called for some system of surveillance since it would be impossible to reconstruct such works of art : 'We no longer have the genius of that age. Industry has replaced art.'[10] He contrasted the ruination of historically meaningful monuments with the construction of meaningless modern buildings that had 'the ridiculous pretension to being Greek or Roman in France'.[11] This article, entitled 'De la destruction des monuments en France', was not published until December 1831.[12] That was about nine months after the first edition of *Notre-Dame de Paris*. It was followed within less than three months by 'Guerre aux démolisseurs!', published on 1 March 1832 in the *Revue des deux-mondes*. This was both more explicit in calling for a solution to the problem of preservation and more confident in justifying the value of such expense over and against that for new building. Hugo mocked the recent architecture of Paris, describing the Chapelle Expiatoire as 'hunch-backed' and 'rachitic', the Madeleine as 'the second volume of the Bourse'.[13] But none of this would have been new to readers of Hugo, for just about one year previously he had said the same things in the chapters 'Notre-Dame' and 'Paris à vol d'oiseau' of *Notre-Dame de Paris*, which first appeared in March 1831. What was new in 'Guerre aux démolisseurs!' was the expression of the belief that if France did not preserve its medieval architecture it would never again have any architecture worth preserving. Hugo based his appeal for the creation of a law to protect and preserve medieval buildings on his belief that 'architecture, alone of all the arts, no longer has a future'.[14]

Such a declaration clearly demanded further explanation in order to be taken seriously. Hugo had actually devoted an entire chapter of *Notre-Dame* to the subject but, for reasons to be discussed below, decided to leave that chapter out of the original edition (in seven pseudo-editions). In December 1832 he made his argument public by including that chapter, along with two other previously unpublished ones, in the 'eighth', or definitive, edition. The chapter was entitled 'Ceci tuera cela' ('This will kill That'). 'Ceci' refers to the printing-press and 'cela' to its victim, architecture. The sentence sealed architecture's fate.

'Ceci tuera cela' is by far Hugo's most important architectural statement and remains the most trenchant statement of French Romantic theory. In 1957 Frank Lloyd Wright called it 'the most illuminating essay on architecture yet written'.[15] But despite its extreme brevity, it has never been carefully analyzed nor has its relation to contemporary Romantic architecture been fully explored. Its oracular content has, however, often been loosely interpreted to serve the purposes of modern architecture and thus has seemed to reflect the very art historical prejudices that have prevented a meaningful evaluation of the architecture of its time.

It is surely not unfair to say that most historians of modern architecture know the chapter in question through Frank Lloyd Wright. Wright more or less paraphrased the entire chapter in his first major architectural pronouncement, 'The Art and Craft of the Machine'. Beginning with that lecture he gave in 1901 at Hull House in Chicago, he referred to 'Ceci tuera cela' in almost all his later books. Hugo became, like Lao-Tse and Whitman, one of the supports of Wright's own philosophical construct. In 'The Art and Craft of the Machine', Wright said that the phrase *ceci tuera cela* 'was to me as a boy one of the grandest sad things of the world'.[16] He was, by his own reckoning, 'fourteen years old when this ... chapter in *Notre-Dame* profoundly affected [his] sense of ... architecture'; and its impact was such that Hugo's 'story of the tragic decline of the great mother-art never left [his] mind'.[17] It most vividly came back to mind, as he said in his *Autobiography* (1932), when he began working in Chicago in the late 1880s. He then re-read the chapter, convinced that 'this essay was one of the truly great things ever written on architecture'.[18] This time Hugo's thought gave added strength to Wright's cause as it reinforced his own opinions: 'Again I felt its force. My own gathering distrust was confirmed. Splendid writing. How "modern" the great romanticist must have seemed in his time!'[19] Wright somehow understood Hugo to have 'prophesied that Architecture, already some five hundred years moribund, would in the latter end of the 19th century or the beginning of the 20th come alive again'.[20] The development of the modern skyscraper 'there, in Chicago, so many years after Victor Hugo's remarkable prophecy,' convinced Wright that 'Naissance had already begun. The sun – architecture – was rising!'[21] Wright fiddled with Hugo's language and turned a prediction of irrevocable doom into an affirmation of resurrection, which would indeed have been ahead of its time. It became through Wright a self-fulfilling prophecy of modern architecture.

Wright's interpretation was not as idiosyncratic and wilful as it may seem. The medieval revival that followed *Notre-Dame* had produced a body of work and theory that appeared to many to have prepared the way for modern architecture. Could not Hugo, therefore, have been referring only to classical architecture? Beaux-Arts classicism was the bête noire, especially for Frank Lloyd Wright and especially after the Chicago Fair of 1893. Wright was particularly impressed with the fact that 'the amazing Frenchman [Hugo] had disposed of the European Renaissance as "that setting sun all Europe mistook for dawn"'.[22] Classical buildings were 'lifeless' copies and Wright saw in them nothing 'but the impassive features of a dead face'.[23] Wright loved to mock American Beaux-Arts classicism by referring to how 'the "academic" mistook a setting sun for dawn!'[24] In the 1920s, Lewis Mumford, one of Wright's most articulate champions at the time, carried this anticlassical version of Hugo to an extreme by giving it an almost plausible literal twist. 'The real misdemeanor of the printing-press,' according to Mumford, 'was not that it took literary values away from architecture, but that it caused architecture to derive its value from literature.'[25] Mumford translated that to mean quite simply the printed architectural treatise, which first appeared in the

Renaissance. This caused architecture to 'live ... by the book'.[26] Medieval buildings display 'the imprint of a happy spirit'; once classical treatises appeared, the rules of 'the Five Orders became ... unchallengeable' and architecture 'became a mere matter of grammatical accuracy and pronunciation'.[27] The availability of treatises by Palladio, Vignola and Chambers, among others, destroyed architecture's vitality, originality and local variety. Classicism became the 'imperial' death mask.[28]

Frank Lloyd Wright, for his part, almost never referred to the relationship between architecture and that product of the printing-press, the book, which as we shall see was the focus of Hugo's theory. Wright chose to read the printing-press as a metaphor for the machine and implied that Hugo was really referring to the overall effect of the machine on art. Wright introduced his paraphrase of 'Ceci tuera cela' in the Hull House lecture by asking his audience to 'assume Architecture in the old sense as a fitting representation of Traditional art, and Printing as a fitting representation of the Machine'.[29] Hugo's account of the death of architecture thus became the death of 'all art immediately fashioned upon the early handicraft ideal'.[30] The machine killed architecture by allowing for interminable 'restatement' of the same hackneyed ideas in conventionalized forms. These forms, previously executed by hand in one material, were moulded and fashioned by machines in other, less appropriate materials. They were 'cheapened', 'butchered' and rendered meaningless by such mechanical reproduction.[31] In effect, only the 'structural tradition' involved in conventional masonry architecture had died.[32] The revival of architecture depended on the ability of architects, 'no longer tied to the meager unit of brick arch and stone lintel, nor hampered by the grammatical phrase of their making', to derive new forms from new materials and structural systems.[33] Wright pointed to the steel-framed skyscraper as 'the first sane word that has been said in Art for the Machine', and thereby gave Hugo's prophecy another familiar modern ring.[34]

The idea that the revival of architecture would be assured not simply by the abandonment of classicism but also by the adoption of new materials of construction had already been imposed on Hugo's 'Ceci tuera cela' by Emile Zola. In *Le Ventre de Paris*, published in 1874,

Zola described the Halles Centrales of Paris as the only contemporary building that could be called 'original, ... that was not copied from anything and that had grown naturally out of the soil of the age'.[35] It was a 'timid revelation of the 20th century'.[36] Its unmitigated use of iron made it seem vigorous and alive in comparison with its stone neighbour, the church of St-Eustache. Zola saw in this contrast of materials the death of traditional art and the birth of 'modern art' and thought by that to bring Hugo up to date: 'It is a curious juxtaposition, ... that bit of church framed by this avenue of cast iron. ... *Ceci tuera cela*, iron will kill stone, and the time is drawing near ... '[37]

To continue to ascribe to Victor Hugo such clairvoyance is a totally irrelevant kind of historical hindsight. In 1830 Hugo was certainly not expecting an architectural revival to result from the use of iron or the abandonment of one style for another, or, for that matter, for none. There is in fact no evidence in 'Ceci tuera cela' that he was looking that far ahead. He was concerned with analyzing what had happened to architecture and why it seemed at the time, not just to him but to every young Romantic, to have reached such a low ebb. It can surely be said that no period in the history of French architecture was more fallow than the first three decades of the 19th century. The work of Lebas, Debret, Peyre, Godde, Caristie and Gau, to name just a few of the most illustrious architects of the Restoration, hardly inspired much confidence in the future. At the moment when the idealism of post-Renaissance classicism was becoming so diluted as almost not to warrant discussion, Hugo focused on the ever-decreasing range of architectural expression and questioned the medium's capacity for embodying significant social content.

A review of 'Ceci tuera cela' is imperative for our understanding of 19th-century architecture. In an age which seems to have consistently doubted the medium's efficacy and constantly restricted its discussion of architectural problems to questions of style or materialistic matters, Hugo's essay opened architecture up to the type of literary-symbolic interpretation that critics such as Daly and Ruskin were to develop so profoundly. But the intimate relationship between architecture and literature, which sustained such critical analysis, was rarely applied to contemporary buildings in any positive way. The need to see Hugo's theory in relation to the architecture of his time may, therefore, become all the more obvious when it is realized that Henri Labrouste actually played a part in the complicated story of the publication of *Notre-Dame*. Surely the most important outcome of that was his Bibliothèque Ste-Geneviève, which was designed and built just a few years later and was the first significant architectural response to the issues raised by Hugo.

II

Hugo began thinking about *Notre-Dame de Paris* as early as 1828, but four years were to elapse before the book was published in its final form.[38] On 15 November 1828 he signed a contract with the publisher Charles Gosselin, agreeing to deliver the manuscript by 15 April of the following year. Perhaps because of his financial situation, aggravated by the birth of a third child in October 1828, Hugo turned his energies to the more lucrative field of theatre. In 1829, he wrote *Un Duel sous Richelieu* (*Marion de Lorme*) and *Hernani* without, it appears, working any more on his projected novel. If Gosselin was annoyed at the fact that the deadline for *Notre-Dame* had gone by without a word from Hugo, he was further angered by the fact that Hugo sold the rights to *Hernani* to another publisher without having given Gosselin first option, which he had previously agreed to do. From that point on, time and money began to play significant roles in the story of *Notre-Dame*. Following some vague threats of a law suit, Hugo finally signed another contract with Gosselin on 5 June 1830, in which it was stipulated that he would deliver a two-volume manuscript by 1 December of that year.[39] If he missed that deadline the penalties would be extremely stiff. While Hugo's fee for the novel was set at 4,000 francs, with royalties to begin after three years, he would be fined 1,000 francs for every delay of eight days beyond 1 December. After two months, 2,000 francs more would be added to the accumulated sum of 8,000 francs that Hugo would owe Gosselin. The maximum penalty of 10,000 francs would be reached on 1 February 1831. Beyond that date, however, Hugo was still legally bound to sell the manuscript to Gosselin. The contract stipulated that only in a certified case of illness 'or some other serious

122 Bibliothèque Ste-Geneviève: façade, engraved after a drawing by Labrouste. (From the *Revue générale de l'architecture et des travaux publics*, XI, 1853)

circumstance impossible to specify in advance' would an extension be granted.[40]

Hugo got back to work on *Notre-Dame* in June 1830 and actually began writing on 25 July. He completed just a few pages when he was interrupted once again. On 27 July the Revolution broke out, and his daughter Adèle was born on the following day. He then began working on things more directly connected with current events and thus wrote a letter to Gosselin on 5 August asking for an extension. Hugo claimed that one of those unspecified 'serious circumstances' had occurred. Fearing that his house, located just off the Champs-Elysées, might be ransacked during the final day of the Revolution, he said that he sent most of his important personal effects and manuscripts to his brother-in-law's house on the rue du Cherche-Midi. In the haste of this move, 'he had lost an entire book of notes, which had cost

him more than two months' research and which were indispensable for the completion of *Notre-Dame de Paris*'.[41] Hugo asked for a two-month extension. Gosselin agreed but warned that he would hold Hugo rigorously to the final deadline of 1 February 1831.

Hugo then bought, according to his wife, a bottle of ink and a thick grey sweater which 'covered him from his neck to his big toe'.[42] He locked up his going-out clothes and began to write feverishly on 1 September 1830. Apparently, his only distraction was to receive some friends for an hour or so in the evening, to whom he sometimes read sections of the novel in progress. By early October, he had completed the first two Books and part of Book VI.[43] He saw the work advancing rapidly and perhaps a chance to increase his fee. On 4 October he questioned Gosselin about the possibility of adding a third volume to the two called for in the contract and wondered how much more money that would mean for him. Hugo claimed that he was merely following his original outline but that he could keep the novel to two volumes 'by omitting the historical developments'.[44] He would, however, only decide to 'amputate' if Gosselin had any objections. Three days later, Gosselin responded that in no circumstances could Hugo expect an increase; that if necessary each of the two volumes could be enlarged; but that this might in the end negatively affect the author's profits.[45] This exchange of letters has given rise to much speculation concerning the ultimate composition of the first 'edition' of the novel; but there is no evidence of what Hugo specifically had in mind nor of what he decided to do, if anything.

Hugo completed the manuscript on 15 January 1831, but the story does not end there. The preface and the chapter 'Paris à vol d'oiseau' had not yet been written. And when the book was published on 16 March, it lacked three chapters, at least two of which had already been written. These two, 'Abbas beati Martini' and 'Ceci tuera cela', had been finished by mid-November of the previous year. Why they were deleted is a question that has often been asked but never conclusively answered. Part of the problem has been to establish precisely at what point Hugo decided against including them.

Hugo gave the first section of the manuscript to Gosselin on 17 January 1831. He was to have from four to six weeks to read and correct the proofs. A series of letters between Hugo and Gosselin, dating from 16 to 19 January, shows that Hugo tried to gain time. Gosselin made it clear to him that he would not play along. On 19 January he told Hugo that he would come by to pick up the final section of the manuscript and that he wanted a brief summary of the novel in order to publicize the forthcoming work.[46] Hugo responded the same day, apparently having decided not to pursue his delaying tactics, and in his summary wrote that 'Louis XI appears in one of the chapter'.[47] Hugo was obviously referring to the chapter 'Le Retrait où dit ses heures Monsieur Louis de France' (Book X, chapter 5). Since Louis XI also appears in 'Abbas beati Martini', albeit incognito, it is almost certain that by 19 January Hugo had decided to withhold that chapter as well as its companion 'Ceci tuera cela'. 'Paris à vol

d'oiseau', the second most important chapter on architecture in the book, was written between 18 January and 2 February. The preface was written last and was given to Gosselin on 9 March, just a week before publication. Both 'Paris à vol d'oiseau' and the preface can be seen as postscripts, substituted at the last moment for what was excluded. They both rephrase, the former illustratively and the latter cryptically, the main theme of the missing chapters.

The first edition was divided into seven pseudo-editions. On 17 December 1832, Eugène Renduel, who had bought out part of Gosselin's rights to Hugo, published what was in effect the second edition of the novel, though it is called the 'eighth'.[48] It is this edition which included, for the first time, the three missing chapters as well as a prefatory 'Note' by Hugo explaining the omission. The composition of the nine Books of the original edition was somewhat altered and their number was increased to eleven to incorporate the three additional chapters. They are consecutive. The first, 'Impopularité,' which may or may not have been written at the time of the others, was almost certainly rewritten in 1832.[49] It is by far the shortest of the three and Hugo placed it at the end of a reconstituted Book IV. He made a separate and new Book V for the other two. The new Book IV, with its addition, was made out of the last five chapters of the original Book III. This left Book III to consist of just two chapters, both dealing with architecture, 'Notre-Dame' and 'Paris à vol d'oiseau'. Book V, in which the new chapter 'Abbas beati Martini' introduces the architectural theory explained at greater length in the following chapter 'Ceci tuera cela', was thus set in place like a pendant to Book III. Book V is, however, shorter than Book III.

In his 'Note ajoutée à l'édition définitive (1832)', dated 20 October 1832, Hugo stressed the fact that the additional chapters were 'not new' and 'were written at the same time as the rest of the work'. He had not previously included them for the 'very simple reason' that they had been lost:[50]

At the time when *Notre-Dame de Paris* was first being printed, the folder containing these three chapters went astray. This meant either rewriting them or doing without them. The author reckoned that the only two of the three chapters long enough to have some importance were chapters on art and history which in no way affected the underlying drama or story, that the public would not notice they had gone and that he alone, the author, would possess the secret of this lacuna in the text. He chose to go ahead. Also, if we are to make a full confession, his laziness recoiled from the task of rewriting three lost chapters. He would have found it quicker to write a new romance.

Now, the chapters have been found again and he has taken the earliest opportunity of restoring them to their place.

Hugo's disarmingly simple explanation has always been doubted. Despite some hints that he may have had political or religious reasons for holding back the chapters, it is generally agreed that his motive was ultimately of a practical nature.[51] Yet different versions of that have been suggested. One opinion emphasizes the 'philosophical' nature of the contents and points to Hugo's later statement in the 'Note' admitting that for those many readers who are only interested in the plot of the novel the 'rediscovered' chapters would 'be judged of small worth'.[52] According to this theory, Hugo withheld them for commercial reasons and only replaced them once the popular success of the book was ensured.[53] This view is difficult to sustain given the fact that only the last of the three chapters, 'Ceci tuera cela', can in any way be called didactic. 'Impopularité' is only a page or so long and the middle one, 'Abbas beati Martini', which introduces Louis XI, in disguise, into the cell of the archdeacon Claude Frollo, to be told by him about his 'hermetic' alchemical studies, is as exciting and dramatic as any other part of the story. It should, however, be noted that while Hugo obviously considered the three chapters a sequence that would stay or go as a block, it was 'Ceci tuera cela' that concerned him especially. This is the only one of the three he referred to specifically in the 'Note'. In fact, the 'Note' is a kind of apologia for its inclusion.

More often than not, Hugo's decision to exclude the chapters is linked to Gosselin's refusal of his request, of the previous 4 October, to lengthen the novel to three volumes.[54] According to this view, Hugo then 'amputated' the 'historical developments', meaning the three chapters, just as he warned Gosselin he would do. It is true that both 'Abbas beati Martini' and 'Ceci tuera cela' can be called 'historical developments', or even embellishments, of the plot, but

their combined length is less than that of the two other chapters about architecture, which form Book III. 'Paris à vol d'oiseau', which is certainly as discursive as any in the novel, is the longest chapter of these pendant Books, and it was written after Hugo's decision. Furthermore, thanks to Jacques Seebacher's recent research, it is now clear that the two chapters of Book V were only begun a month after the October exchange of letters; and no evidence has been brought forth to prove that Hugo was even contemplating them at that time.[55] Even so, it is hard to imagine they would have caused the need for a third volume, especially since Gosselin had told Hugo he could increase the length of the two volumes he was allowed.

One is naturally led to the conclusion that in October 1830 Hugo was sending up a trial balloon hoping for a short-term gain. It has been suggested, however, that Hugo had a more far-reaching objective. Having had an extremely disagreeable relationship with Gosselin up until then, and expecting to change publishers as soon as his contract expired, Hugo was preparing to 'reserve' parts of the novel so that at some later date a new publisher would be convinced he was getting almost a 'new novel'.[56] This hypothesis, which seems somewhat plausible at first, is once again complicated by the fact that the chapters in question had not even been planned. Furthermore, why did Hugo then write a whole new chapter on architecture to replace the excluded one, once the manuscript had been handed over to Gosselin? The answer that by January 1831 Hugo was on better terms with his publisher and gave him the new chapter as 'compensation' for the 'reserved' ones makes little sense.[57]

When 'Paris à vol d'oiseau' is compared with 'Ceci tuera cela' it is evident that Hugo's exchange of the one for the other must have involved a substantive question of architecture. And here is where Henri Labrouste enters the picture to provide the missing link. A manuscript biography of Henri Labrouste, prepared shortly after his death in 1875 by his son Léon, reveals that, during the course of writing *Notre-Dame*, Victor Hugo asked Labrouste to criticize the sections about architecture. The discussions that resulted may have been a major reason for Hugo's withholding the chapters in question:

On his return from Rome [in January 1830], Henri Labrouste was welcomed and sought after by the independent artists of his time, who were all to become great masters, and, in particular, by Victor Hugo, whose plays Labrouste's students went to cheer. It was at the time he was writing *Notre-Dame de Paris* that Hugo gave Labrouste some of his work in order to get his advice on the technical and architectural sections. After an initial exchange of critical comments, their discussions became more frequent. Finally, with his work progressing rapidly, Hugo decided to withhold the chapters he wished to have another look at, since the publisher was applying pressure and the fiery genius of the great master himself could not bear the idea of any further delay. Eventually, the work appeared incomplete, and it was only later that the reconsidered chapters were released for publication.[58]

Léon Labrouste's account of his father's contact with Hugo supports my theory that Hugo's retention of the chapters is not to be explained by his letter to Gosselin of 4 October 1830. While many factors may have been considered, the final decision was determined by a recognition of the consequence of what he had written and, therefore, the desire for some more time to think about it and make sure it was what he would stand by. Faced with an inflexible deadline, Hugo only decided at the very last moment, shortly before 19 January 1831, to withhold 'Ceci tuera cela'. He then immediately set about writing 'Paris à vol d'oiseau', which would illustrate in piquant terms his pessimistic view of recent architecture without, however, abstracting it into a historical necessity. Whatever second thoughts Hugo had about the way in which this was expressed in 'Ceci tuera cela' were thus satisfied for the time being. And, finally, the loss of that theory was recompensed by its epitomization in the preface.

There seems to me to be no reason whatsoever to doubt the veracity of Léon Labrouste's account, but it is at first glance curious that such an important occurrence seems to be recorded nowhere else. On the other hand, we know of another young architect who was asked by Hugo to help him in preparing *Notre-Dame*, and of whose collaboration no evidence remains. The case of Charles Robelin (1797–1887) is somewhat different in that he was a life-long friend of Hugo, and some of their correspondence has been preserved and published. Yet, as pointed out by Jean Mallion in his *Victor*

Hugo et l'art architectural, Hugo never acknowledged his debt to Robelin, and there is no evidence for it except the posthumous accounts of family and friends, the first published mention appearing in 1891.[59] All these agree that Robelin merely provided Hugo with information upon which to base the chapters in *Notre-Dame* dealing with architecture. While it is conceivable that Hugo might then have asked his friend to read and criticize what he had written, it is perhaps more likely that he would have tried to get someone else's opinion. Furthermore, it appears that, from late in 1829, Robelin was away from Paris a good deal of the time, having been placed in charge of the restoration of the Cathedral of Besançon. Had Hugo asked his friend Robelin for the name of the bright young architect to consult on such a matter as a revolutionary view of architectural history, that name, in 1830, would certainly have been Labrouste's.

Robelin and Labrouste surely knew one another. Robelin's career at the Ecole des Beaux-Arts was neither distinguished nor protracted, but it did overlap with Labrouste's.[60] He was a student of Alavoine, who was a friend of Henri's brother Théodore and the first architect for whom Henri Labrouste was to work on his return from Rome.[61] Robelin entered the second class of the Ecole des Beaux-Arts on 3 April 1824. At that time, Henri Labrouste was the leading student. While Robelin was never promoted to the first class, Henri Labrouste won the Second Grand Prix in 1821, in his second year, the Prix Départemental in 1823 and the Grand Prix in 1824. Labrouste then spent the next five years in Italy as a *pensionnaire* of the Académie de France in Rome, which culminated in his celebrated restoration of Paestum of 1828–29. Robelin at the same time began a career of minor restorations, and more importantly for us, it was during these years that he made Hugo's acquaintance and became a member of his *cénacle*. 12 16

Labrouste returned to Paris in late January 1830. While Hugo was involved in the production of *Hernani*, for which the future students of Labrouste and Duban were drafted to do battle,[62] Labrouste and Duban themselves began to lead the young generation of Romantic students at the Ecole des Beaux-Arts in a series of efforts to reform the system of teaching. By the time Hugo began writing *Notre-Dame*,

Henri Labrouste had made a name for himself in Paris as a Young Turk. In the revolutionary atmosphere of July 1830, Labrouste was, in the words of one of his students, 'carried in triumph through the streets round the Ecole' by the members of his recently formed *atelier*.[63] One of the original group that petitioned him to take them on was J.-B.-A. Lassus, who was soon to restore St Germain l'Auxerrois, Notre-Dame and the Ste-Chapelle, and who was to terminate a career devoted to the revival of Gothic architecture with the publication of the *Album de Villard de Honnecourt*, which he dedicated to Henri Labrouste.[64] There was also in that first group of students A.-G. Gréterin, who was to restore St Séverin with Lassus, and F.-G. Klotz, who was to devote his life to the restoration of the Cathedral of Strasbourg. They were later joined, over the years, by such other medievalists as Boeswillwald, Millet, Bossan, Verdier and de Baudot. One might justifiably argue, *pace* Viollet-le-Duc, that the combination of training in Labrouste's *atelier* and inspiration from Hugo's early writing produced the vanguard of France's medieval revivalists.

Quite apart from the sheer quality and integrity of Labrouste's student designs, what catapulted him to fame and assured for him an anti-establishment reputation was his restoration of the Greek temples at Paestum, done in 1828–29. The work was exhibited in Paris in 1829 and, as I have described elsewhere, was bitterly criticized by the Académie for its un-traditional, anti-classical position.[65] In his obituary of Lassus, Alfred Darcel remarked that the budding Gothicists who were 'stricken by the Romantic fever' and were to be 'stirred by the splendid pages of Victor Hugo's *Notre-Dame de Paris*' found 'fuel for their attacks on the classicists in the drawings done by a student in Rome, Henri Labrouste'.[66]

Labrouste's restoration sent mini-shock waves through the French art world in 1829, which had repercussions throughout 1830. Horace Vernet continued to defend Labrouste's cause to the Académie and was so angered over their intransigency that he offered to resign his post as Director of the Académie de France in Rome. This climactic event in the drama made the Paris newspapers in the autumn of 1830.[67]

At the time Hugo was writing *Notre-Dame*, there was no architect of his own generation who was more notorious or promising than

123   H. Labrouste. Restoration of the 'Basilica' (Temple of Hera I) at Paestum, 1828–29: interior perspective. (Beaux-Arts)

Henri Labrouste. There was surely no other architect who had shown himself more sensitive to the issues involved in that theory of architecture underlying *Notre-Dame de Paris*. Labrouste's explanation of his restoration of Paestum was based on a regressive theory of history applied to a limited sequence of buildings.[68] He defined the degeneration from a 'primitive' state of 'purity' to that of conventional representation by the replacement of sculptural form by the written word. He linked that to the replacement of a religious programme by a secular one. He imagined the Temple of Hera I, 123 which he considered to be the latest of the three buildings, to have been a kind of public notice-board whose walls functioned, in his words, like the pages of an 'album', receiving the transient inscriptions of the town's citizens.[69] The building was beholden to the painted word for its meaning. Since there was no remaining evidence of this, Labrouste tried to evoke what the building signified by a liberal restoration of Greek graffiti.

While it may be coincidental, it was the sight of a transient bit of graffito, Greek in content though Gothic in form, which Hugo claimed in the preface to *Notre-Dame* to have generated his novel.[70] He wrote that he had seen the word 'ΑΝΑΓΚΗ', meaning 'fatality', inscribed on a wall in one of the towers of the Cathedral, but by the time he returned a few years later it had disappeared. The 'grim and fatal import'[71] of that word, now reprinted on the first page of the novel, situated it in space and described its underlying theme. The story of unrequited love ends fatally in tragedy and death. The chapter 'ΑΝΑΓΚΗ' contains the scene in which the archdeacon Claude Frollo inscribes the word on the wall of his hideaway in the tower and thus relates the fictional events to an existing spot in the building.[72] But that telltale sign had disappeared, and this foretold for Hugo the possible disappearance of the building itself. In restoring the vanished word to the first page of the book, *Notre-Dame*, Hugo indicated that his concern for the fate of French medieval architecture was a fundamental reason for writing the novel. His choice of reprinting a word on a piece of paper as the symbolic first step towards restoring the building, Notre-Dame, placed the book and the building in a reciprocal relationship and defined their different spheres of influence. In 1482, the word was carried by the building; by 1830, the power that the word had gained over the building, as a result of being mechanically printed, provided it with a durability to which the building was now beholden.

This theme of conflict between two different media of artistic expression, considered as tools of communication, was expanded and made explicit in the chapter 'Ceci tuera cela'. The two chapters devoted to architecture included in the original edition, aside from setting the scene for the novel, contained a plea for preservation and an expression of Hugo's profound distaste for post-Gothic architecture. But 'Ceci tuera cela' went deeper; it attempted nothing less than to explain the cause of the 'necessary decadence of architecture'.[73] According to Hugo, it clarified the historical 'system' of the novel and revealed its 'hidden' meaning to those who cared to read between the lines.[74] 'Ceci tuera cela' recounted the death of what is in effect the leading character of the book – the building.

III

The simple, powerful and symmetrical phrase 'Ceci tuera cela' provides the link between the two 'added' chapters that compose Book V. It is uttered in despair by the archdeacon Claude Frollo at the end of 'Abbas beati Martini', just after explaining the purpose of his 'hermetic' research to the disguised King Louis XI. The scene takes place in Frollo's canonical cell in the cloister of Notre-Dame. The king

has been brought there by his physician, Jacques Coictier, to ask Frollo for medical advice and a casting of his horoscope. Frollo denies the value of both medicine and astrology and, to the king's astonishment, declares that only alchemy holds the answers. But he admits that he has hardly begun to decipher its scripture: 'I do not read, I spell out!'[75] Louis XI asks if he can join Frollo in trying to read these texts and Frollo proposes an architectural tour of Paris:

> We shall content ourselves with the fragments of the book of Hermes which we have here. . . . But especially shall I make you read one by one the marble letters of the alphabet, the granite pages of the book. We shall go from the portal of Bishop William and Saint-Jean-le-Rond to the Sainte-Chapelle. . . . And together we shall spell out the façades of Saint-Côme . . . and Saint-Jacques-de-la-Boucherie . . . [76]

Louis XI does not seem to get this connection between buildings and books and asks Frollo what he means by a 'book'. The archdeacon opens his window and points to the cathedral. He then stares at that 'enormous two-headed sphinx' and becomes silent as he senses the inevitable failure of his studies.[77] He points to a printed book lying open on his desk, 'and looking sadly from the book to the church', he says, 'Alas, . . . this will kill that.'[78] When Coictier remarks that this book, published in 1474, is neither 'new' nor especially 'dreadful', Frollo says that what is significant is that it is printed: 'Alas and alack, small things overcome great ones! . . . the book will kill the building!'[79] The chapter then closes as Louis XI reveals his identity and invites Claude Frollo to visit him at his palace the following day for the first of what were to become frequent meetings between them.

At this point Hugo interrupted the story with the chapter 'Ceci tuera cela' in order to explain the archdeacon's 'enigmatic words'.[80] Hugo offered two interpretations of Frollo's words, the first explicit and integral to the story, the second implicit and eccentric. From the point of view of a priest living then, the liberating power of the printed book would mean the rooting out of faith and superstition and thus the destruction of not just any building but the church in particular. This would have widespread political and social consequences; it meant that 'one power was going to succeed another power'.[81] The agent of this change, which in France would lead to the absolute monarchy of Louis XIV, was Louis XI, who, Hugo wrote, 'began the wholesale demolition of the feudal edifice'.[82] This was foreshadowed in *Notre-Dame* by the king's violation of the cathedral's right of sanctuary which, Hugo noted, determined the outcome of the story.[83]

This institutional revolution was only the first and most obvious meaning of Frollo's words. Hugo's second interpretation was, in his own words, more original, more subtle and more modern. From this point of view, admittedly that of the Romantic artist and historian, the liberating power of the printed book would mean the replacement of the 'book of stone' by the 'book of paper' as society's primary form of artistic expression and thus the death of architecture in general.[84] The invention of movable type meant 'one art was going to dethrone another art'.[85] 'Ceci tuera cela' provided the historical evidence for this radical view.

The discussion traces the history of architecture from its birth in the simple raised stones of pre-literate cultures to its death in the imitative classicism of post-medieval Europe. The turning point occurs in the 15th century. Gutenberg's invention of the printing-press is 'the greatest event in history. It was the mother of revolutions.'[86] Gutenberg is the central historical figure whose 'luminous press' brings to an end the 'reign of architecture' and inaugurates the 'reign of printing'.[87] This division of history into two main periods structures the chapter and divides it approximately in half.

Architecture is obviously for Hugo not simply building. The questions of construction and function, as they are normally understood, are totally irrelevant. Architecture is a literary form of expression, giving permanence to human thought in monuments known as buildings'.[88] The architect is like a stylus who writes, 'at the dictate of the general idea of an epoch, ... those marvellous books which were also marvellous buildings'.[89] The distinction between books and buildings is intentionally vague. Hugo speaks of stone books and paper books; thought can either 'translate itself into a building' or 'become a book'.[90] But whereas a built thought and a printed thought can literally be synonymous, ideally they can not be synchronous. The difference between a book and a building is historical. Throughout the course of history, humanity has known 'two books, two registers, two testaments: masonry and printing, the bible of stone and the bible of paper'.[91] Prior to the 15th century, the books that most fully expressed human thought were made of stone and are called buildings: 'In fact, from the origin of things up to and including the fifteenth century ..., architecture was the great book of mankind, man's chief form of expression. ...'[92] It was 'the chief, the universal writing', and no idea of any importance came into being without being 'inscribed in stone'.[93]

Hugo denied the prevalent neoclassical theories of the origin and function of architecture, expressed most notably by Durand and Quatremère de Quincy.[94] Architecture did not derive from the need for shelter nor, as Quatremère claimed, from the ideal form of the primitive hut. Rather, architecture arose from the same impulse that gave birth to writing: 'Architecture began like any other form of writing.'[95] Early societies chose the medium of stone to perpetuate the thoughts and ideals that had previously been transmitted by oral tradition, for it was the most 'visible, durable and natural' one.[96] But the early forms of architecture were not imitations of nature. A column was not a tree wrought in stone but was 'a letter'; an arch was not two bent and joined trees but was 'a syllable'; a pyramid was not simply a mountain shape but was 'a word'.[97] Each architectural form evolved as a linguistic form and, when combined with others, conveyed more complex meanings. A capital resting on a column was not an artful arrangement of leaves growing out of its support but rather brought one idea to bear on another in the form of a 'hieroglyph'.[98]

The history of architecture is a history of writing. The earliest raised stone slabs or menhirs were 'letters' and thus the first step was the creation of an 'alphabet'.[99] Soon stones were joined with other stones to form 'granite syllables' which were combined to make 'words'.[100] The dolmen and the cromlech are 'words'; the Etruscan tumulus is a 'proper noun'.[101] Later, at Carnac, on the coast of Brittany, these 'words' were strung out to form 'a sentence'.[102] Such aphoristic constructions proved 'no longer adequate to contain' the growing complexity of symbolic expressions, and they were finally elaborated into 'books': 'The symbol needed to expand into a building.'[103] Architecture alone had the capacity to organize and convey all this information, and the books written by the architects of ancient Egypt, India and Israel 'fixed all this vacillating symbolism in a form at once palpable, visible and eternal'.[104] The Temple of Solomon gave both form and substance to Hebrew religious thought: 'The idea that engendered them, the word, was not only the foundation of all these buildings, it was also in their form. The Temple of Solomon, for instance, was not merely the binding of the sacred book, it was the sacred book itself.'[105] The inscribed walls of the temple made the religious teachings legible while encasing the Ark of the Covenant, which was their architectural embodiment: 'Thus the word was enclosed in the building, but its image was on the envelope like the human figure on the coffin of a mummy.'[106]

The subject-matter of the 'books of granite' which ushered in the 'age of architecture' was religious myth, symbolism and dogma.[107] That was no reason to assume, as most Romantics did, a causative relation between religious faith and architectural efflorescence. All major civilizations go through a cycle from theocracy to democracy, beginning in religious 'unity' and ending with individual 'liberty'.[108] Until the end of the 15th century, architecture was quite simply 'the total, the sovereign, the tyrannical art'.[109] No expression of thought was beyond its reach, and every civilization, whether at the beginning or end of its cycle, found the medium of architecture 'ready to write at its dictation'.[110]

While architectural books could be either religious or secular in content, their expression ranged from the 'dogmatic' to the 'seditious'.[111] All products of theocratic thought, be it Hindu, Egyptian or Romanesque, are unchanging, conventional and hieratic in form: 'You are conscious always of the priest and nothing but the priest.'[112] All products of democracy, be it Phoenician, Greek or Gothic, are progressively varied and beautifully natural in form, expressive of 'liberty, the people, man'.[113] Gothic cathedrals are transparent, 'accessible to every soul, ... as easily understood as nature'; Romanesque churches are opaque, 'they are murky books which initiates alone can decipher'.[114] The difference between theocratic and democratic architecture is the difference between a 'sacred and a profane tongue'.[115]

Hugo chose to describe the medieval European cycle as a specific case of a general phenomenon. The development from Roman-

esque to Gothic architecture was a response to the declining authority of the church and the increasing power of the commune and the bourgeoisie. Gothic churches no longer reflected the dogmatic spirit of a priestly caste but, rather, the free spirit of the people. The building of cathedrals and churches was the only outlet for the expression of this new freedom, and naturally 'whoever was then born a poet became an architect'.[116] All the intellectual energy of medieval society focused on architecture and received its expression in built form: 'The other arts all submitted to the allegiance and discipline of architecture.'[117] The architect summed up 'in his own person' all means for making contemporary thought legible and available to everyone.[118] He became the poet-editor of the epic-journal of his era and literally built with a 'freedom of architecture' akin to the modern 'freedom of the press'.[119]

The power of Gothic architecture and the freedom it enjoyed were not peculiar to it but were characteristic of the terminal stage of any civilization in the 'age of architecture'. Nevertheless, the Gothic period occupies a special place in history, for it not only consummated the medieval cycle; it also brought to a close the 'age of architecture' itself. With the invention of the printing-press in the middle of the 15th century, 'architecture is dethroned'.[120] A new historical era opened and it was characterized by the predominance of a new medium of communication: 'It was the total renewal of man's mode of expression, the human mind sloughing off one form to put on another.'[121] The printed book replaced the built book as 'the human intellect ... deserted architecture for the printing-press'.[122] Architecture lost its hegemony and hence its *raison d'être*.

The struggle for primacy between printing and architecture lasted less than a century. Architecture was doomed for essentially the same material reasons that had once given it the advantage over the manuscript. The printed book was 'more lasting and resistant than architecture'.[123] Books were also 'simpler' and 'easier' to produce than buildings and they could thus be made 'more quickly' and reach more people with less expense and effort.[124] The book's mechanical reproducibility made it seem virtually 'indestructible'. Where thought had previously been given the 'resistance' and strength of stone, it now became 'indelible' on paper; where it had been 'durable', it now became 'immortal'.[125] The book's reproducibility also gave it the power of numbers. Thought in built form has a limited sphere of influence; in print it becomes 'ubiquitous'.[126]

A corollary of the book's 'ubiquity' is its transparency and insubstantiality: 'In its printed form, thought is ... volatile, elusive.'[127] A building embodies thought and makes that thought substantial. The substance itself is felt to be pregnant with meaning and thus the body of the building is considered sacred. The idea of a building is 'the form of that idea'.[128] The physical form of a printed book bears no impress of its content: 'Words are not things.'[129] The words printed on its pages represent thought in such an abstract way as to desanctify the medium. This intrinsically modern quality of the printed word ultimately made the book seem more efficacious and, therefore, more suitable as a medium: 'Henceforth the elusive will reign supreme. Nothing nor anyone will be able to seize a thought as one might lay hold of a body. Thought is bodiless.'[130]

The printing-press was both an agent of secularization and a harbinger of democracy. Architecture had always been fundamentally religious in being a form of materially sanctified thought. The invention of printing thus made all previous history seem like one long preliminary stage of theocracy as 'the human mind, volatilized by the press, evaporate[d] from the theocratic receptacle.'[131] As feudal and ecclesiastical authority declined, 'thought itself was everywhere being set free'.[132] The very substantiality of architecture proved recalcitrant to the containment and expression of the rapid developments of modern thought. By contrast, the disembodied form of the printed word could project ideas as volatile, elusive images – a possibility denied the constructed word by the laws of tectonics.

Following the invention of movable type, architecture's evolution was cut short. A process of decomposition and disintegration of architectural form occurred in proportion to the development and expansion of the printing industry. Already, by the second half of the 15th century, 'architecture gradually dried up, it atrophied, and was denuded'; but only in the 16th century did 'architecture's malady' become manifest.[133] The two major symptoms were classicism and the specialization of the arts.

Ironically, these had always been mistaken for signs of a rebirth: 'This was the decadence we call the Renaissance.'[134] The Renaissance is a misnomer. Its architecture 'was no longer the essential expression of society', for the reuse of Greek and Roman forms was a graft of foreign tissue serving only to conceal the decay.[135] Whatever vitality architecture preserved during that moment of transition is attributable to the survival of the Gothic spirit, 'that sun which was setting behind the giant press of Mainz, [and which] still shed its dying rays for a time that hybrid mass of Latin arcades and corinthian colonnades'.[136] This distinction between form and content was hardly understood at the time and, from the mid-16th century on, architects laboured under the illusion that the spirit of revival was contained in the classical forms: 'It was this setting sun which we take to be a dawn.'[138] In his design for St Peter's, Michelangelo 'piled the Pantheon on the Parthenon'.[137] It was the last building based on an 'original' idea, but it was 'a despairing idea'.[139] Having nothing else to express, architects 'imitated' and 'parodied' works such as this during the following two centuries.[140] The Val de Grâce, the Panthéon, St Paul's in London and St Isaac's in Leningrad represent the 'last ravings of a great art in its decline, which relapsed into infancy before it died'.[141]

As architecture was 'abandoned' by creative thought during the Renaissance, the other arts disengaged themselves from the former ruling body of architecture and began to flourish on their own.[142] Once architecture became 'merely one art among others', it no longer had arms to do battle with printing.[143] The printed book moved in for the kill: 'The printed book ate its way into buildings like a worm, and bled and devoured them.'[144] Buildings were reduced to the 'cold and inexorable lines of the geometer', and began to look like nothing so much as 'the bone-structure of some emaciated invalid'.[145] In the process, architecture was denuded of all significance: 'It became mean, impoverished, null. It no longer expressed anything. . . . '[146]

During the three centuries of architecture's 'desperation' and 'misery', the printed book grew into the strongest force of the modern world.[147] By the end of the 18th century, it had destroyed not only architecture but the *ancien régime* itself. In the 19th century, it would help 'rebuild' society.[148] The printing-press was relentlessly spewing forth 'fresh materials' for work.[149] Swelling the continuing stream of individual books was now the collective effort of a new force – the daily newspaper.[150] By 1830, the entire human race was on the 'scaffolding' of the colossal 'metropolis of the universal mind' that was being built of paper and ink.[151] Mankind's 'second Tower of Babel' was rising as an inviolable sanctuary for the products of human intelligence.[152]

Writing in the heat of the events of the summer of 1830 and recalling the role of the printing-press in the Revolution of 1789, Hugo saw absolutely no reason to think that architecture would play any part in the shaping of modern society. He saw no hope whatsoever for its revival and concluded categorically: 'Let there be no mistake, architecture is dead, dead beyond recall, killed by the printed book.'[153]

Hugo's verdict flew in the face of the classical utopian tradition, which ascribed to architecture an inexhaustible regenerative power. That tradition, having just produced two of its most splendid visions in Ledoux's Ideal City of Chaux and Fourier's proposal for a phalanstery, flourished in the first third of the 19th century as never before. It should, therefore, have come as no surprise to Hugo that, within less than two years of its publication, 'Ceci tuera cela' was singled out for a scathing attack by Victor Considérant, one of Charles Fourier's leading apostles. Considérant's denunciation of Hugo's theory came as the conclusion to his description in 1834 of the architectural wonders of the phalanstery. He ridiculed the 'foolishness' and 'childishness' of the belief that 'man could no longer create poetry except with pens!'[154] He refuted the idea that architecture had always been, 'uniquely' and 'simplistically', a form of poetry.[155] Considérant warned artists against listening to those who maintain that architecture is 'dead and buried', for architecture's vitality depends upon the social programme it is called on to fulfil: 'The ASSOCIATIVE ARCHITECTONICS [of the phalanstery] . . . opens up for art . . . an unexpected and unprecedented future.'[156] Considérant ended by advising Hugo to eliminate the added chapters from future editions, for 'such chapters do not do credit to his intelligence'.[157]

Hugo, of course, never took Considérant's advice. But he had already softened the eschatological tone of 'Ceci tuera cela' with the curiously apologetic 'Note' he wrote in October 1832 to accompany the definitive edition. In that, he began by defending his belief in the 'almost inevitable' death of architecture as 'a view, unhappily, deeply rooted in him and deeply pondered'.[158] As if in response to specific criticism, he then added that he 'very much wants the future one day to prove him wrong'.[159] Finally, he backed down enough to admit that while he was 'afraid' his dire conclusion would prove true, he could no longer be sure.[160] There was evidence, especially in the student ateliers, of much 'embryonic' talent and no reason not to expect it to germinate: 'The seed is in the furrow, and the crop assuredly will be a good one.'[161] Hugo noted that it was 'particularly' among the students of architecture that 'there is today so much life, so much potential, so much what one might call predestination'.[162] 'Execrable' teachers were, despite themselves, producing 'excellent' students![163]

While it is possible Hugo received criticism from several people before deciding to publish 'Ceci tuera cela', the nature of the disclaimer in the 'Note' definitely points to his discussions with Labrouste. All the optimistic references directly relate to the latter's interests and concerns as one just beginning his professional career. Labrouste would certainly have agreed both with Hugo's characterization of the leading teachers as 'execrable' and with his overall description of the 'current decadence' of architecture. But he would have presented to Hugo, in return, a much more encouraging view of the future, backed up by an intimate awareness of the changes taking place.

In a letter to Louis Duc of 1 July 1831, Labrouste spoke of 'the odious abuses and privileges which have placed education . . . in the hands of a few charlatans and condemned art to a shameful stagnation'.[164] Soon after the July Revolution, Labrouste had described to Duc the 'disgust' and 'discouragement' felt by students at the Ecole des Beaux-Arts as a result of 'the insufficiencies of a sterile architecture which could no longer express their feelings'.[165] Labrouste organized his own atelier in the summer of 1830 in an effort to remedy the existing situation. By the autumn of 1832, the effects of the new Romantic ideas were beginning to be felt. Despite his involvement in the abortive reform of the Ecole in 1831 and the ostracism of his atelier by the official jury, Labrouste never wavered in his commitment to revitalize French architecture nor his confidence in the ultimate success of this effort. It is extremely doubtful that Hugo's abstract argument could have dimmed his hopes. Quite the contrary, Labrouste's convictions were probably reinforced by having to confront Hugo's views.

Indeed, shortly after that experience, Labrouste wrote to Duc that if the study of history was to serve a 'truly useful' purpose it should lead to 'encouraging conclusions'.[166] He characterized as 'poisonous' any view of history that results only in 'depressing and discouraging thoughts'.[167] As an example of a more healthy optimism, Labrouste referred to an article by Charles Magnin, published on 15 July 1832 in the *Revue des deux-mondes*, in which the Romantic critic said he believed that before long architecture would be restored to its rightful role as 'the leading art, the one on which all the others depend'.[168] Magnin, Labrouste wrote, 'has not lost hope . . . As for me, neither have I.'[169]

Magnin's argument followed Hugo's closely in tracing the decadence of contemporary architecture back to its roots in the early Renaissance. But Magnin assumed, in contrast to Hugo, that the loss of religious unity and faith during the 15th century was the ultimate cause of architecture's 'decomposition'.[170] This allowed him to conclude that architecture would return to give moral sustenance to mankind when, out of the 'impalpable cloud of ideas that surrounds us, some system of belief will take shape, something lasting, and which deserves to be expressed in that monumental language'.[171]

Magnin's views were those of most Romantic architects and critics. The problems of contemporary architecture were blamed on the lack of religious or social unity.[172] Architecture had lost its direction and purpose because there was no longer any coherent body of myths or beliefs or moral or social principles to express. The 19th century's incapacity to originate an architectural style was symptomatic of the situation. A belief in architectural resurgence was therefore most often linked with a Utopian social or religious programme.

Labrouste might well have read Magnin's article as an antidote to Hugo. It echoed his own sense of hope and thus answered his main criticism of Hugo. But compared with the audacity and rigour of Hugo's argument, Magnin's was conventional and sentimental.

Hugo's description of the 'death of architecture' was grounded in a dialectical understanding of history. It grew out of his previous analysis of the modernity of the drama in the 'Preface' to *Cromwell* and paralleled Hegel's contemporary discussion of the successive primacy of each of the arts. While Hugo defined the nature and limits of architecture as a medium transformed by cultural change, Magnin profferred an idealistic, unchanging image of architecture as a passive receptacle for religious thought. To agree with Magnin's rosy view of the future provided very little to build on, since all one could really do was wait. Ironically, an understanding of the limitations Hugo placed on architecture could serve a direct and positive end by forcing the architect to reconsider the expressive character of the medium.

'Ceci tuera cela' was not just a message of doom. It laid the ghost of architecture inherited from the Renaissance, but, in so doing, revealed another conception of it. Hugo himself provided the key in elaborating on what the future held in store for the art of building. The broad vision of a 'reign of printing' succeeding the 'reign of architecture', with books taking over the representative function of buildings, was, of course, the central theme of the chapter. But obviously something related to what had been called architecture would still exist. Buildings would, of necessity, continue to be built. Hugo even allowed that a 'fine' building or two might result, and admitted that an 'architect of genius' could come forth in the near future (*ecce* Frank Lloyd Wright!).[173] Even a 'masterpiece' was possible, 'now and again'.[174] But none of this would betoken a rebirth of architecture, for the advent of an architectural genius would simply be an 'accident' of history and the great building would always remain an 'isolated' example.[175]

The fact was that architecture had lost its original significance and was no longer *archi-tecture*. Since the leading talent and major energies of society were inevitably to be channelled through another medium, architecture had ceased to be 'the social, the collective, the dominant art'.[176] Buildings might still perform important functions and even affect people emotionally; but *building* would no longer be a force for social integration nor its symbolic expression: 'The great poem, the great edifice, the great creation of mankind will no longer be built, it will be printed.'[177]

124 Bibliothèque Ste-Geneviève: Reading Room, looking east from the west end, with the term representing Day in the right foreground.

The 'death of architecture' was in effect a redefinition of architecture, both as a medium and as a mode of expression. It was not so much that architecture as a medium had lost its dominion over the other arts but rather that the architectural mode of expression had lost its hold over the medium itself and now failed to define it. The four-hundred-year history of the disintegration of architectural content was to be matched by a collateral erosion of architectural form.

The message of 'Ceci tuera cela' was that the proliferation of printed matter would alter the form of buildings as radically as their significance. Architects would have to readjust their sights accordingly. If buildings were to express anything, they would have to cease being 'architectural' and become 'literary' in character: 'And in future, should architecture accidentally revive, it will no longer be master. It will be subject to the law of literature, which once received the law from it.'[178] The poems written in ancient India, Egypt, Greece and medieval Europe during the 'age of architecture' were architectural in form and 'resemble buildings'.[179] In the future, buildings would be literary in form and resemble books. Whereas books had once been verbal constructions, now buildings would become a form of imprinted matter. The literary analogy would impose its characteristic distinction between form and content and dispel the illusion of unity in the articulate figures of classical speech.

There is no way of being sure what Labrouste thought of this when he read it in manuscript in late 1830 or early 1831. Aside from the disagreement over the question of architecture's future prospects, there is no evidence of what each said to the other. The manuscript of 'Ceci tuera cela' contains no substantive changes.[179a] Did Labrouste fundamentally agree with Hugo's reasoning? It is just a matter of guessing whether he immediately realized the positive implications of Hugo's thought or whether that only happened over the next few years.

IV

Six years after 'Ceci tuera cela' was published, Labrouste received his first important commission. The Bibliothèque Ste-Geneviève was designed in 1838–39 following the govern-   103 ment's decision to move the library from the attic of the nearby Lycée Henri IV, which it had occupied since the 17th century, when it was the library of the abbey of Ste-Geneviève.[180] The new library was built from 1843 to 1850, during which time Labrouste worked out in detail the building's decorative programme. The ground floor of the two-storeyed building is divided in half by a vestibule, which separates the book-stacks on the left from the collection of manuscripts, prints and drawings and rare books on the right, and leads to a stairwell at

121, 124 the rear. The entire upper floor is a book-lined Reading Room, originally gas-lit and with seating for over four hundred. The great majority of its users, by 1840, were the students in the Latin Quarter, and the building was therefore designed by Labrouste as a 'Bibliothèque d'Etude' rather than a research library.[181]

The Bibliothèque Ste-Geneviève is a long, unrelieved, narrow box of a building that stretches along the north side of the Place du Panthéon like a blind Roman aqueduct. In its utilitarian blandness, it contrasts sharply with Soufflot's domed and colonnaded church, 'the finest spongecake ever made out of stone' according to Hugo.[182] Nothing would seem to illustrate more perfectly Hugo's contention that modern architecture had succumbed to the deathly grip of a 'cold' geometry which turned buildings into mere 'polyhedrons' and gave them the emaciated look of skeletons.[183] But unlike the classical buildings Hugo had in mind, Labrouste's library does not 'conceal this bareness' with superfluous pediments, porticoes, pilasters and cartouches.[184] It is flat, chaste and uniform. All its decorative elements are contained within clearly defined outlines that form the dominating framework of the structure. The decoration seems to be appliquéd or printed on the surface, and the repetitive and mechanical quality of it gives one the impression of looking at a sheet of newsprint.

122 Labrouste's own perspective rendering of the library, published as an engraving in the *Revue générale de l'architecture*, makes the building look as if it had just rolled off the presses.[185] The continuous surface that wraps around the volume is rigidly compartmented. An overall grid of vertical and horizontal lines contains the composition like a 'form' arranged and locked in a 'chase'. Within each bay thin vertical 'rules' divide the surface into 'columns' of print. These are enclosed in 'boxes' by

125 Bibliothèque Ste-Geneviève: cast-iron patera with the library's monogram, on the ground floor of the façade.

vertical 'margins' and horizontal decorative 'slugs'. The whole composition is underlined by a continuous reglet, much as the day's headline stories might be set off from the *feuilleton* below. Black iron dots in the spandrels make a line of punctuation above; while, below, the iron disks, or paterae, supporting the

125 garland fillet are impressed with the interlaced SG of the library's book-stamp.[186] The metal biting into the cream-coloured stone leaves a black deposit on the surface like print on paper and stamps the building as a book.

The most striking aspect of the exterior decoration is the series of 810 names of authors inscribed in chronological order on the tables set in the arcade. The insistent regularity of the approximately 7,000 letters made this seem a meaningless and 'puerile' device to many of Labrouste's contemporaries.[187] The letters were originally painted red, which intensified the papery quality of the surface and the literalness of its decoration. The young architect Achille Hermant thought the façade looked like a 'calendar', a reference made all the more pointed by the recent publication of Auguste Comte's *Calendrier positiviste*.[188] The writer Théodore de Banville felt that the idea was good but that it was done 'too naïvely, like a page of writing'.[189] Hermant, however, considered both the idea and the execution too simple and mechanical: seen from up close, the names are just 'words'; seen from a distance they become simply 'embroidery on the stone'.[190] Such abstraction was the unavoidable result of imitating the medium of print in stone, and Labrouste did it deliberately.

The inscriptions are a sign or quick-reference

directory. Labrouste likened the façade to a 'monumental catalogue'.[191] The columns of print list the contents of the building and the names spell out the reflexive relationship between outside and inside. As Labrouste explained, 'the names of the principal authors or writers whose works are in the library' are written in large letters at just the place on the façade 'that corresponds to the bookshelves inside containing their books.'[192] The decorative horizontal friezes define the tops of the two levels of the shelves; the thin, embedded lotus columns mark the positions of the shelf uprights; and the individual letters fill out their lines like books leaning against one another, or, as the critic for the *Journal des débats* wrote, 'like the title placed on the spine of a good book'.[193]

The straightforward character and arrangement of the letters is crucial in making the reflexivity of form and content as transparent and as abstract as that which obtains in reading a book. The building's external form is read as the binding, its title being the table of contents. One is reminded of Hugo's description of the Temple of Solomon where 'the word was enclosed in the building, but its image was on the envelope'.[194] But then, as Hugo pointed out, in the 'age of architecture' the building 'was not merely the binding of the sacred book, it was the sacred book itself'.[195] The 'principal decoration' of the Bibliothèque Ste-Geneviève advertises the fact that the building is only a functional form of packaging.[196] The printed books inside are the building's content and give it form: 'The books themselves', Labrouste explained, 'are the most beautiful ornament of the interior.'[197]

The conflict between the book and the building and the historical consequences described by Hugo determined both the iconography of the Bibliothèque Ste-Geneviève and its formal structure. The central theme of enlightenment is epitomized in Raymond 127, Balze's circular tapestry entitled *L'Etude*, set 129 in the centre panel of the main door of the Reading Room. Labrouste proposed the subject of the tapestry to Balze after working closely with him and his brother Paul throughout the second half of 1849, installing their 135 copy of Raphael's *School of Athens* in the library's stairwell.[198]

126 A variant of the executed design, produced by Balze in the following year, depicts a pensive female figure, representing Study,

placed between a book and a building.[199] The building is a diminutive version of the library. The book, opposite it, is opened out on a globe, and the figure taking notes is leaning on the building, using it as a prop. Compared with the building, the book is gigantic, and, though slender, it conceals the globe from the figure. The globe, traditionally used in library design as a symbol of knowledge, is here used as a lectern.[200] It is, like the library, a functional piece of furniture. The open book becomes the source of universal knowledge. It cuts across the setting sun, 'that sun which was setting behind the giant press of Mainz', and is bathed in a circle of light that excludes the face of the building, 'that hybrid mass of Latin arcades'.[201] As night is drawn over the scene by a genie whose torch is dying out just above the building, a second genie illuminates the book.

On a simple level, the link between artificial illumination and intellectual enlightenment alludes to the fact that the Bibliothèque Ste-Geneviève was alone among French libraries in being open after dark.[202] But Balze's design points to another level of the building's meaning. The attainment of knowledge is symbolized by the light of a book contrasting with and, literally, emerging out of the darkness of a building. The book on the globe has just been plucked from its shelf formed by an arcade of the building. The building is just a bookcase. Balze rendered the purport of Labrouste's imagery explicit by showing the building as a container or binding having no independent or ideal content. The books in their cases are separated by inscribed piers, like the sarcophagi of the Malatesta court humanists in the lateral 128 arcade of Alberti's S. Francesco at Rimini, recalling the source of the library's style in the delicate literary classicism of the quattrocento.[203]

The design chosen to be executed at the 12ʒ Gobelins factory in 1850–53 differs in some important respects from the one that Balze later published as a lithograph in 1864 and 126 again, somewhat modified, in 1876.[204] Most of the changes are compositional, opening it up and giving a greater sense of breadth and scale to the central figure. The most significant iconographical difference is the replacement of the model of the Bibliothèque Ste-Geneviève by a funereal antique altar. In compensation for the disappearance of the building, the references to reading have been increased. The

126　R. Balze. *L'Etude*, drawn in 1850 and lithographed in 1864. (Coll. Léon Malcotte, Paris)

127　Bibliothèque Ste-Geneviève: tapestry in the Reading Room of *L'Etude*, by R. Balze.

128　H. Labrouste. Detail of the lateral arcade of S. Francesco at Rimini, 1830. (Bibliothèque Nationale)

129　Bibliothèque Ste-Geneviève: Reading Room, looking north to the main door. In the centre is the tapestry of *L'Etude*.

130　Bibliothèque Ste-Geneviève: vestibule, with the monument to Ulrich Gering *in situ* in the stairwell at the end.

more solemn figure now holds two notebooks; and a second book has been placed behind the one on the globe. It is opened on a lectern and is silhouetted against the setting sun. The 'luminous press of Gutenberg' divides darkness from light in both versions, while the unqualified and increased presence of books in the executed one makes the symbolic meaning of the concept even more pronounced.[205]

The tapestry is the last major element of the library's decoration to be seen by someone using the building. In it, architecture has been overshadowed and disembodied by the book. It is significant that, for the spot seen immediately on entering the building, Labrouste originally planned a decorative relief glorifying the invention of the printed book. The vestibule of the library is deep and cavernous, and it takes the eye some time to adjust to its relative darkness. Straight ahead, before the stairs split, a high raking light comes down from a hidden source and dramatically spotlights a flat section of the rear wall of the stairwell. The bank of steps leading up to the landing makes a high pedestal for it. Probably some time after the middle of 1848, Labrouste sketched an idea for a plaque to be set in the wall where a commemorative inscription was finally placed.[206] It shows three busts aligned as in a Republican Roman funerary relief. Only the central figure's name is spelled out: 'GUTTEMBERG'. The two flanking figures were undoubtedly to be Johann Fust and Peter Schoeffer, Gutenberg's collaborators in Mainz. There is a halo of writing around Gutenberg's head, which subordinates the two other figures to him.

The trinitarian composition of the relief, its axial placement within an arch, and the dramatic lighting would have served to enshrine Gutenberg. At the end of the nave formed by the piers of the vestibule, his image might well have illustrated Hugo's description of the 'saviour' who emerged from the 'terrible darkness' to bring 'deliverance to man through the printing-press':[207]

> Gutenberg is a redeemer ... Printing is the discovery of the inexhaustible. ... This prodigy has saved the human intellect ... Nothing can be accomplished without him. He marks the transition from slavery to freedom.
> ... Gutenberg is like a second Father of the creations of the mind.[208]

The dedication of the focal point of a Parisian building, albeit a library, to Gutenberg and the glorification of him and his two German assistants seems an extraordinary idea for the time. It is true that a monumental bronze statue of Gutenberg by David d'Angers was erected in Strasbourg just a few years earlier (1840), and had caused a great show of public interest.[209] But Gutenberg lived and worked in that city, whereas he had no connection whatsoever with Paris or the former library of the abbey of Ste-Geneviève. In the end, parochialism held sway, and the relief portraying Gutenberg was rejected in favour of a bureaucratic inscription recording the essential stages in the library's history – its establishment in 1624, its nationalization in 1790 and the completion of its new building in 1850. The administrator of the Bibliothèque Ste-Geneviève, Balard de Lancy, provided Labrouste with the wording of the inscription in May 1850; and it was engraved with the same red-painted letters used for the names of the authors on the façade.

The inscription on the rear wall of the stairwell is seen after the names on the upper part of the façade and reads like the lower section of the title page in a book. It spells out the provenance and present location of all copies of the works of authors listed in the 'monumental catalogue'. Ironically, the bust of Gutenberg would have been a more abstract form of information than print, for it would have located the source of the riches of the library's collection in the invention of printing itself. Gutenberg's image would have appeared between the name of the author outside and his books upstairs as a persistent reminder that 'nothing can be accomplished without him'. His presence, like an earlier age's image of Christ or a monarch, would have given body to the meaning of the building.

By a fortuitous circumstance of history, Labrouste was able to realize this intention, though much later and through a different persona. In the 1860s, Ferdinand Denis, who succeeded de Lancy and Frédéric de Brotonne as head of the library, thought to erect a

131   H. Labrouste. Study for a plaque in the stairwell of the Bibliothèque Ste-Geneviève, 1848–49. (Bibliothèque Nationale)

132 H. Labrouste. Study for the pedestal of the Gering monument, 1872–73. (Bibliothèque Nationale)

133 Bibliothèque Ste-Geneviève: bust of Ulrich Gehring by Daumas, 1870, 1872–74: pedestal by Labrouste, 1872–74. (Shown *in situ* below the inscription in the library stairwell. Now in the Dépôt des Oeuvres d'Art de l'Etat, Fonds National d'Art Contemporain, Paris)

monument to honour Ulrich Gering, the man who introduced printing to Paris.[210] Gering was brought to Paris in the late 1460s by the rector of the Sorbonne to establish the first printing-press in France in one of the university's buildings on the slopes of the Montagne Ste-Geneviève. In 1470, he published his first book, *Gasparini Barizii Pergamensis epistolae*, and was accorded French citizenship by Louis XI. Gering died in 1510, and left part of his estate to the Collège de Montaigu, the building torn down to make way for Labrouste's library. It was believed by many, including Denis, that Gering was buried in the school's chapel and that his remains were, therefore, under the library. Denis felt that no more appropriate spot could be found to erect a memorial to the man. Labrouste used the opportunity to rededicate the building to the product of the printing-press.

At the suggestion of Denis, the sculptor Louis Daumas did a bust of Gering, which was 13 exhibited in the Salon of 1870. He carved a marble version in 1872–74 and Labrouste designed a pedestal for it.[211] The monument was set up in 1874 against the lower portion of the rear wall of the stairwell, just below the inscription, where the Gutenberg plaque was to have been. It was removed in the early 1950s to make way for an entrance to a public toilet.[212] As a post-construction addition that once had great significance and then disappeared, it reminds us of the word 'ΑΝΑΓΚΗ'.

Daumas' hoary image of Gering gave Gutenberg's Parisian alter ego a patriarchal air. Labrouste's base of hard-cut, contrasting, geometric elements raised Gering's head above the frame of the inscription, and its abstractness emphasized the fleshiness of the bust. Under Gering's name, Labrouste placed a stone replica of the first book printed in Paris. He gave it prominence by placing it at the point where a lower block of stone intersected the pedestal and by treating it in an overly realistic manner. The print on its soft pages was coloured and the book seemed even more palpable than Gering, whose image was blurred by the field of print behind him.

Labrouste turned the Gering memorial into an honorific lectern that was a monument to his book. The book was opened to its title page, revealing the date, 1470. It was tilted back to catch the light and was directly in 130 the line of sight of a person entering the build-

134 Bibliothèque Ste-Geneviève: vestibule, looking south-west, showing busts of Poussin, Corneille and Racine below painted trees by Alexandre Desgoffe.

having a half-indoor, half-outdoor quality. The piers stand like trees with green iron boughs under a ceiling once painted blue like the sky. The illusion of an outdoor pavilion or grove, like Plato's Academy, is completed by the painted trees appearing just above the low side walls.[213] Two rows of busts, facing one another, are set on these podia under the 'shade' of the trees.[214] They represent eminent French writers, scientists, philosophers and artists, and are arranged chronologically from the entrance to the stairwell.[215] A succession of busts of famous men, placed against bookcases, was the

conventional way of decorating galleries and [16] Labrouste abstracted that sculptural from its direct association with books, it chronologically and condensed it ree-dimensional sign. The busts inside the letters of the 'monumental cata- utside into three-dimensional images, the vestibule into a 'living catalogue'. usts are divided by engaged piers into groups of three. The triple image of the Guten- 131 berg plaque would have linked the two rows in a group portrait in the middle, raised as if on a dais. The single point of focus provided by Gering is compensated for by his book. Either sculptural image would have located the historical 'transition' from the manuscript to print at the turning point of the building; and the building's circulation spine would have described the connection between the individuals, named and carved below, and their mass-produced books in the Reading Room above.

The iconography of the Bibliothèque Ste-

135 Bibliothèque Ste-Geneviève: upper landing, with copies of Raphael's *School of Athens* and *Philosophy* by the Balze brothers.

136 Bibliothèque Ste-Geneviève: stairwell, with the tondo of *Jurisprudence* left of the entrance to the Reading Room.

Geneviève is set out in chapters or 'sections', each written in a different medium. The Gering monument completed the sculptural definition of the library's vestibule, and, being slightly elevated, it also introduced the final two parts of the sequence. The upper landing 14? of the stairwell is defined pictorially. The 148 Balzes' copy of the *School of Athens* hangs just 13? above where Gering was, as an illusionistic counterpart to the arches that open opposite 13(it into the book-lined Reading Room.[217] Copies, in the form of tondos, of the figures of Theology, Jurisprudence, Philosophy and 13? Poetry, also from the Stanza della Segnatura, are set like medallions in the upper corners of the two facing walls and complete the painted decoration of the stairwell.[218]

Because the *School of Athens* is at floor level and is seen so close-up and in such a tight space, it loses its historical distance and invites one to imagine that all learning and knowledge have been placed within the reach of everyman. Any anxiety over how to begin sifting through the 'Babel' of information produced by the invention of printing is at the same time allayed by the sense of order in the broad divisions of scholarship outlined by the *School of Athens*. The four tondos give an even clearer picture of the public library's method of organizing its collection. The subject classifications of the tondos correspond almost exactly to the five main divisions of the library's catalogue at the time, which were theology, jurisprudence, history, arts and sciences, and belles-lettres.[219] And although Labrouste knew that the Raphael figure represented Philosophy rather than History, he seems to have so utterly convinced himself of its significance in his building that he almost always called it History.[220] Labrouste intended the correspondence between the pictorial and printed versions to be legible, for inside the Reading Room, in the two blind arcades directly behind the 138 tondos, he placed what are in effect the printed 139 versos of these medallions. They spell out the five main subject classifications of the catalogue.

The paintings on the walls of the stairwell turn that preparatory space into an 'illustrated catalogue raisonné' prefiguring the actual cata-logue of printed books on the other side of the wall. Directly opposite the door, against the southern arcade, is the library's Main Reference Desk. It is pedimented and looks 137 like an Early Christian ambo.[221] It was designed to house the multivolume catalogue of printed books, arranged both by author and by subject. It faces the circular tapestry of *L'Etude* below 129 the level of the subject headings of the printed medallions.

The images referring to the library's catalogue progress from the primary and more objective level, an engraved and carved 'author cata-logue', to the higher and more subjective level, a painted and printed 'subject catalogue'. The names on the exterior walls are translated into busts, as Raphael's figures are transcribed back into words on the interior walls. The unfolding sequence recalls Hugo's description of the transformations of the lithic word in the Temple of Solomon: 'From each of its concentric ring-walls the priests could read the word translated and made manifest to the eye, and could thus follow its transformations from sanctuary to sanctuary until, in its ultimate tabernacle, they could grasp it in its most concrete yet still

137   Bibliothèque Ste-Geneviève: Main Reference Desk in the Reading Room.

architectural form: the Ark.'[222] In the Temple of Solomon, the sacred tabernacle was a product of architecture. In the Bibliothèque Ste-Geneviève, the tabernacle is the wooden Reference Desk containing the modern library's 'bible of paper' – the 'most concrete' form of the building's catalogue.

138 Bibliothèque Ste-Geneviève: copy in the stairwell of Raphael's *Jurisprudence*, by the Balze brothers (see ill. 136).

139 Bibliothèque Ste-Geneviève: medallion in the Reading Room, back-to-back with the tondo of *Jurisprudence*.

V

It might be argued that the literary symbolism of the Bibliothèque Ste-Geneviève has less to do with Hugo than with the fact that the building is a library. But just a brief list of some of the most important early 19th-century libraries, such as Jules de Joly's for the Chambre des Députés (1828–38), Schinkel's project for the National Library of Berlin (1835), Smirke's British Museum (1823 *et seq.*), Gärtner's Munich Staatsbibliothek (1832–43), Visconti's projects for the Bibliothèque Nationale (1829 *et seq.*) and Cockerell's Cambridge University Library (1837–42), should indicate that the imagery of Labrouste's library was at the very least unconventional.[223] In order to see how the formal structure of the building gives further evidence of the effect of 'Ceci tuera cela', the most telling comparison would be with the archetypal neoclassical library design, Boullée's project of 1785 140 for the reconstruction of the Bibliothèque Nationale. Labrouste owned an engraving of the Boullée project; it may very well be that its simple, open, amphitheatric space influenced his conception of the Bibliothèque Ste-Geneviève. Raphael's *School of Athens* is central to both designs, and the way each architect used it gives the clearest indication of how their conceptions of architecture differed.

Boullée proposed to transform the court of the Bibliothèque Nationale into an 'immense skylit basilica' of a Reading Room.[224] He covered it with a coffered barrel vault terminating in 'triumphal arches' that frame allegorical statues of classical divinities, the one visible in the drawing being Minerva. Four rising tiers of bookshelves define the floor as an arena and turn the room into a 'vast amphitheatre', in which, according to Boullée, the nation's 'literary riches could be presented' in a 'spectacle of books'.[225] The entrance was to have been through a portico of colossal Corinthian columns, facing on a public square at the far end, and forming a noble proscenium.[226]

Boullée intended the building to be inspirational – an 'imposing' image of man's

140 E.-L. Boullée. Project for the reconstruction of the Bibliothèque Royale (later Nationale),
1785: reading room. (Bibliothèque Nationale)

intellectual achievements.[227] He wanted the architectural 'tableau' presented by the room to embody the elevating thought its books contained, and so he peopled it with figures in antique dress. They are reading, discussing, drawing and explaining their discoveries to one another, and are supposed to convince us that the 'spirits' of the classical authors are there in the room inspiring in us 'the desire to follow in the footsteps of these great men'.[228] The books themselves are not enough and are represented as actors in an architectural equivalent of a stage set.

Boullée believed that architecture could vie with painting, poetry and the theatre in producing images of public significance. Indeed, he felt that architecture had the advantage in that a building could give concrete reality to images which a painting or a poem could only suggest or evoke in the mind.[229] But, by the same token, architecture was therefore a secondary or dependent form of expression. Boullée always spoke of his projects for buildings as 'tableaux' or 'images' and thought of himself as a painter.[230] He prefaced his essay on the art

of architecture with the epigraph 'Ed io anche son pittore.'[231] His project for the Bibliothèque Nationale was in fact an attempt to embody the meaning of Raphael's School of Athens in architecture by consciously imitating the painting: 'Profoundly struck by the sublime conception of Raphael's School of Athens, I sought to realize it.'[232]

Boullée's use of the School of Athens is diametrically opposed to Labrouste's. To begin with, Labrouste used a copy of it, whereas Boullée imitated it. In the Bibliothèque Ste-Geneviève, the copy takes its place as one of the many signs on the building's walls. In Boullée's project, the image of the School of Athens transforms the whole building into a single, pronounced metaphor. In the Bibliothèque Ste-Geneviève, the School of Athens is read as part of a sequence of what might best be called descriptive passages. Its placement is significant and it requires an active effort on our part to determine its contextual meaning. In Boullée's project it is a constructed figure of speech that 'imposes' an ideal meaning on the audience of passive spectators.

135

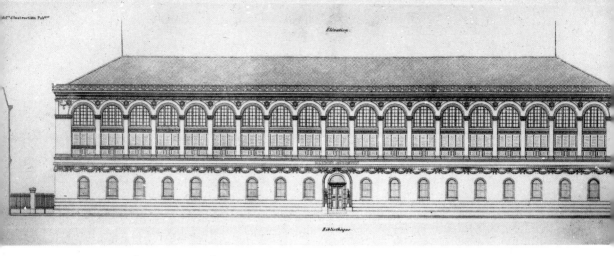

141   Bibliothèque Ste-Geneviève: façade. (From Gourlier et al., *Choix d'édifices publics*, III, 1850)

Boullée's library presents a pre-Gutenberg world in which, as he said, 'the service will be almost as prompt as the spoken word'.[233] While some of the figures in togas consult manuscripts and one looks at a globe, most are gesticulating in one way or another, engaged in animated discussion or declaiming their thoughts aloud. The schema of the *School of Athens* gives this world an illusion of time-lessness and placelessness. That appearance of classical unity depends on a belief in the ultimate reciprocity of idea and substance. It is a theatrical or pictorial form of illusionism which must be viewed utterly vicariously if it is to be accepted.[234] The time that elapses is unlike the time spent in reading. It is the virtual time of listening to music, going to the theatre, or looking at a painting. The image projected by the building is perceived all at once, like the appearance of an image on canvas or the sound of a voice.

If history painting was the model for Boullée's architecture, the printed book was the model for Labrouste's. The formal structure of the Bibliothèque Ste-Geneviève is serial rather than epiphanic. When the building was finished, one of the librarians described it as a series of graphic signs that are revealed progressively and read in time. Henry Trianon noted that 'the decorative system of the architect develops grad-ually'.[235] He particularly remarked on the legible character of the decoration: 'In the spherical cavity of each [patera] can be *read* the monogram of Sainte-Geneviève'; 'on the façade . . . can be *read* the names of 810 writers'; the small stone patera 'located right above the

entrance has the resounding date 1848 *inscribed* in its cavity'; and 'in climbing the nine steps leading to the first landing, on the rear wall, just below the large painting [of the *School of Athens*] of which we can as yet only see the frame, we *read* the following inscription . . .'[236] It is especially noteworthy that Trianon even described some of the pictorial decoration as a written form of expression. He noted that the painted trees of the vestibule are all of different species, chosen in relation to the bust they frame, and called that 'a noble and gracious commentary to write above the heads of great men'.[237] The idea was doubly significant in his eyes, for the running commentary underscored the temporal sequence of the building's struc-ture: 'It was, moreover, a way of turning the vestibule of the new library into an elegant route leading to worthy studies and fruitful meditations.'[238]

The meaning of Labrouste's library unfolds progressively. One sign or image crops up after another as in turning over the pages of a book. The cumulative effect is best understood as a series of sections.[239] The exterior compresses many layers of information into a hard cover or binding. All the repetitive decorative elements are arranged in horizontal strata and overlap one another. At the entrance, below and just in front of the inscribed 'tables of contents' of the upper storey, the name of the building is engraved on the forward plane of the string-course just above and in front of the dated and monogrammed paterae. The paterae are con-nected by a garland which cuts across the embossed arch of the ellipse of the door and

147

134

122
141

125

appears to tie it to the plane. Within the flattened jambs are two embossed lamps, signifying the fact that the library is open in the evening. They are pressed against the surface like dried leaves on the page of an opened album. Placed on each side of the door, they make bookmarks out of conventionalized lamps of learning.

The interior of the library opens up into a lean, hard, almost brittle, three-dimensional grid. Here the images are no longer laminated but are rather spaced out. The grid, though more substantially expressed in the vestibule than in the Reading Room, is present throughout the building as an abstract linear network. Especially when reduced to thin black lines of iron, it both completely dematerializes the building and locks the various floating images in space. The cast-iron arches of the vestibule and Reading Room are like the mechanically set lines of print on a page and provide an overall framework for the sequence of thoughts expressed. The interior is opened up and relieved of tectonic focus by the leanness of the structure, and the continuity of space gives the eye the sense of freedom that the mind has in following out a thought or construing an image from words printed on paper.

The dematerialization of the structure and the opening up of the space in the Bibliothèque Ste-Geneviève is progressive and culminates in the room designed for reading books. The ethereal image of *L'Etude* describes the goal of the 'route' mapped out by the other signs along the way. It too is insubstantial: like a word on paper, it lacks real physical presence. Like everything else in the building, it just describes what is actually happening in the space around it – the act of reading which the building was designed to accommodate.

The programme of the Bibliothèque Ste-Geneviève could not be summed up in one transcendent metaphor. Unlike the generalized personification of learning which Boullée offered, Labrouste provided a series of images which suggest that learning is a matter of progressive discovery on one's own. The images present the idea of knowledge as being the result of a process of study. The building could only aid that process, and that is why the type of book it refers to, as a building, is the catalogue. A catalogue is a tool. In adopting its synoptic and referential form, Labrouste gave the Bibliothèque Ste-Geneviève a functional expression that makes the building a 'machine à lire'.

142   Bibliothèque Ste-Geneviève: entrance.

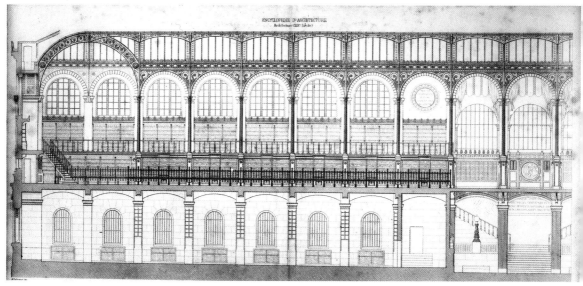

143   Bibliothèque Ste-Geneviève: longitudinal section of western half. Engraved after a drawing by Labrouste. (From the *Encyclopédie d'architecture*, V, 1855)

The printed word presented a model so absolutely antithetical to traditional architectonic expression that indeed it could for a time stand for all that might later be meant by 'the machine' and functionalism. The 'meagreness' of the Bibliothèque Ste-Geneviève was functional and seemed to prove Hugo's contention that the book 'ate its way into buildings like a worm, and bled and devoured them'.[240] But functionalism did not necessarily mean the end of all forms of symbolic expression, as Labrouste's colleague Constant-Dufeux wrote in 1848, shortly after being given a tour of the library by Labrouste at the time it was being 'decorated':

No! It is incomprehensible how you can, at one go, remove poetry from architecture; how you can deny it the expression of general ideas that can only be achieved through allegories and symbols. No! It is incomprehensible how you can want to reduce architecture to the expression of material facts it would often be incapable of rendering. In the lengthy pages of a story, it is possible to say everything and tell everything. In the limited space of a supporting pier or wall, you need to find a concentrated form of expression that can epitomize a thousand ideas in one single sign.[241]

Labrouste took Hugo's thought one step further than Hugo deemed possible. If architecture was just a tool then the architect could give that tool an expressive surface celebrating the building's function. Recognizing that a building's meaning lay outside itself, Labrouste gave the Bibliothèque Ste-Geneviève a functional meaning by placing the reader in a context that allows his act to take on existential significance.

Boullée's library has fundamentally nothing to do with its actual context. In no way does its imagery extend to the rue de Richelieu site or refer to the programme of a Bibliothèque du Roi, nor is its expression limited by either of those conditions. The imagery of the Bibliothèque Ste-Geneviève, inside and out, finally derives from the fact that it is a long, narrow building sited east–west with its main façade facing the Panthéon to the south, and that it is a public library, used mainly by students, and open until 10:00 pm.

The flat, continuous arcading of the library is a foil for the domed and porticoed Panthéon. It was designed as a background building, much as the Camposanto in Pisa is for the Duomo.[242] In contrast to the Panthéon's idealization of national history, the contents of the Bibliothèque Ste-Geneviève are presented in tabulated form as a universal history of civilization. The 810 inscribed names begin with Moses and end with Berzelius, the Swedish chemist who died in 1848, the year the names were engraved. The series outlines the historical cycle from mythic to scientific thought and, with Berzelius as the last term of reference, indicates the up-to-dateness of the library's collection.

The entrance to the library specifies the context by focusing attention on a matter of local history. The Bibliothèque Ste-Geneviève was absolutely unique in being open in the evening. This began in 1838, as a result of a ministerial decision, and it was because of this that the library had to be moved from its former location in the attic of the Lycée Henri 142 IV.[243] The lamps at the entrance thus condense in one 'sign' the reason for the library's being where it is, its hours of opening and the possibility of enlightenment its use offers.

The single most obvious quality of the Reading Room is its openness and lightness.

The deep, girding arcade is continuous, letting in daylight on all four sides, and acting as a 124 *brise-soleil* for most of the day. One is constantly made aware of the passage of time by the movement of the sun and of the fact that it is the skeletal iron construction that allows for this perception of the cycle of the day. Labrouste clearly felt the importance of that and, therefore, detailed a certain number of the thin stone pedestals of the central spine of columns to underline the building's orientation in relation to the path of the sun.

Originally, the sixteen supports of the cast-iron columns were connected by bookshelves except for the two end ones and the four in the centre. The eight exposed surfaces, four facing east and four facing west, were carved with female terms.[244] Labrouste described the 121, 'heads turned towards the sunrise and the sunset' 145, as 'representing day and night'.[245] In the centre, 146

144   Bibliothèque Ste-Geneviève: transverse section. (From Gourlier et al., *Choix d'édifices publics,* III, 1850)

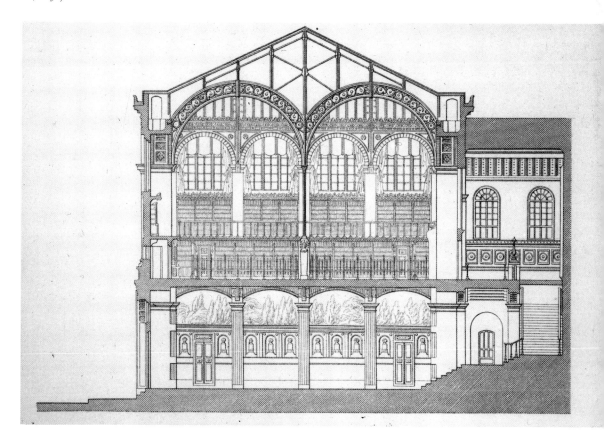

145, 146   Bibliothèque Ste-Geneviève: details of terms in the Reading Room representing Night (left) and Day, carved by Desprez.

137 they mark the open passage from the entrance to the Reference Desk and indicate, by their direction, the extension of the building in space and time.

146 The heads facing west have knitted brows, open eyes and an intense look of concentration. 121, The eyes of the heads facing east are heavy-145 lidded and give the figures a dreamy look. In the centre of the room the opposed images of *vita activa* and *vita contemplativa* describe the cycle of reading and thinking involved in the act of study. But they also point beyond the personal to the daily cycle of nature, for the head representing Night faces east while the head representing Day faces west. This forces us to look beyond each head to the natural source of its disposition. Beyond the sleepy look of Night is the sunset in the west; and beyond the engrossed look of Day is the sunrise in the east.

The figures are not classical representations, like Boullée's Minerva. They do not embody some abstract idea but are labels placed under the real thing. They are arranged back-to-back like the recto and verso of pages in a book. The head facing the sunrise on the terminal 121 pier in the eastern end of the building does not represent Day, as one might expect; rather, it represents Night. Its form was determined by the direction of the plane it occupies in relation to the whole site and not by its position in the delimited space of the building. The terms in the Reading Room refer the imagination to a world beyond themselves and thus seem to occupy the abstract space of print rather than the plastic space of figuration.

The Bibliothèque Ste-Geneviève celebrates the function of study. It gives the individual act of reading a universal dimension while indicating the limits of human knowledge.

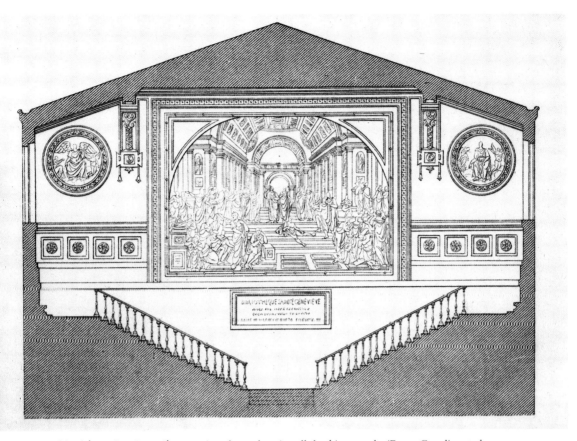

147 Bibliothèque Ste-Geneviève: section through stairwell, looking north. (From Gourlier et al., *Choix d'édifices publics*, III, 1850)

The historical outline of the exterior links the individual's education to the progress of civilization. But that list of authors also circumscribes what has been recorded in print. The cycle of active investigation and passive contemplation is seen as part of the daily cycle of the rising and setting of the sun. But nature's cycle sets the ultimate limits of how much can be learned and known.

The entire structure and decoration of the Bibliothèque Ste-Geneviève locks the building into its site and expresses the fact that nature is inimitable, and that its mechanisms are as intractable as the rising and setting of the sun. The librarian Henry Trianon wrote that Labrouste's forms 'in no way attempt to compete with nature'.[246] Boullée thought of his buildings, in strictly classical terms, as imitating and manipulating nature, and felt that the reason why architecture could do painting or poetry one better was because it was 'the only art that actually brings nature into play'.[247] He meant that architecture could make permanent, in a fictive body, what is naturally insubstantial, evanescent and volatile; and thus he, the architect, 'could be so bold as to say to himself: I make light'.[248] Boullée imagined buildings on paper and said '*fiat lux*'.[249] It is poignant that Labrouste, the first to use iron and gas to make a space that literally turned night into day, would stress the existential limits of intellectual enlightenment.

'Architecture, simply and immediately perceived, is a combination, revealed through light and shade, of space, of masses, and of lines.'[230] This, of course, is not Le Corbusier but Geoffrey Scott, writing in 1914 about the 'fallacies'

171

148 Bibliothèque Ste-Geneviève: section through stairwell, looking south. Engraved after a drawing by Labrouste. (From the *Revue générale de l'architecture et des travaux publics*, XI, 1853)

that governed 19th-century architecture and the values supposed to constitute an 'architecture of humanism'.

Both modernists and traditionalists in the early 20th century agreed on one fundamental point, that architectural form should have a 'purely aesthetic character'.[251] Both modernists and traditionalists criticized 19th-century architecture for being impure and allusive, for being overladen with symbolic decoration and dependent on associationism, in a word, for being too literary: 'Overcharged with literary significance and atrophied in its design, the art of form [architecture] loses the power to impress; it ceases, in any aesthetic sense, to be significant at all.'[252] Geoffrey Scott held that 'the architects of Napoleon built the monument, and wrote the epitaph, of Renaissance art' to which 'the Romantic Movement of the nineteenth century dealt the final death-

blow'.[253] According to Scott, 'the essential fallacy of romanticism was ... that it treated architectural form as primarily symbolic' and 'made architecture speak a language not its own'.[254] Architecture became 'a mirror to literary preferences' and exaggerated the 'secondary question' of 'mere significance'.[255]

The shallow formalism and sentimentality of much of the 'architecture of humanism' of the past seventy-five years, whether traditional or modernist, gives the lie to Scott's revision of Hugo. In the largest sense, then, Wright was correct in his interpretation, for it was the machine that upset the classical equation of form and content and made function the limiting condition. But the dematerialization of structure and abstraction of space that has come to characterize modern architecture, along with the consequent transparency of surface and reflexive relationship between exterior and interior, or container and contained, has its source in that particular object of 19th-century mechanomorphism celebrated by Hugo. By 1830 no other machine could have been said to have affected communication so profoundly as the printing-press and thus to have explained the ever-decreasing sphere of architecture's influence. The analogy of the printed book allowed architecture to break out of the confines of classicism and develop a functional form of expression, and thus ever since Hugo declared the death of architecture as society's principal means of expression, the issue has been to make architecture out of building.

149 J.-l. Hittorff. St-Vincent-de-Paul, Paris, consecrated in 1844: interior looking towards the apse, showing the encaustic frescoes by J.-H. Flandrin and F.-E. Picot executed in 1849–53.

IX

Hittorff's polychrome campaign

R. D. Middleton

AFTER THE FRENCH REVOLUTION, architecture in France entered a lacklustre period. For a short time building activity virtually ceased. Napoleon attempted to act as a great and discriminating patron, he improved the organization of Paris and other French cities, but the architecture he encouraged was of the platitudinous kind – the monumental platitudinous kind. Architecture was reduced then to a range of stereotypes. And this process, fostered by the Conseil Général des Bâtiments Civils, was paralleled in the institutions of learning. J.-N.-L. Durand, who taught at the Ecole Polytechnique from its inception in 1795 to 1830, and J.-B. Rondelet, who was professor of stereotomy at the Ecole Spéciale d'Architecture, later the Ecole des Beaux-Arts, from 1806 to his death in 1829, together reduced architecture to two of its component parts, geometric formality and structural finesse. Their books left little to tell of individual endeavour. The intellectual legacy of the 18th century was compressed into formulae.

The first decades of the 19th century were not inspiring for architecture. The first serious attempt to reinvigorate it was made by Jacques-Ignace Hittorff (1792–1867). His proposals were of the most superficial kind. He thought to apply colour, inside and outside, to buildings. And in support of this programme he undertook detailed and thorough investigations into the use of colour in classical antiquity. For if it could be shown that the hallowed architecture of ancient Greece itself was coloured with paint, no other precedent for his present performance would be required, no further explanation needed. Hittorff was not a rigorous thinker. He was not a talented designer. But his famous fight to establish the importance of colour in classical architecture, and even his own ludicrously inept efforts to apply it to a handful of buildings, is

of the highest significance in the history of 19th-century architecture in France, for he showed that the classical tradition, upon which contemporary architecture was founded, could be reassessed, and reassessed in a fundamental way. His theories served as a catalyst for a group of far more radical reformers – Emile Gilbert, Félix Duban, Henri Labrouste, Louis Duc and Léon Vaudoyer. Such was Hittorff's achievement.

The history of Hittorff's fight to prove that the temples of ancient Greece were highly coloured – his theory of architectural polychromy, as he called it – has been outlined no less than four times in recent years: briefly by myself (1958), in detail by Karl Hammer (1968), circumstantially by David Van Zanten (1970) and at length by Donald Schneider (1971).[1] But though much new information has been adduced, the account published by Hittorff himself in 1851 in his *Restitution du temple d'Empédocle à Sélinonte, ou l'architecture polychrome chez les Grecs* has not been notably advanced. The facts are reasonably well established.

Hittorff's early career was that of a decorator. He was born in 1792 in Cologne, where he was trained as a stonemason, but at the age of eighteen he crossed the Rhine, together with his friend Franz Christian Gau (1790–1853), to study under Charles Percier and to work with François Belanger, then engaged on the construction of the Halle au Blé and the abattoir at Rochechouart. It was rather Belanger's less serious work for the Menus Plaisirs – later the Direction des Fêtes et Spectacles de la Cour – that attracted him. When in May 1818 Belanger died, Hittorff succeeded him in this activity. He was assisted by J.-F.-J. Lecointe (1783–1858), another of Belanger's pupils. Together, in the following years, they designed a number of intricate decors for royal baptisms, weddings and funerals. Soon enough Hittorff foresaw and judged the frivolous prettiness of these decorations to be a defect, or at least a danger – 'he stopped in his tracks', Henri Labrouste noted in 1868, 'and, casting back, he recognized, I believe, that his studies had been inadequate and too soon interrupted'.[2] He determined to enlarge his experience. He decided to travel. He studied English and left in 1820 for England, where he saw the Elgin marbles. The following year he travelled to Germany, where he had for his guide in Berlin none other than K. F. Schinkel, about whom he was curiously condescending, writing in 1824 to Lecointe: 'M. Schinkel has much taste and talent for painting and decoration; he is a man of particular merit, but he lacks the essential to be a good architect.'[3] Nonetheless, Hittorff was much stirred by Schinkel's tomb for Queen Luise at Charlottenburg, a small Doric temple with richly coloured marbles and paintings inside. Towards the end of 1822 Hittorff travelled to Italy, together with another of Percier's pupils, who had moved on to the Fêtes et Cérémonies, Karl Ludwig Wilhelm von Zanth (1796–1857), son of Jérôme Bonaparte's doctor.[4] In Rome, where they arrived in January 1823, they stayed near the Spanish Steps, in the Casa Buti, where Bertel Thorvaldsen (1768–1844), then working on the restoration of the frieze from the temple of Aphaia at Aegina, was in residence, together with other German artists and scholars. Hittorff also met T. L. Donaldson (1795–1888),[5] a Silver Medallist, later a prominent member and president of the Royal Institute of British Architects, who was to remain his close friend through life. Donaldson was a member of that group of English scholars and architects who were hoping to extend the classical tradition through a closer inspection of the antique monuments – William Kinnaird, Joseph Woods, Charles Robert Cockerell and Charles Barry. All had toured and excavated in the preceding decade in Greece. All had noticed traces of colour on Greek temples.

The presence of colour on Greek architecture had not hitherto gone entirely unremarked. In 1762 Stuart and Revett had recorded painted decorations on the frieze of the temple on the Ilissus in the first volume of their *Antiquities of Athens*. William Leake, William Wilkins, and Edward Dodwell, excavating in Greece in the early years of the century, had observed pigment on the remains of several temples. That maverick scholar and collector, L.-F.-S. Fauvel (1753–1838), who arrived in Greece in 1780 and served as French consul in Athens from 1792 to 1831, entertaining most visiting scholars during that period, certainly noticed pigment on the ruins, though his only recorded comment on the subject, as David Van Zanten has observed, was 'pourquoi cela parait-il étrange?' He corresponded with A.-C. Quatremère de Quincy (1755–1843), the rising grammarian of classical orthodoxy, later to become the permanent secretary of the Académie des Beaux-Arts, but made no mention of colour. Somewhat earlier, Léon Dufourny (1754–1818), who settled in Sicily, had noticed colour on the Doric temples there and on his return to Paris in 1794 had shown his notes to Quatremère de Quincy. It was Quatremère de Quincy, surprisingly enough, who first aroused a general interest in the use of colour in antiquity. He was the first to use the word 'polychromie', in October 1806, in a paper addressed to the Académie. His accumulated observations on the subject were published in 1815 as *Jupiter Olympien: ou l'art de la sculpture antique considéré sous un nouveau point de vue; ouvrage qui comprend un essai sur le goût de la sculpture polychrome*. He was concerned with the use of ivory and semiprecious and precious stones, gold and bronze, only touched here and there with paint, and he dealt with sculpture, not architecture, though he did indicate a blue vault with gilded mouldings in one of his hand-coloured plates. Externally, the architecture of antiquity retained the mantle of blanched purity that Winckelmann, Goethe and other 18th-century scholars conferred on it.

Quatremère de Quincy's work certainly stirred Hittorff's imagination. But he was stirred also by the activities of his friend Gau, who had exhibited highly coloured studies of the monuments of Egypt in the Salon of 1822, and in the same year had started to publish *Les antiquités de Nubie*, with equally brilliantly coloured plates. Anxious to make an archaeological discovery on his own account Hittorff took up the challenge offered by Thorvaldsen and by Donaldson and his friends in Rome. Donaldson had started an essay in 1820 in Athens, based on the reports of Kinnaird and Barry, in which he had outlined a system of fairly extensive colour decoration in Greek architecture. Hittorff was no doubt stimulated by this idea, and further stimulated by reports of the discovery by William Harris and Samuel Angell, in March 1823, of

LE JUPITER OLYMPIEN,

VU DANS SON TRÔNE ET DANS L'INTERIEUR DE SON TEMPLE.

A.-C. Quatremère de Quincy. Reconstruction of the interior of the Temple of
Jupiter at Olympia, frontispiece from *Jupiter Olympien*, 1815.

II   H. Labrouste. Drawing inscribed 'Agrigentum 1828' on the reverse. See p. 199. (Académie d'Architecture, Paris, on loan from Mme Y. Labrouste)

III, IV   J.-I. Hittorff, Reconstruction of the 'Temple of Empedocles' at Selinus, 1830: elevation and section. From *Restitution du temple d'Empédocle à Sélinonte, ou l'architecture polychrome chez les Grecs*, 1851. See pp. 186–87, 188, 206–07.

V   G. Semper. Reconstruction of the painted decoration of the Parthenon in Athens, for *Anwendung der Farben*, 1836. See p. 210. (Semperarchiv, Eidgenössischen Technischen Hochschule, Zurich)

VI   M.-G.-B. Bindesbøll. Thorvaldsen Museum, Copenhagen, 1839–44: interior court. See pp. 209–10.

VII   J.-I. Hittorff. Cirque National, Paris, 1840: façade elevation, from *L'Architecture polychrome chez les Grecs*, 1851. See p. 189.

VIII   J.-I. Hittorff. St Vincent-de-Paul, Paris: elevation of the portico showing proposed painted panels, 1844, from *L'Architecture polychrome chez les Grecs*, 1851. See pp. 191, 208–09.

IX   L. de (K. L. W.) Zanth. La Wilhelma, near Stuttgart, 1842–51: interior,
from *La Wilhelma, villa mauresque* . . . , 1855. See p. 190.

X   O. Jones. Messrs R. and C. Osler's Gallery, 45 Oxford Street, London, 1858:
nterior. See p. 213. (Victoria and Albert Museum, London)

XI P.-J. Jollivet. Detail of *The Last Supper*, Volvic panel from the façade of St-Vincent-de-Paul, Paris, 1852–60. See pp. 191–92. (Dépôt de la Ville de Paris, Ivry)

coloured metopes from the temple 'C' at Selinus. In July, Hittorff left for Sicily together with Zanth and Wilhelm Stier (1799–1857), who was hired as an additional draughtsman. In Palermo Harris had died from malaria on 16 March, and Angell showed them the metopes then being trans-shipped. Another of Percier's pupils, Leo von Klenze (1784–1864), got wind of these findings, and there was an undignified rush to win the polychrome honours. Von Klenze, however, had as travelling companion the Crown Prince Ludwig of Bavaria, and was hampered.[6] His folio *Der Tempel des olympischen Jupiter von Agrigent*, published in 1827, was the result of no more than ten days spent on the site. Hittorff had more time at his disposal, and money; he hired nineteen workmen and set to excavating at Selinus. Both there, where he uncovered the 'Temple of Empedocles', and at Agrigentum, he found what he was looking for, ample evidence that paint had been used as a decorative medium in antiquity. He recognized this as a sanction for his need to apply decorative trimming and pattern in his own work. He was naturally excited. He wrote on 14 December 1823, from Agrigentum, to Baron François Gérard, the painter, to describe his discoveries. From Selinus, on 30 December, he wrote to Ludwig von Schorn, editor of the *Kunstblatt*, to outline a theory of polychrome architecture. And, having decided that the mural paintings of Pompeii constituted a further development and extension of the classical colour system, he wrote from Naples on 17 February 1824 to Percier, and on 5 April again to Schorn to elaborate his ideas. In Rome, he prepared his first restoration studies of the temples of Agrigentum and Selinus, and put them on display. P. O. Brønsted, the Danish archaeologist, was impressed, and P.-N. Guérin, director of the Académie de France, became his support. Thorvaldsen confirmed that Hittorff's discoveries were similar to his own observations on the Aegina marbles. Even in France, Désiré Raoul Rochette (1790–1854), newly appointed professor of archaeology at the Bibliothèque du Roi – later *secrétaire perpétuel* of the Académie des Beaux-Arts in succession to Quatremère de Quincy – having read Hittorff's letters in the *Kunstblatt* tentatively explained to his students the nature of Hittorff's new colourful image of antique architecture. Winckelmann's whited sculpture seemed a thing of the past. On Hittorff's return to Paris in June 1824

Raoul Rochette inspected his drawings and restorations and declared himself satisfied. But he soon became Hittorff's bitterest opponent. On 24 July Hittorff read a paper to the Académie des Beaux-Arts in which he described his experiences in Sicily and, in particular, his findings at Agrigentum and Selinus. In the following year Raoul Rochette read a 'Mémoire sur la peinture encaustique' in which – in deference perhaps to the memory of Winckelmann and no doubt under the influence of Quatremère de Quincy, who can hardly have approved of the manner in which Hittorff was extending his own polychrome theories – he minimized the importance of the new discoveries and disparaged Hittorff's scholarship. Hittorff was much disturbed. In the prospectus, printed in 1826, to the first partial edition of the *Architecture antique de la Sicile* that he and Zanth were to bring out between 1827 and 1830,[7] he wrote with reference to the newly discovered temple at Selinus:

> Among the ruins of this building, as in all of those of the city, there are numerous fragments of sculpture and architecture painted in different colours or covered with coloured stucco. The traces of this system leave no doubts as to the practice adopted by the ancients of colouring their sculpture and architecture, enlivening with colour and painted ornament not only the insides of their temples, but also the external walls of the cella, the columns, architraves, metopes, cornices, pediments and even the tiles.

Confirmation for Hittorff's ideas came, moreover, in the form of the published accounts of a whole range of architects and scholars who had recently studied the temples of antiquity. The sculptor Johann Martin Wagner and the philosopher F. W. J. Schelling had published brief observations on the marbles of Aegina in 1817, *Bericht über die Aeginetischen Bildwerke im Besitz der Kronprinz von Baiern*; von Klenze's *Versuch einer Wiederherstellung des toskanischen Tempels nach seiner historischen und technischen Analogien*, printed in Munich in 1822, elaborated their notion that polychromy was a survival of the practice of painting primitive wooden temples; Harris and Angell's *Sculptural metopes discovered amongst the ruins of the temples of the ancient city of Selinus in Sicily* appeared in London in 1826; Otto Magnus von Stackelberg's *Der Apollotempel zu Bassae in Arcadien* in Rome in the same year; P. O. Brønsted published his

Voyage dans la Grèce in Paris, between 1826 and 1830; and Joseph Woods issued his *Letters of an architect from France, Italy and Greece* in London in 1828. But by far the most authoritative work was William Kinnaird's new edition of the *Antiquities of Athens*, published in London in four volumes between 1825 and 1830. In the first volume Kinnaird included his own observations on the colouring of the Parthenon; in the fourth volume, which was also issued in large format in 1830 as a supplementary volume to the original edition, were Cockerell's 'Temple of Jupiter Olympius, at Agrigentum' and Donaldson's 'Temple of Apollo Epicurius, at Bassae', reports that can hardly have failed to convince even the strongest of Hittorff's opponents that colour had been used on Greek temples.

The related problem of the use of colour in Roman and particularly in late Roman antiquity was also studied at this period with particular zeal by Hittorff and Raoul Rochette. Hittorff entered negotiations in 1824 with Schorn and his Stuttgart publisher, J. F. Cotta (1764–1832), to provide a French edition of Sir William Gell and J. P. Gandy's *Pompeiana* (1817–19) with forty-two new plates, but this was to be published in Paris, in 1827, by Firmin Didot as *Vues des ruines de Pompéi*, with texts for the two additional parts by Hittorff and plates by H. Roux, six of them coloured. In the following year Raoul Rochette – who had travelled to Italy and Sicily in 1826 to inspect for himself the ruins of antiquity – issued the *Maison du poëte tragique à Pompéi*, with J. Bouchet. Most of Raoul Rochette's plates were brilliantly coloured, as were many in the third and fourth volumes, of 1829 and 1838, of François Mazois' magnificent *Ruines de Pompéi*, begun in 1812. These last two volumes were issued under the guidance of Gau. All these works were hand-coloured; they were expensive and limited thus in range. When Barré and H. Roux published their more popular *Herculanum et Pompéi: Recueil général des peintures, bronzes, mosaïques, etc.* in eight volumes, in 1839 and 1840, they could include no more than one coloured plate; it was not until Raoul Rochette and Roux issued their *Choix des peintures de Pompéi* in seven parts, between 1844 and 1853, that the glories of late Roman decoration were revealed to the world in the relatively cheap and gaudy brilliance of the chromo-lithograph.

By the end of 1827 the first five parts of

Hittorff and Zanth's *Architecture antique de la Sicile* had been issued. These included only three modestly coloured plates showing details from the Selinus temples. Raoul Rochette reviewed them in July 1829 in the *Journal des Savants*, praising the accuracy of Hittorff's measurements, applauding his powers of observation, but emphatically rejecting the idea that the temples of Selinus were as fully covered with paint as Hittorff cared to believe. Raoul Rochette's firm dismissal was probably part of a mounting campaign, instigated by Quatremère de Quincy, to oppose the radical revision of accepted concepts of classical antiquity in which the *pensionnaires* at Rome were then indulging. The use of colour was only a part of the heretical re-interpretation, but it was an important part. Henri Labrouste had introduced it for the first time in his highly controversial restoration studies of the temples of Paestum, exhibited at the Villa Medici in the spring of 1829, before being sent on later in the year to Paris. These had been the subject of a bitter exchange of letters, during May and June, between Quatremère de Quincy and Horace Vernet, director of the Académie de France. His use of colours, as Labrouste was later to acknowledge, was strongly influenced by Hittorff's propaganda, though it was rather the Etruscan tombs at Corneto, which Baron von Stackelberg, together with Baron August Kestner and the architect Joseph Thürmer had been exploring since early 1827, and had made known in drawings exhibited in Rome in the following year (though they saw to it that the site was, officially at least, restricted), that provided the vital, visual inspiration for Labrouste and his friends, especially Félix Duban, who was soon to be recognized as leader of the Etruscan movement.[8] Raoul Rochette had managed to penetrate to the site in July 1827 and, defying Stackelberg's interdiction, had published an analysis of the paintings in January and February 1828 in the *Journal des Savants*. Hittorff himself was to be much influenced by the new discoveries, which he no doubt saw in Stackelberg's own renderings, which the archaeologist was hoping to have published by Cotta, and which he took on his travels through Germany, France and England in 1829. Hittorff was at last sufficiently stirred by Raoul Rochette to make public a coherent theory. On 3 April 1830 he read the paper 'De l'architecture polychrome chez les Grecs ou restitution complète

123
161

du temple d'Empédocle dans l'acropole de Sélinonte' to the Académie des Beaux-Arts and the Académie des Inscriptions et Belles-Lettres, and presented to them his restoration studies. These drawings were exhibited later at the Salon. In the same year he read the paper to the Société Libre des Beaux-Arts (a society of which he was a founder, formed in October 1830 to foster the reorganization of the Académie and the Ecole des Beaux-Arts). Variants of the paper were published in the *Annali dell'Istituto di correspondenza archeologica* (1830), the journal of an institute founded in Rome in 1829 by Stackelberg and his friends, and the *Journal de la société libre des Beaux-Arts* (1836), with a commentary there by Hittorff's associate Edmé Miel. This paper constituted Hittorff's first real manifesto. In it he adopted a stand more extreme than Raoul Rochette could have thought possible. He sought to persuade his audience to imagine a Greek architecture of rich and ravishing beauty; the mechanical smooth-

III
IV ness of white marble made soft with a coat of pale yellow paint, the surface modulations made lively with patterns of bright blue, green, red and gold paint – an image which does not today seem either tempting or satisfying. This he illustrated in the seventh part of *Architecture antique*, one of the last to be issued. In this same year, one might note, Hittorff's rival, Leo

150 von Klenze, presented his vision of Greek poly-chromy in the form of a painted plaster relief of a restored temple front, set high on the wall, above the pediment sculptures from Aegina restored by Thorvaldsen, displayed in the newly opened Glyptothek in Munich. Raoul Rochette showed surprising tolerance in dealing with Hittorff's proposals, in July 1830, in a 'Mémoire sur les peintures chrétiennes des cata-combes'. He found himself unable to accept Hittorff's theory, though he accepted that colour had been made use of in antique archi-tecture. Even in his more famous reply to Hittorff, 'De la peinture sur mur chez les anciens', printed in the *Journal des Savants* in June, July and August 1833, Raoul Rochette showed no more fight. He preferred that colour be restricted to painted panels, independent of the architecture.

When Hittorff's drawings of the restoration of the 'Temple of Empedocles' were exhibited at the Salon in 1831, they provoked those out-bursts of rapturous applause that are usually reserved for works of popular appeal. Percier

150   L. von Klenze. Relief of a Doric temple front, in the Aegina room of the Glyptothek, Munich.

declared himself enchanted. Scholars and stu-dents whose knowledge of Greek architecture was not greatly inferior to our own vied with one another in upholding Hittorff's ideas – or some aspect of them at least. Discussion became international. The philologist Gottfried Her-mann published *De veterum Graecorum pictura parietum conjecturae* in Leipzig, in 1834, as a rebuke to Raoul Rochette. Gottfried Semper, who had worked in Paris with Gau, issued his *Vorläufige Bemerkungen über bemalte Architektur und Plastik bei den Alten* in Altona, in the same year, in support of Hittorff, though he sug-gested that the pigment employed by the Greeks to soften their marble was vapoury red rather than yellow. In 1835 Franz Kugler published his less fanciful interpretations in Berlin, *Über die Polychromie der griechischen Architektur und Skulptur und ihre Grenzen.* He upheld Raoul Rochette, however, rather than Hittorff. In England, Lord Elgin's erstwhile secretary, William Richard Hamilton (1777–1859), read a translation of Kugler's pamphlet in 1835 to the Royal Institute of British Architects, and in the following year formed part of a select committee, which included such men as C. R. Cockerell, T. L. Donaldson, S. Angell, and Charles Eastlake (who had travelled in Greece with Barry and Kinnaird) and the chemist Michael Faraday, appointed to examine the Elgin marbles for traces of colour. Hittorff himself took part in their discussions, in June 1837. F. C. Penrose and Cockerell were actively interested in the use of colour in antiquity in the years that followed, but it was not until 1854, when Owen Jones and Matthew Digby Wyatt designed the highly coloured Greek Court in the Crystal Palace at Sydenham, that any widespread interest was provoked in England.

France was the centre of the controversy. Hittorff, having outlined his theory, wisely withdrew from the battle. He published a translation of Kinnaird's supplementary volume to the *Antiquities of Athens*, between 1830 and 1832, in which incidentally he cited Labrouste as an authority; and he replied briefly to Raoul Rochette in the *Journal des Savants* in May 1835, when that critic (in the January issue) used a review of *Antichità della Sicilia* by the Duca di Serradifalco (who had been excavating at Selinus) as a pretext to ridicule once again the idea of a complete system of colour application in Greek architecture; but Hittorff reserved his energies rather for the *Restitution du temple d'Empédocle à Sélinonte, ou l'architecture polychrome chez les Grecs* – his famous confession of faith in the use of colour in architecture, both
III ancient and modern – with plates begun in
IV 1846 but published only in 1851, long after the fighting was over. Four years later he commemorated his achievements, fittingly, in the construction of a model of the temple at Selinus, dedicated now to Melpomene, commissioned by the fantastic Plon-Plon, Prince Napoleon, as a gift for Rachel the actress. The paintings in the cella were by Ingres, the cult statues by Barré, father and son, and Simart. The cost was 800,000 francs – a sixth of the cost of the church of St-Vincent-de-Paul. The small temple was one of the wonders of the Salon of 1859.

Hittorff's defender during the 1830s was J.-A. Letronne (1787–1848): one of the first to review Quatremère de Quincy's work on chryselephantine sculpture in the *Journal des Savants*, in November 1817, and later professor of classical archaeology at the Collège de France. In 1835 he published his well-known *Lettre d'un antiquaire à un artiste sur l'emploi de la peinture historique murale chez les Grecs et les Romains* – a carefully framed indictment of Raoul Rochette. Rochette, aiming by then to succeed Quatremère de Quincy, was much angered by the slurs cast on his critique. He read another *mémoire* to the Académie in January 1835 and wrote no less than three articles for the *Journal des Savants* (published in November 1836, in January and February 1837 and in July and October 1837) to reassert his authority; and in both his *Peintures antiques inédites* of 1836 and his *Lettres archéologiques sur la peinture des Grecs* of 1840 reiterated his rude dismissal of Hittorff's theories. Letronne wrote only two further articles, both published in the *Journal des Savants*, in May 1837 and in June and July 1837, but he wrote to greater effect. He laid bare Raoul Rochette's arguments, without committing himself on Hittorff's far-reaching proposals. Raoul Rochette wrote elegantly, as Henri Labrouste was later to observe, but facetiously, 'with a certain lightness, which, rather than serving to diminish in importance the facts he was discussing, revealed that he had not studied sufficiently well the numerous ruins which still retained definite traces of original colouring'.[9]

But it is a mistake to discuss Hittorff's hypotheses in archaeological terms; his ideas were based on an aesthetic ideal to which facts were purely subservient. He was concerned simply to bring the forces of the past to bear on the present. And, if we are to judge by his *Restitution du temple d'Empédocle*, he attached small importance to historical study beyond its relevance to the present: 'the aim of my studies', he wrote, 'whether directed to ancient or modern architecture, has always been to find elements of use in my professional career'.[10]

He designed by analogy. For almost all his architectural works, and even for his most daring structural experiments, he found a historical precedent. But if he felt impelled to turn thus to the past for inspiration, he rarely copied directly from his historical models; he used his observed facts only as points of departure for the creation of a number of highly personal, odd and often ridiculous buildings. He was unable to master his themes. His first attempts to interpret polychromy in contemporary terms were made in the Champs-Elysées in Paris, where he added bright paint to the porticoes of both his Rotonde des Panoramas (1838–39),

VII and the Cirque National (1840), and other such informal buildings, cafés and restaurants erected there in the following years. Later, in 1852, he applied coloured paint on the façade of the Cirque d'Hiver in the Boulevard des Filles-du-Calvaire, but his studied and really serious endeavour to show how the classical style of the 19th century might be transformed by the use of colour in conformity with antique

VIII precedent was the design of St-Vincent-de-
149 Paul.[11] This church, sited high above the Place Franz Liszt in Paris, was started within a few months of his return from Rome. The foundation stone was laid on 25 August 1824. However, building proceeded slowly. The foundation drawings are dated 8 July 1827. After the financial crisis of 1828 work stopped altogether, to be taken up again in 1831 and not to be completed before October, 1844, when the church was consecrated. The double curved

157 ramps, so important a feature of the composition, were designed only in 1839.

The commission was awarded first, in 1823, to J.-B. Lepère (1761–1844), whom Hittorff agreed to join while yet in Rome, in May 1824, and whose daughter (her mother was born Elizabeth Fontaine) he married in December. The design is chiefly Hittorff's, reworked in 1833, when the towers were added, as is the programme for the painted decorations, both inside and out. But the *mémoire* submitted to Rambuteau, Préfet de la Seine, in January 1838 and published in *L'Artiste* in January 1842 – a manifesto, as it were, of the architect's role as artistic co-ordinator – was signed by both Hittorff and Lepère. Lepère was then in his seventy-seventh year.

The stained glass, made by C.-L. Maréchal (1802–87) and Gugnon, was designed by Hittorff in 1842 and installed by 1844. The general tonality was red and yellow. Mindful of the recommendations made in M.-E. Chevreul's *De la loi du contraste simultané des couleurs* of 1839, Hittorff determined to develop the interior colour scheme only when he could judge of the effect of the light cast through the stained glass. Owen Jones (1807–74) judged of his success when he spoke of the church at the

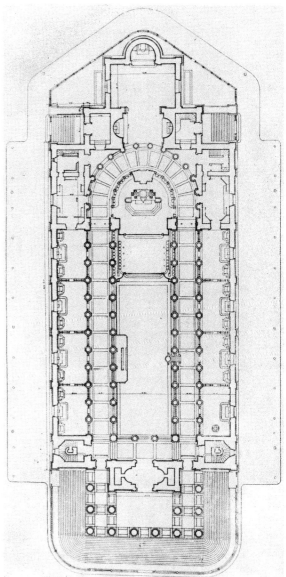

151 St-Vincent-de-Paul, Paris: plan.

Royal Institute of British Architects in 1850 – 'decidedly the most perfect specimen of modern decoration in any country'.[12] But neither Hittorff nor the congregation were so easily satisfied; they found the effect too gloomy, and the borders were changed to grisailles in 1852. The columns of the nave were coated with yellow *scagliola*, a process introduced into France and perfected by P.-L.-C. Ciceri (1782–1868), a pupil of Belanger, who had worked often enough before with Hittorff (and also Daguerre,

on stage decorations). The entablatures and most of the ornamental mouldings were gilded. The exposed trusses over the nave and coffered roof panels were painted in red, blue and gold, a self-conscious paraphrase of those at Messina and Monreale, in Sicily – a sort of latter day expression, Hittorff imagined, of Greek polychrome architecture. It was a notion that he adapted to any rich and colourful work. His friend Zanth, for instance, had as early as 1837 designed a fantastic and costly villa, La Wilhelma, in the moorish style for King Wilhelm I of Wurttemberg, erected outside Stuttgart between 1842 and 1851;[13] and Hittorff had managed to judge that to be in the tradition of Greek architecture: 'the rational approach,' he wrote in his *Restitution du temple d'Empédocle*, 'which is basic to it, has guided the flight of his imagination, and in following this line Zanth has remained confident that, though building an arabian palace, he was continuing in the path of the noble authors of the most beautiful buildings of Greece'.[14] In this Hittorff was clearly guided not by reason but by slack aesthetic ideals.

152 St-Vincent-de-Paul, Paris: detail of the coffered timber ceilings of the nave roof (top) and of the upper gallery.

153 Messina Cathedral: plan and elevation of one bay of the polychrome timber roof. (From M.-P. Morey, *La Charpente de la Cathédrale de Messine*, 1841)

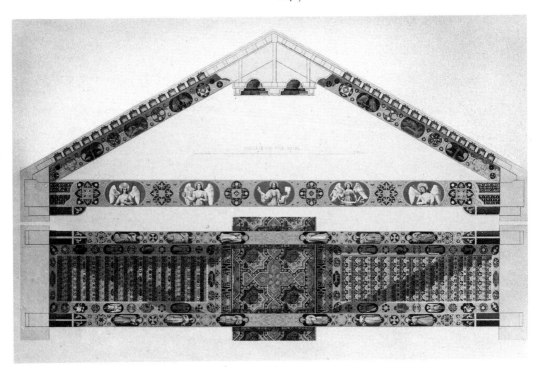

149 The great encaustic frescoes running along the nave and apse of the church, conceived as a sort of Panathenaic procession, were begun only in 1849, finished in 1853. Hittorff intended at first that they should represent the life of St Vincent, with his apotheosis in the sanctuary, above a frieze of the seven sacraments. The commission was offered in September 1845 to Ingres, but he demurred; it was taken up in July 1848 by his pupil, J.-H. Flandrin (1809–64), who painted the nave, and his friend, F.-E. Picot (1786–1868), a pupil of Vincent and David, who was responsible for the apse. Flandrin depicted a procession of pilgrims entering Jerusalem, rather than the life of St Vincent, while Picot substituted a Christ enthroned for the saint's apotheosis; the latter was then represented in stained glass instead, by Maréchal, in an oculus at the west end of the church.

The feature in which all Hittorff's accumulated ideas were to be most splendidly expressed,
157 however, was the west front. In 1844 he
VIII proposed that the whole of the portico wall be covered with thirteen large painted panels, with additional touches of paint in the pediment and on the entablature mouldings and fascias, the whole intended, once again, to conjure up Grecian glories. The proposal was breathtaking.
156 The iconography was, of course, to be Chris-
XI tian, the Holy Trinity in the central panel above the door, flanked by scenes from the Old Testament on the left, the New Testament on the right. The panels, consisting of sheets of volcanic rock as used at the time for pavements, were to be painted in bright enamel and baked: a new process known as *lave d'Auvergne* or *Volvic*, based on that evolved by Bernard Palissy and rediscovered and perfected by the glassmaker F.-H.-J. Mortelèque (1774–1844).[15] This technique was to prove well suited to the application of Hittorff's ideas about polychromy.

Mortelèque's first experiments using the new process had been some roughly painted cameos, which were shown at Sèvres in 1820, but seven years later he had managed to develop the technique to the extent of painting a medium-sized panel. The following year his process was taken up by the Comte de Chabrol, then Préfet de la Seine, who was from Volvic: in 1829 he showed specimens of the work to the Académie des Beaux-Arts and enthusiastically recommended its use. He himself commissioned street signs in the new material and an altar

154 St-Vincent-de-Paul, Paris: interior, showing the timber ceiling. (Lithograph made before the Flandrin frescoes were painted)

front – three medallions, of Faith, Hope and Charity – for the church of Ste-Elizabeth, painted by David's pupil, Abel de Pujol (1785–1861). Mortelèque gave over his interest at this time to his son-in-law, Hachette, who continued the experiments. Hittorff too seems to have taken up an active interest in the firm. In 1834 he and Hachette exhibited a copy of a Raphael madonna, painted by Robert, at the Exposition des Produits de l'Industrie Francaise, and were awarded a gold medal. The next year Hittorff completed a commission offered in 1832 to Ingres for altar fronts for the church of Notre-Dame de Lorette, where he worked with Lebas. He also introduced *lave d'Auvergne* into a café opposite the Bourse, and in the following years experimented with it again and again, making table-tops, fireplace surrounds and decorative panels, which he put on show at the exhibitions of 1839 and 1844. He proclaimed the process to be the most fitting means of applying his polychrome theories. In 1840 Félix Duban incorporated four enamelled roundels of Volvic in the forecourt of the Ecole des Beaux-Arts, and more were to follow.

P. Perlet (1804–1843), a pupil of Gros and Ingres, did a painting of Christ using Volvic for the church of St-Leu. But the idea did not catch on. It was taken up, however, by a pupil of Gros, Pierre-Jules Jollivet (1803–1871),[16] a successful if vulgar painter, who adopted the technique for a Virgin and Christ for the Emperor of Russia and then, prompted by Hittorff, persuaded the new Préfet de la Seine, M. Rambuteau, to commission the first of the panels for St-Vincent-de-Paul. Hachette built a whole range of new kilns. 'La Sainte Trinité' was in place over the central doorway by 31 May 1846, when it was described in rapturous terms in *Le Moniteur*. Hachette died in that year,[17] and though his wife took over the firm there was an inevitable interlude of disruption, prolonged by the partial destruction of the works in the street fighting of 1848. Mme Hachette thought to sell the patent to the Sèvres manufactory, but nothing came of the negotiations. Jollivet took up the cause again in an article in the *Revue générale de l'architecture* in 1851, and in the next year was commissioned to paint a further six panels, enough to cover the whole of the projecting wall of the portico. These were all set in place in March 1860. On the left-hand side of the door were scenes of the Birth of Christ, the Baptism, and the Last Supper, on the right the Creation of Eve, the Temptation and the Expulsion from Paradise. Adam and Eve were shown naked. The clergy were scandalized, in particular the archbishop, who demanded an explanation first from the curé and then from the Préfet de la Seine, the Baron Haussmann. Haussmann was no friend of Hittorff: they were continually engaged in suits of law and other battles of will. Haussmann set up a committee of investigation, which reported on 5 June 1860 that though the offending nudity might be masked, the strident colours would remain always at odds with the calm grandeur of the architecture. Haussmann was anxious to remove the panels at once, though he did nothing.[18] Jollivet wrote the same day to the archbishop to plead for their retention. So many letters of protest poured in from angry parishioners, however, that he complained yet again to Haussmann and in May or June 1861 the panels were finally removed, with the hope that five at least might be set up inside the church. They remained instead in the crypt, where they were inspected in 1909 by Selmersheim, among others, before being removed to a depot at Ivry, where they are now.

Jollivet launched a full-scale attack on the

155   The painter P.-J. Jollivet at work in his studio. (From E. Texier, *Tableau de Paris*, II, 1853)

156   St-Vincent-de-Paul, Paris: panels of Volvic from the façade, painted by Jollivet. At the top is the Trinity, 1846; below are the panels installed left and right of the door in 1860. (Dépôt de la Ville de Paris, Ivry)

clergy in a pamphlet, *De la peinture religieuse à l'extérieur des églises à propos de l'enlèvement de la décoration extérieure du porche de Sainte-Vincent-de-Paul*, issued in 1861, followed in the next year by a more tempered plea, *Peinture en émail sur lave. Sa raison d'être et sa défense contre les obstacles opposés à son adoption.* His final remarks, written in Deauville, appeared in 1867.[19] He had already built a house and studio for enamel painting for himself in 1856, designed by Anatole Jal, at 11 Cité Malesherbes,[20] in which he partly realized Hittorff's ambition to have a highly coloured façade of Hachette's enamelled plaques, but apart from this and a handful of other less spectacular applications of Volvic, Hittorff's propaganda was without considerable effect.

Certainly colour was not to be applied to building in the way he had proposed, though Charles Garnier, it is fair to note, would not have succeeded in lavishing gold mosaic and gilt on the façade of so important a work as the Paris Opéra without Hittorff's campaign. It acted also as the liberating stimulus for that fashion for luridly coloured glazed bricks and tiles set by Eugène Train's Collège Chaptal of 1863 to 1875, and even more perhaps by the splendidly coloured iron-framed Menier chocolate factory at Noisiel-sur-Marne, designed in 1869 by Jules Saulnier and built between 1871 and 1873. And books such as Jules Lacroux's *La brique ordinaire au point de vue décoratif*, in two volumes, 1878 and 1886, and Pierre Chabat's *La brique et la terre cuite*, the first series of 1881, the second of 1886, attest to the popularity of this colourful vogue.

But the real significance of Hittorff's campaign, however shallow his archaeological studies, however facile his arguments and comic his attempts to realize a polychrome decoration, was his demonstration that attitudes to antiquity

158   A. Jal. 11 Cité Malesherbes, Paris, 1856.

could be radically revised, and revised in a liberating way. He dispelled, virtually single-handed, the torpor into which architects had sunk. It was his very lack of success that inspired others to pursue more thoughtful and sensitive interpretations.

157   St-Vincent-de-Paul, Paris: façade,

159, 160   J.-I. Hittorff. St-Vincent-de-Paul, Paris, consecrated in 1844: side elevation, and front and back elevations. (Universitätsbibliothek, Cologne)

Architectural polychromy: life in architecture

David Van Zanten

Life, like a dome of many-coloured glass,
Stains the white radiance of Eternity

Shelley

Accretion

At the beginning of the 19th century, French architectural students were trained to draw the Greek and Roman orders with the greatest finesse. They refined a technique of graded monochrome ink wash that enabled them to bring out the modelling of these forms in an intense, unmoving light. This way of seeing architecture was essentially sculptural. Appropriately, the overseer of artistic theory and education was a sculptor, Antoine-Chrysostome Quatremère de Quincy – *secrétaire perpétuel* of the Académie des Beaux-Arts and friend of Canova. Quatremère asserted that the columnar, Greco-Roman temple had a 'natural' prototype in the primitive post-and-lintel hut, the equivalent in architecture of the human body in sculpture, and that the three Greek orders were three expressive modes by which architecture could communicate a narrow, conventional range of ideas.

> Nature has provided sculpture with the means to determine relationships, the proportional system of the human body . . . controlling the slightest changes in proportion by fixed ratios between the parts . . . . Architecture, in its way, has set up a similar system . . . so that a building becomes, almost, an organic body, subject to rules that serve as its basis and rationale . . . . The study of the human body in its various forms revealed to sculptors those differences dependent on age and type that inform the various modes established by Polycletus, and which one can see upheld in antique statuary. Architecture has its parallel in the orders. There are three styles: the Doric expresses strength; the Ionic, grace; the Corinthian, combining the first two, expresses nobility and majesty.[1]

As the student sculptor was to study the proportional modes and nuances of Greco-Roman statues, so the student architect was to study the ancient marble column with its base and entablature. The orders were the universal, eternal vocabulary of architecture: 'They are the fixed types of beauty and truth which, like nature, allow of variety but not change'.[2]

When, on 7 October 1826, Quatremère made this statement in his eulogy of the deceased architect M.-J. Hurtault, students present hooted him down so that troops had to be called in to restore order.[3] Quatremère had deprecated the varied, incidental architecture of Paris streets in the eulogy, praising only the statuesque severity of Greco-Roman colonnades, but it was precisely the incidental street architecture that the students were discovering and studying. With their discovery of this world of transient and immediate adornment the students were coming to see Quatremère's orders as the mere dry bones of a dead architecture, bleached white in the Mediterranean sun.

> Those who went to study the remains of the Greek and Roman monuments [the painter and critic Gabriel Laviron wrote of Quatremère's generation in 1834], finding ruins and stones washed by the rain of two thousand years, without any trace of their early splendour, returned home to put up buildings washed in advance, the better to imitate their models. They should have built ruins if they wanted to be truly authentic. Indeed, if the Bourse, the Madeleine and a host of other recent buildings were to fall into ruin and become covered in vegetation, they would look more like Greek buildings than they do in their present condition.[4]

What Laviron thought had been stripped away by time and weather was the original painted polychrome decoration of the ancient temples and all the ancillary adornments that once had clothed them. He had come to see Quatremère's venerated models as mere naked ruins.

Laviron moved on the fringe of a group of Parisian architects[5] who had formulated a radical, 'romantic' conception of architecture in the late 1820s.[6] Their leader was Henri Labrouste, who, after winning the Grand Prix de Rome in 1824, worked out his ideas as a *pensionnaire* in Rome (1825–29), embodying them in his *envois*, yearly studies sent back to Paris, and refining them in conversations with his fellow *pensionnaires*, Félix Duban, Louis Duc, Léon Vaudoyer, Théodore Labrouste (his older brother) and Marie-Antoine Delannoy.[7]

The earliest decisive statement of Labrouste's ideas was his fourth-year *envoi* of 1828, reconstructing the three temples at Paestum, a Greek colonial site south of Naples.[8] These drawings caused a great stir, yet at first glance one might wonder what was so extraordinary. They appear to be precise records of these remarkably well-preserved remains with no obvious flights of graphic imagination. The external painted decoration is restricted to the terracotta coronas. Neil Levine, however, has pointed out the importance of the fact that in his accompanying text Labrouste arranged the buildings chronologically with the 'Temple of Neptune' as the oldest, the 'Temple of Ceres' the next, and the 'Basilica' as the most recent.[9] This is a scrambling of the order accepted before and since,[10] which, based on the assumption that the orders increased progressively in elegance, puts the squat 'Basilica' first, the 'Temple of Neptune' second and the 'Temple of Ceres' third. Labrouste, however, places the 'Temple of Neptune' first because it is the most precise rendition of the paradigm of the Attic Doric temple, the memory of which, he argued, would have been freshest among the colonists immediately upon their arrival in Italy. The 'Temple of Ceres' he placed next because it departs from that paradigm in its proportions and details and in its use of two kinds of stone, indicating a greater knowledge on the part of the colonists of the local environment. Finally, he places the 'Basilica' third because in it the Attic paradigm is completely deformed and used not for a temple at all but for a civil assembly hall.[11] By thus arranging the chronological sequence, Levine explains, these three buildings are made to communicate Labrouste's conception of architectural evolution – one in which the Greek Doric style, removed from its natural and social

habitat, disintegrates. The implications of this were obvious to any architect in 1828; if Greek architecture was too delicate an organism to survive transplanting to Italy in the 5th century BC, how could it possibly be expected to survive transplanting to Paris in the 19th century AD? Greek architecture, Labrouste was saying, is dead, and it died the moment it was uprooted from its natural environment, 2,500 years earlier.

This negative demonstration is not the only message of Labrouste's drawings, however. They also contain a second idea, one clearly demonstrated in the most striking of the sheets, the longitudinal section of the 'Basilica'. Labrouste has sliced the building down its long axis so that its central spine of columns reads as a flat, white silhouette, joining with the white silhouettes of the floor and roof structure to become the skeleton of the building. All the subtleties of the sculpted stone shapes of the orders disappear, only the structural diagram remains, with the walls of the 'Basilica' in another, rendered plane. These walls, Labrouste shows, are no longer those of a temple but those of an assembly hall, which have started to accrue unto themselves a new meaningful decoration: inscriptions recording events, vignettes, the rules of assembly and military trophies. He speaks of 'the need to place here, most conspicuously, a painted sign relating to the rules of assembly; the walls of the portico, I imagine, would also be covered with painted notices, serving as a book'.[12] As the conventional form vocabulary of the Greek temple withers, Labrouste shows another immediately comprehensible decorative vocabulary evolving to clothe the skeleton of the old architecture with the flesh of a new one.

In the same group of *envois* was the second-year project of Léon Vaudoyer, parallels of the temples of 'Hercules' at Cori, of 'Fortuna Virilis' at Rome and of 'Minerva' at Assisi in the Doric, Ionic and Corinthian orders respectively. Vaudoyer had completed research for this project while travelling with Labrouste in the summer of 1828. His reconstructions show the temples completely devoid of polychromy, indeed even stripped of the stucco coatings that each temple bears to this day. And to that the Académie objected: Vaudoyer's removal of the stucco coating changed the proportions of the temples and simplified their detailing; it implied, as Vaudoyer insisted, that the temples were later dressed up with stucco

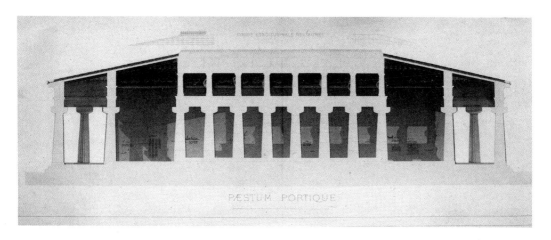

161 H. Labrouste. Reconstruction of the 'Basilica' at Paestum, 1828: longitudinal section.
(Beaux-Arts)

and paint to make them conform to the fuller, more colourful taste of the Empire.[13] Vaudoyer's *envoi*, like Labrouste's, subverted the idea of the forms of the orders as self-sufficient and eternal.

It takes a close reading and analysis of Labrouste's Paestum *envoi* to comprehend its implications. It was executed, however, for public exhibition and for the scrutiny of the Académie; it is mild and discreet compared with a series of reconstructions of ancient cityscapes Labrouste was executing for himself at the same time, most particularly the one inscribed 'Agrigentum 1828', on its back.[14] The dress of trophies of the 'Basilica' section drawing here is joined to a brilliant pervasive painted polychromy and that polychromy is shown laid over the architectural substructure as a sort of shell. The watercolour represents a palace (in the right middleground), a tomb (in the middle) and a temple (at the left) set on a terrace ringed by a defensive wall. Each monument is formed and painted to be distinct from the other: the tomb has a pyramidal top and is painted a rich red with a portrait of the deceased on its entablature; the temple is pedimented with a ship's prow and seahorse acroteria (indicating its dedication to a sea deity?); the palace is open in two tiers of pilastraded loggias (one fictive, the other real) overlooking the landscape. None of these, however, is a canonical Greek building: their half-columns and piers show the slow disintegration of the Attic vocabulary while the Etruscan arches in the fortifications seem to place the scene (as its inscription implies) in Magna Graecia or Sicily. Yet it is the polychromy that emphasizes the reminiscences of the Attic models: the half-columns of the temple are painted to stand out from the wall, as if free-standing; the lower pilastrade of the palace is set off by a painted ground with a dipping upper edge that suggests a curtain hung between the piers.[15]

Around these buildings runs a crenellated terrace pierced by a city gate. Here polychromy appears in another, fiercer guise. The walls are painted red and blue, perhaps as a religious symbol or a defensive charm like the multi-coloured rings of fortifications Herodotus described at Ecbatana.[16] Over the gate are strapped three shields, two spears and a broken chariot wheel: bits of battlefield litter to frighten an enemy. A line of triglyphs is painted on the red wall behind, but is chipping off with the stucco. The similar Etruscan gate at Perugia has a line of triglyphs carved in the masonry above it, with shields in the metopes. Labrouste seems to have been suggesting that such carved motifs had their origin in the effort to make permanent the more primitive and immediately meaningful painted and attached adornment.

Labrouste's fellow *pensionnaire*, Félix Duban, executed similar watercolour fantasies,[17] among them one inscribed 'A Pompéia', developing 162 the same themes as the 'Agrigentum', only more gently. An interior room is shown divided from a city street by an architectural screen. A portion of that screen is formed of a bas-relief represent-

162 F. Duban. *A Pompéia*, *c*.1828. (Coll. Neil Levine)

ing a man and a woman turning to look at each other, the man reaching towards the woman and pouring a libation. This is the conventional representation of a marriage ceremony in Roman reliefs, lacking only the figure of a deity sometimes included between and above the figures, consecrating the bond.[18] What is interesting is that this relief is set immediately beyond a double seat, while to the right the goddess Roma is painted on the wall above an altar dedicated to her.[19] The room is clearly arranged for a marriage ceremony to be acted out before its depiction in the relief. Across the street, a small house is being decorated with a garland and a high, blue, draped wainscoting:[20] is this the house the newly-weds will occupy after the ceremony and is the relief the commemoration of the parents' marriage before? (Duban himself was married in Rome in 1828, about when this watercolour would have been executed.)[21] If this interpretation is correct, Duban, like Labrouste in the gate in his 'Agrigentum', is showing how architectural decoration accumulates: how it starts from an event in the builders' lives; how it first takes the form of temporary adornments draped over an

architectural skeleton; and how it finally takes permanent form in the architecture.

The younger partisans of Labrouste and Duban studying in their *ateliers* (opened in 1830 and 1832, respectively) understood polychromy as a clothing of a structural skeleton with objects, inscriptions and scenes communicating the building's social function and history. In 1835, Gabriel Toudouze, a pupil of Labrouste, executed a project for an amphitheatre. The articulation of the naked brick *cavea* is simplified, but the door is set off in a field of rusticated masonry (the joints picked out in paint) below a broad panel defined by carved Corinthian columns and painted with a scene of a bullfight.[22] One's eyes are drawn from the skeletal surfaces of the *cavea* to the flesh of the rusticated doorway, then finally to the expressive face of the painted panel, and there the conventional vocabulary of building is replaced with the pictorial imagery of paint and the building speaks. The panel is like an X-ray view illusionistically permitting the eye to penetrate the walls and to perceive the activity that brought the building into existence.

The discretion of these early *envois* did not last long. A series of studies sent back from Rome between 1830 and 1836 by a group of younger *pensionnaires* expressed the concept of an accretive polychromed architecture with ever-increasing extravagance. Théodore Labrouste's fourth-year *envoi*, of 1831, reconstructing the temples of 'Hercules' and of 'Castor and Pollux' at Cori, starts the series, to be followed in 1832 by the even more interesting fourth-year *envoi* of Marie-Antoine Delannoy, reconstructing the Tiber Island in Rome.[23] This depicts a precinct of Aesculapius as a crowded jumble of public and private buildings, the two growing around each other like the houses and churches of the Ile de la Cité in Paris. The houses are bizarrely painted, pointing up the garishness of the painting of the temples; the street walls are marred with graffiti, imputing the nature of similar inscriptions in the religious precincts; the shops are hung with wares, implying a parallel with the ex-votos in the temples. Delannoy insists upon reducing the Roman temple, which to the neoclassicists was the highest and most serious form of architectural art, to the level of street architecture – and in 1826 it had been Quatremère's refusal to admire the incidental architecture of Paris's streets that had roused the students to protest.

163

164

11

163   G. Toudouze. Amphithéâtre au système de ceux des Romains, *projet rendu* for the second
class of the Ecole des Beaux-Arts, 1835: elevation. (Bibliothèque Nationale)

164   T. Labrouste. Reconstruction of the 'Temple of Hercules', Cori, 1831: elevation. (Beaux-Arts)

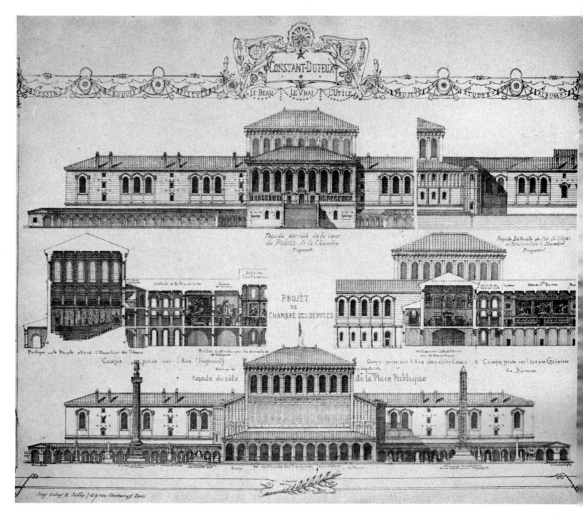

165   S.-C. Constant-Dufeux. Chamber of
Deputies for France, 1835: from bottom to top,
elevation of the main or public façade; sections
(from front to back; longitudinal through the
conference hall and through the galleries); and
elevations of the rear and part of the side.

167   S.-C. Constant-Dufeux. Chamber of
Deputies for France: plan, reproduced upside-
down so that the entrance front, with the
projecting Chamber, is at the bottom. Above it, in
axis, is the conference hall, dividing two
courtyards surrounded by galleries and by offices
for the nine Bureaux, archives, etc.

166   B. Poyet. Façade of the Chamber of Deputies,
Paris, 1806–08.

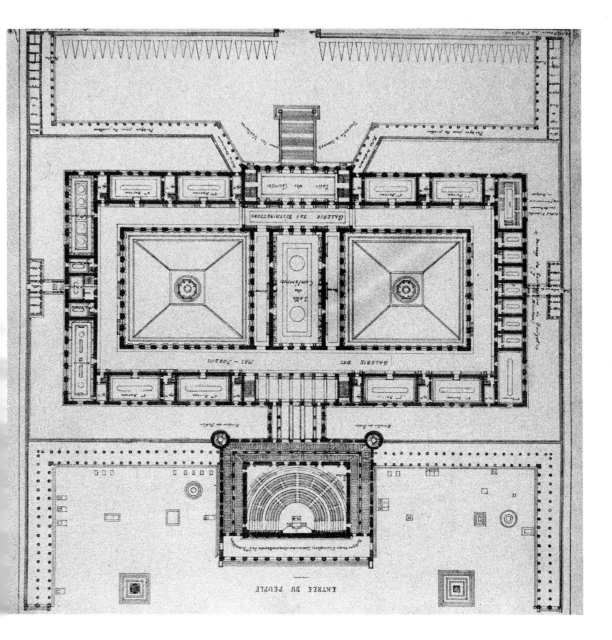

The fourth-year *envois* were archaeological studies. As such, they posed the problem of polychromy historically. The fifth-year *envois* were modern projects based on programmes devised by the *pensionnaires* themselves. Those of Duban, Labrouste and Vaudoyer were somewhat tentative and discreet,[24] but in 1835 165, Constant-Dufeux executed an extraordinary 167 design for a new Chamber of Deputies.[25] The project was obviously made with the old Chamber of Deputies, then being extended, in mind.[26]

The first thing evident in comparing the two 166 façades is that the monumental columnar temple front that constitutes the whole elevation of the

Napoleonic building has, in a sense, slipped down Constant-Dufeux's façade to become a series of short Doric half-columns embedded in an arcaded portico. The majestic file of statuesque shafts topping a high cascade of steps has been transformed into a low, functional cloister at street level serving to keep the rain off visitors arriving at the building. And as that colonnade has slipped down, it has revealed the blank, boxy volume of the Chamber itself – its front ornamented only with a lengthy inscription head CHARTE CONSTITUTIONELLE. The Chamber is pierced with a ring of large arched windows and crowned with an arched cornice

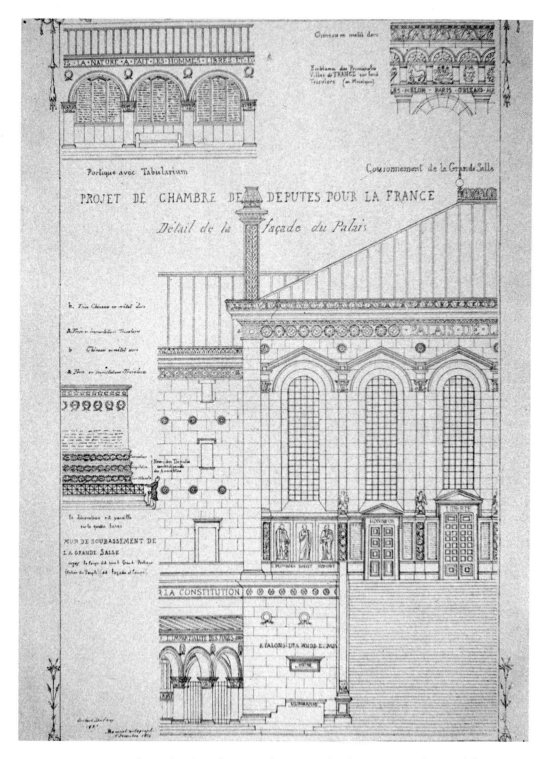

168 S.-C. Constant-Dufeux. Chamber of Deputies for France: details. From top to bottom, left to right, they show: part of the inscribed 'tabularium'; cornice of the Chamber, with gilt metal cresting and emblems of the cities of France on a tricolor ground, in 'mosaic' (painted porcelain); plinth of the Chamber; and the rear or private entrance.

containing painted porcelain plaques bearing the arms of the cities of France. The roof is hipped to cast off the rains and snows of the north; the windows are expansive to admit an ample flow of the feeble northern light.[27]

Behind the Chamber lies a second, larger, less open and decorated volume. Constant-Dufeux rephrased and regularized the 1830 constitution of France as his programme, and the layout of the building is the direct result:

> The chamber will be composed of 450 deputies who will debate in public session. The chamber will be divided into nine sections, of eighty members each, called Bureaux; each Bureau will appoint one or two of its members for committees . . . . The Bureaux and committees will prepare the deputies for general debates; their work will be done in private, thus the Bureaux *must* be housed in a separate building, removed from the noise of traffic by enclosing walls or porticoes.[28]

Thus the building divides into two distinct parts, one public, one private. The private part faces inward and is externally little decorated (although apparently sumptuous inside). The public part faces outward – functional in its square volume, low portico, protruding stair towers and tall windows – gathering to itself a characterizing decoration. Crowned with the sparkling porcelain emblems of the cities of the nation, the constitution itself inscribed on its brow, the Chamber pushes out into a public space filled with political memorials and monuments: a column 'à la mémoire des victimes de la Révolution'; the Monument Desaix; a 'sépulture aux citoyens morts en Juillet 1830'; and the obelisk of Luxor (set up in the Place de la Concorde in 1836). An arcaded 'tabularium' – a wall for inscriptions and memorials – embraces this space on three sides. In the space or under the sheltering porticoes the public might wait for the opening of the session, then flow into the building through the broad corridors surrounding the Chamber and climb the spiral staircases to the two tiers of tribunes. The inner wall of that annular corridor Constant-Dufeux has shown stepping forward in a series of four tall benches. In a detail drawing he shows that these benches are decorative bands inscribed with all the names of the deputies in the Constituent Assembly, the Legislative Assembly and in the Convention – the three original Revolutionary legislatures of France. The Chamber of Deputies is thus made to rest physically upon the memory of the Revolution and the first representatives of the people. Constant-Dufeux's building embodies the history and organization of the French government, as a Gothic cathedral once embodied that of the Christian doctrine: in its pattern of volumes it states the structure of the political system, in its decorative dress it communicates its spirit. Founded upon the legislators of the Revolution; its constitution open for all to read; the names and history of its people gathered about it in memorials and inscriptions increasing year by year.[29]

Nonetheless, despite all the details and the immediacy of choosing as his programme the French constitution of 9 August 1830, Constant-Dufeux's Chamber of Deputies is only a more elaborate and explicit version of Labrouste's 'Basilica' of 1828. Some motifs are identical: the 'tabularium' for memorial inscriptions; the replacement of the pediment by a hipped roof; the cluster of monuments. Both are new building types created by the skeletalization of traditional forms and by their reclothing in a new, immediately meaningful dress of brightly coloured inscriptions, emblems and memorials.[30]

Articulation

In the light of this series of reconstructions and designs, the accepted idea of the discovery of ancient Greek polychromy in 1830 must be re-examined. Only since 1968 have these particular drawings been exhumed, studied, put on display and published.[31] Prior to that, the architectural polychromy of the 1830s was thought to have been chiefly the obsession of Jacques-Ignace Hittorff.[32] And, indeed, Hittorff proposed a very thorough painting of the Greek temple, and proposed it early (1823–30),[33] proclaimed it loudly and published it extensively in a series of papers culminating in his massive *Restitution du temple d'Empédocle à Sélinonte, ou l'architecture polychrome chez les Grecs* (usually known by the second part of its title), of 1846–51.[34] He made it the subject of general discussion through a noisy debate with Desiré Raoul Rochette (soon to be Quatremère's successor as *secretaire perpétuel* of the Académie des Beaux-Arts).[35] A closer look at his ideas, however, particularly in comparison to those of Labrouste and the *pensionnaires*, reveals that Hittorff only inflected contemporary neoclassicism; that – as Labrouste himself noted – Hittorff's disagreement with the Académie was not serious[36] (a point underlined by the fact that Hittorff was elected to that body in 1853 whereas Labrouste had to wait until 1867 to occupy the very place vacated by Hittorff upon his death).

Hittorff took as his point of departure the idea that Greek architectural polychromy must have been as orderly, balanced and harmonious as the forms that it articulated. That is, Hittorff proposed that just as there was believed to be a set, conventional order (preferably expressed through the classical orders) in the forms, so there should be a set, conventional order in the polychromy. He recognized the archaeological fact of the existence of this polychromy, but imagined it as an extension of the received concept of Greek architectural form. He wrote in presenting his reconstruction in 1830:

My main aim ... has been, by bringing together the facts and supporting evidence, to show that architectural polychromy was invariably used by the Greeks, and that it was accepted in all their buildings as the most appropriate means of adding charm and elegance to the majesty of their temples – qualities of poetry that are always associated with this people and their gods. I wished to demonstrate that this system, which achieves its effects through the freshness and vividness of colour, was the only way by which an artist, erecting buildings under the clearest of skies, lit by the brightest of suns and surrounded by the most brilliantly coloured vegetation, could bring his work into harmony with the inexhaustible richness of nature; and that when applied in its entirety to an antique building, it implied no betrayal of the perfection and beauty of Greek art.[37]

The implication of Hittorff's insistence upon speaking of a 'system' of polychrome decoration is evident in the final clause, in which he asserts that the system must be imagined in its entirety and thus seems to refer to the contemporaneous reconstructions of the *pensionnaires* and to refute them, putting forward a principle very different from that of haphazard accretion.

Hittorff's theory centred on the reconstruction of the painted decoration of a single small Greek temple at Selinus in Sicily that he excavated during the winter of 1823–24. Like all Sicilian temples, it was of rough local limestone, stuccoed and painted. He believed it to have been dedicated to the local philosopher-god Empedocles. He exhibited his reconstruction before the Académie des Beaux-Arts on 3 April 1830, reading an explanatory paper,[38] and again at the Salon in 1831. It finally became the centrepiece of his *Architecture polychrome chez les Grecs*. What is important about the reconstruction is that Hittorff did not find evidence for many of the painted details in his excavation itself but instead extrapolated them from parallels in other ancient buildings. The anta capitals, for example, he copied from those found at Aegina and Rhamnus, the pattern of the mosaic floor from a similar floor in the museum at Catania, the rinceau pattern in the pediment from the 'Tomb of Jehoshaphat' in Jerusalem, and the painting of the exterior and interior cella walls from the Roman paintings at Pompeii and the Etruscan paintings just discovered in the tombs at Tarquinia.[39] To Labrouste, concerned in his Paestum reconstruction with the disintegration of Doric architecture when removed from its Attic habitat, such a composite reconstruction, using pieces from sites located all over the Mediterranean and from at least five different centuries, was unthinkable. To Vaudoyer, convinced that the limestone buildings of Italy only subsequently received their coatings of stucco and paint, the reconstruction of a system of polychromatic decoration integral to the original construction was historically naïve. But Hittorff did not share their vivid historical sense; he saw the forms of architecture, not the life that they embraced.

He believed that there was a system of polychromy as there was one of form, the two in harmony and mutually reinforcing. One could restore the painted decoration of the 'Temple of Empedocles' from a number of examples just as one could restore the system of forms of a Greek temple from many sources, the relationship of parts being constant within certain limits, the limits of the orders. And one could judge the correctness of the temple's polychromy with an eye already trained to judge the correctness of Greek architectural form – that is, in terms of balance and harmony. Hittorff reports that he invited his old teacher Charles Percier to examine his restoration of the 'Temple of Empedocles'. 'I wanted to begin at once to explain how I had started and where I had found the models for my restoration, but the noble head of our profession, an artist to the depths of his soul, interrupted me to say, with his firm gentleness, "First let me look, my friend: it is a work of art that you want me to judge, and one can appreciate such works only by eye".'[40] After a half-hour's silent inspection, Percier turned and shook Hittorff's hand. The architecture of the ancient Greeks was also the modern Frenchman's architecture: it could be judged by the modern architect as by the Greek. 'These forms are the very language of architecture: the ancients invented them only because they came first'.[41]

Hittorff in his paper of 1830 attributed at least four functions to Greek architectural polychromy: to harmonize the structural surfaces with the paintings and coloured sculptures adorning the temples; to harmonize all this with the brilliant colours of the Mediterranean environment; to stress the architectural forms; and to make more precise the expression of the building's character.[42] The first three relate to his concept of polychromy as a part of the system of the orders. His friend Ernest Beulé, the third *secrétaire perpétuel* to the Académie, noted: 'Hittorff understood that paint, applied artistically to a building, revealed the details, set off the forms, and underlined the ideal character, just as the fresh colour on the face of a young girl is, if not her beauty, at least the light of her beauty'.[43] The last of the four functions, however, is more interesting: here a desire to warm icy neoclassicism, which is necessarily implicit in studying colour at all, becomes unmistakably evident.

> As a result of accepted ideas on the character of Doric architecture, one might note a certain disparity between the severity of the form and this richness of detail, but reflection will reveal that this is no more than apparent. Far from being in opposition to the rationale of the Greeks, the system lends itself to the variety required as a result of using the Doric order for temples dedicated to a variety of gods. The range of colour application provides an infinite means to express the magnificence of temples, according to the local or universal significance of the god. They could thus make distinctions clear, without changing the universal type of their architecture of the best period . . . .
> The degree of richness of the painted ornament gave the required degree of splendour to sacred buildings, depending on the lustre one might wish to confer on the gods.[44]

Hittorff denied that the orders expressed particular character (citing the fact, which became increasingly obvious as the Greek temples were studied, that the Doric order had been used for all deities in Attica); he suggested instead that the degree of richness of decoration served that purpose. And from this Hittorff proceeded to note one of the most peculiar features of his reconstruction of the 'Temple of Empedocles': an Ionic entablature set over two Doric columns.[45] He explained this in 1830,[46] and again in his *Architecture polychrome chez les Grecs*: 'The choice of orders is unimportant in establishing the character of Greek and Roman sanctuaries; but if the principle had existed, would not the mingling of strength and elegance expressed by the Doric entablature and the Ionic column have been fittingly exhibited whenever these two qualities were combined in the same god, as in the case of Diana and Pallas, Bacchus and Apollo, or even when it was necessary to express symbolically the union of human nature and the divine, as with deified mortals?'[47] Empedocles, significantly, was a philosopher deified – just such a *mortel divinisé*. In a lecture on Agrigentum in 1859, Hittorff went on to assert that the combination of the Doric and Ionic elements in such a situation 'could not be more positive, more rational'.[48]

Following his explanation of the character of a building in his 1830 paper, Hittorff suggested that this expression of character through the mélange of parts was a general historical principle, although he refuses to explain himself: 'I will not enter here into a detailed analysis of this development, expressive of a particular period in the history of art, preferring to deal with it later at proper length'.[49] Fortunately, Hittorff did develop these ideas further, in an entry, 'Architecture', in the *Encyclopédie des gens du monde*, of 1833: 'The architecture of all nations and all periods is a continuous process of imitation of that preceding it, never losing its traces, despite the differences in buildings of different ages'.[50] Applying this to Greek architecture, Hittorff saw the concept as modifying Quatremère's absolute distinction between Egyptian architecture, evolved, Quatremère thought, from the 'type' of the cave, and Greek, based on that of the hut. Hittorff wrote:

> Though Greek architecture is, more than any other, imprinted with the character of the hut, it is no less evident that the oldest temples of Greece, with their columns of stone and marble, have proportions so close to those of the Egyptian temples and so very different

from those of the indigenous trees of Greece that Greek architecture, in so far as its rules and proportions are the most perfect, owes them alone to the use of marble and stone, and to the rational forms that the nature of these materials has imposed, so that despite their differences in origin, Egyptian and Greek architecture have such close similarities in their architectonic natures that we might believe them to have a common origin.[51]

Furthermore, if the Greek temple was in some sense a *déduction imitative* of the Egyptian sanctuary, so was every subsequent architecture.

In tracing the different origins of this art and the wide varieties it has produced, one becomes aware that no particular architecture can serve as an exclusive study and model for building at another period, for other customs, for another climate.... All these styles – Greek, Egyptian, Moorish – compared one with another and with those which derive from them, offer particular beauties and effects unknown to the ancients.[52]

Here, however, Hittorff offers a restriction, modifying his last sentence with the words: 'a fact that one must apply with care, with established rules and proven precepts, to arrive at a coherent and homogeneous whole'.

Thus the quality of modification implicit in Hittorff's theory of polychromy as expressive of specific character was paralleled by a theory of modification, or more precisely, of mélange in architectural detailing, specifically in that most conventional element, the order. This led him to accept mélange as a general principle in architecture, operating in relation to the individual volumes that made up architectural ensembles. In the 1859 paper on Agrigentum cited above – in fact the official discourse at the annual *séance publique* of the Académie des Beaux-Arts – Hittorff praised the mélange in an ancient Greek tomb of the pyramid and the temple form.

This study establishes that, in addition to the pyramid's connotation of permanence and its association with death, the Hellenes in using the form for a tomb attached to it another notion both proud and sublime: to raise on the tops of their temples a replica of the famous tombs of the kings of Egypt, always set on the ground, and to discover in this union of a Greek sanctuary and an

Egyptian pyramid the most accomplished of sepulchral monuments. In a like manner Bramante's genius thought to place the Pantheon of ancient Rome on top of a Christian basilica, to create the most imposing of all Catholic churches.[53]

Here Hittorff opposed Quatremère de Quincy once again: in his *Dictionnaire de l'architecture* of 1832, Quatremère had scorned this very arrangement: 'what can be the meaning of this circular temple on a rectangular one, whose external mass seems designed only to adorn the outskirts of a town, and whose internal articulation seems to belong to the aerial regions?'[54]

At the time Hittorff started preaching these ideas, just after 1830, he was redesigning and completing a major building in Paris embodying them, the church of St Vincent-de-Paul of 1831–44. This had been begun in 1823 by Hittorff's father-in-law, Jean-Baptiste Lepère, as a simple double-aisled basilica with a projecting portico of ten columns and a tower attached to the rear of the apse.[55] Construction had languished, and when it was recommenced in 1831 Hittorff added two towers over the first outer aisle bays (two lower towers were projected over the last two outer aisle bays as well, but were not carried out),[56] widened the apse so that it embraced the inner two aisles, deepened the portico and enriched the details with polychromatic decoration (which in the end was never completed externally).

159, 160, 151, 149, VIII

It was immediately recognized that Hittorff's façade was intended as an integration of Gothic and Greek elements, two great traditions of Western architecture.[57] This is, of course, an equivalent of the pyramid and the temple combined in the tomb at Agrigentum that Hittorff was to praise in 1859. But it was also recognized that while the constituent elements were from more than one historical source, they were all dressed up in a classical vocabulary of pilasters and mouldings and proportioned with classical breadth and monumentality. Even if none of the constituent elements had been Greco-Roman in historical origin, the building would nonetheless have been classical in its composition and decorative detailing. Hittorff has indeed adhered to his own requirement of 1833 that while a modern building must be a mélange it must also be *un tout homogène* following in its composition *règles certaines* and *préceptes éprouvés*.

The presence of the paired 'Gothic' façade towers was to identify the building as a church and to the same end Hittorff planned painted angels and crosses on the friezes to stress its Christian character. This polychromatic decoration, however, was entirely subordinated to the sculpted forms of the architecture (so that one does not even notice today that it was not carried out) and would have functioned in the same way as the angel heads carved in the rinceau of the portico frieze or the crosses in the anthemion pattern on the necking of the Ionic columns: as an embellishment of the conventional system to communicate specific character.

We observed earlier that Hittorff lacked Labrouste's historical consciousness in his combination of examples from all antiquity to make III up his *système* of the 'Temple of Empedocles' IV polychromy. Here, in the church of St Vincent-de-Paul, we see him carrying out the same ahistorical combining of motifs from the whole span of styles, as if each element was a fixed sign in a set architectural vocabulary, which expanded with the passage of time, but from which no signs fell out of use – that is, in which temporal distance and the resultant decay were absent. And just as in the case of polychromy, Hittorff felt that greater or lesser emphasis might be obtained by the inclusion or exclusion of parts of the decorative system, as long as the system was itself preserved intact; thus in St Vincent-de-Paul he suggested one might combine a variety of elements as long as they were fitted into a conventional compositional framework. Yet, despite his insensitivity to temporal distance – to the individuality of each architectural epoch and to its subsequent disintegration – Hittorff also went against many of the details of Quatremère's classical doctrine. Hittorff's and Quatremère's ahistoricism are not the same. Hittorff's was mechanistic, the orders were understood as an abstract geometric grid into which a series of neatly fitting signs might be inserted. Quatremère's ahistoricism admitted only one form: the compositional grid and its constituent element, the column. Hittorff did not destroy the rules of neoclassical architecture, but he did destroy the spirit, for his division of design into abstract composition and elements to be composed begins the separation of form from content, which was to receive its clearest and most radical expression when Labrouste combined this separation with a real sense of temporal distance, cultural uniqueness and decay in his Paestum drawings.

Dematerialization

To the educated public in 1830, Hittorff seemed the champion of architectural polychromy; to the young 'romantic' artists, Labrouste and his friends so appeared. But in the end, the profoundest adherents of the idea were found in a third place, in the loose community of young German and English architects who visited Paris and absorbed the bright ideas circulating in the *ateliers*.

Franz Christian Gau, born in Cologne, conducted a private architectural school in Paris in the 1820s, which attracted foreigners unwilling to take the entrance examination of the Ecole des Beaux-Arts. The Dane, M. G. B. Bindesbøll, studied with him in 1823 and later, from 1826 to 1830, Gottfried Semper.[58] Semper then set out for Rome and Greece accompanied by the Frenchman Jules Goury, from Leclère's *atelier*. Returning to Hamburg in 1833, Semper left Goury in Athens to continue his explorations with the Briton Owen Jones, and they continued on to Constantinople, the Levant, Egypt and finally to Granada. There, in 1834, Goury died of cholera, but not before completing with Jones a painstaking study of the Alhambra, published under their joint authorship by Jones from 1836 to 1845.[59]

These men had one thing in common: a fascination with the element of colour in architecture. Gau, although he had impressive intellectual credentials and seems to have been pivotal in bringing polychromy to the general consciousness,[60] has not left us a coherent theory, in spite of producing two major publications and one important building.[61] Goury died before he could make public a compendious study of architectural polychromy, known and admired by Semper.[62] Bindesbøll, however, went on to erect the Thorvaldsen Museum in Copenhagen, painted inside and out; Semper to conceive the great theory of his *Stil*; and Jones to build a remarkable series of painted iron and glass structures during the 1850s.

The Thorvaldsen Museum was begun as a series of projects executed for Thorvaldsen's amusement in Rome during the winter of 1836–37. Many are brilliantly polychromed, if derivative.[63] The museum became a reality in 1839, when Bindesbøll was commissioned to transform the royal stables at Charlottenbord Palace in Copenhagen into a repository for the sculptor's work, recently given to the state. He

169, 170   M. G. B. Bindesbøll. Thorvaldsen Museum, Copenhagen, 1839–44: façade, and detail of painted frieze.

169 added a monumental hall at the front of the utilitarian brick building and carried its file of 'Etruscan' doors around the exterior, picking out the insistent rhythm in ochre, white, red and blue. Then, interwoven with the pattern of blank door embrasures, he stretched around
170 the sides and back a painted frieze depicting the transportation of Thorvaldsen's work to Co-
VI penhagen by ship. In the interior court, around Thorvaldsen's tomb, the frieze is expanded to occupy the entire wall surface up to the cornice, with oaks, palms and laurels.

The Thorvaldsen Museum is not a conventionally composed building; historians have sought a historical model in vain.[64] Indeed, it is self-contradictory: the 'Etruscan' door motif makes no sense on the sides and back; the frieze has slipped down from the entablature to the ground level, addressing the viewer with unexpected immediacy. The rhythm of forms, the colours, the illusions are too insistent and vivid. The building has two interwoven scales: that of the file of doors, large and made larger for being underlined in colour; and that of the frieze, small and made smaller by its illusionism.
II It is a built fantasy, like Labrouste's 'Agrigentum' in its simultaneous strangeness and immediacy. Bindesbøll has permitted paint to transform his architecture; he has not, like Hittorff, used it to articulate a neoclassical composition.

Semper's formulation of his monumental theory began while studying Greek polychromy with Goury in Italy, Sicily and Greece in 1830–33.[65] He embodied his first ideas in two publications: a folio of chromolithographed plates, *Die Anwendung der Farben in der Architektur und Plastik* (published in 1836 at his expense and discontinued after the first fascicle) and a pamphlet of 1834 serving as the folio's introduction, *Vorläufige Bemerkungen über bemalte Architektur und Plastik bei den Alten*. In the plates, he showed the Greek temples painted red, set off with V touches of green, purple and gold.[66] In the pamphlet, he put forward an explanation of painted architecture based on a careful intellectualization of Labrouste's accretive idea.[67] He attempted to demonstrate how decorative colour and form evolved dialectically and how both derived from real objects originally attached to primitive huts and temples. He used the example of the bead moulding, proposing that it evolved thus: 1) the actual braided hair of a sacrificial victim was suspended in the temple; 2) a representation of this braid was painted flat on the wall as a symbol; 3) that representation was etched into the wall to preserve it from weathering; 4) beads were painted on this carved moulding; 5) the moulding was carved in relief and painted, at first flatly, later with shadows and highlights; 6) beads were carved into the moulding, heightened with paint.[68] In 1851, Semper published his *Vier Elemente der Baukunst* (alternatively entitled *Über Polychromie*) refining and generalizing this idea. Here he proposed that architectural decoration was determined by the memory of one of the primitive crafts that had originally been combined in the making of buildings – those of masonry (the foundation), of carpentry (the roof structure), and of weaving (the walls).[69] Although the primitive hut was long ago superseded by the homogeneous masonry structure, Semper theorized that the decorative motifs carved into its surfaces retained the memory of masonry patterns in the foundations, rafters in the ceilings and textile patterns in the walls. Finally, in his massive (and incomplete) *Stil in der technischen und tektonischen Künsten* of 1860–63 Semper codified this into his theories of *Stoffwechsel* and *Bekleidung*. The first concept was that the decoration of a particular element of a building remained the same regardless of the material in which it was rendered, being derived from the primitive craft that originally produced that element. The second concept was that architectural construction was clothed (literally, *bekleidet*) with this decoration and thus was only a framework for what was a fantasy – although a structural fantasy.[70] What is fascinating about Semper's slowly unfolding theory is that behind it lies the image of Labrouste's 'Agrigentum': architecture as a structural skeleton clothed with a meaningful (rather than conventional) decoration.

The first two decades of Jones's career were principally devoted to the production of his *Alhambra*, for which he perfected the technique of chromolithography for the huge, precise plates at the cost of his personal fortune.[71] In 1850, however, he was appointed superintendent of the works for the erection of the Crystal Palace and set to work on the first and most celebrated demonstration of architectural polychromy applied to a modern ferro-vitreous building.

His work on that project fortuitously coincided with two meetings of the Royal Institute of British Architects on 12 and 26 January 1851, devoted to the discussion of ancient Greek architectural polychromy. Hittorff, Semper and Jones all attended,[72] and *The Civil Engineer and Architect's Journal* recorded the deliberations in detail.[73] Hittorff's *Architecture polychrome chez les Grecs* was summarized by T. L. Donaldson. Semper (whose reconstruction drawings of painted Greek temples were exhibited on the walls of the hall) explained that he believed them to have been painted red in a 'transparent enamel' with decorative details picked out in contrasting colours to produce a strong, glowing effect. (He had earlier in his *Vorläufige Bemerkungen* described Greco-Roman polychromy as being applied in small areas and of brilliant hue so as to mix visually.)[74] Jones stated his own belief to be 'that the columns [of the Parthenon] were coloured gold .... It must have been done by gilding upon the stucco.'

He explained: 'There was already evidence, which could not possibly be controverted, that the Parthenon was partially coloured, and he considered that it might be assumed, in fact, that it was entirely coloured. Not only portions of colour, but actual painted forms had been traced upon the mouldings, and he believed that the colours that bounded these forms must have been of the greatest possible intensity, as otherwise they would have been indistinguishable, and perfectly useless at the height from the ground at which they were placed. These, indeed, could not have been tints, but positive colours.'[75] Later in the discussion Jones added that 'notwithstanding the use of such positive colours', he assumed that they were 'so well balanced ... as to produce a bloom which would be satisfactory in its effect.'[76]

Jones's remarks were the application to the Parthenon, that standard of architectural perfection, of a whole theory of architectural polychromy, which was sketched out more fully, if less dramatically, in his contemporaneous writings and designs.[77] The 'positive colours' that he imagined covering all the surfaces of the Parthenon were the primary colours: red, yellow and blue. The gilt columns were the yellow component of the triad (gold being the cognate of yellow), Jones evidently applying to the Parthenon the system of colouring he had reconstructed for the Alhambra.[78] The implied parallel of the Alhambra and the Parthenon explains the last of Jones's remarks, that the primaries were 'so well balanced and harmonized as to produce a bloom':[79] he believed that the primaries at the Alhambra were applied in precise proportion so that they produced a quasi-musical harmony that blended visually into a vibrant white when seen from a distance. He was using the word 'bloom' in the sense of 'glowing with warmth or with a warm colour' (Webster's definition).

Jones subsequently designed a series of painted buildings in which he applied the primaries to achieve this 'bloom' of chromatic harmony.[80] To decorate the huge iron and glass Crystal Palace in 1850–51 he refrained both from using ornamental castings and from painting the individual structural members, covering all the spidery elements instead with narrow stripes of red, yellow and blue separated by white. The white was to impart purity of hue, in accordance with the chromatic researches of Michel Chevreul; the primaries to achieve

II

171   O. Jones. Crystal Palace Bazaar, London, 1858. (From the *Illustrated London News*, 1858)

chromatic harmony (applied in the proportion of three parts yellow to five red to eight blue, perfect balance according to the researches of George Field).[81] The desired visual result (evidently achieved) for the vast open interior of the building was the slow passage from vivid colour outlining the forms of the elements in the foreground to an atmospheric, vibrant white – Jones's 'bloom' – as the hues mixed in the distance. In a later building, the Crystal Palace Bazaar, opened in 1858, Jones sought to create this same effect of space pervaded by a chromatic glow by more direct means: a ceiling of stained glass triangles of red, yellow and blue in Field's harmonic proportions. So perfect was the balance that Jones asserted a scientifically white light would actually be projected on the goods sold inside so that their colour could be correctly judged by the customers. Gas fixtures were hung between two layers of the ceiling to illuminate it at night so that it would work as a huge, unvarying source of a pervasive, pure light. Jones used the same system in Osler's glass shop of the same year and we can judge the effect sought from his watercolour rendering.

The largest and most celebrated of this series of buildings was St James's Hall, a concert theatre, of 1855–58. Although built with a self-supporting iron skeleton, it was not ferro-vitreous, the deep barrel-vaulted ceiling being of papier-mâché. This was divided into lozenge-shaped fields of stylized floral ornament and painted bright red, blue and gold, while a cloud of star-shaped gas fixtures was suspended below it projecting upward a brilliant illumination, intended to cause the surface to glow and light the room by reflection – in the same manner as the glass ceilings of the Crystal Palace Bazaar and Osler's shop. Here at St James's Hall, however, the vibrant chromatic 'bloom' that was made to fill the room was not in order to permit the correct judgment of textile colours or to produce sparkling reflections on glassware, but rather to reinforce the aural waves of musical harmony projected through the room by the orchestra. The whole interior became a sort of static colour organ.

Jones's proposition that the Parthenon was painted in positive colours with gilt columns, made before the members of the Royal Institute of British Architects that evening in January, 1851, thus seems comprehensible enough: he was imagining the harmony of its forms complemented by a harmony of colours.

Yet there is something a little odd about his statement of this old idea: gilding is a very intense sort of yellow; a 'bloom' is a very special sort of colour balance; the Alhambra is a very unusual source for the reconstruction of Greek architectural decoration. Jones may seem to agree with Winckelmann (and Hittorff) that Greek art was characterized by simplicity and balance, but he has transformed the particular nature of that simplicity and balance. Just how, is evident in a description of the effect of Greek temple polychromy written in 1851 by his friend Semper:

> The prevailing colours of the temple burned with all the glowing beauty of the setting sun. The colour may be defined as of a yellow-red, very vapoury, resembling that of the finest terracotta. In fact, the general appearance of the temple would precisely resemble the appearance of a fine day in an Eastern climate.[82]

Jones would have imagined the glow as a vibrant white, but would otherwise have agreed Semper and Jones imagined that a brilliantly enamelled or gilded Greek temple when seen on its acropolis in the intense Mediterranean sun would simply have disappeared into some sort of vibrant 'bloom', precisely resembling 'the appearance of a fine day in an Eastern climate'. Sparkling in the rising or setting sun, it would have reflected the rays and become itself a sunrise or sunset: an analogy for these great natural phenomena.

In thus rephrasing Semper's statement, we have emphasized the idea of comparing a building to an atmospheric effect. Semper, however, specifically related the colouring of a Greek temple to that of a fine day in an *Eastern* climate,[83] that is, he imagined a harmony between the temple's colouring and the particular atmospheric quality of the environment. He thus implies that a building erected in another environment would have a different chromatic 'bloom' in harmony with the atmospheric quality of that environment.[84] And Jones said as much at the RIBA in 1851, when he noted, 'At present we transplanted a Greek temple into England'; in his opinion, the 'colouring on it would be more out of place than the building itself'.[85] The form of a Greek temple was derived in part from the materials chosen and the trabeated technique of construction adopted in their assembly, that would remain largely the same whether executed in Greece

172   O. Jones. St James's Hall, London, 1855–58.

or in England. What would be most dramatically different would be the atmospheric environment – misty and dark in England rather than clear and bright – and since that determined the building's colouring, the colouring would be entirely different.[86]

Jones refined this concept one step further. He asserted that the polychromatic 'bloom' of a building not only varied with the atmospheric quality of its environment, but also in response to the cultural maturity of the society producing it. Primaries were preferred by young, recently founded societies; secondary colours by older, declining societies.[87] This makes evident another aspect of the polychromatic 'bloom' that Jones and Semper saw embracing the great buildings of history: the 'bloom' was internally generated,

taking on a different particular nuance depending upon the cultural and atmospheric 'soil' out of which it grew, just the way the hue of the hydrangea varies with the acidity of the ground in which it is planted. As the polychromed religious building resembled a sunrise, gilt and gleaming upon its promontory, so it also resembled a flower revealing in its colouring the particular nature of the environment in which it grew. The buildings of the history of architecture in their pristine, polychromatic state, if imagined all at once in the historical mind's eye, would seem like flowers in a varied landscape, very much like what W. W. Hudson at the end of the 19th century evoked with his imaginary 'rainbow lily':

> Now I knew why these autumnal flowers were called rainbow lilies, and remembered how Yoletta had told me they gave a beauty to the earth which could not be described or imagined. The flowers were all undoubtedly of one species, having the same shape and perfume, although varying greatly in size, according to the nature of the soil on which they grew. But in different situations they differed in colour, one colour blending with or passing by degrees into another, wherever the soil altered its character. Along the valleys, where they first began to bloom, and in all moist situations, the hue was yellow, varying, according to the amount of moisture, from pale primrose to deep orange, this passing again into vivid scarlet and reds of many shades. On the plains the reds prevailed, changing into various purples on the hills and mountain slopes; but high on the mountains the colour was blue; and this also had many gradations, from the lower deep cornflower blue to a delicate azure on the summit, resembling that of the forget-me-not and the harebell.[88]

All these majestic images evoked by Jones and Semper, however, make one fear for what modern architecture might hope to produce. Jones's England lacked the limpid atmosphere of Greece, its 19th-century society was not necessarily a young and vigorous one that would find the clear harmony of primary colours sympathetic. Yet Jones's iron and glass interiors were blazing worlds of red, blue and gold – seeming to announce the rebirth of the Greek spirit in sooty London – and in these very words are the explanation of that non-sequitur: Jones's polychromy was not external, but internal. The exterior of the Crystal Palace was merely painted blue and white, evidently to blend with the blue-grey of the London sky.[89] The Crystal Palace Bazaar, Osler's shop and St James's Hall had no exteriors to speak of because of their enclosed London sites. Yet these interior volumes were so broad, light and open as to seem exterior spaces through the use of the new industrial materials of iron and glass and gas lighting. Filtered through the glass exterior sheathing of his buildings the mists dissolve and the weak light of London is transformed into the pure light of Greece, made more brilliant as it plays over the red, blue and gold painted surfaces. Jones's friend César Daly wrote of one of his interiors: 'On entering the room we changed latitude, the artist seemed to have repeated the miracle of Prometheus in snatching fire from the sky to light up his work . . . he has imprisoned the sun in this building'.[90]

Here are all the qualities implicit in Jones's and Semper's evocations of Greek architectural polychromy, but now applied in a modern interior decoration in London. And the fact that the new industrial techniques have made it possible to 'capture the sun' explains why Jones uses the colours of a young, vigorous age in his ferro-vitreous buildings: he saw the 19th century as the beginning of a new period in human history, the opening of the industrial, scientific, commercial age.[91] Its architecture might rightly reflect – and revel in – this renaissance, when finally what the Greeks accomplished on their acropoli in harmony with nature the English could now achieve in the hearts of their great industrial cities in command of nature.

All of this seems to explain an obscure depiction of the objectives of an unnamed group of London architects pronounced by John Ruskin before the Architectural Association in 1857.

> If your style be of an ideal kind, you shall wreath your streets with ductile leafage, and roof them with variegated crystal – you shall put, if you will, all London under one blazing dome of many colours that shall light the clouds round it with its flashing as far as the sea.[92]

He was clearly referring to the ideas of Jones. He was right in calling it 'ideal' with its Neoplatonic scientific underpinning. And he is not exaggerating the boldness of Jones's objectives or the wonder of his imagery. The amazing thing is that Jones in his actual designs succeeded to the degree that he did.

Conclusion

I have tried to show here how distinct were these various interpretations of ancient Greek architectural polychromy. Yet it is remarkable how they all intertwine: how they all lead back to the *ateliers* in Paris around 1830; how one is the visualization of a theory while another is its verbalization; how the same motifs constantly recur. All these men were reacting to the realization that it no longer seemed convincing to believe that architecture communicated its meaning through a narrow series of fixed, conventional modes, the orders. Instead, they sensed that a building was the container of some sort of life that engendered it – causing it to be needed in the first place, determining its plan, dressing up its walls, infusing itself into its surfaces. Hittorff was the least adventurous (as well as the oldest); he felt that this life could be expressed through a greater variety in the traditional system of the orders. Labrouste was perhaps the most rebellious and visually impressive: his 'Agrigentum' and its numerous offspring depict architecture almost overwhelmed by the life it contains. But Labrouste's conception of an accretive polychromy was perhaps the least fertile, at least in its direct application. It was left for Bindesbøll to paint a modern building as Labrouste had the imaginary ancient palace of his 'Agrigentum', for Semper to explain precisely how an accretive decoration might evolve, and for Jones to transform the idea of coloured decoration from an applied covering into a glowing aura expressive of the cultural soil in which the structure had grown and in grand harmony with the light and air of its surroundings.

173 E. Duthoit. Notre-Dame-de-Brébières, Albert, designed in 1883, completed
in 1896, statue installed in 1897.

XI

'The synthesis of all I have seen':
the architecture of Edmond Duthoit (1837–89)

B. Bergdoll

VIOLLET-LE-DUC'S *Entretiens sur l'architecture* close with a characteristic 19th-century concern for the dichotomy between contemporary society and architecture. Architects, Viollet-le-Duc insists, must seek a style based on the rational use of modern materials and structural techniques or they will find their role in society taken over by engineers 'who start from purely scientific facts and construct an art which derives from those facts and from the conditions imposed by our own age.'[1] The challenge, as well as the contradictions, of Viollet-le-Duc's theory are reflected in the work of the young architects he trained in the 1850s and 1860s. The career of Edmond-Clément-Marie-Louis Duthoit, one of Viollet-le-Duc's closest and most favoured pupils, was especially shaped by the thought and work of the mentor of the 'Ecole Rationaliste'. Although Duthoit, like many of the young architects who worked with Viollet-le-Duc on his restoration projects, attempted to create an individual style, his approach to design can only be understood in terms of the doctrine of Viollet-le-Duc.[2]

Viollet-le-Duc never abandoned his conviction that French 13th-century Gothic was 'both the perfect expression of rational construction and the most instructive example for the 19th-century architect. Increasingly however he denounced the imitation of its forms in favour of a quest to use its principles as the basis for a new architecture.[3] Like many, he considered the 19th century a transitional period in search of a characteristic style. He developed the argument that a new style could not be invented; it must evolve from an understanding of the past applied to the needs of the present. The experimental spirit which he believed to have directed medieval architects in their development of an architecture in perfect harmony with the needs and conditions of its society was the example he upheld as an appropriate model for modern architects.

The *Entretiens*, as the direct result of Viollet-le-Duc's campaign for reform of the Ecole des Beaux-Arts,[4] have architectural education as a central theme. In the late 1840s and 1850s, J.-B.-A. Lassus and Viollet-le-Duc first sought to provide an alternative training through the ambitious restoration projects at the Ste-Chapelle and Notre-Dame. In the tradition of the medieval *chantier*, the student would learn about the essential skills of construction and the qualities of materials necessary for the evolution of a modern architecture founded upon a rational method. Viollet-le-Duc proposed the parish church as the most suitable model for emulation: a rational ideal most clearly expressed only later in *Eglises des bourgs et villages*, published by his pupil Anatole de Baudot in 1867. The construction of parish churches, like the restoration of medieval monuments, they hoped would serve as the beginning of a new organic era in architecture through a reintegration of architecture and the building crafts. A challenge to the centralized control of the Académie d'Architecture, the Ecole des Beaux-Arts and the Conseil des Bâtiments Civils was implicit in their programme.

The attack on the enshrined classical ideal of the Académie had begun within its own ranks among the generation of architects who were *pensionnaires* at the Villa Medici in the 1820s. In Rome, a new attitude towards the architectural past and its relevance to modern architecture had been formulated, as Neil Levine has shown,[5] in the projects of Labrouste, Vaudoyer and Duban. Influenced by the historical schema of the Saint-Simonists, they analyzed architectural history in terms of transitional or synthetic periods and organic periods, wherein style and society were in perfect harmony. The incorporation of Byzantine, Romanesque and Gothic elements in Vaudoyer's Marseille Cathedral and the superimposition of diverse but mutually supportive historic precedents in Labrouste's Bibliothèque Ste-Geneviève are the results of an attempt to synthesize a modern style from a dynamic view of the past. This inclusivist attitude to history was not only the basis for the architecture of the so-called 'romantic rationalists', but was also the legacy to many of the students trained by Labrouste, Vaudoyer, Duc and Duban.

Viollet-le-Duc accepted this view of history; but he insisted on the unique relevance of Gothic to the dilemma of the modern architect. This left his pupils in an historicist quandary. Nurtured by a thorough appreciation of Gothic, they were nonetheless impelled to forge something new. Viollet-le-Duc detailed the principles of medieval construction but offered only the cumbersome illustrations of the use of iron structural members in public buildings as suggestions of the type of experimentation required for the development of an appropriate modern architecture. He did not purport to offer a final form; he merely sought to establish a base for individual interpretation:

> Young people who wish to learn the practice of a science or an art rightly ask that they should be shown a recognized path. The teacher who points out all possible paths but does not tell us which is the right one, or prove why one is right rather than another, is not really a teacher at all. He is creating confusion and darkness in minds which have come to him seeking order and light. But this road should not be a narrow rut – it should be broad, open to everyone, so that each student can follow it according to his own inclinations, his own ideas and his own special talents.[6]

Predictably the responses of Viollet-le-Due's pupils were varied and often as tentative as Viollet-le-Duc's own much-maligned designs. In 1856 Anatole de Baudot led a group of pupils from Labrouste's disbanded *atelier* to ask Viollet-le-Duc to open one. This was to be short lived. The majority of Viollet-le-Duc's most important pupils and associates, though they might have begun in his *atelier*, were trained rather on the *chantiers* of the Commission des Monuments Historiques and Service des Edifices Diocésains.

De Baudot used iron columns in his church at Rambouillet of 1864 as supports for the vaulted nave. His writings, likewise, continually echo the themes of the *Entretiens*. After Viollet-le-Duc's death in 1879, he boldly pursued the search for an architecture based on new materials in his experiments with reinforced brickwork and concrete.[7] Emile Boeswillwald's use of iron and brick at Masny reflects both his training in Labrouste's *atelier* and the influence of Prosper Merimée and Viollet-le-Duc, with whom he travelled in the 1850s. While Eugène Millet remained faithful to the style and *chantier* system engendered at Notre-Dame, other architects in the 'Ecole Rationaliste', such as Paul Abbadie, sought to apply Viollet-le-Duc's method to an interpretation of Romanesque and Byzantine sources. Edmond Duthoit is a rare case of an architect trained primarily in Viollet-le-Duc's office. His small *oeuvre*, in which a wide exposure to Early Christian, Byzantine, and Arab architecture is combined with the Gothic ideals taught by Viollet-le-Duc, is an ideal subject for assessing the fate and possibilities of Viollet-le-Duc's programme for modern architecture.

Indeed, Duthoit's training exemplifies Viollet-le-Duc's enthusiasm for the revival of regional craftsmanship in the years before his ill-fated lectures at the Ecole des Beaux-Arts in 1864. Had it not been for Viollet-le-Duc's interest in the young Duthoit, he would probably have continued in the family tradition, training with his father and uncle as a decorative sculptor. The heir of a long line of sculptors in Lille, Duthoit's grandfather, Louis Duthoit (1766–1824) had established the family workshop in Amiens in 1796.[8] Edmond Duthoit emphasized the hereditary nature of the family craft in an article on his father and uncle, 'les frères Duthoit': 'One could say that they began to sculpt and draw the day their little hands could hold a pencil or lift a chisel.'[9] Largely self-taught, it was to the cathedral that Duthoit's father, Aimé (1803–1869), and his uncle, Louis (1807–1874), 'went in order to learn from the humble 13th-century carvers of images the secret of their simplicity and naive grandeur. . . . Here too the masters of the 16th century taught them how to group their figures in wonderful scenes filled with nature and life.'[10] This home-grown appreciation of a late medieval world was especially attractive to Viollet-le-Duc, who conceived of the brothers as 'les dernièrs imagiers du Moyen Age' and their workshop as a survival of a medieval *chantier*.

But they were not simply traditional artisans. Duthoit was proud to point out the family's early role in the renewed appreciation of Gothic:

> When only 13 or 14, the two brothers had studied and understood by intuition the historical and artistic value of medieval works, twenty years before the learned researches of Montalembert, Merimée, Vitet and du Sommerand had drawn attention to those monuments that had been underrated and misunderstood for so many centuries.[11]

Contemporaries of Arcisse de Caumont and other such provincial antiquaries, the Duthoits were already learned amateurs active in Picardy when a Commission of the Comité des Arts et Monuments visited Amiens in 1838 and sought their advice. Aimé Duthoit was a founding member of the Societé des Antiquaires de Picardie in 1836, and from that date the brothers collaborated as illustrators for many of the Society's publications. They also provided illustrations for some of the principal publications of the Gothic Revival, including Didron's *Annales archéologiques*, the *Revue de l'art chrétien* and Baron Taylor's great series *Voyages pittoresques dans l'ancienne France* (1826–64), through which they may first have met Viollet-le-Duc, another contributor. Their collection of topographical views done during travels in the Somme was so extensive that in the 1870s Louis attempted to collect them into 'un dictionnaire en images' similar to the picturesque works of Taylor.

Despite an *oeuvre* of some eight thousand drawings, the brothers made their reputations chiefly as ornamental sculptors and decorators often working on restorations under other architects. Their *atelier* was very busy. There is little exaggeration in Duthoit's statement: 'In the *département* of the Somme there were very few districts that did not possess one of their works: every church, every public building, almost every private house had some memento of these artists' visit.'[12] Amiens Cathedral, however, remained the focus of their activity. The brothers had been working on the restoration of the portal under the local architect François-Auguste Cheussey (1781–1857) for eight years, when Viollet-le-Duc was appointed in 1849 to the restoration of the cathedral.[13] The Duthoits were then assigned the entire sculptural restoration, thus beginning a long association with Viollet-le-Duc during which countless designs were executed in the Duthoit *atelier*. Work on the exterior continued until 1866. Between 1860 and 1869 several chapels, including the Chapelle de la Vierge, were decorated in the polychromatic manner that Lassus and Viollet-le-Duc had pioneered in the 1840s at the Ste-Chapelle and Notre-Dame. Aimé Duthoit and his wife, Geneviève Pauchet (1813–89), lived in the house over the Duthoit workshop at 11, rue Dominique (now rue Emile Zola), where Edmond was born and where he and his sister Marie (1839–1917) grew up. That the tradition of the family craft and a taste for medieval art were, if not innate, at the very least engendered from an early age, is illustrated in the memoirs of Edmond's nephew, the architect Pierre Ansart:

> In 1837 a son was born, who received the Christian name of Edmond, and to commemorate this happy event, the lady of the house ordered a chapel vaulted in the style of the 15th century to be built in the attic.[14]

If the family's hopes for Edmond were clearly expressed in this monument, their aspirations were no less apparent in the iconography of the chapel's altar, which reproduced a bas-relief from Amiens Cathedral of Christ among the doctors. On the advice of a canon in the cathedral, Duthoit was given a Jesuit education, first at the Collège de Brugelette, then at St-Clement, Metz and, finally, after 1850, at the newly founded Collège de la Providence in Amiens. Not until 1857, at the age of twenty, when Viollet opened his *atelier* in Paris, did he begin his training. The short-lived *atelier* was intimately connected with Viollet-le-Duc's restoration projects, especially at Notre-Dame. Paul Gout, another pupil, recalled that, after the *atelier* was closed, Viollet-le-Duc 'kept de Baudot and Duthoit near him and introduced them to the Notre-Dame workshop. Both of them, plus Maurice Ouradou, used to work in the office during the morning and spend the afternoon at the cathedral'.[15] Viollet-le-Duc, Gout noted, was a reluctant and impatient teacher; his pupils learned more from practical experience than actual instruction. As Viollet-le-Duc intended, Duthoit had entered an equivalent of the family workshop, where he gained a command of medieval detail and valuable experience in both construction and restoration.

The earliest work that can be attributed to him is the great ciborium for the chapel of the Petit Séminaire de St-Riquier. The frères

174

174   E. Duthoit. Ciborium for the chapel of the Petit Séminaire de St-Riquier, 1861. (From the *Gazette des architectes et du bâtiment*, 1865)

Duthoit were at work at the church and former abbey of St-Riquier between 1844 and 1863, during which time its disparate 18th-century buildings were consolidated and a new chapel 'en style byzantin à coupoles'[16] constructed for the seminary. The Duthoits' role in the decoration provided the perfect opportunity for Edmond to test his newly learned skills in ecclesiastical design, although in keeping with the new building his ciborium was designed in a Romano-Byzantine style. First drawn in 1860, it remained unexecuted when Duthoit left for Syria at the end of the following year. He modified the design in minor details during his voyage,[17] although the initial drawings had already gone to the Parisian goldsmith Alexandre Chertier,[18] who executed the iron-framed copper ciborium and the stone altar with its glittering bronze ornaments and brightly coloured enamels in 1862. Not surprisingly the ciborium is based on Viollet-le-Duc's work, and may be related to his designs and his illustrations in the first volume of the *Dictionnaire du mobilier français* (1858). The brackets on each side of the cupola, with their sense of organic vitality and sinuous movement, are derived from a favourite form of Viollet-le-Duc's, illustrated, for example, in the article 'Tabernacle'. The use of abstracted plant forms reflects Viollet's doctrine that ornament, like architecture, should be based on rational principles that might be related to natural models. Indeed, it was during these years that a method of deriving ornament from the study of flowers and leaves – in the manner already formulated by Pugin – was being taught at the Ecole Nationale de Dessin by Viollet-le-Duc's friend and assistant, the architect Victor-Marie-Charles Ruprich-Robert (1820–87). It is possible that Duthoit may have attended these courses, although he was already familiar with the theory as formulated in the article 'Floral' in the *Dictionnaire* (vol. 5, 1861), where the importance of naturalistic abstraction in all rational styles was stressed.[19]

In turning to a Romano-Byzantine type, Duthoit had a choice of models among recent ciboria exhibited at the Exposition Universelle of 1855: Viollet-le-Duc's impressive altar for the cathedral at Clermont-Ferrand, which included certain Byzantine details in its rich ornamentation, and the round-arched arcading and small canopy of Questel's altar for St Martin d'Ainay, Lyon – described by the *Ecclesiologist* as 'in pure Byzantine style'[20] –

which is in fact closer to Duthoit's ciborium. The stylistic mixture and richness of Pierre Bossan's early ecclesiastical designs, such as that for the high altar of the church at Couzon-sur-Saône (Rhône) of 1855, already seem the closest comparison with Duthoit's style. The ciborium was published in great detail in the *Gazette des architectes et du bâtiment*, where it was praised by de Baudot.[21] It is interesting to speculate whether Duthoit would have continued this Romano-Byzantine style if he had not soon become immersed in those archaeological studies which were to be a significant source for its later development.

An architectural tour was no less a part of his training and view of architecture than that of the winners of the Prix de Rome. Although he had visited medieval monuments in France with Viollet-le-Duc, the ideal opportunity for him to travel with a knowledgeable mentor arose in 1861, when the archaeologist and epigraphist, the Comte Melchior de Vogüé (1829–1916) required a skilled draughtsman for a six-month expedition to Syria and the Lebanon. Viollet-le-Duc, who probably knew de Vogüé through another Near-Eastern scholar, his close friend Ernest Renan, recommended Duthoit. Duthoit's first letter home reveals his personal goals in undertaking the journey: 'It has been agreed between M. de Vogüé and me that I shall come home via Constantinople, Greece and Italy. So that is settled, as long as I am not too tired' (21 December 1861).

De Vogüé's expedition, like most of the government-sponsored missions in the 19th century, was neither exclusively, nor even primarily, architectural. Exploiting the movements of the French army, scholars amassed volumes of information in Egypt, Greece, Asia Minor, Syria and, finally, in North Africa. The expedition to the Peloponnese in 1829, directed by the architect Abel Blouet, illustrates the comprehensive nature of these expeditions. His *Expédition scientifique de la Morée* (1831–38) not only includes polychromatic reconstructions of such important monuments as the Temple of Jupiter at Aegina, it also juxtaposes buildings from antiquity with monuments of the Byzantine era in Greece. The philosophy of the generation of architects who succeeded Blouet as *pensionnaires* at the Villa Medici in Rome in the 1820s is reflected in his explanation that 'good examples from all periods and all countries provide profitable lessons'.[22] This attitude marks a break with 18th-century architectural publications intended more to enshrine the classical past than to analyze architecture in its context. Charles Texier, a pioneer in studies of post-classical architecture, offered an even broader range of styles in his *Description de l'Asie Mineure* (1839–49), with its brightly coloured reconstructions and measured drawings of details from classical, Byzantine and even Arab-influenced structures. Views of Byzantine buildings were thus already available when the first book devoted to that style, Couchaud's *Choix d'églises byzantines de la Grèce*, appeared in 1842. In the 1850s, attention focused on Byzantium itself, beginning with Gaspard Fossati's *Aya Sofia, Constantinople as recently restored by the order of H.M. the Sultan Abdul-Medjid* (London 1852) and W. Salzenberg's *Altchristliche Baudenkmale . . .* (Berlin 1854), both studies of Sancta Sophia, and culminating in Texier and Pullan's great *Architecture byzantine* (1864), which appeared in both English and French.

De Vogüé's journey forms part of a controversy over the existence and nature of Phoenician and Jewish culture. Félicien de Saulcy had travelled extensively in the Holy Lands and published in 1858 his *Histoire de l'art judaïque*, arguing the contribution of Jewish civilization to the development of architecture in the eastern Mediterranean. Viollet-le-Duc drew on de Saulcy's finds in his account of Early Christian and Byzantine architecture in the sixth *Entretien*, published in 1860. In that year his friend Renan undertook his mission to the Lebanon and Syria in search of the elusive remains of Phoenician civilization. Aided by French troops, he excavated extensively but concluded, on the basis of the scant evidence unearthed, that no distinctive Phoenician or Jewish style could be discerned in the Holy Lands.[23] These cultures, he concluded, continued to draw on the vitality of Egyptian art in their artistic and architectural expressions. His spirits dampened by the death of his sister in a Maronite hut in the Lebanon, Renan entrusted de Vogüé with further investigation of the Phoenician issue in Cyprus, a former Phoenician colony. De Vogüé had received government sponsorship to resume his own studies of Early Christian architecture, which he began on a trip to Syria and Jerusalem in 1853, recounted in *Les Eglises de la Terre Sainte* (1860). In addition to Duthoit, he was accompanied by the Anglo-French epigraphist

William Henry Waddington,[24] who had begun collecting coins and inscriptions in Asia Minor as early as 1850. Duthoit summarized the goals of the mission as ' . . . to make an exact survey of Jerusalem, to trace the exact course of the old fortifications and to show the connection between Jewish and Egyptian architecture, especially for the study of the funerary monuments in the Valley of Jehosephat' (21 December 1861). All of these tasks culminated in the text and plates of the two great works published after their return: de Vogüé's *Le Temple de Jérusalem* (1864–65) and the highly respected *Syrie centrale: Architecture civile et religieuse du Ier au VIIe siècle* (1865–77), the standard reference for half a century until the Princeton expeditions in the first decade of this century.[25] *Syrie centrale* offered illustrations of a severe round-arched style to French architects seeking an alternative to the Gothic, but its influence – in the tradition of the new analytical view of the past – is more important as a case study of the dynamic transformation of alien traditions into a locally expressive style. De Vogüé not only recorded the remains, he also analyzed the character and evolution of Early Christian architecture and assessed its relevance to 19th-century architects. He summarized the confluence of Roman, Persian and native Syrian architectural traditions and their modification by regional social requirements and building materials. Any style, Viollet-le-Duc had maintained, is 'the manifestation of an ideal based on a principle'. The way to define the Syrian style was to isolate the intellectual structure which supported its physical forms:

The architects who raised the innumerable monuments of this country belonged to the true Greek tradition – not so much because of the forms they adopted as because of the principles that they applied. In their own works they could rival neither the delicacy of taste nor the exquisite perfection of the classical epoch, but they did recapture the spirit that had inspired the creations of the early Greeks, a spirit that was logical, practical and sincere. Foes, like them, to all sorts of artifice, rejecting the use of mortar, they relied only on the laws of statics for the solidity of their works, and the organization of their outline; if they borrowed decorative motifs from the Greek orders, if at the same time they took the arch and the vault from the Romans, they used these elements with great discretion, eliminating unnecessary features, and subordinating their dimensions to the material at their disposal, and the purposes for which the buildings were intended.[26]

The echoes of Viollet-le-Duc were no less pronounced in Duthoit's article, which accompanied a reconstruction of the east end of the monastery of St Simeon Stylites in the *Encyclopédie d'architecture*: 'They created a new art, a rational architecture, whose salient feature is the subordination of form to function and the logical use of the materials employed.'[27]

A further goal of the mission cited by Duthoit was the study of mosques in order to prove that 'Islamic architecture is due not to the Arabs but to the Greeks'. The notion of a 'true Greek tradition' had become a recurring thesis in the writings of architectural historians and critics. It proposed a continuity of the rational method of Greek architects throughout the Middle Ages. Not only did this thesis result in an architectural history which shifted the focus of developments away from Italy to the Near East, but it formed the basis for a new relationship of 19th-century architects to the monuments of the past. Challenging the academic insistence on the universal validity of an immutable classical ideal, the 'romantic rationalist' architects sought to appreciate the local significance of all historical styles. This new view of history was nonetheless not without an ideal. Wherever an architecture was to be found wherein materials, structural system and programme determined form and decoration, Greek rationality was proclaimed. Greek craftsmen had been relied upon in the eastern Roman Empire and thus their logical approach to construction and design is to be detected in what Viollet-le-Duc and de Vogüé called the Greco-Roman style of Syria. Byzantine and Sicilian Romanesque architecture were repeatedly singled out as two vital styles in which the elements of several traditions were synthesized into a new expression appropriate to its specific context.

Hittorff had already challenged the sanctified view of classical architecture in his study of the polychromy of the antique Sicilian temples during the 1820s. In *Architecture moderne de la Sicile* (1835), he proposed that the richly decorated interiors of Sicilian medieval cathedrals were no less an expression of Greek rationality than the polychromy of antique temples. Quite probably, he claimed, they were even the work of Greek craftsmen. As early as 1838, Ludovic Vitet, the first Inspecteur Général des Monuments Historiques, proposed the study of Byzantine or néo-Grec architecture as a fecund example of 'the critical spirit' which might 'deliver us from these exclusive imitations'.[28] As Neil Levine has argued, this appeal paralleled the new synthetic eclecticism of the 'romantic rationalists'. The desire for a synthesis of historical traditions is central to the work of Vaudoyer as well as Labrouste, and the prototype of Byzantine architecture is an important element in the eclectic vocabulary of Vaudoyer's Marseille Cathedral as well as in the historical allusions of the Bibliothèque Ste-Geneviève. Labrouste's understanding of the principles of Byzantine and medieval architecture and his appreciation of these principles in an architecture whose overall imagery remained classical was an important lesson to his pupils, who formed the nucleus of Viollet-le-Duc's *atelier*. Vitet's successor as Inspecteur Général des Monuments Historiques was Prosper Mérimée, who not only sponsored Viollet-le-Duc's early restoration at Vézelay, but sparked his historical investigation of medieval architecture. Indeed, through Vitet and Mérimée a particular historical attitude came to prevail in the Commission des Monuments Historiques, which forms an important element in Viollet-le-Duc's own schema. Vitet's 1838 analysis is paraphrased and embellished in the sixth *Entretien*, in which Viollet describes the Byzantine synthesis of Roman structure, Eastern ornament and Greek rationality as the source of a new architectural expression:

> Byzantine art is thus not, as one has so often been told, a product of the decadence of Roman art: it is an art which carried Roman constructional principles as far as they can go, abandoning those second-hand decorative motifs that the Romans had used and gathering new ones that were truer, more logically derived from the structure, and applied them with Greek intelligence. Far from being an art in decline, it is an art rejuvenated, capable of embarking on another long career and fathering principles hitherto unknown.[29]

Félix de Verneilh's *Architecture byzantine en France* (1851) had established the close links between Byzantium and the distinctive Romanesque churches of Aquitaine, especially that of St-Front at Périgueux; but he saw these as an isolated case of direct Byzantine influence. Viollet-le-Duc, however, viewed the Eastern influence as crucial in the development of French Romanesque. In a letter of 1853 he protested to de Verneilh: 'I see Byzantine everywhere during the 11th and 12th centuries, and our architecture is more or less saturated with it'.[30] French Gothic architects had, however, studied the Byzantine style more critically to derive 'their own principles'.[31] It was precisely this method that Vitet had recommended as the key to finding a new style in the 19th century. Although Viollet-le-Duc was defensive of the French national style as 'the revival of the old Gaulish spirit, a spirit that can become impassioned with an idea',[32] he, nonetheless, was intrigued by the notion that archaeology might reveal a continuous tradition of rationality in architecture. He recognized the importance of Byzantine architecture as the source for Greek rationality in both medieval and Islamic architecture:

How is it that after the establishment of the Eastern Empire, the Byzantines were able to apply new forms to Roman structure without any apparent transition? To ask that question, and to resolve it, is to find the key to the whole of medieval art, both in the East and in the West.[33]

Duthoit left for Syria anxious to help de Vogüé find that answer. Their voyage can be followed in letters written by Duthoit to his mother in Amiens. Enthusiastic, impressionable, and indeed somewhat overwhelmed by de Vogüé's ambitious plans, the young architect, however, did not lack confidence in his own skills: 'He [de Vogüé] can't complain of me as an artist. We have been travelling with painters . . . and not one of these gentlemen could draw a single figure without a model, whereas I could dash off a dozen.' Clearly, with companions such as Gérôme and Cabanal on board, Duthoit lacked neither self-confidence nor Viollet-le-Duc's disdain for the Ecole des Beaux-Arts. The group assembled in Marseille and sailed just before Christmas 1861. En route to Syria they called at Malta and Alexandria, the destination of the painters. In early January they arrived in Beirut. Despite de Vogüé's priorities, time was limited in Syria, for official arrangements had been made for them to begin work in Cyprus in February. Moreover, their start was delayed nearly two weeks by administrative bungling during which time Duthoit prepared designs for two chapels for French monastic orders in Beirut.

These were a chapel for the Capuchin monastery and the Eglise de l'Orphelinat, the chapel of the Lazarist monastery and hospital. Duthoit did not, of course, supervise construction. He returned to Beirut in 1865 to find the churches complete and ready for furnishing and ordered the necessary fittings from Parisian workshops. Neither church, however, was executed according to his design. In fact he was so horrified with the Capuchin chapel that he disowned it: on 23 May 1865 he exclaimed,

What a disappointment! It is absurdly built, and I certainly can't be proud of having had anything to do with the design of this church. I have explained to the Capuchin fathers my way of seeing things, but they seem so pleased with what they have done that it's impossible to make them realize their mistake.

The initial designs for the Lazarist chapel alone survive. These were published in 1866 in the *Gazette des architectes et du bâtiment*,[34] although in a slightly modified form. The aisleless chapel consists of four vaulted bays with internal buttresses pierced to form side aisle passages, and a rounded apse. This straightforward plan is well adapted to the confined site between the hospital and monastery. The public entrance is to the west, where Duthoit made an adventuresome, if still immature and awkward, attempt on the elevation to design something both original and in keeping with the traditions of Beirut. Both the polychromy and the forms of fenestration reflect medieval mosques as well as Ottoman architecture in the area. Indeed, the following year Viollet-le-Duc's campaign against the Ecole des Beaux-Arts was triggered when the Prix de Rome was awarded to a classical design for a Governor's Palace in Algeria.[35] Duthoit admitted that he had begun with a medieval model and attempted to modify it in relation to the Arab style, writing on 20 January 1862:

I tried to make it appropriate to the country. I drew on the traditional building technique and on the many different kinds of ornament, so that, although basically my work is really Romanesque, it has an unusual Islamic flavour that has captivated a lot of people here.

Although the arbitrary and somewhat crowded disposition of horseshoe arches and pierced-stone fenestration on the façade seems to con-

175 E. Duthoit. Église de l'Orphelinat (Lazarist chapel), Beirut: sections across the chancel (left page) and along the nave, dated 19 January 1862. (Coll. M. Robert Duthoit)

tradict the doctrine of Viollet-le-Duc in its lack of correspondence with internal disposition, Duthoit nonetheless derived the plan from the site, programme and structural system. Not surprisingly, echoes of Marseille Cathedral, which was rising over the harbour when Duthoit set sail, are to be detected here. Both the synthetic eclecticism of Vaudoyer's cathedral and the motifs Duthoit experimented with in this building were to preoccupy him two decades later when he was next given an opportunity to design a church.

De Vogüé, whom Duthoit reports as being enchanted with the church, was no doubt impressed by Duthoit's industry and initiative. His trust in his draughtsman developed quickly and Duthoit soon led several excursions into the Syrian desert to record monuments and measure sites. In early February 1862 the group travelled together to Cyprus, but de Vogüé and Waddington soon returned to Syria leaving Duthoit behind in charge of a government team of excavators. Duthoit also recorded inscriptions and collected fragments of architecture and sculpture – including the famous Vase of Amathus – which were later installed in the

Louvre galleries formerly named after the explorers. Following Renan's programme, Duthoit supervised a great number of excavations including the ancient city of Idalium, the Early Christian city of Soli and Amathus. Already fascinated by the richly decorated churches of the East, Duthoit studied a great number of Cypriot medieval churches and published examples in the *Gazette des architectes et du bâtiment*.[36]

In June he travelled to Jerusalem where he spent the summer assisting de Vogüé in his study of the Holy Sepulchre. De Vogüé had begun the study ten years earlier but was unable to gain admission to the mosque. Renewed negotiations were successful and the group spent each morning working in the temple wearing traditional Muslim dress. By the end of the summer, Duthoit was anxious to begin his personal travel as de Vogüé had confided that Viollet-le-Duc had implored him to retain his pupil 'for as little time as possible'. Duthoit reflected proudly on his six-month trip: 'I am bringing back more than 1,200 drawings, and almost all of them are of unpublished buildings. That is twenty times as much as M. Ernest

Renan did, and he had two professional artists with him, and hundreds of people to help him, *chasseurs à pied* to carry out his excavations, and what excavations! a whole army of moles!'[37]

After finishing work in Cyprus, Duthoit travelled to Greece, where he visited the classical monuments around Athens. 'The Parthenon is truly beautiful', he told his parents, 'but in spite of myself I am a Goth at heart.' Although he recognized the Greek genius in its original manifestation, he thought medieval art more vital and thus, by implication, capable of development:

> ... I could not help comparing this perfect monument to our cathedrals. The two arts are very different. The art that governed the composition of every tiny detail of this temple represents a genius at its peak, and therefore already old. Geniuses are not often young men. The Parthenon is the achievement of a culture that has reached its culmination and is more ready to descend than to mount higher – one more step and it will find itself at the beginning of decadence. The effort that has made it so refined and so sophisticated is about to become affectation, pretentiousness; I am already aware of an element of artifice, even slickness – still so well hidden that the result is truly artistic, but that is how it is going to end. The art of our cathedrals, on the other hand, is forever young; it is a great rush of enthusiasm, a blaze of youth which is short-lived but which instantly flares up to the sky. It lacks experience and wisdom, but it produces masterpieces from the start.[38]

Too hurried to reach Rome, Duthoit nevertheless visited Sicily, where the Romanesque cathedrals offered decoration richer than any he had yet experienced. Sicily, the cradle of 19th-century theories of polychromy, had also excited Viollet-le-Duc in 1836 during his grand tour. He had seen 'this architecture that is half Islamic, half Norman, half classical'[39] as an important precursor of French Gothic:

> It is here, where the transition from Islamic to Gothic architecture is so marked, that one can most easily understand how the extraordinary technique of combining structural effects was transmitted to the Gothic masons. Certainly they would never have been able to do it had they not had predecessors profoundly versed in that knowledge.[40]

Duthoit's tour had filled out and documented the transition from the antique to the medieval that Viollet-le-Duc had discerned in Sicily. Viollet-le-Duc applauded his pupil for having demonstrated 'the transition from Greek and Roman art to Byzantine'[41] as the final link in the history of Greek architectural rationalism.

Upon his return, Duthoit resumed his position in Viollet's *agence* and devoted himself to preparing some of his studies for submission to the Salon. In both 1863 and 1864, he exhibited carefully executed and accurately measured watercolours of the remains and reconstructions of the monastery of St Simeon Stylites, which gained him both medals and critical notice.[42] Both Robin Middleton and H.-R. Hitchcock have suggested the influence of these studies on the round-arched forms of Emile Vaudremer's St-Pierre de Montrouge, designed in 1864.[43] In the following year the first *livraisons* of *Syrie centrale* were available to French architects.

Further Salon entries came as a result of Duthoit's own mission to the Near East, an appointment he accepted, on Waddington's recommendation, in 1865 from the Ministre de la Maison de l'Empereur et des Beaux-Arts, Henri Courmont, the close friend of Mérimée and Viollet-le-Duc. He was there from May to November supervising excavation at the antique city of Assos in Asia Minor, a site first surveyed by Charles Texier in 1833, which the Turks were about to dismantle to build their forts in the Dardanelles. He himself surveyed the Byzantine military architecture there. Although he considered a publication on this subject or on the monuments of Cyprus, which he visited during this period to arrange transport of the Amathus vase, he satisfied himself with the exhibition of drawings from Rhodes and Syria at the Salons of 1868 and 1869. These voyages established archaeology and architecture as his separate but related careers – a pattern characteristic for those architects trained by Viollet-le-Duc.

Returning once more to Viollet-le-Duc's *agence*, Duthoit was given greater responsibility and, like another pupil, Denis Darcy (1823–1904), he was especially relied upon for Viollet-le-Duc's châteaux commissions. The transformation of the ruins of the immense medieval château of Pierrefonds into a fantastic neo-medieval château combining modern technology with historicist fantasy, established Viollet-le-Duc as an expert in a domestic Gothic Revival. Duthoit may have assisted on the project,

176

176 E. Duthoit. *Ruins of the Monastery of St Simeon Stylites, Syria*, watercolour shown at the Salon of 1864 (detail). (Coll. M. Robert Duthoit)

which began in 1858, the year in which the first volume of Viollet-le-Duc's *Dictionnaire raisonné du mobilier français* appeared. This work, devoted not only to furniture but to all the minor arts – and even the social customs – of the Middle Ages, served to establish some principles of design but was more important as a source book for the creation of neo-medieval interiors. Its impact was not confined to France. William Burges might have been disappointed by his visit to Pierrefonds in 1873, but he continued to make use of the *Dictionnaire*.[44] Its influence is easily detected in his furnishings, although his work at Cardiff Castle and Castell Coch in Wales is more original and charming in its playfulness. Even King Ludwig II of Bavaria visited the Imperial château in 1867 in search of ideas for his own extravaganza, Schloss Neuschwanstein.[45] Although incomplete, Pierrefonds remained the focus of medieval fantasy in France and its grandeur has often obscured more successful work undertaken elsewhere.

Marquis Lodoïs de Mauvesin clearly had Pierrefonds in mind when he asked Viollet-le-Duc to restore the Château de Roquetaillade at Mazères (Gironde) and to provide both fashionable neo-medieval interiors and modern convenience. The château, one of the best and most complete examples of the English type of fortified castle in Gascony, was built in 1316 by Cardinal Gaillard de la Mothe, nephew of Pope Clement V and ancestor of Mauvesin's wife.[46] There has been some confusion over the attribution of the work at Roquetaillade,[47] but the château's archives provide a complete chronology and illustrate the procedure Viollet-le-Duc followed in such commissions. In 1864 Duthoit was sent to Roquetaillade to prepare measured drawings. Exterior restoration was begun while Duthoit was in the Middle East in 1865 but continued under his supervision until 1867. A set of notes taken by the Marquise de Mauvesin records Viollet's comments on a visit of 1866, probably undertaken en route to inspect the work at St Sernin at Toulouse. She reports that Viollet 'wanted to take M. Duthoit, of whom he is very fond, away with him, so in fact he is staying and then coming back which is very useful for us'.[48] Viollet referred to Duthoit as 'mon jeune aide de camp' in correspondence and from 1867 all the bills were approved and signed by Duthoit, 'architect in charge'. Moreover, he conducted a detailed correspondence covering all aspects of the interior decoration with the Marquise for over a decade which reveals how quickly the commission became his own.

177   E. Duthoit with Viollet-le-Duc. Château de Roquetaillade, Mazères: exterior, restored in 1865–67.

Léon Drouyn's *La Guienne militaire* (1865) provides a view and description of the château before Viollet-le-Duc's restoration according to his oft-quoted dictum that restoration is 'to restore a building to a state of, completeness which may never have existed at any one time'.[49] The accumulation of the centuries was swept away and replaced by the perfect regularity of that ideal moment. With the exception of the regularization of the fenestration and the addition of the machicolated porch over the north-east entrance, his work was largely repair and decoration. As at Pierrefonds, a willingness to incorporate modern materials in medieval restoration is frankly expressed in the iron beams that support the drawbridges spanning the moat.

With the construction of only one interior wall, the ground floor of the medieval fortress was transformed into a Second Empire show-piece. The stairhall, with its beautifully carved stone staircase and delicately poised umbrella vault painted in light brown and blue and picked out in red, replaced a single grand stair-case of the 17th century. The treatment of the painted walls reflects Mérimée's thesis that painting should accentuate structure as well as Viollet-le-Duc's belief that painting should respect the natural light source.[50] The ornate bronze chandelier, in the spirit more of such eclectic designers as Jank and Hoffman at Neuschwanstein than of the increasingly more restrained designs of Viollet-le-Duc, was designed by Duthoit in 1872 and executed by Chertier in 1874.

Unlike the ceremonial grandeur of Pierre-fonds, Viollet-le-Duc's dining hall of 1867–68 at Roquetaillade is domestic and relatively free of historical allusions. It is the realization of his unexecuted projects for the private chambers at Pierrefonds where the grand imagery of the public spaces is relaxed for something more practical and comfortable. It is probably this room that is recalled in his recommendations for decorating a dining room in the *Histoire d'une maison* (1873), where canvas wall paintings set in frames are recommended because they could be easily removed and cleaned. Even the woodland imagery of the Roquetaillade can-vases is described in the later text. The arches spanning the room are painted with abstract

178

patterned borders and spiralled vine motifs in the spandrels. This spiral form recurs repeatedly in Viollet's designs, regardless of material. Duthoit had already quoted the medieval source in bronze at St Riquier. In the thirteenth *Entretien* Viollet-le-Duc translated it into an iron brace as a suggestion of how a new style might be derived from medieval principles. Indeed the sinuous organic line of this motif was to be exploited fully by Art Nouveau designers.

At the Salon of 1868, Duthoit exhibited a series of finely executed drawings and sparkling watercolours showing the projected interiors, including some grand projects for the first floor rooms, which were never realized. As was often the case with Viollet-le-Duc's disciples – including A. de Baudot, M. Ouradou and E.-E. Millet – a project originally conceived in conjunction with Viollet-le-Duc was entirely credited to the pupil or assistant most concerned with its realization; perhaps an implicit acknowledgment that his architecture failed to meet the demands of his writing. Duthoit's distinctive mixture of Gothic and Islamic details is already reflected in his watercolours. The two rooms wholly designed by Duthoit in 1868–69 are much closer to the whimsicality of Pierrefonds in their bold mural painting, fanciful medieval chimney pieces and decorative wooden ceilings. Although Duthoit made an attempt in the 'masculine' Chambre Verte and the 179 'feminine' Chambre Rose, which flank the dining hall, to transform Viollet-le-Duc's style by integrating elements from his travels, he saw all these elements as compatible in terms of universal principles of decorative design. The ceiling of the Chambre Rose features hexagonal and triangular panels forming interlocking star patterns in a manner similar to a Muslim example from the Archiepiscopal Palace of Alcalá in Spain, published by Boeswillwald in 1863.[51]

Duthoit's designs for two suites of bedroom furniture are his most individual contributions to the decoration of the château. The pieces were all made by Tricot and Jeancourt in Paris and published in detail in the *Gazette des architectes et du bâtiment* in 1869. Whimsical details such as the dogs' heads on the Chambre Verte chairs are derived from the *Dictionnaire du mobilier*, in this case the throne of Charles V. But few of Duthoit's designs are direct imitations, as de Baudot noted in his review:

178   E. Duthoit with Viollet-le-Duc. Château de Roquetaillade: stairhall, with chandelier executed in 1874.

One notes that, unlike our manufacturers of *Gothic* and other furniture, the designer has tried above all to capture the spirit of the products of that age, and if his design is intelligent it is because he has taken the inner principle, and not the outer form, as the point of departure. He has proceeded methodically, concentrating first of all on those functional qualities which every piece of furniture has to have, choosing a particular form only insofar as it fits the required shape, suits the material used, and lends itself to straightforward construction. In this way he has been able to make his furniture interesting and – as they say nowadays – amusing.[52]

179   E. Duthoit. Château de Roquetaillade: Chambre Rose, 1868–69.

Duthoit himself had emphasized the need for furniture rationally conceived and free of ostentation in his criticism of the furniture displayed at the *Exposition universelle* of 1867: 'the real problem is rather to devise furniture for everyday use that is simple, elegant, comfortable, solid and at a price that people can afford'.[53] Taking up the philosophy of Lassus and Viollet-le-Duc, he discussed 'our duty to fight with all our strength against this debased eclecticism, this laziness, that is making its appearance in modern designs'.[54] If the chairs and tables meet these lofty demands in their revealed construction and simple painted decoration, the hanging armoires deliberately evoke medieval forms, neglectful even of initial function. The Noyon armoire recalled here had been illustrated by Viollet-le-Duc and used extensively as a model by Burges. Duthoit's furniture, however, has neither the muscular vigour nor the solid craftsmanship of English work of these years.

Of Viollet-le-Duc's numerous other châteaux commissions of the 1860s, Duthoit was charged with supervision and eventually the execution of two. Comte Charles de Saint-Victor approached Viollet-le-Duc late in 1860 for a restoration proposal for the Château de Chamousset (Rhône), near Lyon. As at Roquetaillade, Duthoit was sent to prepare measured drawings, which survive at the château, of the medieval building, a rather lacklustre defensive château of the 15th century, parts of whose fabric date back to the 12th century. In February 1861, Viollet-le-Duc and Duthoit drew up two alternative schemes to recast the château in an image more befitting the Second Empire's notion of the medieval familial seat. The imagery of Pierrefonds is clearly recalled in the first, with its central block treated as a massive keep and emphasis on defensive features such as machicolations throughout. In the other project Viollet-le-Duc suggested a more domestic imagery with richer profiles, turrets, unexpected juxtapositions of scale, and use of vernacular references. This project does not yet include the extensive use of half-timbering, as in the central belvedere, which makes Chamousset so distinctive among Viollet-le-Duc and Duthoit's châteaux; that treatment is closer in spirit to Viollet-le-Duc's smaller outbuildings such as the stables at Roquetaillade and indicative of his romantic attraction to the wooden vernacular of the Vosges and Alpine regions. Interspersed among Viollet-le-Duc's sketches for naturalistic and whimsical carvings preserved in the Archives du Rhône are several more timid sketches by Duthoit, thoroughly imitative in style. Yet a group of plaster models of the carvings survives at Chamousset which may have been prepared by Duthoit, his own background in the Amiens workshop of the frères Duthoit leading him to prefer three-dimensional sketches for the stonecarvers.

The new service wing and walls around the château, which create a picturesquely fragmented sequence of framed views for the arriving visitor, are already indicated in Viollet-le-Duc's 1861 plans, but the work does not seem to have begun for several years. It would seem that Duthoit was initially charged with the supervision of the *chantier* at Chamousset around the same time he began work at Roquetaillade. In a letter from his 1865 trip, Duthoit asked his uncle Louis to see to the pacification of Saint-Victor until the architect's return from the Middle East. Even after Duthoit had returned to France, work at the château progressed slowly and extended over nearly two decades. Many sketches by Viollet-le-Duc for interior details reveal that he prepared the early designs for the sculptural decorations, carved mouldings and painted ornamentation and that he continued to collaborate, providing an occasional sketch even once the work was largely Duthoit's. A watercolour project by Duthoit for an interior stencilled in the manner of Pierrefonds is similar to those displayed in the Salon for Roquetaillade. Again the magnificent neo-medieval appointments were completed only in a handful of rooms, although brightly painted beams and stencilling are to be found throughout the château. The impressive collection of wooden furniture at Chamousset is bolder in its use of chamfered members and revealed construction than the ungainly furniture for Roquetaillade.

If Chamousset and Roquetaillade are closely related to the neo-medieval whimsy of Pierre-

fonds, the more exotic decoration of the Château d'Abbadia (d'Arragori), a newly designed château in the style of the late 14th century built to Viollet-le-Duc's designs on a cliff overlooking the Atlantic north of Hendaye (Basses-Pyrénées), clearly reflects Duthoit's own tastes and travels.[55] The château was commissioned by the explorer and astronomer Antoine d'Abbadie d'Arast (1810–97)[56] who, like many of Viollet-le-Duc's clients, was a friend of Napoleon III. The château incorporates both a richly ornamented chapel furnished in the style of Notre-Dame, with many Islamic details, and an astronomical observatory. Duthoit's work was coordinated with that at Roquetaillade and he even reused many of his designs at both châteaux. He first visited the site in June 1864, but in the absence of drawings or plans the progress of the work is difficult to estimate. The only surviving drawings are for ornamental carvings by Viollet-le-Duc and furniture by Duthoit. The building was nearing completion in 1870 when Abbadie invited Napoleon to lay the final stone; a hole remains unfilled beneath one of the château's windows.

Duthoit designed most of the furnishings between 1867 and 1869, though several pieces for the chapel were not designed until 1879. The stencilled walls and painted decoration are similar to Roquetaillade, but Duthoit's flexibility as a furniture designer is apparent in contrasting the simple, slightly coarse furniture for Roquetaillade with the intricately carved late Gothic and Islamic pieces he designed to harmonize with Abbadie's 'remarkable collection of furniture and objects brought back from the Orient'.[57] Abbadie's enthusiasm for Basque culture and his extensive travels throughout Africa and the Middle East are reflected in the juxtaposition of a suite of 'chambres espagnoles', 180 in a florid late Gothic style, with the 'salon arabe', a pleasure chamber similar in spirit to the Summer Smoking Room created by Burges for the Marquis of Bute at Cardiff Castle. Near the Spanish border, Duthoit had every justification for mingling Gothic and Islamic decoration, but he kept the styles distinctly separate. Viollet-le-Duc had attempted to incorporate Islamic details already in the mausoleum he designed in 1867 for the Duchess of Alba near Madrid.[58] Duthoit's furniture for the 'chambres espagnoles' confines Gothic detailing to inset carved panels and rich cresting, in the manner

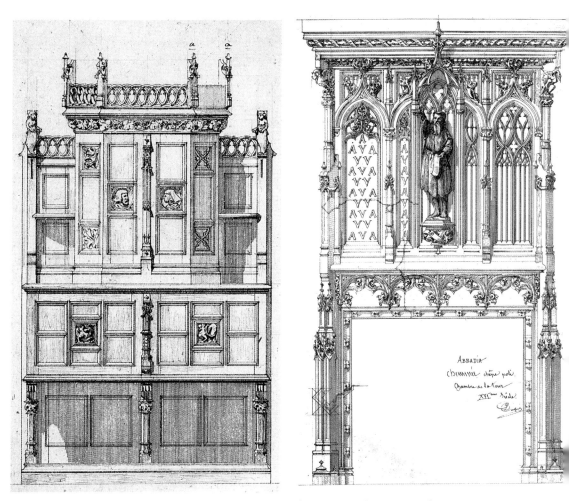

On the fireplace drawing, handwritten text:

ABBADIA
Cheminée chêne poli.
Chambre de la Tour
XVIème Siécle

180–182 E. Duthoit. Designs for furnishings for the Château d'Abbadia, near Hendaye:
sideboard for the 'chambres espagnoles', dated October 1870; fireplace for the Chambre de la
Tour; and (below) dressing table for the Chambre de la Tour. (Coll. M. Robert Duthoit)

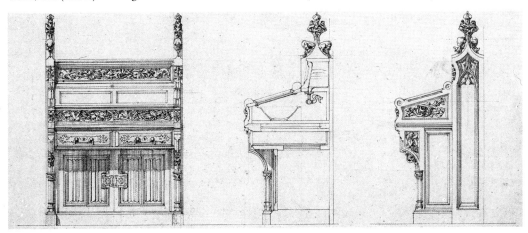

183 E. Duthoit. Design for an altar for the Chapelle du Sacré-Coeur, church of Berteaucourt ▷
les Dames, dated December 1875. (Coll. M. Robert Duthoit)

184 E. Duthoit. Project for the decoration of the Chapelle de la Ste-Vierge, Notre-Dame,
Boulogne-sur-Mer, dated 28 September 1872. (Coll. M. Robert Duthoit)

of Viollet-le-Duc. The Chambre de la Tour is a
display of late Gothic detailing. The intricately
carved oak chimney piece might be related to
archaeological details in the *Dictionnaire*, but
it is more ornate than much of Viollet-le-Duc's
work. The closest parallel to the exuberant
carving and rich profiles of such pieces as the
toilette is the furniture designed for Schloß
Marienburg near Hannover by Edwin Oppler,[59]
a German pupil of Viollet-le-Duc. The stylistic
juxtaposition and rich overall decoration at the
château remains closest in spirit to Burges. The
Château d'Abbadia, indeed, like Cardiff Castle,
is as much a reflection of the passions and eccen-
tricities of its owner as of the imagination and
talent of its designer.

Duthoit's independent work during these
years consisted largely of restorations under the
auspices of the Commission des Monuments
Historiques, for which he served from 1866 as
Inspecteur in the Somme and Oise *départements*. After his father's death in late 1869 and
the outbreak of the war in 1870, Duthoit, his
wife and their two young sons left Paris to
return to the family home in Amiens, abandon-
ing in the eyes of his anonymous biographer 'a
brilliant future and the reputation that his talent
had assured him at Paris'.[60] The most notable
work of these years was the restoration of
Senlis Cathedral, in 1866–67, where he restored
the choir, decorated two chapels in the chevet,
providing altars in the manner of those executed
by the Duthoit *atelier* for Viollet-le-Duc during
the same year, and installed a new sacristy in
the octagonal chapel adjacent to the south
transept. He also painted the walls and vaults in
brightly coloured abstract patterns. The robust
altar for the late 11th-century church at Ber-
teaucourt-les-Dames (Somme), which Duthoit
restored in 1875, is one of his boldest designs in
its original combination of painted and sculpted
elements and its adaptation to the Romanesque
style.

Duthoit's stylistic flexibility is nowhere more
apparent than in several commissions in the
classical style undertaken jointly with his uncle
in the early 1870s. As early as 1872 they began
decorating several chapels in the recently completed Notre-Dame of Boulogne-sur-Mer,
which had been built under the direction and
to the designs of the ambitious Monseigneur
Haffreingue. In addition to the impressive neo-
baroque altar which fills the north transept,
Duthoit designed the Chapelle de St Joseph and

collaborated with Louis Duthoit and, after his
uncle's death in 1874, the sculptor Eugène
Delaplanche on a monument to the Monseigneur. His major contribution to the church
was the design for the Chapelle de la Vierge,
which continues the classical vocabulary of the
attenuated nave with an enriched applied Corinthian order. The focus of the chapel is Louis
Duthoit's oak statue of the Virgin, which
replaced the miraculous cult statue burned
during the Revolution. It stands in a grotto
framed by Duthoit's aedicular high altar and
dramatically lit from above. Although a successful essay in Italian High Renaissance design,
Duthoit's chapel nonetheless reflects Viollet-le-
Duc's doctrines in the disposition of abstracted
organic ornament to reflect the structural
system.

Such commissions were undertaken in the
intervals between annual trips to North Africa
for the Commission des Monuments Historiques. An initial expedition had been conducted
after the French conquest of Algeria by A.-H.-A.
Delamare in 1840–45,[61] but the securing of the
boundaries of the colony and the organization
of departmental government there led to more
determined efforts to conserve Algerian monuments. Duthoit was appointed by the Ministre
de l'Instruction Publique in 1872 to survey the
architecture of Algeria in order to establish
restoration priorities. After four months in
North Africa he was forced by the overwhelming late summer heat to return to Paris,
but his enthusiasm for Islamic architecture was
undaunted. Reappointed annually until 1880,
when he was appointed to the newly created
post of Chef des Monuments Historiques en
Algérie, Duthoit spent nearly half of each year
supervising the recording and restoration of the
major mosques at Tlemcen, Mansourah and
Sidi-Bu-Madyan. In 1880 Duthoit and Boeswillwald, Inspecteur Général des Monuments
Historiques succeeding Mérimée, followed the
French troops upon the conquest of Tunisia,
in order to survey the rich remains of the Roman
Empire.[62] Although work continued on Muslim
monuments, the focus of attention and excite-
ment shifted to the antique remains. The principal site was Timgad (Thamugadi), the so-called
'African Pompeii'.[63] Annual campaigns, beginning in 1881, unearthed an entire antique city
with later Byzantine and Islamic additions.
Although these antique excavations received
considerable attention – de Vogüé even visited

the site in 1888 – Duthoit's role was principally administrative. He was increasingly absorbed by his small architectural practice in Amiens and his African sketchbooks continue to reflect his preference for Islamic architecture and his fascination with its rich ornamentation.

Duthoit considered the plan and structure of Islamic buildings of less significance than the complicated interlaces and geometrical patterns which were signs to him of a highly developed understanding of the principles of decorative art. Hundreds of Islamic designs were recorded by his assistants in transfer rubbings. Following the analytical approach of Viollet-le-Duc, he sought to untangle these interlaces on grid paper in order to penetrate to their generative principles. Ornament alone seemed to provide him with a justification for restoring buildings that lacked the structural finesse or the rationality of French Gothic: 'The more one admires the fertile imagination and decorative skill of the Arabs, the more one regrets the lack of care which those artists took to give their works the solidity that they deserve, and the more one curses the irresponsible owners of these marvels who are letting them decay and disappear.'[64] Indeed, by the 1870s, Islamic ornament had become virtually symbolic of rational principles in decorative design. Islamic buildings had been widely studied in Spain and Egypt from early in the century. Murphy's *Arabian Antiquities of Spain* had appeared as early as 1811, and was followed by the studies of Joseph-Girault de Pragny (1804–93) in France. The French imagination had been early aroused by Napoleon's expeditions in Egypt. The notion however that Islamic architecture offered the best lessons in decorative design was pioneered by Owen Jones. His friendship with Semper and his travels with Goury have already been described by David Van Zanten (p. 209). His ideas became known in France when excerpts from his book on the Alhambra appeared in the *Revue générale de l'architecture* in 1844. The structural polychromy of Cairene mosques had already served as an important source for permanent polychromy in European architecture.[65] Pascal Coste (1787–1879), from Marseille, was architect to Mohammed Ali from 1818 to 1828, after which he built a number of churches in his native city and prepared his great work on Egyptian monuments, *L'Architecture arabe* (1839), with many measured details of ornamental woodwork and painting. Later, Coste

travelled to Persia and published volumes on its Islamic architecture. Owen Jones's approach to Islamic ornament, as the prime manifestation of universal laws of two-dimensional design based on principles of colour and geometry, was widely taken up in France. Racinet's *Ornement polychrome* (1869–87), an encyclopedic compilation of historical styles, emulates Jones's format, though it incorporated examples drawn from French research. His section on 'le style Mauresque' is based on Duthoit's studies of Algerian mosques, some of which were exhibited at the Exposition Universelle of 1878 and at the Salon of 1879. Archaeological copies of Islamic buildings at the Expositions of 1867 and 1879 greatly popularized the style, but it was during these years that the studies of Duthoit, Jules Bourgoin (1838–1907) and Léon Parvillée (d. 1885) in France deepened the analytical approach to Islamic ornament. Jules Bourgoin had studied Islamic art in Egypt before his appointment to teach the theory of ornament at the Ecole des Beaux-Arts. In 1868 he began to publish the first of several books on the style, *Les Arts arabes*, in which lavish colour plates are accompanied by a section analyzing the underlying geometrical principles of the complex ornamental patterns, some of which are analyzed on grids to highlight their regularity and simplicity. Moreover he specified the relevance of these Islamic principles in deriving novel ornament from natural forms, a method later expanded in his treatise, *Théorie de l'ornement* (1879). This method had already been formulated as a medieval principle in Pugin's writings, particularly *Floriated Ornament* (1849), and was taken up in the work of such Englishmen as Christopher Dresser. It was a technique much praised by Viollet-le-Duc and taught by Ruprich-Robert, who like Pugin and Ruskin in England saw it as the principle of the medieval sculptors. Viollet-le-Duc praised Bourgoin for demonstrating the geometrical qualities of Islamic art in the preface and in the review he wrote for *Les Arts arabes*, and noted the English precedent:

That is the great lesson. The arts of design have their philosophy; one has to know how to see beneath the outward forms, to analyze the creative principles: this is the only way of creating in our turn. They already understand this in Germany and England, where they do not think it necessary to forbid artists to think.[66]

Viollet-le-Duc went on to argue that the style had its origins in the inventive ornamentation of central Syria, studied earlier by Duthoit. In his preface to Parvillée's *Architecture et décoration turques* (1873), Viollet-le-Duc discussed the unity of the style throughout the world of Islamic rule and congratulated Parvillée for confirming the mathematical principles of ornament and proportion already explored by Duthoit and Bourgoin. Viollet saw these principles as common to Islamic and medieval design because of their common roots in Byzantine architecture. It was precisely this mixture of the three related styles that Duthoit would attempt to formulate into an original style in the five churches he designed between 1875 and his death in 1889.

Work was resumed at Roquetaillade after the Franco-Prussian War, but no effort was made to take up the ambitious schemes for the first floor. The desire to emulate Pierrefonds seems to have collapsed with the Empire. The restoration of the derelict Romanesque Chapelle de St-Michel, however, occupied Duthoit between 1875 and 1877. Following Viollet-le-Duc's recommendations of 1866, he restored the apse and ceiling and then concentrated on decorating and furnishing the interior. But rather than introduce new details into a model derived from Viollet-le-Duc's style, as he had in the château interiors, Duthoit sought to develop an independent style drawing on the decorative richness of Islamic and Byzantine models. He intended to rival the splendour of Viollet's polychromatic restorations. Here Duthoit had the advantages of an ample budget and a single unified space – just as Lassus and Viollet-le-Duc had enjoyed at the Ste-Chapelle three decades earlier.

Islamic details, such as the scalloped arcades and claustral screens of the organ gallery and the geometric patterning of the wall-painting, had already been a prominent feature of Boeswillwald's Xifre House in Madrid (before 1874) and his two polychromatic churches in the south of France: St-Martin at Pau and the richly painted 'chapelle du palais', off the Avenue de la Reine Victoria at Biarritz (1864). Although the lavish chromolithographic publication of the painted decoration at Biarritz appeared in the *Revue Générale* only in 1877, Duthoit had no doubt visited the building at the time of his visits to the nearby Château d'Abbadia. Unlike Boeswillwald's brick chapel, where a profusion

185   E. Duthoit. Château de Roquetaillade: interior of the Chapelle de St-Michel, 1875–77.

of diapering, tiles, and polychromatic brick prepares us for the richness of the painted interior, Duthoit's simple stone exterior provides an austere contrast to the jewel-like interior, a contrast he admired in Byzantine churches and Islamic mosques. Indeed, it is the decorative painting of nearly every surface, rather than architectural elements, which creates the 'grands effets de l'ensemble',[67] described by Viollet-le-Duc as the appropriate treatment for a painted interior. In the chapels of Notre-Dame Viollet had even incorporated certain Islamic details in the ornament. St-Michel is articulated by a painted framework of dado, mouldings and ornamental ceiling friezes, as well as by niches on the side walls with figures of St Joseph and the Virgin. Originally the apse was the highlight

237

186   E. Duthoit. Church at Bryas, 1880–84.

Hittorff's revised design of 1833 incorporates the present painted and gilt open timber ceiling, recalling Sicilian prototypes of the sort that Hittorff and Zanth later published in *L'Architecture moderne de la Sicile* (1835). Ceilings such as that of Palermo Cathedral are also recalled in Emile Vaudremer's St Pierre de Montrouge. The Roquetaillade ceiling is based on the more elaborate ceiling of Messina Cathedral, the 153 tripartite format of which lends greater prominence to the patterns of interlocking panels. Duthoit had visited Messina in 1862. Viollet-le-Duc had been so impressed by the ceiling on his trip to Sicily in 1836 that he drew it in detail, as had Labrouste before him. Furthermore, in 1841 the Nancy architect Mathieu-Prosper Morey (1805–78), a fellow pupil of A. Leclère, whom Viollet-le-Duc had encountered in Palermo and Rome in 1836 and 1837, had published an exquisite set of chromolitho- 153 graphic plates of the ceiling and its details.[68] Boeswillwald's 1863 article on the panelled ceiling of the Archiepiscopal Palace in Madrid recommended Islamic models for providing 'a great richness of effect by the simplest of means'.[69] In the same year he erected a painted open timber ceiling with panels of overlapping stars in his chapel at Biarritz. Here, and in the canopy of the pulpit of St-Martin at Pau, Boeswillwald used painted, recessed cupolas of metal set in the ceiling as at Messina to give greater glittering reflections. This feature is also used by Duthoit at Roquetaillade. He was to make the Messina type ceiling his own in his church designs.

Duthoit's altar, with its coloured marble inlays, bronze cresting, jewels, and translucent enamels, is the focus of the chapel. Its mixture of Romanesque, Byzantine, and vaguely Islamic details comes closest to the exuberant designs of Pierre Bossan such as those for the basilicas at Louvesc (1865) and Fourvière at Lyons, which drew heavily on the almost claustrophobic decoration of Sicily. Earlier, Duthoit had admired Boeswillwald's high altar for the Cathedral at Quimper, exhibited in 1867, where Islamic elements 'mingle agreeably with pointed forms'.[70] Appropriately, the consecration ceremony of the newly decorated chapel, on 13 June 1877, was presided over by the Baron Jules de Verneilh, friend of Viollet-le-Duc and brother of the art historian who had first established the path which led from Constantinople to the south-west of France.

of the scheme, with figures of St Genevieve and St Louis set on a gold ground giving the effect of a mosaic semi-dome. In relying solely on a rich overlay of two-dimensional pattern, Duthoit, like his Byzantine and Sicilian predecessors, had compromised neither the purity of the structure nor the effect of the ornament.

The chapel is dominated by its boldly painted and ornamented ceiling truss with inset panels of Islamic motifs. Trussed timber ceilings had been a common roofing solution in basilican churches in France since St-Vincent-de-Paul in Paris. Lepère had originally projected a flat panelled ceiling for the great church, but

Partly by reusing several Roquetaillade designs, Duthoit was able to complete both the chapel of the Château d'Abbadia in a similar style and the simple Romanesque church in the small village of Champeaux (Deux-Sèvres) in the late 1870s. Champeaux has a simple aisleless nave of three bays preceded by a narrow vestibule and terminated by a rectangular sanctuary flanked by square sacristies. With its plain west tower over the porch entry, it expresses the modest ideal of the parish church put forward by Viollet-le-Duc as the path to a new architecture and is perhaps best compared with such de Baudot designs as the Romanesque style church at Privas (Ardèche).

186, Duthoit's church at Bryas (Pas-de-Calais),
187 built between 1880 and 1884, to replace a medieval structure much damaged in the Revolution, was financed by the Comte de Bryas and his wife Ursula de Vogüé, sister of the archaeologist. The exterior of the church is dominated by a massive tower, a landmark in the flat, wooded landscape around Bryas. Its placement over a porch, open on three sides, repeats the favoured arrangement of Viollet-le-Duc as an expression of the civic, indeed secular, role and significance of the belfry, as opposed to the spiritual realm of the nave behind.[71] The simplicity and boldness of detail, massive forms and reduced 13th-century French Gothic vocabulary all recall two of the most important French Gothic Revival churches of the mid-1860s: Viollet-le-Duc's at Aillant-sur-Tholon (Yonne) and de Baudot's at Rambouillet, both of 1865. Duthoit has profited from such models. His tower is confidently and vigorously massed with a clear sense of interpenetrating volumes and a subordination of bold details to the overall composition. Moreover, he has followed the credo of regionalism in using brick, the common building material of the north of France.

188, The church for Souverain-Moulin (Pas-de-
189 Calais), of the same years, continues the approach of Bryas; but brick construction is more imaginatively expressed, both in the wall planes and buttressing and in the stepped corbelling. As at Bryas, the tall, narrow proportions are wholly Gothic in spirit but here combined with details reinforcing a humble scale such as a bell-cote and the timber dormer in the south elevation; a motif also used by R.-P. Pullan in his small Swiss churches. The church was commissioned by the Comtesse de Béthune-

187 E. Duthoit. Church at Bryas, 1880–84: transept end.

Sully in memory of her husband and daughter and built at the entrance to the hamlet near the château. The interiors of both churches – that at Souverain-Moulin never completed – reflect Duthoit's desire to incorporate original details into the Gothic Revival type. Both are simply painted to accentuate their structure and ornamented with a few whimsical animal carvings such as the corbels of the Bryas pulpit. Rather than the overall Sicilian richness of the château chapels, these village churches are filled with light. The Messina type timber ceilings, steeper in slope and lighter in tonality, seem almost to hover above the crisp space below. Indeed the English critic P. G. Hamerton cited Souverain-Moulin as an example of the skilful solution to 'the difficult problem of making Gothic acceptable and cheap at the same time'.[72] If he could cite Duthoit as representative of the viability of the Gothic Revival as late as 1891, it could only be through ignorance of his last building.

188, 189 E. Duthoit. Church at Souverain-Moulin, *c*.1883: view, elevation of the chancel end, and cross-sections of the nave and the transept. (From A. Raguenet, *Monographies de bâtiments modernes*, n.d.)

IGLISE de SOUVERAIN-MOULIN

(Pas-de-Calais)

Mr E. DUTHOIT. Architecte

à Amiens.

FAÇADE POSTERIEURE

COUPE SUR LA NEF   COUPE SUR LE TRANSEPT

Echelle de 0.000 p.e mètre

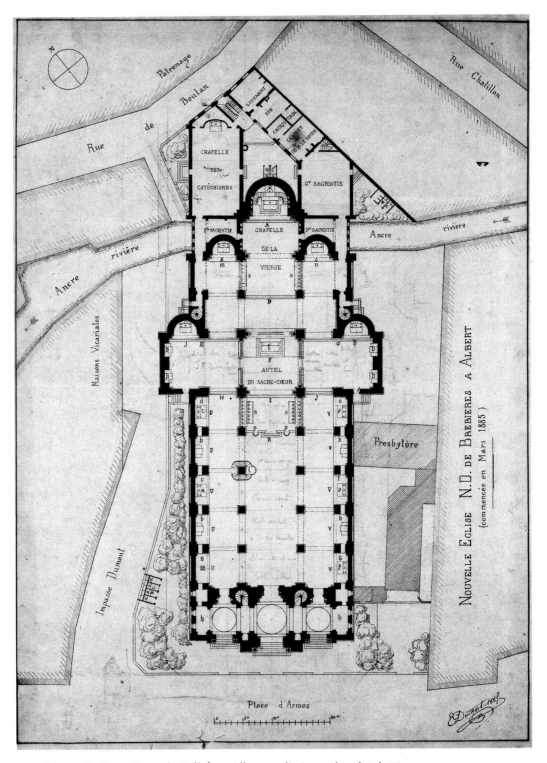

190   E. Duthoit. Notre-Dame-de-Brébières, Albert: preliminary plan, dated 1885.

Although reconstructed after its destruction in the First World War, the Basilica of Notre-Dame-de-Brébières at Albert (Somme) remains the clearest testimony to Duthoit's desire to respond to Viollet-le-Duc's challenge for an original architectural style. The unique form of the Basilica reflects also the individualism of the group of great pilgrimage churches built in France during the 19th century, from J.-E. Barthélemy's Notre-Dame-de-Bonsecours at Rouen of 1842, a herald of the serious Gothic Revival, to Paul Abbadie's great Romano-Byzantine Sacré-Coeur, on Montmartre. The pilgrimage to Albert enjoyed a popular revival as a result of this general Catholic Revival and its accompanying enthusiasm for shrines and relics. The venerated statue of the Miraculous Virgin, the object of the pilgrimage, had been found, according to legend, by a sheep grazing on the banks of the Ancre river, around the year 1000. The statue had been installed in 1727 in the ancient parish church of Albert. The revival of the pilgrimage however made the modest structure inadequate for the crowds who came each September. The move to rebuild the church was due to the determination of a young clergyman, the Abbé Anicet Godin (1840–1913),[73] who had served as curate in St-Jacques, Amiens, from 1863 to 1882, during which time that church had been decorated by the Duthoits and given a new Chapelle du Catéchisme by Edmond Duthoit (now demolished). Appointed Doyen d'Albert in 1882, Godin immediately began efforts to replace the church, whose unstable tower was a threat to the nave walls. He was determined to raise funds for construction privately. In 1883 he approached Duthoit for plans for the new building, leaving the style to the architect's discretion but suggesting a Roman basilican plan. The parish magazine commented tersely on Godin's method: 'He shut his eyes, but he opened his hands.'

Duthoit's first plans were presented in September 1883 and modified only in detail in the working drawings of 1884. Several unusual conditions prolonged construction, which continued actively for the next thirteen years, although the building was not complete in furnishings and details until the first decade of the present century. The entire site was purchased in February 1884, foundations were begun in May and the first stone laid on 13 July of that year. In addition to the marshy site, which necessitated very deep foundations,

the length of the new building required that it span the narrow Ancre river, which was diverted from its course while a bridge supporting the Lady Chapel was constructed. By early 1888 the main fabric of the building, with the exception of the porch and tower, was essentially complete and Duthoit began to design the decoration and furnishings. The major altars and much of the furniture were complete when he died on 10 June 1889, from a heart attack. Indeed, he is reputed to have continued drawing details feverishly in his sickbed, having told Godin prophetically after preparing the initial plans: 'Now I can die – there is your church'.[74] Henri Bernard (1849–1929), Duthoit's chief assistant and designated successor, continued the work using Duthoit's plans for the tower and porch, which were begun in October 1893 after destruction of the old parish church, which had been used during construction. Bernard was assisted by Duthoit's son, Louis, who entered his father's office in November 1888. Completed in November 1896, the tower was crowned on 13 July 1897 by the figure of the Virgin raising the Child to heaven, by the Amiens sculptor Albert Roze.

The construction of the basilica came close to recreating the cherished ideal of the medieval *chantier*. A profusion of craftsmen and artists made individual contributions to the decoration. All the mosaics were executed by Facchina, the Italian artist originally brought to Paris for Garnier's Opéra, after cartoons drawn by Duthoit: Albert Polart, a pupil; and the religious painter François Grellet. Grellet also executed the processional frieze of 130 saints, which originally extended through the nave, transepts and apse and included portraits of Duthoit and Godin. The figurative sculpture was divided between Roze and Delaplanche, whose Notre-Dame-de-Brébières – shown at the Salon of 1889 – terminates the vista down the long nave. The *orfèvrerie*, including the monstrance shown at the Exposition Universelle of 1889, was divided between Poussielgue-Rusand and Chertier. Indeed Duthoit complained: 'the architect's job all too often is only to put right the mistakes of his colleagues'.

Nonetheless, the basilica is nothing if not the individual statement of its creator. Duthoit himself described it in terms of an architectural autobiography:

After having been brought up and having studied in a milieu that was passionately devoted to the Middle Ages, I went on to analyze Roman architecture in Italy and Greek architecture in Athens, the Islands and Asia Minor. In Cyprus, Rhodes and Palestine I saw almost all that survives of Phoenician monuments. Egypt I only touched on, but in Syria, Constantinople, Sicily, southern Italy and finally in Algeria and Tunisia I was able to study the earliest manifestations of Christian art. From Constantinople to Spain, along the whole length of the Mediterranean, I drew or at least visited an incalculable number of Islamic buildings, or buildings deriving from that style . . .

The architecture of the church at Albert is meant to show the effects of all these experiences – it is the synthesis of all I have seen. If you look hard you can recognize where the details come from. The tower is the minaret of Tlemcen or Seville; on the palaces of Siena and Florence, at the top of their towers, one can see console cornices which (at a distance) are terribly like the cornices of the new church; those of the apses with their semi-domes and their corbels look to central Syria; the clerestory is found in all the basilicas of Syria, Italy, Sicily and Corsica. The large horseshoe arches that separate the nave from the aisles are borrowed from the great mosque of Tlemcen; the great mosque of Kairouan gave me the shape of the abacus blocks; my portal recalls the arrangement that I particularly admired in the mosque at Tunis. Finally, I should be very happy if a tourist looking at the decoration of the apse should be reminded of that of the church at Monreale, near Palermo. I cannot give a name to this mixture; all the elements that go to make it up are good: may their combination not be disagreeable to visitors.[75]

Indeed, every detail reflects the diversity of Duthoit's travel and study and it would be fruitless to attempt a more exhaustive account here of the specific sources than that offered by the architect. Despite his insistence on individual sources, they are all given unity by the idea of a Christian basilica, the development of a brick architectural vocabulary and the search for a synthesis of post-classical architecture. As Duthoit intended, his forms are not merely reproduced but reinterpreted, so that they are original in form but rich in allusion:

Whoever has seen a lot should remember a lot. That is how it is with me. All these forms float in my memory and I cannot think of them in isolation; whether I like it or not,

my Islamic feels Gothic and my Gothic has an after-taste of Islamic or Byzantine.[76]

Notre-Dame-de-Brébières is the culmination of Duthoit's attempt to reconcile the diversity of his architectural experience with desire for a coherent style based on rational principles.

The basilican form, like the pre-existing Romanesque walls at Roquetaillade, was an inspiration serving to set aside the models of the Gothic Revival in search of a new abstraction of historical prototypes. Viollet-le-Duc had discussed the form and development of the basilica in the historical lectures of the *Entretiens sur l'architecture* and also in his *Histoire d'un Hôtel de Ville et d'une Cathédrale* (1878), in which he even offered an illustration of an Early Christian basilica in Gaul. But Viollet repeatedly emphasized the unique relevance of the perfected form for contemporary architects. The great vaulted cathedrals of Picardy and the Ile de France were the apogee of structural rationality, only imperfectly expressed in earlier medieval architecture. Byzantine and Romanesque architecture, however, were of dominant concern in academic ecclesiastical architecture and remained in the forefront with the development of a Romano-Byzantine style in the hands of Abbadie, Vaudremer, and others. Sustained by the rationalist *Traité d'architecture* (1850–58) of the engineer Léonce Reynaud and the studies of his colleague Fernand de Dartein (1838–1912) in northern Italy,[77] even conservative academic architects looked to Lombardic Romanesque for an Italian alternative to the Gothic Revival. If this compromise position led to few noteworthy buildings, Romanesque and Byzantine architecture were vital stimuli to the radical group within the Académie who sought to learn from the experimental spirit of transitional styles. The basilica had been reinterpreted in a number of important churches including two prominent Parisian buildings which are recalled in the design of Albert. Hittorff's St-Vincent-de-Paul is commemorated in the Raventine frieze by Grellet, which consciously emulates the famous frieze by Flandrin between the superimposed colonnades of the great Parisian church. The frieze at Albert is, however, integrated into an arcuated nave elevation similar to that used by Vaudremer in St Pierre de Montrouge, whose western tower over a central porch, incorporation of transepts into a basilican plan and reliance on a combination of Syrian,

191   E. Duthoit. Notre-Dame-de-Brébières, Albert: interior, before destruction in the First
World War. (Courtesy of M. Robert Duthoit)

Sicilian and Byzantine forms were important prototypes. Albert, however, lacks both the sculptural coherence and the solemn monumentality of Vaudremer's most successful work.

A precedent for great stylistic freedom and decorative richness had been established by several great pilgrimage churches in the 1860s and 1870s. Abbadie's restoration of St Front, Périgueux, the key monument in the connection between French and Byzantine architecture, provided the model for his own great church of Sacré-Coeur. The stylistic mixture and design attitude of Pierre Bossan (1814–88), a pupil of Labrouste, is however a more instructive comparison. His productive career culminated in the two great basilicas at Louvesc (Ardèche) (1865) and Fourvière at Lyons (1872–96). Notre-Dame de Fourvière at Lyons is especially remarkable for its almost overwhelming accumulation of sparkling ornament and material. Like Duthoit, Bossan had been impressed by the decoration of Sicilian churches, the spirit of which permeates his later work. But Bossan felt that it was the role of the architect's developed aesthetic sense to select and adjust the elements of his composition according to the dominant character of the building. As his disciple Saint-Marie-Perrin explained, each building has a physiological type. As in nature the parts must accommodate themselves to conform to the demands of the whole: 'Each element renews itself, modifies itself, assumes a balance of its own, and the composition, full of freshness and youth, appears as a harmonious and living unity.'[78] Although Bossan denied that his approach was eclectic or governed by anything so whimsical as taste, he obscured his design rationale in a committed Christian mysticism. To Viollet-le-Duc such an approach remained eclectic:

A certain school, tired of the more or less faithful imitations of the architecture of the past, has had the notion that one can put together a new architecture by choosing whatever seems attractive in these earlier models. This is a dangerous error. A *macaronic* style cannot be a new style ... it can never be the manifestation of a principle and an idea.[79]

Duthoit had been taught to believe that every element in a building must be the direct manifestation of structural requirements. Viollet-le-Duc felt that the lessons of history were the logical methods of its architects. The notion

that to comprehend a form, even those used by Gothic architects, it was necessary to understand its genesis and development was central to the 'romantic rationalist' point of view. Vaudoyer's cathedral and its pendant across Marseille harbour, Notre-Dame-de-la-Garde (1854–65) by his principal pupil Henri Espérandieu (1829–75), are both based on a historical analysis of the development of Christian architecture. Built during the 1850s and 1860s, they were seen by critics as monuments of the 'Romano-Byzantine' style, but their formal vocabulary is even wider in historic scope. The impact of these buildings on Duthoit's early work has already been suggested and one cannot but be struck by the similarities between Espérandieu's campanile-like tower and that at Albert. Both Marseille churches have basilican plans which incorporate Byzantine, Romanesque and French Gothic elements. Marseille, the gateway between France and the Mediterranean, was the ideal location for buildings which represent a dialogue between French architecture and its Byzantine sources.

The re-evaluation of Byzantine architecture as a particularly vital moment in the early Middle Ages was the vortex of the synthetic eclecticism of Vaudoyer, and, as Neil Levine has suggested, the néo-Grec of Labrouste. Their new view of architectural history was pioneered in the writings of Ludovic Vitet, who also set the tone for the Commission des Monuments Historiques and thus might be seen as a theoretical forebear of Mérimée and his protégé Viollet-le-Duc. As early as 1830, in a review of two Italian works on Lombardic architecture, Giulio Corder de Conti di S. Quinto's *Dell'italiana architectura durante la dominazione longobarda*, and Sacchi and Sacchi's *Della condizione economica morale e politica degli italiani nei bassi tempi ...* , Vitet challenged the academic admiration of Roman architecture and maintained that in Byzantine architecture was to be found a reawakening of the rational spirit of antique Greek architecture and the fountainhead of both medieval Christian and Islamic architecture.[80] By 1838 he had come to see Byzantine architecture as an antidote for contemporary architectural malaise. Seeing the East as 'an untapped reservoir that we should do well to exploit',[81] he characterized Byzantine architecture in terms analogous to the synthetic historicism of later architectures, predicting that in 'this new, fertile union of memories from Rome and the Orient

... the lifeless genius revives, and on all sides rise up monuments like nothing we have ever seen before.'[82] Both its critical relationship to the past and its experimentation were valuable examples for 19th-century architects.

Through Labrouste's *atelier* and Albert Lenoir and Léon Vaudoyer's popular history of architecture, which appeared in the *Magasin pittoresque* between 1839 and 1852, this new attitude influenced a whole generation of architects. The travels of Labrouste's pupils, Bossan and Couchaud, to Sicily, Turkey and Greece reflect a new interest in post-classical architecture Couchaud's *Choix d'églises byzantines de la Grèce* (1842) saw a continuity of spirit in that nation's monuments: 'The creative genius of ancient Greece, which shone so brightly centuries ago, finding itself oppressed by the domination of Rome, had to rekindle itself at another flame – that of Christianity.'[83]

The notion of a Christian tradition in architecture continuing the rationality of Greece to new ends is a central theme of Vaudoyer's history as well. Although he acknowledged – as Viollet-le-Duc was to proclaim in his early articles of 1844 to 1846 in Didron's *Annales archéologiques* – that Gothic 'should be considered the most powerful expression of Christian thought'[84] he maintained that an investigation of its development was necessary in order to understand its final forms. This development is the history of the basilican form. Vaudoyer recognized the dependence of Early Christian architects on Roman prototypes, but he regarded Christianity as the cause of 'a complete transformation in the arts'.[85] Following Vitet's example, he saw Byzantium as the source from which the new Christian style 'begins to free itself ready to be transformed and to spread across the whole of Europe'.[86] Rather than Gothic, he proposed French Romanesque as 'a purer expression of Christianity'.[87] In the sixth *Entretien*, Viollet not only posed the questions which Duthoit investigated in Syria the following year, but discussed the instructive value of the embryonic forms of an architectural style. There he saw the Greek genius as fundamental to the early development of medieval architecture.

In Marseille Cathedral, forms are not juxtaposed but rather used with this new analytical insight. David Van Zanten has discussed the building as an exegesis of its own history, as a summary of 'the history of architecture in the sense that its abstract configuration showed clearly the historical evolution through which its type coalesced'.[88] Espérandieu continued this synthesis in Notre-Dame-de-la-Garde, where the forms which Vaudoyer had singled out as characteristic of Western Christianity – bell towers and a Latin cross plan – are detailed with Byzantine and even Arab elements. Duthoit, too, sought a historical synthesis based on an analysis of the tradition of the basilican form. Respecting the highest ideals of Viollet-le-Duc, he selected expressive forms from the history of the Greek rational spirit, a history his own researches had expanded and documented. The Greek spirit, like the Christian tradition, was nothing less than the capacity to accommodate new elements and specific demands by the consistent application of rational principles.

At Notre-Dame-de-Brébières, Duthoit learned from the past to create something entirely personal, and he hoped new. All the elements may be related to the rational tradition he traced during two decades of travel and restoration. If the building's total impression seems unresolved, Duthoit nevertheless considered his borrowings carefully, hoping to realise a synthetic unity, as recommended by Vitet: ' ... there are certain dissonances that one can neither prepare for nor repair; one must therefore choose and put together only those forms that can live together in harmony. In designing a building one must visualize the general characteristics of this or that great family of monuments, but at the same time one must not be afraid of drastically modifying the type that one has chosen, to give it a contemporary character.'[89] De Vogüé's analysis of the use of stone in Hauran monuments, which he had seen as Greek-influenced, is reflected in the pierced stone fenestration of the porch. The Messina type timber ceiling had been seen by Morey as the very embodiment of Greek rationality in both construction and decoration. Morey reiterated the argument of Hittorff and Henry Gally Knight[90] in describing the Sicilian synthesis of Islamic, Byzantine and Norman elements as the source of a new expression. All of these elements formed a unity because 'the genius of Greece still floats over the whole and dominates it'.[91] This view of Sicilian Romanesque repeats the argument used by Vitet, Mérimée, Vaudoyer and even Viollet-le-Duc in analyzing Byzantine architecture. The lessons of such synthetic styles did not sanction a mere

153

juxtaposition of diverse elements, but illustrated how previous traditions could be reinterpreted to realize something new and related to a different context.

The tower at Albert, which dominates both the church and town, perhaps best illustrates Duthoit's effort to superimpose forms drawn from several manifestations of the rational tradition. Although Vaudoyer distinguished the 'clocher' as 'the symbolic form of the Western church',[92] a rich combination of Eastern and Western tradition underlies the unique form of Duthoit's belfry. It rises over a porch/narthex with three shallow domes decorated in mosaic as at Abbadie's Sacré-Coeur. The dual civic and spiritual significance of the church tower in Viollet-le-Duc's secularized history of the Middle Ages and in his own church designs reaches a brilliant climax in Duthoit's combination of porch and tower at Albert. Both the civic campanile of Siena's Palazzo Pubblico and the spiritual beacons of Algerian brick minarets are used to reinforce and enrich the traditional symbolism of the French belfry. The tower recalls all of these forms simultaneously without reproducing any of them. It is the summation of a sequence of interpretations of a single form, or 'the synthesis of all that I have seen'.[93]

The same attitude is reflected, to some extent, in most aspects of Duthoit's summary history of the basilican form. He was unable to realize the same degree of historicist abstraction throughout, but many details reveal his particular strength in ornamental design. Beginning at Roquetaillade, Duthoit sought to integrate and adapt the geometrical patterns of Byzantine and Arab ornament to a French context. While the interior of the basilica at Albert recalls Sicily in its lush decorative conglomeration, many details are strikingly original. Particularly in the late designs for the decoration of the Chapelle de la Vierge, Duthoit submitted natural forms to geometrical stylization realizing a sinuous linear design of an almost proto-Art Nouveau character. Both his pupil Bernard and his son would develop an Art Nouveau stylistic vocabulary strongly tinged with medieval reminiscences, best seen in Louis Duthoit's Hôtel Bouctot-Vagniez (1908–11) at Amiens.

If the interior reflects Viollet-le-Duc's description of Byzantine 'grands effets de l'ensemble' in its articulation of surface through colour and pattern, the exterior is closer to his observations on Islamic architecture:

... the method of applying decoration to the exteriors of buildings springs from the same principle: large plain surfaces and, at certain points, very brilliant but very delicate ornament, the sunlight bringing out the most minute details.[94]

Unlike Vaudoyer or Espérandieu, who used a marble cladding derived from Sienese architecture, Duthoit contrasts frankly expressed brick construction with mosaic and faience highlights. The development of an appropriate architectural expression for brick occupied many of the architects in Viollet-le-Duc's circle. Certain details such as the corbel table cornice are echoed at Albert. Boeswillwald's more determined efforts to forge a brick style at Biarritz and particularly in his church and presbytery at Masny (Nord) of 1860 were valuable prototypes. Motifs such as the inverted V-shaped lintels in the side elevation of the Albert tower are derived from Boeswillwald and were used extensively by many of Viollet-le-Duc's disciples including de Baudot, Gout and Narjoux in his brick schools throughout Paris. The source of the motif was no doubt Viollet-le-Duc's restoration of the tower of St Sernin at Toulouse. This treatment, as much as it today seems a mere conceit of the Viollet-le-Duc school, reflects the recurring hope among 19th-century architects that new geometrical forms appropriate to their building materials might be the source for a new style, as the pointed arch had given birth to Gothic.

Duthoit's inconclusive synthesis must be seen as his final response to Viollet-le-Duc's challenge and his expression of the recurring anxiety of the 19th century: 'Is the 19th century condemned to end without having had an architecture of its own?'[95] Inspired both by the new view of history developed by Vitet and the 'romantic rationalists' and by the options offered in the Romano-Byzantine style, architects trained in the Gothic *atelier* at Notre-Dame searched further back into history hoping to find suggestions for the future. Increasingly they favoured simplified styles over the structural complexity of Gothic. De Baudot had used a simplified Romanesque style in several parish churches before turning to concrete as the material for modern architecture in his Lycée in the rue de Sevigné, Paris. The lectures he gave at the end of the century reflect a loosening of Viollet-le-Duc's insistence on Gothic and echo Vitet's call of 1838 for a re-evaluation of

17

Byzantine architecture: 'in fact it would be very useful to revive the spirit of innovation that animated the Romanesque architects'.[96]

In characterizing Romanesque buildings as 'combinations of Roman, Byzantine and Syrian',[97] de Baudot cites the key elements of Duthoit's synthetic historicism. Viollet-le-Duc had challenged his pupils to plant the seeds for a new architecture, but insisted that their method must be based upon a style which was both rational and suited to the French context. Duthoit's entire career was devoted to the study of medieval architecture in all its manifestations. He had helped trace its rational principles from the rekindling of the Greek spirit by the forces of Christianity to the perfected Gothic of the Cathedral of Amiens. He had witnessed the flexibility of those principles as they had accommodated a variety of climates, societies and religious beliefs. At Albert he attempted to create an architecture both individual in form and universal in its evocation of the rich history of the basilican church. If his work has none of the structural experimentation of de Baudot's quest for a new style, it nonetheless represents a notable attempt to forge a modern architecture from the heritage of the past.

Notes

II Durand and the continuity of tradition

I am deeply indebted to the archivists, curators and librarians who helped me in the preparation of my doctoral thesis on Durand for the University of Göttingen, supervised by Prof. Th. W. Gaehtgens. I also would like to thank Bridget Ikin (London). Without the help of Alix Blanchette (Paris) I could not have written this article. Her support went far beyond rendering it into English
1 A complete bibliography will be included in my doctoral thesis. Among recent titles are: M. Tafuri, *Theories and History of Architecture*, London, 1980 (tr. from the original Italian edition, 1968); J. Rykwert, *On Adam's house in paradise*, New York 1972; N. Pevsner, *A History of Building Types*, Princeton and London 1976; M. Foucault, B. Barret Kriegel, A. Thalamy, F. Béguin, B. Fortier, *Les Machines à guérir*, Paris 1976; R. Chafee, A. Drexler, N. Levine, D. Van Zanten, *The Architecture of the Ecole des Beaux-Arts*, New York 1977; R. D. Middleton, D. Watkin, *L'Architettura moderna*, Milan 1977 (English ed. 1980); L. Pelpel, *La Formation architecturale au 18ᵉ siècle en France*, CORDA, Paris 1978; B. Hamburger, J.-C. Paul, A. Thiebaut, *Dimensionnements*, Paris 1979; A. Braham, *The Architecture of the French Enlightenment*, London 1980
2 W. Szambien, 'Das Landhaus des Jean-Nicolas-Louis Durand (1760–1834) in Thiais', *Architectura*, 1, 1978, pp. 73–87
3 'Builder': L. Hautecoeur, 'Conférence', *Architecture française*, 37, November 1943, p. 6: 'functionalist': A. Hernandez, 'Jean-Nicolas-Louis Durand und die Anfange einer

funktionalistischen Architekturtheorie', *Architekturtheorie*, Internationaler Kongress in der TU Berlin 1967, pp. 135–51; tr. as 'J.-N.-L. Durand's Architectural Theory: a Study in the History of Rational Building Design', *Perspecta*, vol. 12, 1969, pp. 153–60; 'rationalist': L. Hautecoeur, *Histoire de l'architecture classique en France*, vol. V, Paris 1953, pp. 259–62; 'revolutionary architect': J.-M. Pérouse de Montclos, *Etienne-Louis Boullée, 1728–1799, De l'architecture classique à l'architecture révolutionnaire*, Paris 1969, pp. 214–16; 'utilitarian': *The Age of Neoclassicism*, Catalogue of the Exhibition, London 1972, pp. 970–71 (article by J. Wilton-Ely); Rykwert, *op. cit.*, pp. 43–45; 'architect of the bourgeoisie': H. Wirth, 'Clemens Wenzeslaus Coudray (1775–1845), Architekturtheoretische Anschauungen', *Wissenschaftliche Zeitschrift der Hochschule für Architektur und Bauwesen Weimar*, 5/6, 1975, pp. 473–83; C. Schnaidt, 'Le Tombeau d'Alberti', *La Nouvelle Critique*, 97, 1976, p. 34; P. Melis, 'Architettura e revival del cristallo nella città contemporanea da Joseph Paxton a Kevin Roche', *Psicon*, 6, 1976, p. 86; 'last exponent of classical architecture': E. Kaufmann, 'Die Architekturtheorie der französischen Klassik und des Klassizismus', *Repertorium für Kunstwissenschaft*, XLIV, 1924, pp. 197–237; 'begetter of modern functionalism': see note 6 and E. Kaufmann, *Von Ledoux bis Le Corbusier. Ursprung und Entwicklung der autonomen Architektur*, Vienna 1933, pp. 50–54; 'baroque tradition': E. Kaufmann, *Architecture in the Age of Reason. Baroque and Post-Baroque in England, Italy and France*, New York 1968 (1955), pp. 210–15; 'rise of the engineer': P. Collins, *Changing Ideals in Modern Architecture, 1750–1950*, London 1971 (1965), p. 192

4 *Recueil et parallèle des édifices de tout genre, anciens et modernes, remarquables par leur beauté, par leur grandeur ou par leur singularité, et dessinés sur une même échelle*, Paris Year VIII (1799/1800), which was accompanied by a text by J.-G. Legrand; *Précis des leçons d'architecture données à l'Ecole polytechnique*, 2 vol., Paris Year X–XIII (1802–5); revised edition: *Nouveau Précis*, 1813; *Choix des projets d'édifices publics et particuliers composés par MM. les élèves de l'Ecole polytechnique par Durand et Gaucher*, Paris 1816; *Partie graphique des cours d'architecture faits à l'Ecole Royale polytechnique depuis sa réorganisation*, Paris 1821. In my text I refer to Durand's publications as *Recueil*, *Précis*, *Nouveau Précis*, *Choix* and *Partie graphique*
5 L. Benevolo, 'Considerazioni sull'architettura neoclassica', *Quaderni dello Istituto di storia dell'architettura, Saggi di storia dell'architettura in onore del professor Vincenzo Fasolo*, Rome 1961, pp. 293–98; Hernandez, *op. cit.*; J. Guillerme, 'Notes pour l'histoire de la régularité', *Revue d'esthétique*, 3, 1971, pp. 383–94; W. Oechslin, 'Monotonie von Blondel bis Durand, Reduktion einer architektonischen Aesthetik?', *werk-archithese*, January 1977, pp. 29–34; Szambien, *op. cit.*
6 H.-R. Hitchcock, *Architecture, Nineteenth and Twentieth Centuries*, Harmondsworth, Middlesex, 1975 (1958), pp. 47–73: 'The Doctrine of J.-N.-L. Durand and its application in Northern Europe'
7 All three scientists taught at the Ecole Polytechnique. Gaspard Monge (1746–1818) was a personal friend of Durand's as shown by the obelisk at Thiais. See Szambien, *op. cit.*, notes 3, 43. Durand's architectural teaching was considered as a part of the descriptive geometry developed by Monge. Durand refers

to Joseph-Louis Lagrange (1736–1831) in his *Nouveau Précis*, p. 63 For J.-H. Hassenfratz (1755–1827) see Pelpel, *op. cit.*, p. 638

8 A. Détournelle, Review of the first volume of Durand's *Précis*, *Journal des Arts*, 235, 5 brumaire Year XI (26 October 1802), p. 172

9 A. Rondelet, *Notice historique sur la vie et les ouvrages de J.-N.-L. Durand*, Paris 1835, pp. 5–6. As well as Monge, Leroy was mentioned on the obelisk. See note 7

10 Three drawings at the Ecole des Beaux-Arts, not published in the collection of A. Prieur and P.-L. van Cléemputte, *Collection des prix que la ci-devant Académie d'Architecture proposoit et couronnoit tous les ans . . .* , Paris, n.d.

11 M.-J. Peyre, *Oeuvres d'architecture*, Paris 1765, pl. 3, 4. Van Zanten, *op. cit.*, p. 112, gives the date of 1756, but is in disagreement with A. M. Vogt, *Boullées Newton-Denkmal, Sakralbau and Kugelidee*, Basel and Stuttgart 1969, p. 337

12 Prieur and Van Cléemputte, *op. cit.*, pl. 1–4, include these two projects. They do not include Barbier's and Durand's contributions

13 Pérouse de Montclos, *op. cit.*, p. 165, fig. 93. Boullée's Museum, discussed p. 163, illustrated in figs. 76–80, has more to do with Percier's Académies than with Durand's project

14 Pérouse de Montclos, *op. cit.*, p. 165, dates it 1784/85

15 Durand reproduced it in his *Recueil*, pl. 55

16 Discussed by Hitchcock, *op. cit.*, p. 51, and Pevsner, *op. cit.*, pp. 124–26; for Klenze see O. Hederer, *Leo von Klenze*, Munich 1964

17 D. Dolgner, 'Clemens Wenzeslaus Coudray (1775–1845), Studienarbeiten der Pariser Zeit', *Wissenschaftliche Zeitschrift der Hochschule für Architektur und Bauwesen Weimar*, 5/6, 1975, pp. 485–500, pp. 492–93, notes 20 and 21, fig. 7. Fig. 7 gives Durand's museum. In the copy the plan is reduced to a pure outline, a *parti*

18 See W. Szambien, 'J.-N.-L. Durand, Une méthode de composition architecturale', lecture given in March 1978 at the CERA, Paris, to be published

19 Prieur and Van Cléemputte, *op. cit.*, pl. 35, 36; the original plan of the project is at the Ecole des Beaux-Arts and has been published in Van Zanten, *op. cit.*, p. 125

20 Such windows, copied after

Roman baths, are among Durand's most typical motifs. Their frequent use gives evidence of Durand's Palladianism.

21 See the drawing by A. Huet, dating from 1833/34, Bibliothèque Centrale de l'Ecole polytechnique, XII C/10

22 A. Détournelle, *Recueil d'architecture nouvelle . . .* , Paris Year XIII (1804/05), pl. 47–49. Explaining his elevation, Détournelle writes: 'Des cazernes conviennent à deux régiments de Cavalerie, et pourroient être placées à l'entrée de Paris sur le bord de la Seine, un peu au dessus de l'Hôpital de la Salpêtrière. L'Auteur qui fut adjoint au génie militaire Chargé de cazernement de Paris et qui a Habité pendant 4 ans diverses Cazernes, a cherché dans Ce projet, en se conformant aux ordonnances, à donner une disposition salubre, et à éviter mille défauts observés jusqu'à présent. Nota. dans le précis des leçons d'Architecture 2.eme Volume planche Vingt, Durand m'a fait l'Honneur d'Insérer comme exemple, Ce projet il le présente différemment, que l'Original, connu et exposé l'An 8.au salon, je le reproduis aujourd'hui sans me permettre le plus léger changement.'

23 See Rondelet, *op. cit.*, p. 5

24 Some of Boullée's drawings for his 'Recueil d'architecture privée', fragments of which I discovered recently, indicate that the interdependence between Boullée and Durand was not limited to public buildings. See W. Szambien, 'Notes sur le recueil d'architecture privée de Boullée', *Gazette des Beaux-Arts*, March 1981, pp. 111–24

25 These projects are published by Pérouse de Montclos, *op. cit.*, figs. 84 and 85 (Lequeu, Temple de la Terre), 87 (Labadie, Cénotaphe à Newton, 1800), 88 (Gay, Cénotaphe à Newton, 1800), 89 (Delespine, Tombeau en l'honneur de Newton, 1785); Vogt, *op. cit.*, p. 108 (Delespine), 110 (Moreau, Cénotaphe, 1785), 114b (Labadie), 115 (Gay), 116a (Vaudoyer, Maison d'un Cosmopolite, 1785), 116b (Sobre, Temple de l'Immortalité), 118 (Lequeu, Temple consacré à l'égalité), 119 (Lequeu, Temple de la Terre); J. de Caso, 'Remarques sur Boullée et l'architecture funéraire à l'âge des lumières', *Revue de l'art*, 32, 1976, pp. 15–22, fig. 11 (Molinos, Champ de repos, Year VII (1798/99); Prieur and Van Cléemputte, *op. cit.*, pl. 57, 58 (Lefèvre, Bibliothèque publique, 1787).

Some of the projects which are mentioned here are certainly published elsewhere. There are no doubt other such projects by Boullée's followers unpublished or unrecorded

26 See W. Szambien, 'Aux origines de l'enseignement de Durand: les cent soixante-huit croquis des *Rudimenta Operis Magni et Disciplinae*', *Etudes de la revue du Louvre*, 1, 1980, pp. 122–30

27 Collection Baderou, Rouen, 975-4-1256, A4–10. The one flanked by columns is A8. A4 and A5 appear to have a square plan

28 *Cf.* L. Portiez, *Rapport sur les concours de sculpture, architecture et peinture ouverts par les décrets de la Convention Nationale*, Paris, n.d. (1795)

29 Dolgner, *op. cit.*, p. 489 and note 11. Coudray made the drawings for the engravings of the second volume of the *Précis*

30 For Leroy (1724–1803) see H. Ottomeyer, *Das frühe Oeuvre Charles Perciers, Zu den Anfängen des historismus in Frankreich*, unpublished thesis, Munich 1976, pp. 25–28, 33–34, 321–22; *Piranèse et les Français*, Catalogue of the Exhibition, Rome, Dijon, Paris 1976, pp. 220ff.

31 J.-D. Leroy, *Les Ruines des plus beaux monuments de la Grèce . . .* , Paris 1758, 1ere partie, p. vj. Leroy, not trusting the translations of Vitruvius and noting discrepancies between the rules of proportion and the actual remains of ancient buildings, proposed that architects should unite to establish new rules

32 R. Fréart Sieur de Chambray, *Parallèle de l'architecture antique et de la moderne . . .* Paris 1650, 2nd ed. 1702; G.-P.-M. Dumont, *Parallèle de plans des plus belles salles de spectacle d'Italie et de la France*, Paris, n.d. (1765?)

33 Leroy, *op. cit.*, 2nd ed., 2 vol., Paris 1770, vol. I, pl. I. This plate goes back to the 'Plan des églises les plus remarquables . . .' published by Leroy in the *Histoire de la disposition et des formes différentes que les chrétiens ont données à leurs temples depuis le règne de Constantin le Grand jusqu'à nous . . .* , Paris 1764. Robin Middleton has drawn my attention to an earlier comparative plate of this kind, 'Parallèle général des édifices les plus considérables depuis les Egyptiens, les Grecs jusqu'à nos derniers modernes, dessinés sur la même Echelle par J.-A. Meissonnier', engraved in Dumont's *Détails des plus intéressantes parties de la Basilique de St Pierre de*

Rome ... Paris 1763, BN Cab. Est., Ha 36. The drawing probably dates from before 1750, as Meissonier died in that year.

34 V. Louis, *Salle de spectacle de Bordeaux*, Paris 1782, pl. XXII

35 L.-A. Dubut, *Architecture civile, Maisons de ville et de campagne* ... , Paris, Year XI (1803), 'Table figurée et parallèle des plans ... '; C.-P.-J. Normand, *Recueil varié de plans et de façades, motifs pour les maisons de ville et de campagne, des monumens et des établissemens publics* ... , Paris 1823; L. Bruyère, *Etudes relatives à l'art des constructions* ... , 2 vol., Paris 1823–28, 10e livraison, pl. 3, 4. The title 'Parallèle' continued to be used (for example: J.-C. Huet, *Parallèle des temples anciens, gothiques et modernes*, Paris 1809)

36 H. Lemonnier (ed.), *Procès-verbaux de l'Académie royale d'architecture*, 10 vol., Paris 1911–29, vol. VIII, pp. 351, 379, 388, 391, vol. IX, pp. 14, 26, 74

37 *Précis*, vol. II, p. 26

38 *Précis*, vol. I, 1802, pp. 73–74: *Nouveau Précis*, pp. 61–62. Even the fourth one is taken from Vignola, although Durand indicates that it derives from Serlio. Durand also used Fréart de Chambray, *op. cit.*

39 *Précis*, vol. I, 1802, p. 65: *Nouveau Précis*, p. 53

40 *Nouveau Précis*, pp. 55–56

41 Published in *Europäische Architekturzeichnungen* ... , catalogue of the Exhibition, Munich 1977, pp. 24–27

42 *Nouveau Précis*, pp. 54–55

43 These capitals follow the model of Durand's third order, given in the *Nouveau Précis*

44 *Précis*, vol. I, 1802, 1ere partie, pl. 4, which in the *Nouveau Précis* becomes pl. 5. See also pl. 8 (pl. 9 after 1813) and *Nouveau Précis*, 2e partie, pl. 20

45 P. Collins, 'Origins of graph paper as an influence on architectural design', *Journal of the Society of Architectural Historians*, 1962, 4, pp. 159–62; Guillerme, *op. cit.* Durand himself recommends using grids in the *Partie graphique*, p. 13, and most of the surviving drawings at the Ecole Polytechnique are on paper on which a grid is printed

46 *Recueil*, pl. 16 (*Raccolta e Parallelo* ... , Venice 1833, pl. 41, 42)

47 G.-B. Piranesi, *Il Campo Marzio dell' antica Roma*, Rome 1762. The plans given on pl. 16 of the *Recueil* are all copied from Piranesi's 'Ichnographia', *op. cit.*, pl. V–X. The model

for the ancient Capitol should be below on the left side of pl. VIII. But while the other buildings on pl. 16 of the *Recueil* are free copies after Piranesi, the ancient Capitol is a pure invention of Durand's. J.-G. Legrand writes in his text: 'Les planches 41 et 42 offrent une suite de places et de marchés dont la richesse et la disposition grande et majestueuse peuvent servir de modèles à ceux qui voudraient, à l'instar des Romains, composer des édifices de ce genre; et quoiqu'on ne puisse pas assurer que ces plans soient bien authentiques et relevés d'après des ruines antiques encore subsistantes, toujours est-il vrai qu'on y retrouve la marche simple et les formes sévères employées par les anciens.' (*Raccolta e Parallelo* ... , *loc. cit.*, p. 86; J.-G. Legrand, *Essai sur l'histoire générale de l'architecture* ... , Paris 1809, pp. 104, 105.) See also S. Conard, 'De l'architecture de Claude-Nicolas Ledoux, considérée dans ses rapports avec Piranèse', *Actes du colloque Piranèse et les Français*, Rome, 1978, pp. 161–76

48 Bibliothèque Centrale de l'Ecole Polytechnique, Carnet de Fransoz, 1822

49 *Recueil*, pl. 28; *Partie graphique*, pl. 29

50 *Recueil*, pl. 45; *Partie graphique*, pl. 28

51 *Partie graphique*, pp. 19–20

52 A. Vidler, 'The Idea of Type: The Transformation of the Academic Ideal, 1750–1830', *Oppositions*, 8, pp. 94–115, p. 108

53 Durand considered that illustrating functions by architectural forms with symbolic meaning is ridiculous. On the subject of prisons, he writes: 'l'architecture ne s'occuperait plus qu'à rendre un tel lieu supportable par tous les moyens possibles, loin de chercher à le rendre horrible par le spectacle ridicule de colonnes enchaînées, entassées, incarcérées en quelque sorte dans les murs, etc'. (*Nouveau Précis*, p. 98). As for character, a most important notion in Boullée's thought (see E.-L. Boullée, *Architecture, Essai sur l'art*, edited by J.-M. Pérouse de Montclos, Paris 1968, pp. 73ff.) Durand only comments that it results automatically from considering the real principles of architecture, such as utility, economy and convenience (*Précis*, pp. 17–18; *Nouveau Précis*, pp. 19–20)

54 G. Semper, *Wissenschaft, Industrie und Kunst*, Mainz 1966, 'Vorlaufige Bemerkungen' (1834), p. 15

55 *Revue générale de l'architecture et des travaux publics*, vol. 6, 1845/46, p. 330. I would like to thank Helene Lipstadt for having brought this quotation to my attention

III Planning and building in towns

This article is based on research done in 1974, with a grant from the DGRST in the IERAU, Paris, under the direction of Bernard Huet. The statistical analysis was done with Gilbert Erouart. Archives Nationales has been abbreviated AN

1 L. Hautecoeur, *Histoire de l'architecture classique en France*, vol. V, Picard, Paris 1953, pp. 112–14

2 The Ministry of the Interior was established by a law of 27 April–25 May 1790. It was to focus in one administration 'tout ce qui peut assurer la liberté, la tranquillité et la prospérité publiques'. After the Convention, it was re-established by a decree of 10 vendémiaire Year IV (2 October 1795). Benezech remained in charge from 12 brumaire to 28 messidor Year V. Among his successors were: François de Neufchâteau, Quinette, Laplace, Lucien Bonaparte, Chaptal, Champagny, Cretet and Montalivet. See: *Recueil des circulaires ... émanées du Ministre de l'intérieur de 1790 à 1830*, Paris 1850; and Charles Gourlier, *Notice historique sur le service des travaux des Bâtiments civils à Paris et dans les départements* ... , Paris 1848; 2nd ed. enlarged by Questel (1886)

3 See the introduction to Emil Kaufmann, *Trois architectes révolutionnaires: Boullée, Ledoux, Lequeu* (introduction and notes by G. Erouart and G. Teyssot), Paris, SADG, 1978 (see the English version in *Oppositions*, 13, 1978, pp. 46–75); and A. Demangeon and B. Fortier, 'The politics of urban space: the city around 1800', *Architectural Design*, vol. 48, no. 8–9, 1978, pp. 8–13

4 J. Guillerme and J. Sebestik, 'Les commencements de la technologie', in *Thalès*, 1966, XII, Paris 1968, pp. 21–31

5 C. Babbage, *La macchina analitica*, M. G. Losano (ed.), Etas Kompass, Milan 1973

6 J.-M. de Gérando, *Des signes et de l'art de penser considérés dans leurs rapports mutuels*, 4 vol., Paris Year VIII

7 D. Richet, *La France moderne:*

l'esprit des institutions, Flammarion, Paris 1973, p. 13

8 E. Bellone, 'Note sulla rivoluzione scientifica nella prima metà dell'Ottocento', *Quaderni di critica marxista*, no. 6, 1970; and J. Guillerme and J. Sebestik, *op. cit.*

9 Quoted by L. Hautecoeur, *op. cit.*, vol. VI, p. 113

10 *Cf.* Lucien Bonaparte, *Arrêté sur l'organisation du service des Bâtiments civils*, 8 vendémiaire Year IX, AN, F¹³ 1555

11 AN, F¹³ 1555. In Year IX, the architects were Raymond, Poyet, Blève, Maréchaux, Delannoy, Legrand, Gondoin, Soufflot, Vaudoyer, Jaillier, Moreau, Duhameau, Molinos. They received a yearly salary of between 3000 and 4000 F. The three council members received 4000 F.

12 Jean Petot, *Histoire de l'administration des Ponts et Chaussées, 1599–1815*, Paris 1958, p. 438

13 An Imperial decree organizing the Corps des Ingénieurs des Ponts et Chaussées, 7 fructidor Year XII

14 R. Chafee, 'The teaching of Architecture at the Ecole des Beaux-Arts', in *The Architecture of the Ecole des Beaux-Arts*, A. Drexler (ed.), Secker and Warburg, London 1977, pp. 76–77

15 *Bulletin des lois*, 11 and 13 January 1811 (nos. 6454 and 6459); and J. Tulard, *Nouvelle histoire de Paris: le Consulat et l'Empire*, Paris 1970; J. Tulard, *Paris et son administration (1800–1830)*, Paris 1976; Petot, *op. cit.*, p. 419

16 Navier, *Notice sur M. Bruyère*, Paris 1833, p. 14; and Louis Bruyère, *Etudes relatives à l'art des construction*, Bance aîné, Paris 1823–28, 2 vol.

17 A. de Laborde, *Projet d'organisation des Bâtiments civils dépendans du ministère de l'intérieur, tendant à l'amélioration de l'architecture en France; remis à son Exc. le Ministre de l'Intérieur, sur sa demande, le 10 Avril 1819*, Paris 1820. By De Laborde, see also *Projets d'embellissemens de Paris et de travaux d'utilité publique, concernant les Ponts et Chaussées*, Paris 1816. See also Rondelet, *Mémoire sur l'architecture considérée généralement avec le projet d'une école pratique qui serait chargée de tous les ouvrages publics*, Paris 1790; and A.-G. Kersaint, *Discours sur les monuments publics*, Paris 1792

18 *Ibid.*; and: 'Les élèves qui n'auraient pas remporté les prix du grand concours, mais qui auraient suivi tous les cours de l'Ecole, pen-

dant cinq ans, et remporté quatre médailles d'architecture, et une pour chaque partie, pourront être également admis parmi les inspecteurs ordinaires', p. 15

19 L. Lebrun, architect, 'Dénonciation du cours d'architecture et du cours de construction de l'Ecole Royale d'Architecture', *Journal du Génie civil*, vol. I, 1828, pp. 473–78; Picolet, 'Architecture, systèmes divers, routines (écoles sans doctrines, et par conséquent, sans résultats utiles)', *Ibid.*, vol. III, 1829, pp. 379–93, criticizing the 'manque de théorie du conseil des bâtiments civils', and the 'poncifs' used by the architects. See also Jeannin, professor of mathematics, 'Des ponts et chaussées et des bâtiments civils; des dépenses de toute nature de ces deux corps; comparaison des résultats qu'ils produisent et discussions des dépenses', vol. V, 1829, pp. 539–57. We are grateful to Helene Lipstadt for drawing our attention to this magazine, whose contributors included among others Charles Dupin, Héricart de Thury, Navier, Alavoine, Durand, Clapeyron, Auguste Comte

20 In the constitution of 1945 an independent Direction Générale de l'Architecture, incorporating the Bâtiments civils et palais nationaux and the Monuments historiques et des sites, was formed within the Ministère de l'Education nationale. Parallel to it was the Conseil général des Bâtiments de France. De Lestang, *Notice historique sur le service des travaux des Bâtiments civils et sur le conseil général des Bâtiments de France (1896–1945), suivie d'une annexe pour la période 1946–1960*, (n.d.). See also *Quatre siècles du service des Bâtiments (1535–1938)*, Exhibition catalogue, AN, Paris 1938

21 *Bourges, politique municipale, morphologie urbaine et typologie architecturale au XIX siècle*, by D. Bérard, J.-P. Braun, B. Leroy, S. Santelli, under the direction of B. Huet, IERAU-DGRST, 1975

22 See the exhaustive study by Robert Triger, 'Les travaux publics au Mans à l'époque de la Révolution et l'ingénieur Bruyère', *Revue historique et archéologique du Maine*, vol. XXXVIII, 1895

23 *Ibid.* (Chap. V, p. 99)

24 *Ibid.* (Chap. IV, pp. 227*ff.*)

25 *Ibid.*, p. 246

26 *Ibid.*, p. 254

27 AN, F²¹ 1900 (Sarthe), no. 29. 'Salle de spectacle au Mans, mars 1838'

28 J. Petot (*op. cit.*, p. 358) refers to this. See also R. Triger, *op. cit.*, chap. V, p. 100

29 Minutes of the Conseil des Bâtiments Civils, AN, F²¹* 2470, 7 pluviose Year IV (27 January 1796). The first meeting of the Conseil des Bâtiments Civils was held on 11 December 1795: 'Le Cᵉⁿ Vaudoyer, membre du conseil et inspecteur de la division des travaux relatifs aux édifices consacrés à l'administration de la Justice et à l'exécution des Lois, a fait lecture d'un rapport sur un projet de prisons à exécuter sur l'emplacement de l'ancien évêché de la ville du Mans . . . .'

30 AN, F²¹* 2473: Proposal by Mr Thomas, architect, living in Paris, for setting up a temple in the church of 'Lacouture', Le Mans, 2 ventose Year 7 (20 February 1799)

31 *Cf.* AN, F²¹ 1900. See also the minutes of the Conseils des Bâtiments Civils (F²¹* 2470–2542), and the departmental series F²¹ 1862–63 (reports by the inspectors-general). On the history of the town of Le Mans, see A. Bouton, *Le Maine, histoire économique et sociale au XIXe siècle*, Le Mans 1974; F. Dornic, *Histoire du Mans et des pays manceaux*, Privat, Toulouse 1975, and L.-M. Auvray, préfet, *Statistique du département de la Sarthe*, Paris Year X

32 In the second half of the century the following buildings were erected: the station (1854), the barracks at Paixhans and Chansy (1870–71), the tram terminus (1888), the post office (1889–91), the stock exchange (1890) and the new hospital (1891)

33 AN, F²¹ 1900

34 AN, F²¹* 2474, 'Rétablissement de la correspondance directe entre lui et les architectes', 16 pluviose Year IX. It should be noted that Mouchelet, in the name of the Conseil des Bâtiments Civils, advised the architect who wished to transform the church of La Couture at Le Mans into a temple, that he should retain 'toute la pureté du gothique' appropriate to this building founded in the 6th century. See F²¹* 2473, *cit.*

35 AN, F²¹* 2475, Meeting of the Conseil des Bâtiments Civils, 18 floréal Year IX (May 1801); 28 thermidor Year X (August 1802) and 16 pluviose Year XI (February 1803)

36 Plans in F²¹ 1900 carry the date 9 pluviose Year XI. The estimate, accepted on the 23 germinal of the same year (April 1803) was 54,780 F.

See F[13] 863. The firm of Duchesne was awarded the contract

37 Report by Barbier Neuville (1 February 1806)

38 F[21]* 2477, 16 November 1807: 101,232.85 F. for the building, 19,238.34 F. for the boundary road, giving a total of 120,471.19 F.

39 In accord with the proposals of the Constituent Assembly of 1791. See J. Godechot, *Les institutions de la France sous la Révolution et l'Empire*, PUF, Paris 1968, p. 153. In Year IX (1800), the total number of people in prison in France was estimated at about 16,000. See 'Extraits de l'état de demandes de fonds pour l'an IX', AN, F[13] 1551, no. 1

40 AN, F[13] 863

41 B. Melossi et M. Pavarini, *Carcere e fabbrica*, Il Mulino, Bologna 1977; M. Foucault, *Surveiller et punir, naissance de la prison*, Gallimard, Paris 1975, pp. 235–260; M. Perrot, 'Délinquance et système pénitentiaire en France au XIXe siècle', *Annales ESC*, 1975, no. 1, pp. 67–91; B. Foucart, 'Architecture carcérale et architectes fonctionnalistes en France au XIXe siècle', *Revue de l'Art*, no. 32, 1976

42 On the 'beginnings' of hygiene in the 18th and 19th centuries, see G. Canguilhem, *La connaissance de la vie*, Vrin, Paris 1975 (2); and J. Guillerme, introduction to the special issue 'Le sain et le malsain', *Dix-huitième siècle*, 1977, no. 9

43 AN, F[13] 1795, no. 7: Guyot's basic salary was set at 1500 F. a year, not including the payments made for each separate job (e.g. 1500 F. for the seminary; 5000 F. for the workhouse in 1816)

44 AN, F[13] 1795 and F[21] 1900. In Year IX (1800) there were in France '28 maisons destinées à recevoir les vagabonds, les femmes de mauvaises moeurs, les fous, les épileptiques et les mutilés', 2400 people in all. These served also as houses of correction (2200 inmates). Serviced by contracts with individual companies they cost the state a million francs a year; see AN, F[13] 1555, no. 1. In 1808 workhouses were officially re-established, with no prisoners included

45 F[21]* 2486: 7 February 1814, the design for the workhouse of the Sarthe by Guyot was accepted, with changes, by the Conseil des Bâtiments Civils. The estimate was 432,703 F.

46 AN, F[13] 1795, no. 3

47 AN, F[13] 1795, no. 2, and F[21]*

2486: the new plan was agreed by the Préfet, Cellerier, before his death, and the engineer Daudin; the report was written by Rondelet, and accepted by the Conseil on 25 July 1814. See the plans in F[21] 1900, no. 16. The estimate was 50,082 F., accepted in September 1814

48 AN, F[13] 1922: letter of 28 September 1816

49 *Ibid.*: 'Note pour le bureau des Bât. civils', 10 December 1816

50 AN, N III Sarthe 31, nos. 1 and 6: report by the chief engineer of the Département de la Sarthe, 25 October 1817, with Cherrier's plan

51 AN, N III Sarthe, 31, nos. 2 and 3: 'Esquisse donnée à l'appui d'un rapport concernant l'établissement dans l'ancien couvent de la visitation du Mans, des tribunaux, des prisons et de la gendarmerie, Le Mans, Mai 1817', Guy de Gisors, with a report by the architect dated 18 December 1817 (copy of the plans in F[21] 1900, no. 19)

52 AN, N III Sarthe 31, no. 3: report by Gisors, *cit.*

53 AN, F[13] 1922: 'Esquisse d'un projet de caserne de Gendarmerie et des prisons dans une partie des terrains et du jardin de la visitation de la ville du Mans, 27 Mars 1818', signed Alavoine (two sketches). And 'Projet des Prisons du Mans, ... rectifié d'après la demande de M. le Préfet du 2 Avril 1818 et selon les Instructions et disposition générale données par le Conseil des Bâtiments civils, par J.-A. Alavoine' (two sketches)

54 AN, F[21] 1900, no. 24 and F[21]* 2516

55 B. Fortier, 'Espace et planification urbaine (1760–1820)', in *Prendre la ville, esquisse d'une histoire de l'urbanisme d'état*, ed. Anthropos, Paris 1977, pp. 79–102

56 See our article 'Città-servizi, la produzione dei bâtiments civils in Francia (1795–1848)', *Casabella*, no. 424, April 1977, pp. 56–65; French version in *Architecture, Mouvement, Continuité*, no. 45, 1978. See also *Le macchine imperfette, architettura, programma, istituzioni nel XIX secolo*, edited by P. Morachiello and G. Teyssot, a conference held at the IUAV, Venice, October 1977 published by Officina, Rome, 1980. The definition of 'heterotopie' is given by M. Foucault, in 'Des espaces autres', *L'Architettura, cronache e storia*, XIII, p. 822. See also G. Teyssot, 'Eterotopie e storia degli spazi', in *Il dispositivo Foucault*, edited by F. Rella, Venice 1977

57 P. Lavedan, *Histoire de l'urbanisme, Renaissance et temps modernes*, Laurens, Paris 1951; P. Morachiello, 'Bruyère, Comacchio e il programma dei Lazzaretti in Italia (1805–1823)', *Casabella*, no. 439, 1978; and P. Morachiello and G. Teyssot, 'State town, the colonization of the territory during the First Empire', *Lotus International*, 24, 1979, p. 24–39

IV Early architectural periodicals

This essay is based on research undertaken by Helene Lipstadt and others with a grant from the Comité de la Recherche et du Développement en Architecture of the Ministre de l'Environnement et du Cadre de vie in France, published as *Architecte et ingénieur dans la presse: polémique, débat, conflit*, CORDA, 1980

1 Jean Tulard, *Nouvelle histoire de Paris: le Consulat et l'Empire*, Paris 1970, p. 185, table showing the amount of stone (*pierre de taille*) brought into Paris during these years. By 1806, it is clear, building had begun again – see *Annales de l'architecture* I, 25 October 1806, p. 502. 'Si, pendant les premières années de l'existence de notre feuille, nous nous sommes plaints de la sterilité des travaux publics, du peu d'empressement que l'on mettait à suivre l'exécution de certains; si, avec toute l'energie qu'on nous connait, nous avons fait sentir que des projets, que des concours, ne suffisaient pas ... maintenant ... nous voyons Paris en quelque soft metamorphosé ... les travaux sont grandement actives de toutes part ..., comme par l'effect d'une sorte de miracle ou bien par magie.'

2 L.-B. [Le Bars], 'Architecture', *Journal des bâtiments* XIII, 29 frimaire Year XII, p. 401.

3 *Journal des bâtiments civils et des arts*, 3 vendémiaire Year IX to 30 fructidor Year X, then *Journal des bâtiments, des monuments et des arts*, 3 vendémiaire Year XI to Year XII, then *Journal des monuments et des arts*, 4 vendémiaire Year XIII to 28 frimaire Year XIII and, finally, from 16 germinal Year XIII, *Annales de l'architecture et des arts* until 10 May 1810, when it was absorbed by the *Journal des arts* (see p. 121 of that issue of the *Journal des arts*, also *Almanach de commerce*, 1811, pp. 198

and 499). The *Annales* reappeared briefly in 1819

4 The first proposals for an art journal were made in Germany in 1755, but four years later, in France, the Abbé Laugier put forward the idea for the Marquis de Marigny's consideration. After taking advice from C.-N. Cochin, who had proposed himself and J.-G. Soufflot as collaborators, he turned it down (see W. Hermann, *Laugier and 18th century French theory*, London 1962, pp. 13–14). The first art journal was German: *Miscelaneen Artistischen Inhalts*, founded in 1779 (see E.-H. Lehmann, *Die Anfange der Kunstzeitschrift in Deutschland*, Leipzig 1932). The first architectural journal, also a German, or rather Weimar, invention, was started in 1789, running until 1796: *Allgemeines Magazine für die Bürgliche Baukunst* (see R. Fuhlrolt, *Deutschsprachige Architektur-Zeitschriften*, Munich 1975). Fuhlrott suggests that the architectural review was an outgrowth of the art review, just as the art review sprung from the literary review, but in France, it is evident, the *Journal des bâtiments* derives rather from the *Almanach des bastimens*, a pocket book for builders compiled by Journault, containing lists of the members of the corporations of the building trade. There are two sets of the *Almanach des bastimens* in the Bibliothèque Nationale in Paris, in the Collection des Almanachs and in the Collection Le Senne. Both include editions for the years 1774, 1776, 1777, 1780, 1784, 1786, 1787, 1790 and 1791

5 *Recueil polytechnique des ponts et chaussées* I, 1 prairial Year XI (21 May 1803) to vendémiaire Year XII (October 1803); II, 1807. The periodical is not listed in the *Catalogue collectif des périodiques* at the Bibliothèque Nationale, Paris, having been miscatalogued as an 'Anonyme'

6 A. Cabanis, *La presse sous le Consulat et l'Empire (1799–1814)*, Paris 1975

7 A. Aulard, *Paris sous le Consulat*, Paris 1903, vol. I, p. vii

8 Archives Nationales, Paris (hereafter abbreviated as AN), F⁷ 3454, fol. 405–15.

9 AN, F⁷ 3457, 'Rapport à son excellence le ministre sur les journaux de 8 Avril 1808'

10 AN, F⁷ 3458, 'Rapport au Ministre de la police', 27 September 1810

11 AN, F⁷ 3452, fol. 380–82

12 *Journal des bâtiments* I, 3 vendémiaire Year IX, p. 2c

13 'Q***', 'Sur la manière d'imiter la bonne architecture grecque', *Journal des bâtiments* II, 6 nivôse Year IX, pp. 3–6; see also Chery, 'Lettre d'un artiste a BONAPARTE', *Journal des bâtiments* I, 29 brumaire Year IX, pp. 1–7

14 AN, F¹³ 508, F.-C. Le Bars à Chaptal, 1 pluviôse Year IX; Rapport, 3 germinal Year IX; Chaptal refuses to support the *Journal*, 8 germinal Year IX; Camille à Chaptal, 15 floréal Year IX; Chaptal à Camille, 3 messidor Year IX; Camille à Barbier Neuville, 16 messidor Year X, and response, 18 messidor Year X

15 Quoted M. Agulhon, *Le Cercle dans la France bourgeoise 1810–1848*, Paris 1977, p. 9

16 Undated prospectus for the *Journal des bâtiments*, bound with vol. XIII of the BN copy

17 F.-C. Le Bars, 1 pluviôse Year IX, AN, F¹³ 508

18 *Journal des bâtiments* XIII, 20 brumaire Year XII, p. 229

19 Undated prospectus for the *Journal des bâtiments*

20 *Journal des bâtiments* IX, 21 vendémiaire Year XI, pp. 89–90; see also XII, 25 thermidor Year XI, p. 247

21 L. Pelpel reproduces the draft of an Act which, in 1780, would have given this development the force of law; see 'La formation architecturale au XVIIIᵉ siècle en France', *Les cahiers de la recherche architecturale* II, March 1978, p. 10; Cf. also T. Shinn, 'Du corps de l'Etat au secteur industriel: genèse de la profession d'ingénieur, 1750–1920', *Revue française de sociologie* XIX, 1978, pp. 39–71

22 Ms. 524 bis (1834)

23 Ms. 524 ter (1049) for proposal; circular sent in response by the Conseil des Ponts et Chaussées, 1 thermidor Year XI, in the Collection Piou, AN: 147 AP5

24 *Recueil polytechnique* II, 1807, pp. 372–77, 'Tableau synoptique des premiers souscripteurs'

25 On Herbert d'Hauteclair see *Recueil polytechnique* II, 1807, pp. 38, 85, and Abbé Letacq and Abbé Vegras, *Statistique de la commune d'Arconnay, rédigée en l'an IX (1801)*, Le Mans 1913, pp. 75–83

26 *Recueil polytechnique* II, prairial Year XII, p. 3

27 'Note des 'rédacteurs', *Journal des bâtiments* VI, 5 pluviôse Year X, p. 184

28 P.-L. Baltard, 'Réponse', *Journal des bâtiments* II, 13 floréal Year

IX, pp. 1–2. The polemic and debate fill the third volume

29 *Journal des bâtiments* XIII, 12 vendémiaire Year XII, p. 59

30 'Note du rédacteur', *Recueil polytechnique* I, Year XII, p. 129

31 See AN, F⁷ and F¹³ references above; see also AN: Minutier Central, Etude IV, 946 (655) 6 brumaire Year XII, and 948 (1037), 16 nivôse Year XII. For exposure by a rival editor, *Annales des bâtiments* IV, 1819, pp. 287–88

32 *Journal des bâtiments* XIII, 8 vendémiaire Year XII, pp. 33–39

33 On Houard, see AN: Minutier Central, Etudes: III (1189), 23 February 1788; XI (801), 25 fructidor Year VII; XVI (945), 15 brumaire Year X; XX (797), 13 prairial Year XI; XX (798), 12 messidor Year XI; XVI (953), 29 frimaire Year XII; XVI (961), 6 messidor Year XIII; *Recueil polytechnique* II, 1807, pp. 38, 85, 272. In the Bibliothèque Historique de la Ville de Paris is a collection of pamphlets by Houard, the most useful of which are 'Moyens et nécessités absolus d'occuper les ouvriers', Paris n.d., p. 18, 'Nouvelle loi promulguée le 7 juillet 1833', Paris n.d., p. 7; 'Le prévoyant régulateur des arts agricoles', Paris 1829, p. 3. There are several editions of Houard's Paris map in the collection of Michel Verne. Houard's lack of familiarity with architects was noted in the *Journal des bâtiments* XIII, 1 frimaire Year XII, p. 282, by Chausson, a mason, who pointed out that Houard had omitted the names of Durand, Guillaumot, Ledoux and Rondelet in his *Almanach général pour l'an XII*. 'Il se dit architecte', Chausson commented, 'mais c'est donc en Chine qu'il a exercé cet art'

34 For one year the *Journal des bâtiments* used the address of the Athénée des Etrangers

35 *Journal des bâtiments* VI, 20 ventôse Year X, pp. 383–86; 23 ventôse Year X, p. 403; VII, 6 germinal Year X, pp. 20–22

36 L. B. [Le Bars], 'Quelques observations sur les grands travaux et les fortes entreprises confiés aux ingénieurs ...', *Journal des bâtiments* XIV, 14 pluviôse Year XII, p. 197

37 E. Charton, *Dictionnaire des professions*, 1840, pp. 43–45

38 *Journal des bâtiments* II, 26 nivôse Year IX, p. 1–2

V The programmes of the architectural section of the Ecole des Beaux-Arts, 1819–1914

1 Thérèse de Puylaroque, 'Pierre Baltard, Peintre et dessinateur', *Bulletin de la Société de l'Histoire de l'Art Français*, Paris 1976
2 See the magazine *Les monuments historiques de la France*, no. 1, 1978, devoted to this subject, in particular Daniel Rabreau's article, which demonstrates the special interest taken at this time in thermal architecture, faithfully reflected in the programmes at the Ecole
3 Exceptions, in a Grand Prix programme, are the greenhouses included in the projects for a House for a Rich Banker by J.-L. Pascal and E. Benard, illustrated in *The Architecture of the Ecole des Beaux-Arts*, A. Drexler (ed.), 1977, p. 236–38

VI The competition for the Grand Prix in 1824

1 This essay grew out of a talk given at the Symposium on the Ecole des Beaux-Arts and French 19th-Century Architecture, held at the Architectural Association School of Architecture, London, in the last week of May 1978. In discussions following the lecture, many helpful suggestions were made by Richard Chafee, Alan Colquhoun, Robin Middleton, Werner Szambien, and David Van Zanten. On a more general level, however, this essay owes a very great deal to Arthur Drexler, for making me look at the student drawings *as drawings* and making me aware of the importance of that; to Jean Paul Carlhian, for a scintillating lecture on the Ecole des Beaux-Arts he gave in April 1978 at Harvard University, which opened my eyes to many of the realities of study there; and to John Coolidge, for a fundamental methodological orientation combined with the most gentle form of practical guidance and help. I would like to thank Mme H. Labrouste for allowing me access to her family papers; M. Paul Dufournet, Curator of the Académie d'Architecture, Paris; and Mme Colomb-Gérard, Archivist of the Académie des Beaux-Arts, Paris. I would also like to express my indebtedness to Mlle

Annie Jacques, Librarian of the Ecole des Beaux-Arts, Paris, for making it possible to study the drawings at the Ecole in the deeply understanding way she did. And, finally, to Lorie Winder goes my warmest thanks for her unstinting help in preparing the manuscript.
Since this essay was finished in the summer of 1979, I was unable to make use of the following two more recent publications: Jean Paul Carlhian, 'The Ecole des Beaux-Arts: Modes and Manners', *Journal of Architectural Education*, vol. 33, no. 2, November 1979, pp. 7–17; and Donald Drew Egbert, *The Beaux-Arts Tradition in French Architecture, Illustrated by the Grands Prix de Rome*, ed. David Van Zanten, Princeton University Press, Princeton, N.J. 1980.
The archival sources from which much of my information is drawn are cited in note 18.
2 This was essentially the point of view of Donald Drew Egbert, under whom I had the good fortune to study as an undergraduate at Princeton University, 1958–63. Egbert was the only American scholar at the time to stress the importance of French 19th-century architecture, and my own interests were strongly influenced by him
3 There is a short description in Richard Chafee, 'The Teaching of Architecture at the Ecole des Beaux-Arts', *The Architecture of the Ecole des Beaux-Arts*, ed. Arthur Drexler, Secker and Warburg, London 1977, pp. 86–88. For a colourful late 19th-century account, see Alexis Lemaistre, *L'Ecole des Beaux-Arts dessinée et racontée par un élève*, Firmin-Didot et Cie, Paris 1889, pp. 232–84
4 See, in chronological order of publication, Reyner Banham, *Theory and Design in the First Machine Age*, Frederick A. Praeger, New York 1960, pp. 14–34; Colin Rowe, 'Character and Composition: or Some Vicissitudes of Architectural Vocabulary in the Nineteenth Century', *Oppositions* 2, January 1974, pp. 41–60; and David Van Zanten, 'Architectural Composition at the Ecole des Beaux-Arts from Charles Percier to Charles Garnier', *The Architecture of the Ecole des Beaux-Arts*, ed. A. Drexler, pp. 111–290. The most complete French discussion of the importance of composition is Julien Guadet, *Eléments et théorie de l'architecture*, 4 vols, orig. pub. 1901–

04; Librairie de la Construction Moderne, Paris [1905]. See also Georges Gromort, *Essai sur la théorie de l'architecture*, Vincent, Fréal & Cie, Paris 1946, pp. 133–274. In English, see John Vreedenburgh Van Pelt, *A Discussion of Composition, Especially as Applied to Architecture*, Macmillan Company, New York 1902; and John F. Harbeson, *The Study of Architectural Design*, Pencil Points Press, New York 1927. It should be noted that, following most of the works cited above, this essay assumes composition to be fundamentally a two-dimensional process of planning
5 Details of the catalogue are: *The Architecture of the Ecole des Beaux-Arts*, an exhibition presented at the Museum of Modern Art, New York, 29 October 1975–4 January 1976, Museum of Modern Art, New York 1975
6 For the projects of 1774–90, see Amant-Parfait Prieur and Pierre-Louis Van Cléemputte, *Collection des prix que la ci-devant Académie d'Architecture proposoit et couronnoit tous les ans*, Paris 1787–c.1796. The plates have been republished in Helen Rosenau, 'The Engravings of the Grands Prix of the French Academy of Architecture', *Architectural History* 3, 1960, pp. 15–180. The premiated designs of 1791–1805 are included in L.-J. Allais, Athanase Détournelle and Antoine-Laurent-Thomas Vaudoyer, *Grands Prix d'Architecture, couronnés par l'Académie d'Architecture et l'Institut de France*, Paris 1806: those of 1803–15 in Louis-Pierre Baltard and A.-L.-T. Vaudoyer, *Grands Prix d'Architecture, projets couronnés par l'Académie Royale des Beaux-Arts de France*, Paris 1818; and those of 1816–31 in Baltard and Vaudoyer, *Grands Prix d'Architecture couronnés par l'Académie Royale des Beaux-Arts de France*, Paris 1834. A final publication of engravings appeared in Liège in 1842. The two series of Armand Guérinet's photographic reproductions are *Les Grands Prix de Rome*, 1st ser.: *Années 1823 à 1849*: and *Les Grands Prix de Rome d'Architecture de 1850 à 1900*. Both were published in Paris but without dates of publication
7 For a checklist, see the catalogue of the exhibition, *The Architecture of the Ecole des Beaux-Arts*, 1975, pp. 38–39
8 This appears to be true for the entire 19th century. For the most complete coverage of the competitions of the latter part of the century,

see Intime-Club, *Croquis d'architecture*, 1866/67–98; *La Construction moderne*, began publication 1885; and *L'Architecture*, began publication 1888. Both *Croquis d'architecture* and *La Construction moderne* often published the complete group of twenty-four-hour sketches, but after 1864 they were no longer the basis for the final renderings. All the twenty-four-hour sketches from 1890 to 1905 were also published separately, along with the programmes, in *Les Esquisses de 24 heures, 1890 à 1905, à l'Ecole Nationale et Spéciale des Beaux-Arts: section d'architecture*, Auguste Vincent, Paris, n.d.

9 The renderings were backed with linen and stored rolled up; the sketches were mounted and bound in volumes, 'Esquisses originales – Grand Prix Architecture', with the overall series number A14 D547. All the drawings are in the library of the Ecole Nationale Supérieure des Beaux-Arts, Paris (hereafter abbreviated as EBA)

10 The sketches for the three prize-winning designs of Henri Labrouste, Léon Vaudoyer and Louis Lepreux are in 'Esquisses originales', vol. 3, 1823–30, EBA. Théodore Labrouste's sketch is also in the library of the Ecole (No. 32081), having been given along with a group of his drawings. It is unsigned and otherwise unidentified except for the endorsement of Pierre Baltard, professor of architectural theory. The four other sketch designs were among the family papers of Henri Labrouste in the collection of Mme H. Labrouste, Paris. Those of Félix Fries, François-Alexis Cendrier and Raphael Lignière are tracings of the original sketches, apparently done by them and offered to the winner Labrouste. Louis Duc's project is only recorded in a small block plan drawn by Henri Labrouste on a sheet which also includes those of Lignière, Fries, Théodore Labrouste and Cendrier. Although Mme Labrouste gave her remaining collection of drawings to the Académie d'Architecture, Paris, in 1975, I was unable to find any but the sheet of block plans there in June 1978

11 Chafee, 'Teaching of Architecture', pp. 77ff. See also Lemaistre, *Ecole des Beaux-Arts*; Henry Guédy, *L'Enseignement à l'Ecole Nationale et Spéciale des Beaux-Arts: section d'architecture*, Librairie de la Construction Moderne, Aulanier et Cie, Paris 1899; and Eugène Müntz,

Guide de l'Ecole Nationale des Beaux-Arts, Maison Quantin, Paris 1889

12 The two-class system was established in May 1819 in accordance with the reorganization of the Ecole begun in 1816 and finally instituted by the royal order of 4 August 1819. For the rules that governed the organization of the Ecole during the period that concerns us here, see *Règlement de l'Ecole Royale et Spéciale des Beaux-Arts de Paris*, Firmin Didot, Paris 1819; Ecole Royal des Beaux-Arts: section d'architecture, *Règlement*, Firmin Didot, Paris 1823; and Ecole Royale des Beaux-Arts: section d'architecture, *Réglement des assemblées et des jugements des concours d'émulation*, Firmin Didot, Paris 1824. For the changes that occurred over the rest of the century, see the collection of documents in Archives Nationales de France, AJ[52] 2, Ecole des Beaux-Arts. Règlements du 4 août 1819 à 1893 (Archives Nationales de France hereafter abbreviated as AN)

13 The Prix Départemental was also sometimes called the Grande Médaille d'Emulation. It too was instituted in 1819

14 Paris, Institut de France, Archives de l' Académie des Beaux-Arts, Pièces annexes des procès-verbaux de l'Académie des Beaux-Arts, 5E 13, 1822, Montalivet, 'Règlement concernant les concours pour les Grands Prix à l'Ecole Spéciale des Beaux-Arts', 5 April 1810; Académie Royale des Beaux-Arts, *Règlements relatifs aux concours ouverts et aux Grands Prix décernés par l'Académie*, Firmin Didot, Paris 1822; Académie Royale des Beaux-Arts, *Règlements relatifs aux concours ouverts et aux Grands Prix décernés par l'Académie Royale des Beaux-Arts*, Firmin Didot, Paris 1835; and *Règlements pour les concours aux Grands Prix de l'Académie Royale des Beaux-Arts*, Firmin Didot Frères, Paris 1846

15 In 1855, the twenty-four-hour sketch was increased to ten days, but this was only a temporary change. See Henry Sirodot, 'Concours des Grands Prix à l'Ecole des Beaux-Arts', *Revue générale de l'architecture et des travaux publics* 13, 1855, col. 186 (hereafter abbreviated as *RGA*). For the later changes, see *RGA* 21, 1863, cols 290–99; *RGA* 22, 1864, cols 64–68; *RGA* 28, 1870/71, cols 258–59; *Gazette des architectes et du bâtiment*, 2d ser., 12, 1883, pp. 247–51, 254–58, 260–62; and Guédy, *Enseignement à l'Ecole*, pp. 391–405

16 In 1864, the competition became a three-stage affair, based on the system previously established for painting and sculpture. The twenty-four-hour sketch became a separate competition for the sole purpose of selecting the ten, rather than eight, finalists. The second stage was another sketch on a different programme, done *en loge* and usually taking two to four days. These sketches were not judged, and the final renderings were based on them

17. For the various changes in eligibility requirements, see AN, AJ[52] 2, Règlements

18 The facts upon which this essay is based derive mainly from unpublished material in two archival sources. The first is the Archives de l'Académie des Beaux-Arts, Institut de France, Paris (hereafter abbreviated as AABA), and consists of the Registres des concours (series 1H); the Procès-verbaux de l'Académie des Beaux-Arts (series 2E); and the Pièces annexes des procès-verbaux de l'Académie des Beaux-Arts (series 5E). The second is the archives of the Ecole des Beaux-Arts, now in the Archives Nationales de France, Paris (AN), forming the series AJ[52]. The documents most important for the Grand Prix competition are the Registres des procès-verbaux des assemblées des professeurs, 1793–1920 (AJ[52] 95–124); and the Registres de présence des élèves aux différents concours, 1821–70 (AJ[52] 159–61)

19 AN, AJ[52] 97–101, 'Troisième Registre' (1 January 1812–20 May 1819)–'Septième Registre' (1 January 1826–10 May 1828). From now on, references to the documents noted above will only be made when there is a direct quotation or special need for clarification

20 The relevant documents for the competition of 1824 are: AABA, 1H 1, 'Registre des concours. Années 1817 à 1827', fols 189–91, 205–06; 5E 15, 'Pièces annexes des procès-verbaux', 1824; AN, AJ[52] 100, 'Registre des jugemens des Prix délivrés en l'Ecole d'Architecture. 1er Janvier. Sixième Registre'; and AJ[52] 159, 'Registre de présence des élèves de 1re et 2e classes aux concours des deux classes, 15 Mars 1821–6 Mai 1828'. The year 1817 will be the starting point for most of the statistical information given here, since the Ecole was reorganized beginning in 1816 and consistent records were kept from that moment on

21 AABA, IH I, fol. 189. It should be noted that the Maison de Campagne was also referred to as a Maison de Plaisance pour un Prince.

22 AABA, IH I, fol. 62

23 AABA, IH I, fol. 88

24 See Louis Hautecoeur, *Histoire de l'architecture classique en France*, 7 vols., A. et J. Picard et Cie, Paris 1943–57, vol. 6: *La Restauration et le gouvernement de juillet* (1955), pp. 111–18; and Charles Gourlier et al., *Choix d'édifices publics projetés et construits en France depuis le commencement du XIXe siècle*, 3 vols, L. Colas, Paris [1825–50], vols 1–2

25 AN, F²¹ 3513, N III Seine 1136–40, and Versement de la Direction de l'Architecture, Albums 5, 6, 40, 108–10; and Paris, Bibliothèque Nationale, Cabinet des Estampes, HC 15d, ve 1180, and Ye 158

26 Félix Pigeory, *Les Monuments de Paris: histoire de l'architecture civile, politique et religieuse sous le règne du roi Louis-Philippe*, A. Hermitte et Cie, Paris 1847, pp. 346–47

27 On the building history of the Cour de Cassation and the Palais de Justice, see Henri Stein, *Le Palais de Justice et la Sainte-Chapelle de Paris: notice historique et archéologique*, D. A. Longuet, Paris 1912; and Félix Narjoux, *Paris: monuments élevés par la ville, 1850–80*, 4 vols, Vve A. Morel et Cie, Paris 1877–84, *Edifices judiciaires* (1880), pp. 1–44. For a contemporary description, see B. Sauvan and J.-P. Schmit, *Histoire et description pittoresque du Palais de Justice, de la Conciergerie et de la Sainte Chapelle de Paris*, G. Engelmann, Paris, 1825

28 See Narjoux, *Edifices judiciaires*, pp. 13–43, pls. 1–22; and Anon., *Documents relatifs aux travaux du Palais de Justice de Paris et à la reconstruction de la Préfecture de Police*, Charles de Mourgues Frères, Paris 1858

29 On the history and function of the Cour de Cassation, see A.-P. Tarbé, *Cour de Cassation: lois et règlements à l'usage de la Cour de Cassation*, Librairie Encyclopédique de Roret, Paris 1840; Ernest Faye, *La Cour de Cassation*, A. Chevalier-Marescq et Cie, Paris 1903; and René David and Henry P. de Vries, *The French Legal System: An Introduction to Civil Law Systems*, Ocean Publications, New York 1958

30 The triple division actually existed on a provisional basis from 1793 to 1795 (Tarbé, *Cour de Cassation*, pp. 27, 261, 269)

31 Tarbé, *Cour de Cassation*, pp. 353–60

32 The programmes for the 1820s are in AABA, IH I; and AN, AJ⁵² 98–102. All the programmes, beginning with the one for 1823, were published in Pierre Lampué's *Programmes des concours d'architecture pour le Grand Prix de Rome*, Alphonse Derenne, Paris 1881. They appear to have been published in conjunction with the Guérinet plates (see note 6 above)

33 AABA, IH I, fol. 10

34 AABA, IH I, fol. 11

35 AABA, IH I, fol. 116

36 AABA, IH I, fol. 238

37 AABA, IH I, fol. 63

38 AABA, IH I, fols 189–90; AN, AJ⁵² 100, fol. 111; and Lampué, *Programmes*, p. 10. Only the copy in the minutes of the Académie will be referred to hereafter

39 AABA, IH I, fols 189–90

40 *Ibid.*, fol. 190

41 *Ibid.*

42 *Ibid.*

43 *Ibid.*, fols 190–91

44 AN, AJ⁵² 100, fol. 108; AJ⁵² 159, n. fol.

45 Académie Royale des Beaux-Arts, *Règlements*, 1822, p. 18

46 Théodore to Henri Labrouste, May 1827, Labrouste family papers, Mme H. Labrouste, Paris

47 This is not always possible to check, but it is definitely true for 1820, 1821, 1824, 1826 and probably 1822. Since the sketches preserved at the Ecole are mounted in bound volumes, one can not see the number on the back. However, Théodore Labrouste's sketch of 1824, which has been preserved loose at the Ecole, is signed by Baltard and identified with the number five on its back; and Théodore was, indeed, ranked fifth at the time

48 The rule was passed at the meeting of 24 April 1824 (AN, AJ⁵² 2, Règlements, fol. 8)

49 AN, AJ⁵² 100, fols 109–110

50 There were also four from the atelier of Delespine, who was shortly to be elected a member of the Académie and would take part in the final judging in September. There were three from Achille Leclère's atelier and two each from those of Barthélemy Vignon, André Châtillon, and the elder Guénepin

51 This was true until 1845, when it was decided that the eight should be arrived at by elimination

52 There is no record of the voting in 1824

53 AN, AJ⁵² 100, fol. 110

54 AN, AJ⁵² 98–100

55 AN, AJ⁵² 237, 'Registre sommier de l'enregistrement de MM. les Elèves', vol. 1, 1 January 1801–1 January 1836, no. 396; AJ⁵² 372, 'Elèves. Architecture', vol. 20. fol. 358. The following biographical information dealing with the student careers of the eight finalists is primarily drawn from the two relevant Registres matricules des élèves de la section d'architecture (AN, AJ⁵² 237, 244); the individual student records (AN, AJ⁵² 353–85); as well as the Registres des procès-verbaux (AN, AJ⁵² 97–103) and the applicable Registre de présence (AN, AJ⁵² 159).

For further biographical information, see esp. Edmond Delaire, *Les Architectes élèves de l'Ecole des Beaux-Arts*, 2nd ed., Librairie de la Construction Moderne, Paris 1907; and Charles Bauchal, *Nouveau dictionnaire biographique et critique des architectes français*, Librairie Générale de l'Architecture et des Travaux Publics; André, Daly Fils et Cie, Paris 1887

56 AN, AJ⁵² 237, no. 477; AJ⁵² 244, no. 477; AJ⁵² 366

57 Henri Labrouste to [Dommey], [May 1825], Labrouste family papers, Mme H. Labrouste

58 AN, AJ⁵² 237, no. 444; AJ⁵² 244, no. 444; AJ⁵² 358, fols 319–20

59 AN, AJ⁵² 237, no. 511; AJ⁵² 363, fol. 319

60 AN, AJ⁵² 237, no. 422. Vaudoyer's individual school record is missing

61 AN, AJ⁵² 237, no. 463; AJ⁵² 244, no. 463; AJ⁵² 373, fols 170–71. Lignière's name was sometimes spelled with an s (Lignières)

62 AN, AJ⁵² 237, no. 349; AJ⁵² 370

63 AN, AJ⁵² 237, no. 417. Henri Labrouste's individual school record is missing

64 This was the youngest during the decade except for Vaudoyer, who won it in 1823 at the age of $20\frac{1}{2}$

65 See Albert Soubiès, *Les Membres de l'Académie des Beaux-Arts depuis la fondation de l'Institut*, 4 vols, new ed., Ernest Flammarion, Paris 1904–15, vol. 3 (1911)

66 The eleven were: H. Labrouste, Vaudoyer, T. Labrouste, Durand, Dommey, Lepreux, Gisors, Duc, Isabelle, Grisart, and Cendrier. Both Labroustes, Vaudoyer, Gisors, and Isabelle became Officiers, while Duc rose to the rank of Commandeur

67 Lemaistre, *Ecole des Beaux-Arts*, pp. 67–68

68 Pierre Baltard, *Observations sur l'état actuel du classement des élèves de la section d'architecture, à l'Ecole Royale des Beaux-Arts, et sur quelques modifications à proposer dans les jugements du Grand Prix et des récompenses à décerner au prix dit Prix Départemental*, P. Didot, l'aîné, Paris 1822, pp. 4–5

69 *Ibid.*, p. 8

70 The only two winners of the Grand Prix in the 1820s who did not come close to winning the Prix Départemental were Duc and Simon-Claude Constant-Dufeux, who won the Grand Prix in 1829

71 Baltard, *Observations*, p. 6

72 *Cf.* Gromort, *Théorie*, p. 158

73 Antoine-Chrysostome Quatremère de Quincy, *Architecture*, 3 vols, in *Encyclopédie méthodique*, Paris (Panckoucke, 1788; H. Agasse, 1798–1825), 1 (1788) pp. 162–63 (s.v. 'Atrium'). Vitruvius's discussion of the atrium is in bk. 6, chap. 3 of his *Ten Books of Architecture*

74 This point was particularly stressed by Jean Paul Carlhian in his talk on the Ecole des Beaux-Arts at the Graduate School of Design, Harvard University, April 1978. *Cf.* Gromort, *Théorie*, pp. 148–59

75 AABA, IH I, fol. 189

76 Vitruvius *Ten Books* 6. 3. 3, 1

77 It was the only one of the eight projects without a pediment

78 It is, however, specifically designated as an atrium on the plan

79 Jean-Nicolas-Louis Durand, *Précis des leçons d'architecture données à l'Ecole Polytechnique*, 2 vols, Paris (by the author) 1802–1805, vol. 2, pt. 3, pl. 6. I am grateful to Werner Szambien for pointing out this connection

80 This is a significant point that I intend to elaborate upon in a future article

81 In 1827 Théodore Labrouste wrote to his brother Henri, soon after being chosen as a finalist, to tell Vaudoyer 'that [he] would very much like to render the plan of [his] garden as [Vaudoyer] rendered his' for an Académie de France in Rome (T. Labrouste to H. Labrouste, May 1827, Labrouste family papers, Mme H. Labrouste)

82 Vitruvius *Ten Books* 6. 3. 7

83 There is, however, some evidence in the sketchy indication of the flutes at the foot of the columns that Labrouste was toying with the idea of giving them a base. The outside edges of the two end triglyphs are likewise slightly fudged and almost give the appearance of being Roman rather than Greek

84 It is actually indicated as the atrium on the rendered plan

85 Again, all the parts of the building are indicated on the rendered plan

86 Académie des Beaux-Arts, *Règlements*, 1822, p. 18

87 Lemaistre, *Ecole des Beaux-Arts*, pp. 199–203

88 Alfred Pommier, 'De la manière dont on étudie un projet dans un atelier d'architecture, et méthode infaillible à suivre un jour de concours pour faire une esquisse de réussite; conseil amical donné au petit nombre d'élèves qui s'acharnent encore sur les médailles et sur les Grands Prix', *La Liberté: journal des arts* 2, no. 15, December 1832, p. 48. I am grateful to Ann Lorenz Van Zanten for bringing this article to my attention

89 It has usually been assumed that the sketch was done *en loge* as in the final stage of the competitions in painting and sculpture. However, that only began in 1864, when a prior twenty-four-hour sketch competition was held to limit the number of finalists, or *logistes*, to ten. Apparently, there were not thirty individual locked rooms, or *loges*, to go round

90 P. Baltard, *A Messieurs les Professeurs de l'Ecole Royale des Beaux-Arts: organisation de l'enseignement dans la section d'architecture*, Firmin Didot Frères, Paris 1839, p. 9

91 T. Labrouste to H. Labrouste, May 1827

92 AABA, IH I, fol. 155

93 The theatre of Bordeaux was designed by Victor Louis and built in 1772–80; the Odéon was designed by Marie-Joseph Peyre and Charles de Wailly and built in 1779–82 (after a fire in 1799, it was rebuilt by Jean-François Chalgrin in 1808; and after another fire, by Peyre's son Antoine-Marie *c.* 1819)

94 AN, AJ^{52} 98. The competition was judged on 29 February 1820

95 *Cf.* Gromort, *Théorie*, pp. 161–69

96 This was, of course, more true of the monthly competitions at the Ecole when the students were less apt to be preparing in advance for certain programmes

97 AABA, IH I, fol. 155

98 *Ibid.*

99 The first stage in the process of judging was in fact sometimes referred to as 'classifying' the projects

100 *Cf.* Van Zanten, 'Architectural Composition', pp. 117–30

101 Prieur and Van Cléemputte, *Collection des prix*, pl. 1

102 For references, see note 6 above

103 The programme was worded almost exactly the same as in 1824 (Lampué, *Programmes*, pp. 121–23)

104 *Cf.* Durand, *Précis des leçons*, vol. 1, pt. 2, pl. 22

105 Claude-Nicolas Ledoux, *L'Architecture considérée sous le rapport de l'art, des moeurs, et de la législation*, the author, Paris 1804, pp. 114, 185

106 AABA, IH I, fol. 205

107 The placement of three major rooms on parallel axes was a solution usually avoided in academic or school projects. For one of the rare examples, see Durand, *Précis des leçons*, vol. 1, pt. 2, pl. 22. Durand's example clearly exhibits the lack of focus and differentiation that were the main reasons for the *parti*'s unpopularity

108 *Cf.* Van Zanten, 'Architectural Composition', p. 118

109 AABA, IH I, fol. 205

110 *Cf.* Robin Middleton, 'Vive l'Ecole', *AD Profiles 17: The Beaux-Arts*, n.d., p. 39

111 See, e.g., Léon Labrouste to Eugène Millet, 20 April 1877, Labrouste family papers, Mme H. Labrouste

112 AABA, IH I, fol. 130

113 T. Labrouste to H. Labrouste, May 1827

114 H. Labrouste to [Dommey], [May 1825]

115 [César Daly], 'Concours pour le Grand Prix d'Architecture et envois de Rome', *RGA* 6 1845/46, col. 78; and *Règlements pour les concours aux Grands Prix de l'Académie Royale des Beaux-Arts*, Firmin Didot Frères, Paris 1846, pp. 61–62

116 'Réorganisation de l'Ecole des Beaux-Arts', *RGA* 21 1863, cols 290–99 (esp. cols 296–97)

117 See note 89 above

118 Académie des Beaux-Arts, *Règlements*, 1822, pp. 19–20

119 *Cf.* T. Labrouste to H. Labrouste, May 1827

120 H. Labrouste to [Dommey], [May 1825]

121 *Ibid.*

122 Académie des Beaux-Arts, *Règlements*, 1822, p. 12

123 Ecole des Beaux-Arts: section d'architecture, *Règlements des assemblées et des jugements*, 1824, p. 5

124 This rule was passed on 29 March 1828 (AN, AJ^{52} 2, fol. 16)

125 Ecole des Beaux-Arts: section d'architecture, *Règlements des assemblées et des jugements*, 1824, p. 5

126 Quatremère, *Architecture*, 1, p. 376 (s.v. 'Etude')

127 Guadet, *Eléments et théorie*, 1, p. 100

128 Sirodot, 'Concours des Grands Prix', col. 186

129 *Cf.* Guadet, 1, p. 137*ff*

130 Pommier, 'De la manière dont on étudie un projet', p. 49

131 César Daly, 'Concours pour les Grands Prix de Rome', *RGA* 6, 1845/46, col. 420

132 See, e.g., those later published in Hector d'Espouy, *Fragments d'architecture antique, d'après les relevés et restaurations des anciens pensionnaires de l'Académie de France à Rome*, 2 vols, Schmid, Paris 1905

133 These were the hours set in 1821. In 1825 they were changed to 11:00 am – 3:00 pm for everyone from October to May, and 10:00 am – 12:00 noon for *logistes* only from June to September (AN, AJ^{52} 1, Ecole des Beaux-Arts, *Règlements*. Extraits de 1797 à 1858)

134 H. Labrouste to [Dommey], [May 1825]

135 [Jean-Baptiste] Boutard, *Dictionnaire des arts du dessin*, orig. pub. 1826, new ed., Edmé et Alexandre Picard, Paris 1838, p. 574 (s.v. 'Rendre')

136 Quatremère, *Architecture*, 3: 281 (s.v. 'Rendre')

137 *Ibid.* (s.v. 'Rendu')

138 This rule was passed on 4 June 1825 (AABA, 2E 7, 'Registre des procès-verbaux')

139 H. Labrouste to [Dommey], [May 1825]

140 AN, AJ^{52} 2, 14 November 1828

141 See Andrea Palladio, *The Four Books of Architecture*, Isaac Ware, London 1778; reprint ed., Dover Publications, New York 1965, bk. 3, pl. 17

142 François Mazois and François-Christian Gau, *Les Ruines de Pompéi*, 4 vols, Firmin Didot, Paris 1824–38, vol. 3, pl. 14 bis

143 L.-P. Baltard, *Introduction au cours de théorie d'architecture de l'année 1841: aperçu ou essai sur le bon goût dans les ouvrages d'art et d'architecture*, Firmin Didot Frères, Paris 1841, p. 12. On the Temple of Zeus at Nemea, see Society of Dilettanti, *The Antiquities of Ionia*, 5 vols, London 1769–1915, vol. 2 (1797) pls 15–18; and Jean-Baptiste Lesueur, *Histoire et théorie de l'architecture*, Librairie Alcide Picard et Kaan, Paris n.d., pp. 291–93. Lesueur dealt with the Doric of Nemea in his discussion of Roman Doric and compared it to

that of the Triangular Forum at Pompeii.

144 France, *Bulletin des lois*, 5th ser., vol. 1, no. 17, September 1814, p. 200. For the English translation, see Frank Maloy Anderson, *The Constitutions and Other Select Documents Illustrative of the History of France, 1789–1901*, H. W. Wilson Company, Minneapolis 1904, p. 459. The text of the Constitutional Charter of 1814 and the Napoleonic Codes would have been easily available to Labrouste in the small handbooks published for law students such as the *Cours du droit français, contenant les cinq Codes réunis, . . . précédés de la Charte Constitutionelle*, Le Prieur, Paris 1819

145 From a speech given to the Convention on 15 brumaire, Year II, quoted in A. Aulard, *Christianity and the French Revolution*, trans. Lady Frazer, 1927; reprint ed., Howard Fertig, New York 1966, p. 104

146 France, *Bulletin des lois*, p. 205; Anderson, *Constitutions*, p. 463. The letters in brackets are hidden by columns

147 The other two codes are the Code of Commerce of 1806 and the Penal Code of 1810

148 France, *Bulletin des lois*, p. 199; Anderson, *Constitutions*, p. 458. The words in brackets are obscured on the right. Naturally Labrouste started the inscription almost a fifth of the way in so the beginning of the sentence would be legible

149 See G. Berthier de Sauvigny, *La Restauration*, new ed., rev. and enl., Flammarion, Paris 1955, pp. 67–74

150 Quatremère, *Architecture*, 1, p. 509 (s.v. 'Caractère')

151 From a speech given to the Legislative Assembly on 4 November 1791, quoted in A. Aulard, *Les Orateurs de la révolution de la Législative et la Convention*, 2 vols, new rev. ed., Edouard Cornély et Cie, Paris 1906, 1, p. 174, note 1

152 This was based on a decision made on 24 April 1824 (AN, AJ^{52} 2, fol. 8)

153 AABA, 2E 7, 'Registre des procès-verbaux', fol. 308

154 This was approved by the faculty on 11 November 1825 (AN, AJ^{52} 2, fol. 12)

155 It was definitively reinstated on 10 April 1886 (H. Guédy, *Enseignement*, p. 392). For the monthly Ecole competitions, it was first decided, on 28 September 1833, that 'the names of the competitors will no longer be *ostensibly* written on

their works' (italics added); then, on 28 November 1846, a rule was passed eliminating any form of identification; but, finally, on 28 August 1847, it was decided that sketch compositions would be anonymous but all renderings would be identified with the name of the student and his teacher (AN, AJ^{52} 1). Since it has generally been assumed that all competitions at the Ecole were anonymous, this whole question should be investigated more thoroughly

156 Académie des Beaux-Arts, *Règlements*, 1822, p. 21. The two commissioners chosen were supposed to have no students of their own in the competition. Thibault was a commissioner with Hurtault every year beginning in 1819 and, since Delespine had just been elected to Hurtault's seat in the Académie, it was natural for him to join Thibault

157 This is from the minutes of the meeting recorded for the Ecole by its secretary Vaudoyer (AN, AJ^{52} 100, fol. 151). In the minutes recorded for the Académie by Quatrèmere, the phrase is 'quelques variations de détails' rather than 'quelques légers changements' (AABA, 1H 1, fol. 205). Usually the wording of the minutes was exactly the same

158 AABA, 5E 13, 1822, 'Règlement pour le Jugement des grands prix', art. 3, fol. 1

159 The record of the morning vote is preserved in AABA, 5E 15, 1824, 'Jugement préparatoire'

160 The two winners by unanimous vote were Gilbert in 1822 and Delannoy in 1828

161 For the record of the 1825 vote, see AABA, 5E 16, 1825, 'Jugement préparatoire du concours d'architecture par la section'

162 AABA, 1H 1–3, *passim*

163 AABA, 1H 1, fol. 155

164 AABA, 1H 1–3, *passim*

165 AABA, 1H 1, fol. 205

166 *Ibid.*

167 AABA, 1H 1, fols 22, 257

168 AABA, 1H 1, fol. 278

169 AABA, 1H 1, fol. 75

170 AN, AJ^{52} 100, fols 150, 154. The number and names of the jurors present were always recorded in the minutes kept for the Ecole by Vaudoyer but never, in the first half of the century at least, in those recorded by Quatrèmere for the Académie

171 For the membership of the Académie at the time, see Soubiès, *Membres de l'Académie*, vol. 2

172 AN, AJ^{52} 100, fol. 152

173 The record of the afternoon

vote is also preserved in AABA, 5E 15, 1824, 'Jugement définitif'

174 In 1820 Villain defeated Quantinet by a vote of sixteen to eight, while in 1825 Duc defeated Fries by a vote of twenty to five. Both were on the first ballot (AABA, 5E 12, 1820; 5E 16, 1825)

175 Eugène Millet, *Notice sur la vie et les oeuvres de Pierre-François-Henry Labrouste*, p. 5, reprinted from *Bulletin de la Société Centrale des Architectes*, 1879/80; and Léon Labrouste, Biography of H. Labrouste, n.d., fol. 2, Labrouste family papers, Mme H. Labrouste

176 In this case Emile Vaudremer was chosen for the Grand Prix by the section while Paul-Emile Bonnet was given a Second Grand Prix. In the afternoon, the entire Académie awarded Bonnet a Premier Grand Prix and Vaudremer a Deuxième Premier

177 Baltard, *Observations*, p. 5

178 *Ibid.*

179 H. L[abrouste], 'Concours pour le Grand Prix d'Architecture', *RGA* 1, 1840, col. 547. All the following quotations are from this article which appeared in cols 547–48

180 [Daly], 'Concours pour le Grand Prix', col. 78

181 *Ibid.*, col. 82

182 AABA, 1H 1, fols 115–16

183 In his talk of April 1978, Jean Paul Carlhian pointed out how the Beaux-Arts plan was thought of as having a bottom and a top and how this naturally could lead to an anthropomorphic interpretation. On the other hand, the subdivisional, or horizontal, treatment of the site referred to earlier presented a much closer analogy to the conventions of landscape painting

184 AABA, 1H 1, fol. 130

185 *Ibid.*

186 *Ibid.*

187 In 1821 Blouet defeated Gilbert on the first ballot by seventeen votes to seven, with Paul Jacot receiving one vote. Gilbert was ineligible for the Second Grand Prix, having won it in 1820. Labrouste received twelve votes on the first ballot for the Second Grand Prix, winning easily over Jacot with six, Tavernier with three, Vaudoyer with two, Fontaine with one and Lefranc also with one (AABA, 5E 12, 1821)

188 Thanks to Annie Jacques, I was able to unroll and study, year by year, all the renderings from these five competitions

189 D. [Etienne-Jean Delécluze],

'Concours pour le Grand Prix d'Architecture', *Journal des débats*, 20 September 1832, p. 3

190 Pommier, 'De la manière dont on étudie un projet', p. 52. For an interesting recent discussion, see Richard A. Moore, 'Academic *Dessin* Theory in France after the Reorganization of 1863', *Journal of the Society of Architectural Historians* 36, October 1977, pp. 145–74

191 Both Fries's and Dommey's upper-floor plans are about half the size of Duc's!

192 Guadet, *Eléments et théorie*, 2, p. 16

193 *Ibid.*, 1, p. 8

194 *Ibid.*, 2, p. 16

195 Quoted in [Daly], 'Concours pour le Grand Prix', col. 78

196 Quatremère, *Architecture*, 3, p. 217 (s.v. 'Projet')

197 *Ibid.*, 3, p. 217; 3, p. 281 (s.v. 'Rendu')

198 Boutard, *Dictionnaire*, p. 276 (s.v. 'Etudier')

199 Such a connection was originally pointed out by James F. O'Gorman in *Henry Hobson Richardson and His Office: A Centennial of His Move to Boston, 1874*, Department of Printing and Graphic Arts, Harvard College Library, Cambridge, Mass. 1974, esp. pp. 16–23

200 *Cf.* Albert Boime, *The Academy and French Painting in the Nineteenth Century*, Phaidon, New York 1971, esp. pp. 79–121

201 Quatremère, *Architecture*, 2, p. 209 (s.v. 'Dessiner')

202 *Ibid.*

203 Guadet, *Eléments et théorie*, 1, p. 108

204 *Ibid.*, p. 7. *Cf.* O'Gorman, *Richardson*, pp. 17–18

205 Guadet, *Eléments et théorie*, 1, p. 7

206 *Ibid.*, p. 101

207 For an analysis of the system of teaching at the Ecole as preparation for actual practice, see Albert Louvet, *L'Art d'architecture et la profession d'architecte*, 2 vols, Librairie de la Construction Moderne, Paris [1913]

208 This was also pointed out by O'Gorman in his illuminating discussion of Richardson's office (O'Gorman, *Richardson*, esp. p. 10)

209 The average age rose gradually from $24\frac{1}{3}$ in the first decade to $25\frac{3}{4}$ in the 1820s. Then in the 1830s it hit 28 but levelled off at 27 in the 1840s and 1850s; $26\frac{1}{2}$ in the 1860s and 1870s; and 27 again in the 1880s. In the 1890s it reached almost $28\frac{1}{2}$, the oldest for the century

VII The building of the Ecole des Beaux-Arts

1 R. Chafee in *The Architecture of the Ecole des Beaux-Arts*, Arthur Drexler (ed.), Secker and Warburg, London 1977, p. 77*ff*; David Van Zanten, 'Félix Duban and the Buildings of the Ecole des Beaux-Arts 1832–1840', *Journal of the Society of Architectural Historians*, October 1978, vol. XXXVIII, no. 3, pp. 161–74

2 S. Thoroude, 'Le couvent des Petits Augustins', *Information d'Histoire de l'Art*, October 1964

3 Bruno Foucart, 'La fortune critique du Musée des Monuments français', *Information d'Histoire de l'Art*, 1959, no. 5, p. 227*ff*.

4 AN, N. III Seine 1128

5 Louis XVIII, 1815–30

6 AN, F^{13} 1118

7 AN, AJ^{52} 443

8 *Inventaire général des Richesses d'Art de la France. Archives du Musée des Monuments français* III, Paris 1897

9 Wanda Bouleau-Rabaud, 'Inventaire des sculptures décoratives et éléments d'architecture', Ecole Nationale Supérieure des Beaux-Arts, xerox copy

10 AN, F^{13} 1115

11 AN, AJ^{52} 443, Decazes's letter dated 24 September

12 AN, F^{13} 1115, Vaudoyer's letter to Chevalier Bruyère dated 1 October 1818

13 AN, AJ^{52} 443, Versement Architecture, N. III Seine 1118

14 AN, AJ^{52} 443, Versement Architecture 49 pièce 3–4

15 AN, F^{13} 1117, Debret's report dated 15 January 1832

16 AN, F^{21} 614

17 AN, AJ^{52} 443

18 AN, F^{21} 614

19 AN, F^{21} 615, Héricart de Thury's letter dated 5 May 1829

20 AN, F^{13} 526, Comte d'Argout's letter dated 31 July 1832

21 AN, F^{21} 615

22 AN, F^{13} 1117

23 AN, F^{13} 526

24 AN, F^{13} 1117

25 AN, F^{13} 1117, Merimée's memorandum dated 22 January 1833

26 AN, F^{13} 1117

27 AN, F^{13} 1114

28 AN, F^{13} 1117

29 AN, AJ^{52} 443

30 AN, F^{13} 1117

31 AN, F^{13} 1117

32 AN, F^{13} 1117

33 David Van Zanten, *op. cit.*

34 AN, Box VIII, 2, elevation of the 'part built between 1820 and 1833' signed Prosper Morey, dated 1842; Box VIII, 3, elevation of buildings, drawing unsigned

35 AN, F^{13} 1117, 'Rapport à Messieurs les membres du Conseil des Bâtiments Civils' and 'Observation sur la translation proposée du portique de Gaillon' published in *Bulletin de la Société d'Histoire de l'Art Français*, 1977, p. 221ff.

36 AN, F^{13} 1116

37 AN, F^{13} 1117

38 BN, Est. Carton Labrouste

39 AN, N, F^{13}

40 AN, F^{13} 1116

41 AN, F^{13} 1116

42 AN, F^{21} 1420

43 AN, F^{13} 1116

44 AN, F^{13} 1116

45 AN, F^{13} 1116

46 AN, F^{21} 1420

47 AN, F^{21} 1420

48 AN, AJ^{52} 443

49 AN, F^{21} 1421

50 AN, F^{21} 1421

51 AN, AJ^{52} 14, with a request that the ground for sale next to the Ecole be bought

52 AN, F^{21} 779

53 AN, F^{21} 775

54 AN, F^{21} 775

55 AN, AJ^{52} 9

56 AN, F^{21} 780

57 AN, AJ^{52} 15, AN, AJ^{52} 9

58 AN, F^{21} 779

59 AN, F^{21} 779

60 AN, F^{21} 779

61 AN, F^{21} 779

62 AN, F^{21} 3059

63 AN, F^{21} 3059

64 Atget's photographs are in the Carnavalet Museum, Paris

65 A. Lenoir and C. Daly, *Revue Générale de l'Architecture* XII, 1864, col. 73

66 AN, F^{21} 780

67 AN, F^{21} 780

68 AN, versement architecture, Box XLVIII

69 C. Muntz, *Guide de l'Ecole des Beaux-Arts*, Paris 1889; P. Smith, A. Braham, *F. Mansart*, London 1973, pp. 92–93 and 243

70 J. Musy, 'Renouveau de l'Ecole des Beaux-Arts', *l'Oeil*, October 1978; B. Foucart, Ph. Canac, C. Marmoz, 'L'Ecole Nationale des Beaux-Arts', *Revue des Monuments Historiques*, April 1979

71 *The Architecture of the Ecole des Beaux-Arts*, cit.; Bruno Foucart, 'Trois siècles de dessins français', *l'Oeil*, October 1978

72 AN, F^{13} 1117, see note 35

73 Carnavalet Museum and B.-N. Estampes, for drawings of Le Vau's work before Duban's restoration

74 R. Jullian, *Le Mouvement des arts du romantisme au symbolisme*, Paris 1979, p. 36; N. de Gary, 'La maison pompéienne du prince Napoléon', *Cahiers des Arts Décoratifs*, no. 1, 1978

75 C. Daly, *Funérailles de Duban*, Paris 1871

VIII   The book and the building

This essay was written in 1977 based on my doctoral dissertation (*Architectural Reasoning in the Age of Positivism: Henri Labrouste and the Néo-Grec Idea of the Bibliothèque Sainte-Geneviève*, Diss. Yale University 1975). It was originally conceived as the final chapter of a monograph on the Bibliothèque Ste-Geneviève which is still in preparation and was supported by a research fellowship from the American Council of Learned Societies in 1977–78. It was first presented as a lecture in 1978.

I am deeply indebted to Mme H. Labrouste and M. Léon Malcotte for their extraordinary generosity in making their family papers available to me. I should also like to thank Mlle Madeleine Boy and the staff of the Bibliothèque Ste-Geneviève, Paris; and M. Jean Adhémar and Mme Bertrand Jestaz of the Cabinet des Estampes of the Bibliothèque Nationale, Paris. I am also extremely grateful to James Ackerman, John Coolidge, Robin Middleton, Vincent Scully and Jacques Seebacher for reading the manuscript and making valuable suggestions.

For Hugo, in my text I have used John Sturrock's translation, *Notre-Dame of Paris*, Penguin Books, Harmondsworth 1978; in my notes I refer the reader to the original French (see note 4).

In the notes Bibliothèque Nationale has been abbreviated as BN, and Archives Nationales as AN.

Part I

1 Perhaps the most well-known critique of the 'literary fallacy' of 19th-century architecture is contained in the second and third chapters of Geoffrey Scott's *The Architecture of Humanism*, originally published in 1914. He singled it out as the first 'architectural fallacy' and called it 'the Romantic Fallacy'

2 Félix Duban officially replaced his older brother-in-law François Debret as architect of the Ecole in the summer of 1832. Henri Labrouste was given the subordinate post of *inspecteur*. The buildings, begun by Debret in 1820, were substantially redesigned and completed by 1840

3 See Jean Mallion, *Victor Hugo et l'art architectural*, Université de Grenoble, Publications de la Faculté des Lettres et Sciences Humaines, 28, Presses Universitaires de France, Paris 1962; and, most recently, Nikolaus Pevsner, *Some Architectural Writers of the Nineteenth Century*, Clarendon Press, Oxford 1972, pp. 195–97 *passim*

4 Victor Hugo, *Notre-Dame de Paris: 1482. Les Travailleurs de la mer*, edited by and with Introductions and Notes by Jacques Seebacher and Yves Gohin, Bibliothèque de la Pléiade, Editions Gallimard, Paris 1975, p. 7, ('Note ajoutée à l'edition définitive [1832]')

5 *Ibid.*

6 See, for example, Eugène-Emmanuel Viollet-le-Duc, 'Du style gothique au XIXe siècle', *Annales Archéologiques*, vol. 4 (1846), pp. 325–53; and Jean-Baptiste-Antoine Lassus, 'De l'art et de l'archéologie', *Annales Archéologiques*, vol. 2 (1845), pp. 69–77, 197–204, 329–35

7 Hugo, *Notre-Dame*, p. 186 (Book V, chap. 2, 'Ceci tuera cela')

8 *Ibid.*, p. 6

9 Victor Hugo, *Oeuvres complètes de Victor Hugo. Philosophie I, 1819–1834: Littérature et philosophie mêlées*, J. Hetzel et Cie., A. Quantin, Paris 1882, p. 279

10 *Ibid.*, p. 322

11 *Ibid.*, p. 318

12 It was originally published with this title in the *Nouveau Keepsake français*, on 17 December 1831, and not, as the editors of the Club français du livre edition of the complete works of Hugo claim, in the *Revue de Paris* in August 1829. When Hugo revised it for *Littérature et philosophie mêlées*, he gave it the same title he had already used for a second article on the subject, 'Guerre aux démolisseurs!', which was published in 1832

13 Hugo, *Littérature et philosophie mêlées*, p. 339

14 *Ibid.*, p. 340

15 Frank Lloyd Wright, *A Testament*, Bramhall House, New York 1957, p. 17

16 Edgar Kaufmann and Ben Raeburn, eds, *Frank Lloyd Wright: Writings and Buildings*, World Publishing

Co., Cleveland and New York 1960, p. 57. Bruce Pfeiffer claims the Hull House lecture was given in 1894 (Olgivanna L. Wright, *Frank Lloyd Wright: His Life, His Work, His Words*, Horizon Press, New York 1966, p. 206). The lecture was originally published in the *Catalogue of the Fourteenth Annual Exhibition of the Chicago Architectural Club*, Chicago 1901, n. pag., where the date of the lecture was given as 6 March 1901

17 Wright, *A Testament*, p. 17

18 F. L. Wright, *An Autobiography*, orig. pub. 1932, Duell, Sloane and Pearce, New York 1943, p. 78

19 *Ibid.*

20 F. L. Wright, *An Autobiography. Book Six: Broadacre City*, Taliesin [October 1943], p. 30

21 Wright, *A Testament*, p. 17

22 Wright, *An Autobiography*, p. 78

23 F. L. Wright, *The Future of Architecture*, Bramhall House, New York 1953, p. 86

24 F. L. Wright, *The Disappearing City*, William Farquhar Payson, New York 1932, p. 14

25 Lewis Mumford, *Sticks and Stones: A Study of American Architecture and Civilization*, orig. pub. 1924, 2d rev. ed., Dover, New York 1955, p. 41

26 *Ibid.*, p. 42

27 *Ibid.*

28 *Ibid.*, pp. 123–51

29 Kaufmann and Raeburn, *Frank Lloyd Wright*, p. 57

30 *Ibid.*

31 Wright, *The Future of Architecture*, pp. 77–83

32 Kaufmann and Raeburn, *Frank Lloyd Wright*, p. 57

33 *Ibid.*, p. 62

34 *Ibid.*

35 Emile Zola, *Le Ventre de Paris*, Livre de Poche, Fasquelle, Paris 1964, pp. 338–39

36 *Ibid.*, p. 339

37 *Ibid.*, p. 338

Part II

38 Among the Hugo papers in the Département des Manuscrits of the Bibliothèque Nationale are (1) the manuscript and preparatory notes ('Reliquat') for *Notre-Dame* (MS n.a.fr. 13378), and (2) Hugo's correspondence concerning the novel's publication (MS n.a.fr. 13404). Jacques Seebacher's recent edition of the novel includes the 'Reliquat' and notes of the changes Hugo made in the manuscript (Hugo, *Notre-Dame*, pp. 503–57, 1093–1253) as well as a historical Introduction (pp. 1045–84) and extremely useful 'Tableau chronologique de la composition' and 'Tableau de concordance' (pp. 1085–93). See also: [Adèle Hugo], *Victor Hugo raconté par un témoin de sa vie*, 3d ed., 2 vols, Librairie Internationale, A. Lacroix, Verboeck-hoven et Cie., Paris 1863, vol. 2, pp. 334–53; [Paul Meurice], 'Notes de l'éditeur', in *Oeuvres complètes de Victor Hugo. Roman – II: Notre-Dame de Paris: 1482*, Imprimerie Nationale, Librairie Ollendorff, Paris 1904, pp. 445–61; Emile Henriot, 'Hugo et "Notre-Dame de Paris"', in *Romanesques et romantiques*, Plon, Paris 1930, pp. 189–96; Flavien Michaux, 'A travers les oeuvres de Victor Hugo – originales, préoriginales, éditions fictives, etc.: *Notre-Dame de Paris*', *Bulletin du bibliophile et du bibliothécaire*, n.s., vol. 10, August–September 1931, pp. 409–18; and Etienne Cluzel, 'Les Premières Editions réelles ou fictives de *Notre-Dame de Paris*', *Bulletin du bibliophile et du bibliothécaire*, November 1948, pp. 524–31

39 The relevant parts of this contract are cited in [Paul Meurice], 'Notes de l'éditeur', p. 447

40 *Ibid.*

41 Hugo to Gosselin, 5 August 1830, MS n.a.fr. 13404, fol. 46^r, BN, Paris

42 [Adèle Hugo], *Victor Hugo*, p. 345

43 See Seebacher's 'tableau chronologique de la composition', in Hugo, *Notre-Dame*, p. 1085

44 Hugo to Gosselin, 4 October 1830, *FC8. H8748. 831 nab v. 1, Houghton Library, Harvard University, Cambridge, Mass. There is a copy of this letter in BN, MS n.a.fr. 13404, fol. 50^r; and it was quoted in full by Emile Henriot in 'Hugo et "Notre-Dame de Paris"', pp. 192–93

45 Gosselin to Hugo, 7 October 1830, MS n.a.fr. 13404, fol. 51^r, BN

46 Gosselin to Hugo, 19 January 1831, MS n.a.fr. 13404, fols 60^r–61^r, BN

47 BN, MS n.a.fr. 13404, fol. 66

48 Both Cluzel and Michaux call the fifth edition of 1831 the 'second real edition' and the eighth the third; and they incorrectly state that the latter was published in October 1832

49 The paper and ink are different from the rest of the original manuscript; however, Seebacher only tentatively dates it 1832

50 Hugo, *Notre-Dame*, pp. 5, 6

51 See Seebacher, 'Introduction' to Hugo, *Notre-Dame*, pp. 1055, 1074, 1127. For Hugo's relations with Lamennais and the Liberal Catholic movement and the possible effect of the encyclical *Mirari vos* of 15 August 1832, see Christian Maréchal, *Lamennais et Victor Hugo*, A. Savaète, Paris [1906]; and Maurice Souriau, *Histoire du romantisme en France*, 2 vols, Spes, Paris 1927, vol. 2, pp. 42–43. For Hugo's relations with the Saint-Simonians, a connection emphasized to me by Robin Middleton, see Marguerite Thibert, 'Le Rôle social de l'art d'après les Saint-Simoniens', *Revue d'histoire économique et social*, vol. 13 (1925), pp. 181–95. For the Saint-Simonian view of art, see especially Emile Barrault, *Aux Artistes. Du passé et de l'avenir des Beaux-Arts (Doctrine de Saint-Simon)*, Alexandre Mesnier, Paris 1830

52 Hugo, *Notre-Dame*, p. 6

53 See Henriot, 'Hugo et "Notre-Dame de Paris"', p. 194; and Léon Cellier, Preface to V. Hugo, *Notre-Dame de Paris: 1482*, Garnier-Flammarion, Paris 1967, p. 18.

54 The connection was first made by Emile Henriot in his article cited above, and was endorsed by Hector Talvart and Joseph Place in their *Bibliographie des auteurs modernes de la langue française (1801–1948)*, Editions de la Chronique des Lettres Françaises, aux Horizons de France, Paris 1949, vol. 9, p. 18

55 Again, see his 'tableau chronologique' and 'tableau de concordance' in Hugo, *Notre-Dame*, pp. 1085–92. It should however be noted that Hugo had developed the major outline of the architectural theory expressed in 'Ceci tuera cela' at least as early as 16 July 1830. After a meeting of that date, Montalembert noted in his journal that Hugo had given him a two-hour lecture on the subject of architecture as 'l'expression de la liberté et de l'activité intellectuelle avant l'invention de l'imprimerie' and its demise 'depuis la presse', quoted in P. de Lallemand, *Montalembert et ses amis dans le romantisme [1830–1840]*, H. Champion, Paris 1927, pp. 122–23. I am indebted to Robin Middleton for this reference

56 J. Seebacher, 'Victor Hugo et ses éditeurs avant l'éxil', in Hugo, *Oeuvres complètes*, Jean Massin (ed.), Le Club Français du Livre, Paris 1968, vol. 6, pp. ix–xv; and Seebacher, 'Introduction', in Hugo, *Notre-Dame*, p. 1055

57 *Ibid.*, pp. 1055, 1126, 1129

58 Undated note by Léon Labrouste, in the family papers of Mme H. Labrouste, Paris

59 On Robelin's involvement in *Notre-Dame*, see Henry Lapauze, 'Lettres inédites de Victor Hugo', *Le Figaro: Supplément littéraire*, 17th year, no. 8 (21 February 1891), p. 1; Edmond Biré, *Victor Hugo après 1852: L'Exil, les dernières années et la mort du poète*, Librairie Académique Didier, Perrin et Cie., Paris 1894, pp. 268–72; Léon Séché, *Le Cénacle de Joseph Delorme (1827–1830)*, vol. 2: *Victor Hugo et les artistes*, Mercure de France, Paris 1912, pp. 132–50; Maurice Dreyfous, *Ce que je tiens à dire: Un Demi-siècle de choses vues et entendues*, vol. 1: *1862–1872*, 4th ed., Société d'Editions Littéraires et Artistiques, Librairie Paul Ollendorff, Paris [1912], pp. 175–83; Maurice Guillemot, 'Le Plus Vieil Ami de Victor Hugo', *Bulletin de la Commission Municipale Historique et Artistique de Neuilly-sur-Seine*, 10th year (1912), 2d part, pp. 23–31; P. Destray, 'Un Témoin nivernais du romantisme: Charles Devieur, dit Robelin, 1796–1887', *La Revue du Centre: Nivernais-Berry, Bourbonnais-Bourgogne, Orléanais*, 3d year, no. 5 (September–October 1926), pp. 129–36; and Mallion, *Victor Hugo*, pp. 64–65

60 The most useful biography of Robelin is in Mallion, *Victor Hugo*, pp. 644–47 ('Charles Robelin: Essai de notice biographique'). See also Charles Bauchal, *Nouveau dictionnaire biographique et critique des architectes français*, Librairie Générale de l'Architecture et des Travaux Publics, André, Daly Fils et Cie, Paris 1887, p. 718. Mallion claims that Robelin entered the Ecole in 1822, but the actual date was 3 April 1824. AN, AJ⁵² 100 and AJ⁵² 239

61 In July 1831, Labrouste worked as Alavoine's *inspecteur* for the fête at the Place de la Bastille commemorating the July Revolution. This involved the design and erection of viewing stands and a temporary cenotaph

62 [Adèle Hugo], *Victor Hugo*, p. 308; and 'Historique d'*Hernani*', in *Oeuvres complètes de Victor Hugo. Théâtre – 1: Cromwell. Hernani*, Imprimerie Nationale, Librairie Ollendorff, Paris 1912, p. 717

63 Anatole de Baudot, *L'Architecture: Le Passé – le présent*, H. Laurens, Paris 1916, p. 197

64 The *Album de Villard de Honnecourt*, edited and annotated by Lassus, was published posthumously under the direction of Alfred Darcel in 1858

65 Neil Levine, 'The Romantic Idea of Architectural Legibility: Henri Labrouste and the *Néo-Grec*', in *The Architecture of the Ecole des Beaux-Arts*, Arthur Drexler (ed.), The Museum of Modern Art, New York 1977, and Secker and Warburg, London 1977, esp. pp. 357–93

66 Alfred Darcel, 'Notice sur Lassus', in *Album de Villard de Honnecourt*, ed. J.-B.-A. Lassus, Imprimerie Nationale, Paris 1858, p. iii

67 See *Journal des débats*, 22 October 1830, p. 3 and 17 November 1830, p. 2; Laure Labrouste [L. Dassy], *Compte rendu sur la restauration de Paestum exécutée en 1829 par Henri Labrouste*, Société de l'Histoire de l'Art Français, J. Baur, Paris 1879; Henri Jouin, 'Notes pour servir à l'histoire de l'Académie de France à Rome', *Nouvelles Archives de l'Art Français*, 3d series, vol. 6 (1890), esp. pp. 225–27; René Schneider, *Quatremère de Quincy et son intervention dans les arts (1788–1830)*, Hachette, Paris 1910, pp. 301–05; and Henry Lapauze, *Histoire de l'Académie de France à Rome*, 2 vols, Plon-Nourrit, Paris 1924, vol. 2, pp. 189–200

68 See Henri Labrouste, *Les Temples de Paestum: Restauration exécutée en 1829*, Restaurations des monuments antiques par les architectes pensionnaires de l'Académie de France à Rome depuis 1788 jusqu'à nos jours, Firmin-Didot, for the French Government, Paris 1877; and N. Levine, 'Romantic Idea of Architectural Legibility', esp. pp. 389–93

69 Labrouste, *Temples de Paestum*, pp. 12–14

70 Hugo, *Notre-Dame*, p. 4

71 *Ibid.*, p. 3

72 'ΑΝΑΓΚΗ' is Book VII, chapter 4

73 Hugo, *Notre-Dame*, p. 109, Book III, chapter 1, 'Notre-Dame'

74 *Ibid.*, p. 6, 'Note ajoutée'

Part III

75 *Ibid.*, p. 171

76 *Ibid.*, p. 172

77 *Ibid.*, p. 173

78 *Ibid.*

79 *Ibid.*

80 *Ibid.*, p. 174

81 *Ibid.*

82 *Ibid.*, p. 408, Book X, chapter 4, 'Un Maladroit Ami'

83 'Note' sent by Hugo to Gosselin on 19 January 1831, summarizing his forthcoming novel, MS n.a.fr. 13404, fol. 66ᵛ, BN

84 Hugo, *Notre-Dame*, p. 175

85 *Ibid.*

86 *Ibid.*, p. 182

87 *Ibid.*, pp. 174, 186

88 *Ibid.*, p. 179

89 *Ibid.*, p. 176

90 *Ibid.*, pp. 179, 183

91 *Ibid.*, p. 187

92 *Ibid.*, p. 175

93 *Ibid.*, pp. 180, 182

94 See Antoine-Chrysostome Quatremère de Quincy, *Architecture*, 3 vols, in *Encyclopédie méthodique*, Panckoucke, Paris 1788; H. Agasse, 1798, 1825, vol. 1 (1788), pp. 109–27 ('Architecture') and 382–86 ('Cabane'); and Jean-Nicolas-Louis Durand, *Précis des leçons d'architecture données à l'Ecole Polytechnique*, 2 vols, pub. by the author, at the Ecole Polytechnique, Paris 1802–05, vol. 1, pp. 1–24. It should be noted that Durand disputed the theory of the hut

95 Hugo, *Notre-Dame*, p. 175. The relation between architecture and writing, especially in the matter of decoration, can be traced back in this context to late 18th-century theory. Writing, however, never supplanted nature as the fundamental source of architectural form. See, e.g., A.-C. Quatremère de Quincy, *De l'architecture égyptienne, considérée dans son origine, ses principes et son goût, et comparée sous les mêmes rapports à l'architecture grecque, Dissertation qui a remporté, en 1785, le prix proposé par l'Académie des Inscriptions et Belles-Lettres*, Barrois l'aîné et Fils, Paris 1803, esp. pp. 48–50, 161–65

96 Hugo, *Notre-Dame*, p. 175

97 *Ibid.*, pp. 175, 176

98 *Ibid.*, p. 175

99 *Ibid.*

100 *Ibid.*

101 *Ibid.*

102 *Ibid.*

103 *Ibid.*, p. 176

104 *Ibid.*

105 *Ibid.*

106 *Ibid.* In this context, one is naturally reminded of Ledoux's projects for a Panarétéon and a Pacifère, both published in his *Architecture considérée sous le rapport de l'art, des moeurs, et de la législation*, the author, Paris 1804

107 *Ibid.*, pp. 180, 182

108 *Ibid.*, p. 177

109 *Ibid.*, p. 184

110 *Ibid.*, p. 178

111 *Ibid.*, p. 179

112 *Ibid.*, p. 181

113 *Ibid.*

114 *Ibid.*

115 Ibid.
116 Ibid., p. 179
117 Ibid., p. 180
118 Ibid.
119 Ibid., p. 179
120 Ibid., p. 182
121 Ibid.
122 Ibid., p. 183
123 Ibid., p. 182
124 Ibid., pp. 182, 183, 186
125 Ibid., pp. 182, 183
126 Ibid., p. 182
127 Ibid.
128 Ibid., p. 386, Book X, chapter 1, 'Gringoire a plusieurs bonnes idées de suite rue des Bernadins'
129 Note by Hugo for Book V of Notre-Dame, in 'Reliquat', 133/24, fol. 424, MS n.a.fr. 13378, BN
130 V. Hugo, Oeuvres complètes de Victor Hugo. Philosophie II: William Shakespeare, orig. pub. 1864, J. Hetzel et Cie., A. Quantin, Paris 1882, p. 173
131 Hugo, Notre-Dame, p. 174
132 Ibid., p. 184
133 Ibid., p. 183
134 Ibid
135 Ibid.
136 Ibid.
137 Ibid.
138 Ibid., p. 184
139 Ibid.
140 Ibid., p. 185
141 Ibid.
142 Ibid., p. 184
143 Ibid.
144 Ibid.
145 Ibid., p. 185
146 Ibid., p. 184
147 Ibid., p. 185
148 Ibid., p. 186
149 Ibid., p. 188
150 Cf. Balzac's Preface to the third edition of Le Père Goriot (dated 1 May 1835): 'Sa Majesté le Journal, cet autocrate du XIXᵉ siècle, qui trône au-dessus des rois, leur donne des avis, les fait, les défait; et qui, de temps en temps, est tenu de surveiller la morale depuis qu'il a supprimé la religion de l'Etat.' Honoré de Balzac, Le Père Goriot, Collection Folio, Editions Gallimard, Paris 1971, p. 401
151 Hugo, Notre-Dame, p. 188
152 Ibid.
153 Ibid., p. 186
154 Victor Considérant, Considérations sociales sur l'architectonique, Les libraires du Palais-Royal, Paris 1834, p. 82
155 Ibid.
156 Ibid., pp. 84, 82
157 Ibid., p. 83
158 Hugo, Notre-Dame, p. 6
159 Ibid., pp. 6 7

160 Ibid., p. 7
161 Ibid.
162 Ibid.
163 Ibid.
164 'Henri Labrouste: Lettres inédites sur l'enseignement de l'architecture', ed. Charles Lucas, La Construction moderne, 10th year, no. 23, 9 March 1895, p. 268
165 Labrouste to Duc, 30 September 1830, in 'Henri Labrouste: Lettres inédites sur l'enseignement de l'architecture', ed. C. Lucas, La Construction moderne, 10th year, no. 22, 2 March 1895, p. 254
166 'Henri Labrouste: Lettres inédites', p. 268. This undated letter was erroneously dated 'end of 1831' by Lucas. It was written either in the late summer or autumn of 1832. The letter refers to an article published on 15 July 1832, and it also refers to the setting up of the agence des travaux at the Ecole des Beaux-Arts. Lucas mistakenly thought Labrouste was named inspecteur under Duban in 1831
167 Ibid.
168 Charles Magnin, 'De la statue de la Reine Nantechild, et, par occasion, des révolutions de l'art en France au moyen âge', Revue des deux-mondes, vol. 7 (1832), p. 213. Labrouste copied out the section of Magnin's article related to Hugo's theory
169 'Henri Labrouste: Lettres inédites', p. 268
170 Magnin, 'Reine Nantechild', p. 213. Magnin noted: 'Ce ne fut que lorsque la foi vint à s'altérer, lorsque Wiclef, Jean Hus et Luther commencèrent à saper le catholicisme et le moyen âge, que les traditions s'affaiblirent ... L'unité fut bannie de l'art comme de la communauté chrétienne ... La foi n'existait plus: l'art qui en était né devait peu à peu disparaître.' (p. 210)
171 Ibid., p. 212
172 Perhaps the most concise summary of this position is to be found in César Daly, 'De la société et de l'architecture à propos de notre architecture funéraire', Revue générale de l'architecture et des travaux publics, vol. 29 (1872), cols 97–107. The idea can certainly be traced back at least to Chateaubriand's Génie du christianisme, published in 1802
173 Hugo, Notre-Dame, p. 186
174 Ibid.
175 Ibid.
176 Ibid., p. 187
177 Ibid
178 Ibid.

179 Ibid.
179a Chief among the changes made by Hugo were the addition of the discussion of hieroglyphics right after the quotation from Moses (Notre-Dame, pp. 175–76); the mention of Phoenician as one of the 'democratic' arts (p. 181); the discussions of the Reformation and of the specialization of the arts (pp. 183–84); and, finally, the entire paragraph describing the demise of French architecture from the 16th through the late 18th century (p. 185). The only reference to criticism received is in the summary of his arguments, set exactly midway through the chapter, in which Hugo added the disclaimer 'as well as many objections of detail' to the introductory phrase: 'If we now sum up what we have so far said all too hurriedly, omitting many proofs as well as many objections of detail, it amounts to this ...' (p. 181). (See BN, MS n.a.fr. 13378)

Part IV

180 For the pre-Labrouste history of the Bibliothèque Ste-Geneviève, see Paris, AN, F¹³ 1066, F¹⁷ 3497 and F¹⁷ 3499; Alfred de Bougy, Histoire de la Bibliothèque Sainte-Geneviève, Paris 1847; and Alfred Franklin, Les Anciennes Bibliothèques de Paris: Eglises, monastères, collèges, etc., vol. 1, in Histoire générale de Paris: Collection de la Bibliothèque Sainte-Geneviève, Paris 1847; and Alfred Franklin, Les ments concerning Labrouste's work, see AN, F²¹ 751, F²¹ 1362–64, F²¹ 3507, and Versement de la Direction de l'Architecture, Album 45; Paris, Bibliothèque Ste-Geneviève, MSS 3910–39 and Rés. Suppl. W. Fol. 19; Paris, Musée du Louvre, Cabinet des Dessins, RF 4141; BN, Cabinet des Estampes, uncatalogued drawings
181 H. Labrouste, 'Bibliothèque de Ste. Geneviève. Project d'un bâtiment à ériger sur l'Emplacement de l'ancienne prison de Montaigu et destiné à recevoir la bibliothèque de Ste. Geneviève' [December 1839], fasc. 1, F²¹ 1362, AN. Note explaining the project submitted in December 1839. Cf. A. de Bougy, Bibliothèque Sainte-Geneviève, pp. 149–54, 188–89; and Léon de Laborde, De l'organisation des bibliothèques dans Paris, huitième lettre: Etude sur la construction des bibliothèques, A. Franck, Paris April 1845, pp. 27–28
182 Hugo, Notre-Dame, p. 134, Book III, chapter 2, 'Paris à vol d'oiseau'
183 Ibid., p. 185

184 Ibid.

185 Revue générale de l'architecture et des travaux publics 11, 1853, pl. 31. The drawing was apparently based on a photograph, taken from exactly the same angle, dated 1852, and among the Labrouste papers recently given to the Académie d'Architecture, Paris

186 The interlaced SG was adopted as the library's book-stamp after the Revolution of 1830. Cf. Franklin, Anciennes Bibliothèques de Paris, pp. 89–92

187 Achille Hermant, 'La Bibliothèque Sainte-Geneviève', L'Artiste, 5th series, vol. 7, 1 December 1851, p. 130; Gustave Planche, 'Le Musée du Louvre', in Portraits d'artistes – peintres et sculpteurs, 2 vols, M. Lévy, Paris 1853, vol. 2, p. 268; and Théodore de Banville, 'Le Quartier Latin et la Bibliothèque Sainte-Geneviève', in Paris Guide par les principaux écrivains et artistes de la France, 2 vols, Librairie Internationale, A. Lacroix, Verboeckhoven et Cie., Paris 1867, vol. 2, p. 1358. The names were engraved by J. Deutsch in September–November 1848. For the complete list, see Bibliothèque Sainte-Geneviève, MS 3939

188 Hermant, 'Bibliothèque Sainte-Geneviève', p. 130. Auguste Comte's Calendrier positiviste, ou système général de commémoration publique destiné surtout à la transition finale de la grande république occidentale was first published in 1849 and, by May 1852, was in its fourth edition. It was incorporated in his Catéchisme positiviste in 1852. Hermant could also have been referring to the Roman perpetual calendar found at Pompeii, drawn by Labrouste in the Museum of Naples in 1826 and published in François Mazois and François-Christian Gau, Les Ruines de Pompéi, 4 vols, Firmin-Didot, Paris 1824–38, vol. 2 (1824), pp. 29, 103

189 Banville, 'Quartier Latin', p. 1358

190 Hermant, 'Bibliothèque Sainte-Geneviève', p. 130

191 H. Labrouste, 'A M. le Directeur de la Revue d'Architecture', Revue générale de l'architecture, vol. 10 (1852), col. 383

192 Ibid.

193 F. Barrière, 'Embellissemens de Paris', Journal des débats, 31 December 1850, p. 1

194 Hugo, Notre-Dame, p. 176

195 Ibid.

196 Labrouste, 'A M. le Directeur', col. 383

197 Ibid.

198 On the commission, see AN, F^{21} 14, F^{21} 678, F^{21} 751, F^{21} 1364

199 The drawing is dated 1850, but the lithograph itself is not dated. The copy in the BN, Cabinet des Estampes (R. Balze – S.n.r.), has a dépôt légal date of 1864. The drawing had to be done before September 1850, since that is when the tapestry was begun. There is a copy of the lithograph in the collection of M. Léon Malcotte, Paris, which is dedicated to Henri Labrouste.

200 The most extreme case of a globe used in a library to symbolize knowledge is surely Boullée's third design for the rue Colbert façade of the Bibliothèque Nationale of 1788, in which the portico of the building is composed of two atlantes supporting a gigantic globe. See Jean-Marie Pérouse de Montclos, Etienne-Louis Boullée (1728–1799): De l'architecture classique à l'architecture révolutionnaire, Arts et Métiers Graphiques, Paris 1969, fig. 102. Cf. N. Pevsner, A History of Building Types, The A. W. Mellon Lectures in the Fine Arts, 1970, The National Gallery of Art, Washington, D. C., Bollingen Series XXXV, vol. 19, Princeton University Press, Princeton, N. J. and Thames and Hudson, London 1976, pp. 91–110; and André Masson, Le Décor des bibliothèques du moyen âge à la révolution, Librairie Droz, Geneva 1972.

It should also be noted here that before deciding to place a copy of the School of Athens in the stairwell of the Bibliothèque Ste-Geneviève, Labrouste not only rejected the idea of a copy of Ingres' Apotheosis of Homer but had originally thought of a 'planisphère' or 'carte du monde' to cover the rear wall. See H. Labrouste, Draft of description of Bibliothèque Ste-Geneviève for Revue générale de l'architecture, n.d., MS 3939, Bibliothèque Ste-Geneviève; and Labrouste to Minister of Public Works, 7 July 1849, F^{21} 1364, AN

201 Hugo, Notre-Dame, p. 183

202 In 1837 the Minister of Public Education, Salvandy, decided that the library should stay open until 10:00 pm. Evening hours began in January 1838. AN, F^{13} 1066, F^{17} 3497

203 Labrouste studied and drew Alberti's church at Rimini in 1830, on his return trip to Paris after five years as a pensionnaire at the Académie de France in Rome. In 1826 he drew the Cappella Pontana in Naples,

a building related to Alberti's in style and the use of inscriptions. (BN, Cabinet des Estampes, Vb 132g and Vb 1321 [1])

204 As noted above, the first version of the lithograph is undated but carries a dépôt légal date of 1864. The second version, dated 1876, is oval rather than round and is a bit simplified in detail. It was published as the fifth of five Etudes and was exhibited in the Salon of 1877 (BN, Cabinet des Estampes, R. Balze – Gr. S.n.r.) The cartoon for the tapestry is now in the Musée de Pont-de-Vaux (Ain)

205 There is no way of telling, from the documents preserved, why one design was chosen over the other. It seems to me, from what is known of Labrouste's personality, that a sense of modesty prevented him from choosing the design with the building. Although it is difficult to be certain, it appears that in the executed design the second book, the one in the background, may be a manuscript rather than a printed book. The juxtaposition would then restate the historical evolution from building to book in purely bibliographic terms

206 BN, Cabinet des Estampes, uncatalogued

207 Hugo, Shakespeare, p. 174

208 Ibid., pp. 173–74

209 See Auguste Bussière, 'La Statue de Gutenberg, à Strasbourg', Revue générale de l'architecture, vol. 1 1840, cols 759–61, pls 20, 21; and Anon., 'Gutenberg', Magasin pittoresque 8, July 1840, pp. 217–20

210 G. Lepreux, 'Le Buste d'Ulric Géring et la Bibliothèque Sainte-Geneviève', Bulletin officiel de l'Union Syndicale des Maîtres Imprimeurs de France, 15th year, 2d series, no. 4 (April 1911), pp. 177–80

211 AN, F^{21} 208, F^{21} 751; and Bibliothèque Ste-Geneviève, MSS 3936–37

212 The bust of Gering is now in the Dépôt des Oeuvres d'Art de l'Etat, Fonds National d'Art Contemporain, Paris

213 The trees were painted by Alexandre Desgoffe, a student of Ingres, in June–September 1850. On 1 April 1850, Labrouste gave Desgoffe 'deux petites Etudes de peintures antiques' to serve as models (H. Labrouste, 'Bibliothèque Ste. Geneviève. 1843. Journal des travaux', MS 3910, Bibliothèque Ste-Geneviève)

214 Labrouste, 'A M. le Directeur',

col. 382. Labrouste described the illusionism of the vestibule as follows: 'le jardin que j'aurais aimé à traverser pour arriver au monument, je l'ai fait peindre sur les murs du vestibule, seul intermédiaire entre la place publique et la bibliothèque. Mon jardin en peinture ne vaut pas sans doute de belles allées de marronniers et de platanes; mais il a l'avantage de présenter des arbres toujours verts et toujours en fleurs, même au mois de décembre; et puis, sans avoir égard au climat de Paris, je pouvais, dans cette terre fertile de l'imagination, planter des arbres de tous les pays, et placer auprès de saint Bernard des palmiers d'Orient, auprès de Racine des orangers en fleurs, auprès de la Fontaine un chêne et un roseau, et des myrthes et des lauriers auprès du Poussin.

'Le vestibule est un peu sombre; mais les lecteurs en le traversant croiront peut-être un instant que cette obscurité n'est autre chose que l'ombrage des arbres qui frappent les regards, et l'on me pardonnera, je l'espère.' *Ibid.*

215 On the left they are· St Bernard, Montaigne, Pascal, Molière, La Fontaine, Bossuet, Massillon, Voltaire, Button, and Laplace; on the right: L'Hospital, Descartes, Poussin, Corneille, Racine, Fénelon, Montesquieu, Rousseau, Mirabeau, and Cuvier. They were carved by the sculptors Elschoët, Merlieux, and Mallet in 1848–50

216 That was, in fact, the way the 17th–18th-century galleries of the former Bibliothèque Ste-Geneviève were decorated. The best view is P.-C. de la Gardette's engraving of the main gallery done in 1773. See also the illustration in Claude du Molinet, *Le Cabinet de la bibliothèque Sainte-Geneviève*, Paris 1692. Another prominent example that comes to mind is Wren's Trinity College Library, Cambridge (begun 1676)

217 The *School of Athens* was set in place in December 1849. It was not, however, originally painted for the Bibliothèque Ste-Geneviève. It was commissioned in 1840 by the Minister of the Interior, Duchatel, as part of a government programme to provide Paris with copies of the masterpieces of Italian Renaissance art. It was exhibited at the Panthéon in 1847–48, at which time Labrouste saw it. As noted above (Note 200), he had originally planned a 'planisphère' to be painted on the rear wall of the stairwell. Apparently, a con-

versation he overheard caused him to change his mind: 'Les personnes attirées au Panthéon par cette Exposition [en 1847] profitaient souvent de l'occasion pour visiter les travaux qui s'exécutaient dans le quartier. Aussi je reçus beaucoup de visites alors et j'entendis un jour un M [onsieur] exprimer l'idée que cette grande muraille qui s'élève au fond du bâtiment de la bibliothèque serait sans doute d'un fâcheux effet à moins qu'on n'y plaçât un grand tableau, l'Ecole d'athènes.' Labrouste, Draft of description for *Revue générale de l'architecture*, MS 3939, Bibliothèque Ste-Geneviève. Given Labrouste's extremely self-effacing personality, it is difficult to know whether or not this account is absolutely true. In any event, it is characteristic of the way the library was designed that certain places or slots were set aside to be 'decorated', and one idea might be tried in two or three different places and then, all of a sudden, be replaced by another one. It is a process that reminds one of 'collage' or, more particularly, of the way a newspaper is 'composed' so that a late-breaking story can be fitted in on the front page simply by removing what is there. In the case of the stairwell, it just happened that 'les dimensions de l'Espace à décorer répondaient à celles du tableau de l'Ecole d'athènes.' *Ibid.*

The choice of the *School of Athens* over a map was unconventional. Labrouste thought, however, that it was not possible to 'trouver un plus beau sujet et un plus beau tableau pour servir d'Introduction' to a library (Labrouste to Minister of Public Works, 7 July 1849, F²¹ 1364, AN). In seeing the connection between Raphael's work and the programme of a library, he anticipated the later art-historical theory that the Stanza della Segnatura was Pope Julius II's library. *Cf.* John Shearman, *The Vatican Stanze: Functions and Decoration*, Italian Lecture, British Academy, 1971, from the *Proceedings of the British Academy*, vol. 57, Oxford University Press, London 1972, pp. 14–17, 44–46. For the *School of Athens* commission, see AN, F²¹ 14, F²¹ 751, F²¹ 1364

218 The tondos were executed by the Balzes in Rome in 1850–51. AN, F²¹ 14, F²¹ 751, F²¹ 1364; Bibliothèque Ste-Geneviève, MS 3919

219 Bougy, *Bibliothèque Sainte-Geneviève*, pp. 191–93

220 See, e.g., Labrouste to Minister

of Public Works, 14 September 1850 and 25 February 1851, F²¹ 751, AN; and Labrouste, 'A M. le Directeur', col. 382

221 The ambos of S. Lorenzo fuori le mura and S. Clemente, which Labrouste drew in Rome in 1830 and 1828, are the ones that immediately come to mind. BN, Cabinet des Estampes. Vb 132s [3] and [2]. The symbolic connection between pulpit and Reference (Catalogue) Desk is self-evident

222 Hugo, *Notre-Dame*, p. 176

Part V

223 *Cf.* Jules de Joly, *Plans, coupes, élévations et détails de la restauration de la Chambre des Députés, de sa nouvelle salle des séances, de sa bibliothèque et de toutes ses dépendances*, A. Le Clerc, Paris 1840; Paul Ortwin Rave (gen. ed.), *Karl Friedrich Schinkel, Berlin*, vol. 3: *Bauten für Wissenshaft, Verwaltung, Heer, Wohnbau und Denkmäler*, by P. O. Rave, Deutscher Kunstverlag, Berlin 1962, pp. 24–37; N. Pevsner, 'British Museum: Some Unresolved Problems of Its Architectural History', *Architectural Review*, vol. 113, no. 675 (March 1953), pp. 179–82, and J. Mordaunt Crook, *The British Museum*, Allen Lane, London 1972; Oswald Hederer, *Friedrich von Gärtner, 1792–1847: Leben, Werk, Schüler*, Studien zur Kunst des neunzehnten Jahrhunderts, 30, Prestel-Verlag, Munich 1976, pp. 112–25; David Watkin, *The Life and Work of C.R. Cockerell*, Studies in Architecture, vol. 14, A. Zwemmer, London 1974, pp. 183–96; and Jean-François Foucaud, *La Bibliothèque royale sous la Monarchie de Juillet (1830–1848)*, Comité des travaux historiques et scientifiques, Mémoires de la section d'histoire moderne et contemporaine, no. 5, BN, Paris 1978

224 Etienne-Louis Boullée, *Architecture: Essai sur l'art*, ed. J.-M. Pérouse de Montclos, Miroirs de l'Art, Hermann, Paris 1968, p. 130. Boullée published his project for the Bibliothèque Nationale separately, in 1785, with a text of three pages and seven engraved plates (BN, Cabinet des Estampes, Ha 43, Ha 55a). This project should not be confused with the one for the Couvent des Capucines site of 1784

225 *Ibid.*, p. 131

226 See Pérouse de Montclos, *Etienne-Louis Boullée*, fig. 99. Boullée prepared a second design for the façade on the rue Colbert with a simple aedicular entrance and niches for statues on either side of the otherwise blank wall (fig. 101). The third project with the atlantes and globe is of 1788 (fig. 102)

227 Boullée, *Architecture*, p. 131
228 *Ibid.*, p. 126
229 *Ibid.*, pp. 34–35, 59
230 *Ibid.*, pp. 47, 55, 72–75, 81, 113, 144–45
231 *Ibid.*, p. 45. The phrase is Correggio's
232 *Ibid.*, p. 126
233 *Ibid.*, p. 131
234 Boullée was aware of the extreme to which he carried this aspect of classical architecture and realized that he had to 'craindre ... d'être ce qu'on appelle *théatrâl*' (*ibid.*, p. 145)
235 Henry Trianon, 'Nouvelle Bibliothèque Sainte-Geneviève', *L'Illustration* 17, no. 411, 10–17 January 1851, p. 30
236 *Ibid.* (italics mine)
237 *Ibid.* Cf. above, Note 214
238 *Ibid.*
239 French architects of Labrouste's generation hardly ever designed in perspective. The section, which is a vertical plan, is abstract and stresses the flatness of the plane. Designing by section caused the architect to think in planar terms and reinforced the analogy of the building's walls with the pages of an 'album' or printed book
240 Hugo, *Notre-Dame*, p. 184
241 Simon-Claude Constant-Dufeux, 'Tombeau de Napoléon', *Revue générale de l'architecture*, vol. 7 (1847–48), col. 301. Directly following Constant-Dufeux's article on Napoleon's Tomb is one on Henri Labrouste's project for redecorating the Pont de la Concorde, a project that had been shelved for almost eight years. Constant-Dufeux had just been taken by Labrouste on the first official visit of the Bibliothèque Ste-Geneviève, along with César Daly and Emile Gilbert, on 11 December 1849 (Labrouste, 'Journal des travaux', MS 3910, Bibliothèque Ste-Geneviève); and it is clear that Labrouste's work was on his mind. He concluded the article on the still unfinished tomb by saying: 'Nous nous bornerons à cet exposé de l'état d'avancement des travaux ... Nous ne voulons pas être de ceux qui, *passant devant une Bibliothèque ou tout autre monument en construction*, portent étourdiment un jugement prématuré, et le qualifient d'épithètes injurieuses, qu'il leur serait bien difficile de motiver suffisamment

en présence d'une oeuvre à l'état d'ébauche.' (Col. 301, italics mine)
242 Labrouste carefully studied the site at Pisa in 1825 and drew both the Duomo and the Camposanto. BN, Cabinet des Estampes, Vb 132 q [1]; and Italian sketchbook in the family papers of M. Léon Malcotte
243 AN, F^{13} 1066, F^{17} 3497; and Bougy, *Bibliothèque Sainte-Geneviève*, pp. 148–51
244 The terms were begun by the sculptor Desprez in September 1848
245 Labrouste, 'A M. le Directeur', col. 383
246 Trianon, 'Bibliothèque Sainte-Geneviève', p. 30
247 Boullée, *Architecture*, p. 34
248 *Ibid.*, p. 35
249 *Ibid.*, p. 91
250 Geoffrey Scott, *The Architecture of Humanism: A Study in the History of Taste*, 2d ed., orig. pub. 1924, Charles Scribner's Sons, New York 1969, p. 157
251 *Ibid.*, p. 51
252 *Ibid.*, p. 64
253 *Ibid.*, pp. 48, 42
254 *Ibid.*, p. 100
255 *Ibid.*, pp. 59, 56. Cf. Harvey Wiley Corbett, architect of London's classical Bush House: 'When printing presses multiplied, however, and the public gradually began to read, the need for satisfaction through the eye began almost imperceptibly to diminish. As the new worlds of poetry, philosophy and history were opened, humanity began more and more to depend on the purely intellectual pleasures, and to pay increasingly less attention to the beauty of objects around them ... There have been, of course, sporadic renascences of the plastic sense, but until the present day the rise of literature has been almost exactly proportionate to the decline of visual enjoyment ...
'[But] with most of us, reading has become a trivial pastime, if not a positive nuisance. We have become weary of sitting with our eyes on a printed page which gives back no aesthetic satisfaction or enjoyment. Our eyes are turning again to the more direct and objective pleasures of the visual arts.
'This resurgence of visual interest finds its first outlet in architecture.' ('Architecture', in *Year Book of the Architectural League of New York and Catalogue of the Forty-Second Annual Exhibition*, 1927, n. pag.)

IX Hittorff's polychrome campaign

1 R. D. Middleton, 'Viollet-le-Duc and the rational Gothic tradition', Ph.D. thesis, University of Cambridge, 1958, ch. I, pp. 157–72, ch. IV, pp. 4–7. K. Schneider, *The works and doctrine of Jacques Ignace Hittorff*, Ph.D. thesis, Princeton University, 1971, University Microfilms 1972, vol. I, pp. 135–229, 296–364
2 H. Labrouste, *Notice sur M. Hittorff*, Paris 1868, p. 4
3 Quoted Hittorff, *op. cit.*, p. 36
4 T. L. Donaldson, 'Memoir of Louis de Zanth', *Transactions of the Royal Institute of British Architects*, 1st series, (*Papers read*), vol. 8, 1857–58, pp. 15–18; E. v. Schulz, *Die Wilhelma in Stuttgart ein Beispiel orientalisierender Architektur im 19. Jahrhundert und ihr Architekt Karl Ludwig Zanth*, Diss. Tübingen, 1976
5 S. Blutman, 'The father of the profession', *Journal of the Royal Institute of British Architects*, December 1967, pp. 542–44
6 O. Herderer, *Leo von Klenze*, Munich 1964
7 This first edition had only forty-nine plates, the second, though still an incomplete edition, was published in 1870 by Hittorff's son, Charles, with eighty-nine plates
8 'Du mouvement en architecture', *L'Artiste* II, 1833, pp. 74–78
9 H. Labrouste, *op. cit.*, p. 8
10 Hittorff, *op. cit.*, p. 814
11 For the history of this church see works by Middleton, Hammer, Van Zanten and Schneider already cited, and H. Doisy, *Les débuts d'une grand paroisse Saint-Vincent-de-Paul Montholon*, Rouen 1942
12 Owen Jones, 'On the decorations proposed for the exhibition building in Hyde Park', RIBA, 16 December 1850, printed in *Lectures on architecture and the decorative arts*, London 1863, p. 10
13 L. de Zanth, *La Wilhelma, villa mauresque de sa majesté le roi Guillaume de Wurtemburg*, Paris 1855
14 Hittorff, *op. cit.*, p. viii, footnote – see also J.-I. Hittorff, *Notice sur Sir Charles Barry*, Paris 1860, p. 17 *et seq.*
15 For the history of *lave*

d'*Auvergne* see, in addition to the works by Middleton, Hammer, Van Zanten, Schneider and Doisy already cited, L. Dussieux, *Recherches sur l'histoire de la peinture sur émail*, Paris 1841, the publications referred to later in the text by P.-J. Jollivet, and his and César Daly's notes and articles in the *Revue Générale de l'Architecture*, vol. IV, 1843, cols 190–93; vol. VIII, 1849, cols 73–80, 129–41, 194–99, 242–50, 313–18, 382–97; vol. IX, 1851, cols 28–35, 55–64, 121–29, 173–81; vol. XV, 1857, cols 237–44

16 Jollivet appears to have been little studied, though there is a detailed entry on his career in the *Nouvelle biographie générale*, (1858), and his ostentatious studio in rue des Saints-Pères is illustrated in E. Texier, *Tableau de Paris*, vol. 2, Paris 1853, p. 45

17 See obituary by Jollivet, *Revue Générale de l'Architecture*, vol. VIII, 1847, cols 352–54

18 Haussmann's critique was prophetic of Adolf Loos's later attack on applied decoration – 'l'enduit coloré non seulement de la surface des murs, mais encore des fûts, cannelures et chapiteaux de colonnes, des murs, mais encore des fûts, cantrises, et voussures des voutes, dont le but est de remplacer la froideur et la monotonie de la pierre par des teintes plates diverses, a, selon moi, le grand tort de cacher aussi la beauté simple et noble des matériaux de taille employés dans la construction. Et quand on agrémente cet enduit d'ornements variés, qui me rappellent ces tatouages dont les peuples barbares couvrent leur nudité, en guise de vêtements, je ne puis m'empêcher de trouver grotesque ce mode prétentieux de décoration.' *Mémoires du Baron Haussmann*, ch. XIV

19 P.-J. Jollivet, *De la polychromie de l'architecture par l'emploi des émaux ... à Deauville*, Paris 1867

20 *Revue Générale de l'Architecture*, vol. XVI, 1858, cols 45–46, 73–78, 115–26, pls 15–19

X Architectural polychromy: life in architecture

1 A.-C. Quatremère de Quincy, 'Architecture', *Encyclopédie méthodique*, 3 vols, Paris 1788–1825, vol. I, p. 119; see also R. Schneider, *L'esthétique classique chez Quatremère de Quincy (1805–1825)*, Paris 1910, and *Quatremère de Quincy et son in-*tervention dans les arts, Paris 1910. The matter of this essay is drawn from my doctoral dissertation, *The Architectural Polychromy of the 1830s* (Harvard 1970), which has been published in the Garland series *Outstanding Dissertations in the Fine Arts*, New York 1975. Many of the points touched upon here are treated at greater length there, but fewer and quite different conclusions are drawn

2 A.-C. Quatremère de Quincy, 'Notice sur la vie et les ouvrages de M. Hurtault, architecte', *Recueil des notices lues dans les séances publiques de l'Académie des Beaux-Arts*, Paris 1834, p. 351

3 *Moniteur universel*, 9 October 1826: the account of the annual *séance publique* of the Académie des Beaux-Arts. 'M. Quatremère de Quincy a reparu à la tribune, et a lu une Notice sur la vie et les ouvrages de M. Hurtault, architecte.

'Pendant la lecture de ce morceau qui était reçu avec intérêt par l'assemblée, quelques jeunes gens placés dans une des tribunes latérales, ont temoigné leur impatience de voir retarder le moment de la distribution des prix. Leurs murmures et leur interruption, dont une séance académique offrit pour la première fois l'exemple, ont excité les exclamations de l'assemblée, et l'agitation générale a suspendu la lecture. Bientôt un détachement de militaires a paru dans la tribune pour imposer silence aux perturbateurs, ou pour les expulser de la salle s'ils continuaient à troubler l'ordre. L'Apparition de cette force armée a été le signal d'un nouveau mouvement: quelques dames effrayées ont franchi la barrière qui séparait leur tribune de l'enceinte. Les militaires se sont retirés, et le calme s'est retabli, plutôt que l'impression produite par une scène si affligeante.' This was the first of a series of student demonstrations that culminated in a strike at the Ecole in 1830, the issue being a good deal more than impatience over the distribution of prizes.

4 G. Laviron, *Le Salon de 1834*, Paris 1834, p. 180

5 Laviron frequented Nodier's *salon* at the Arsenal (together with Lassus and Viollet-le-Duc), participated in the 'Bataille d'Hernani' in 1830 (where the claque in part was drawn from the *ateliers* of Duban and Labrouste [anon., *Victor Hugo par un témoign de sa vie*, Paris 1863, ch. LII], neither *atelier* had, in fact, been founded by then, although the group which was to offer itself to Labrouste under Lassus's leadership was already forming itself and Duban had already several followers, notably Questel, after taking over Blouet's *atelier* in 1829, during the latter's absence in Greece); Laviron was also a friend of the radical 'romantic' architect Bruno Galbaccio. Laviron was always particularly interested in architecture, and once designed a 'Pompeian' house for Gérard de Nerval (G. de Nerval, 'Promenades et Souvenirs', *l'Illustration*, 30 December 1854)

6 The designation 'romantic' has come to be taken very seriously as the 1830s have come under careful historical scrutiny. In 1830 the term was used loosely for almost any radical artist, and the members of the circle of Labrouste did not refuse the designation, as Léon Vaudoyer's letters to his father of 1830–32 show. However, in the 1870s Vaudoyer already felt it necessary to retreat a step, writing in an obituary of his friend Duban, that he in 1830 'devint naturellement le chef de la nouvelle école qu'on désigna alors sous le nom d'école *romantique*. Seulement, hâtons nous de le dire, cette qualification était tout à fait impropre à exprimer les aspirations et les doctrines dont Duban était le promoteur, car cette école, qui déjà comptait de nombreux adeptes, conservait le plus grand respect et la plus entière admiration pour les chefs d'oeuvres classiques; mais en les étudiant d'un nouveau point de vue, elle se proposait d'en déduire un plus grand enseignement, et proclamait en même temps plus d'indépendance dans ses conceptions; son but et son ambition étaient surtout d'imprimer à notre architecture un caractère vraiment national.' 'Discours prononcé aux funérailles de M. Duban', Paris 1871. Neil Levine has proposed the designation 'Néo-Grec' for this group, but it, like 'romantic', is a borrowed term, properly applied to certain poets and painters ('The Romantic Idea of Architectural Legibility: Henri Labrouste and the *Néo-Grec*', *The Architecture of the Ecole des Beaux-Arts*, A. Drexler (ed.), New York and London 1977). The group itself would seem to have tried to avoid dogmatic labels and perhaps we should respect that, and use the term 'romantic' in inverted commas, because it is the broadest term available.

7 The group included all the *pen-*

sionnaires arriving in Rome between 1822 and 1831, that is, Emile Gilbert (1822), Abel Blouet (1823), S.-C. Constant-Dufeux (1830) and P.-J. Garrez (1831) in addition to those listed here.

8 See Neil Levine, *loc. cit.*, and *Architectural Reasoning in the Age of Positivism: the Néo-Grec Idea of Henri Labrouste's Bibliothèque Ste-Geneviève*, Yale University doctoral dissertation, 1975, ch. VII, pt. 3

9 Labrouste's explanatory text is preserved in the library of the Ecole des Beaux-Arts and is reproduced verbatim in *Temples de Paestum par Labrouste: restaurations des monuments par les architectes pensionnaires de France à Rome*, Paris 1877. In what follows I retain Labrouste's designations of the temples for the sake of clarity; subsequent archaeological exploration has proven their dedications to be quite different.

10 For example, C.-M. de Lagardette, *Les Ruines de Paestum ou Posidonia* ... Paris 1798, the source against which Labrouste's work was compared in 1828–29

11 *Temples de Paestum par Labrouste*, pp. 12–13

12 *Ibid.*, p. 14

13 The drawings survive in the possession of the family. Vaudoyer states his intentions in a letter to his father of 22 March 1830

14 The watercolour was exhibited at the Hôtel de Sully in January 1975. See Académie d'Architecture, *Centenaire Henri Labrouste*, Paris 1975, nos 83–86. Also, Pierre Saddy, *Henri Labrouste, architecte, 1801–1875*, Paris 1977, p. 11

15 Such a painted curtain 'stretched' between real or painted pilasters is a familiar Pompeian motif. Here it is also reminiscent of the curtain-enclosed loggia of the palace depicted in the Byzantine mosaics in S. Apollinare Nuovo in Ravenna, which Labrouste and Vaudoyer had seen together in the summer of 1828

16 Herodotus, *History* I, ch. XCVIII

17 Indeed, Duban produced a whole body of such compositions over the length of his career and they were exhibited as a series at the 'Exposition Universelle' in 1855 and at the Ecole des Beaux-Arts after his death in 1872. See C. Blanc, 'Félix Duban', *Les Artistes de mon temps*, Paris 1876; V. Baltard, 'Exposition d'une collection de dessins de Félix Duban', *Revue générale de*

l'architecture XXIX (1872), cols 22–29. See also *The Second Empire: the Arts under Napoleon III*, Philadelphia and Paris 1978, pp. 46–47

18 S. Reinach, *Répertoire de reliefs grecs et romains*, 3 vols, Paris 1912, II, fig. 224; III, figs 42, 263, 265, 402, 501

19 The painting, in fact, seems to be a depiction of a colossal chryselephantine statue of the deity

20 The entire background is in the style of a Pompeian wall-painting. I know of no Pompeian painting that depicts just such a scene, although figures are frequently represented standing on walls or roofs, and garlands are frequently shown decorating structures. However, in the one case where a structure is shown being garlanded it is Venus's throne, which cupids are adorning. Duban would seem to have rendered this motif in this Pompeian style in order to communicate that the little house is being prepared to receive the newly-weds.

21 So we ascertain from a letter by Léon Vaudoyer to his father of 9 December 1828. The *pensionnaires* were not supposed to marry and the letter refers to various difficulties. Perhaps the inscription in Duban's composition citing Aeneas's arrival in Italy (when he married the Latin princess Lavinia, after overcoming great resistance, and thus founded the Roman nation) is a reference to his own problems

22 The programme according to which the design was made seems to have been one for a *rendu* for the *seconde classe* at the Ecole des Beaux-Arts of 1835, 'Un amphithéâtre au système de ceux des Romains': 'l'Usage de ces édifices, est parvenu jusqu'à nous d'une manière trop imparfaite pour que dans les exemples grossiers qu'on pourrait à peine citer, on puisse y trouver un type à imiter.

'C'est donc chez les anciens à Rome et dans les provinces de l'Empire qu'il faut chercher des modèles de ce genre de monument.

'Nos usages moins populaires, qu'ils ne le furent, même au temps de la plus grande splendeur de la puissance romaine, ne nous permettent pas, de nous conformer sans modifications aux dispositions et aux formes des amphithéâtres antiques, et de les composer exclusivement pour la partie destinée aux spectacles, de gradins s'élevant les uns derrière les autres.

'Ainsi il conviendra dans l'intérieur de réunir aux parties disposées en gradins quelques tribunes, ou loges, pour les personnes de distinction et de l'usage des appariteurs des jeux, pour y jouir ou présider aux scènes, aux spectacles gymnastiques, et aux combats simulés qu'on y représentait.

'En dehors, on observa de distinguer sensiblement les entrées des tribunes de celles des gradins, et de pratiquer des escaliers pour les desservir. Enfin des vomitoires pour la sortie à la fin des jeux.' (AN, AJ[52] 128)

23 The fourth year *envois* were retained by the Ecole des Beaux-Arts, but for some reason Constant-Dufeux's project, reconstructing the Capitol in Rome, is missing. Written descriptions of it make it appear to have been the most extraordinary of the series

24 Duban's is known from sketches done after it by J.-L. Lecointe (Ecole des Beaux-Arts, 'Carnets Hittorff'); Labrouste's was exhibited at the Museum of Modern Art in 1975 (Drexler, *op. cit.*, pp. 396–97); Vaudoyer's survives in the possession of the family

25 The original is lost, but it was published (with the views rearranged to fit on only three sheets, it appears) in a set of lithographs for circulation among his friends and students after his death

26 The existing Palais Bourbon was transformed to house the *Corps Législatif* and a Corinthian portico added on its north façade facing the Pont de la Concorde by Bernard Poyet in 1806. Beginning in 1829, the interior was rebuilt and the southern, court façade erected by Jules de Joly

27 The functional inappropriateness to France of the tall columnar porticoes and low-pitched roof of the Greeks and Romans was a constant point of criticism around 1830. Léonce Reynaud wrote in 1834: 'On vit s'introduire chez nous les portiques ouverts, les terrasses, les petites fenêtres à la place des portiques fermés, des toits élancés et des grandes ouvertures du môyen age. Ces nouvelles dispositions ne convenaient ni à nos moeurs ni à notre climat ...' ('Architecture', *Encyclopédie pittoresque* [renamed *Encyclopédie nouvelle*], I, 1834, p. 777)

28 The constitution that Constant-Dufeux included as part of his project is that of France in 1835 (i.e., that accepted by Louis-Philippe on 9 August 1830), except for the specific numbers of certain bodies. It is an architect's programme distilled from the actual political structure of the state, rather than a Utopian document: this project does not attempt to make an independant political statement, aside from the fact that it emphasizes the most democratic branch of the current government. Constant-Dufeux later in his career supported the bourgeois 'party of order', fighting against the workers in the *Jours de Juin* of 1848 and barricading the Panthéon against republican demonstrators at the time of Napoleon III's Coup d'Etat in 1851

29 In 1847, Constant-Dufeux published an article in the *Revue générale de l'architecture* suggesting a Chamber of Deputies as a suitable subject for student competitions at the Ecole des Beaux-Arts, explaining: 'Dans ce projet devrait se résumer notre conviction architecturale, et cet édifice, placé de nos jours au premier rang entre tous, devrait, pour satisfaire à toutes les données du programme, être empreint au suprême degré des caractères combinés de l'art, de la science, et de l'industrie … Aujourd'hui où toute capitale, toute ville, et jusqu'au moindre village, doivent avoir leurs *salles d'assemblées*, pourquoi ne cherche-t-on pas là le motif d'une nouvelle architecture? Pourquoi ne fait-on pas de ces édifices un objet particulier d'études et de recherches, pour constituer un type nouveau … Les Pays-Bas ont su, dans un temps, faire une *architecture municipale*. Serons-nous impuissants pour constituer une *architecture représentative*?' (VII, cols 297–98)

30 At least three further steps were taken by the French 'romantic' architects in the evolution of this idea. First was Duban's completion of the buildings of the Ecole des Beaux-Arts as a museum of French national architecture; see D. Van Zanten, 'Félix Duban and the Buildings of the Ecole des Beaux-Arts, 1832–1840', *Journal of the Society of Architectural Historians*, XXXVII, 1978, pp. 161–74. Second was Léon Vaudoyer's conception of the 19th-century cathedral as a volumetric summation of the evolution of the Christian church since Constantine, demonstrated in his design for Marseille Cathedral; see D. Van Zanten, entries I-23 to I-27 in *The Second Empire*, pp. 64–67. Third was the abstraction and synthesis of the root

forms of the western architectural tradition that Neil Levine asserts was embodied by Labrouste in his design of the Bibliothèque Ste-Geneviève; see N. Levine, *Architectural Reasoning in the Age of Positivism*. Polychromy and Constant-Dufeux's polychromed Chamber of Deputies project formed only one aspect of this conception of architecture, but an early and important part

31 I commenced tracing Duban's compositions while working on my dissertation in 1968; Neil Levine rediscovered the *envois* of Delannoy and Théodore Labrouste in 1969–70; Labrouste's 'Agrigentum' was put on display at the Labrouste Centenary at the Hôtel de Sully in 1975; I explored the Vaudoyer material in 1974–78 and (thanks to Michael Driskel) examined the Toudouze drawings in 1978

32 See K. Hammer, *Jakob-Ignaz Hittorff: ein Pariser Baumeister, 1792–1867*, Stuttgart 1968; D. Schneider, *The Works and Doctrine of Jacques-Ignace Hittorff (1792–1867); Structural Innovation and Formal Expression in French Architecture, 1810–1867*, Princeton University doctoral dissertation, 1970, published in 1975 in the Garland series *Outstanding Dissertations in the Fine Arts*

33 He made the discovery while in Sicily during the winter of 1823–24. He then displayed reconstruction drawings in Rome in 1824 (they now cannot be identified with certainty among his papers in the Wallraf-Richartz Museum in Cologne); read a paper mentioning the evidence of polychromy (but not emphasizing it) before the Académie des Beaux-Arts on 24 July 1824 (text preserved in the library of the Institut de France); and commenced publication of his *Architecture antique de la Sicile*, which was terminated incomplete in 1830 (republished, complete, in 1870), with three chromolithographed plates of polychrome details. His full reconstruction of the 'Temple of Empedocles' was only made public in 1830 – after the storm had broken over the *envois*. Hittorff was the first French architect to study the evidence, but was he the first to realize its significance?

34 *Architecture antique de la Sicile*, Paris 1827–30; 'De l'Architecture polychrome chez les Grecs', *Annales de l'institut de correspondance archéologique*, II (1830), pp. 263–84; 'De l'Architecture polychrome chez les Grecs', *Journal de la société libre des*

beaux-arts, I (1830–31, actually published 1836), pp. 118–55 (a slightly expanded republication of the second citation here); *Restitution du Temple d'Empédocle, ou l'Architecture polychrome chez les Grecs*, Paris 1846–51

35 The controversy is summarized at great length in Hittorff, *Architecture polychrome*, and again by Hammer (*op. cit.*, ch. V)

36 H. Labrouste, *Notice sur Hittorff*, Paris 1868, pp. 7–8. As the successor to Hittorff's chair at the Académie, Labrouste was obliged to present an obituary of his predecessor

37 *Annales de l'institut de correspondance archéologique, loc. cit.*, p. 263

38 At his own request. He also displayed his drawings and read his paper before the Académie des Inscriptions et Belles Lettres in 1830 and before the Société Libre des Beaux-Arts in 1830 or 1831. He was clearly seeking to publicize his idea

39 *Annales de l'institut de correspondance archéologique, loc. cit.*, pp. 268–79

40 *Architecture polychrome*, pp. 6–7. Cf. Van Zanten, *Architectural polychromy*, pp. 102–03, note 124

41 E. Beulé, *Eloge de M. Hittorff*, Paris 1868, p. 4

42 *Annales de l'institut de correspondance archéologique, loc. cit.*, pp. 263–64. See also the introduction to his *Architecture antique de la Sicile*

43 Beulé, *op. cit.*, p. 10

44 *Annales de l'institut de correspondance archéologique, loc. cit.*, pp. 272–73

45 *Ibid.*, p. 273

46 *Ibid.*, p. 273

47 pp. 438–39

48 *Notice sur les ruines d'Agrigente*, Paris 1859

49 *Annales de l'institut de correspondance archéologique, loc. cit.*, p. 273

50 *Encyclopédie des gens du monde*, Paris 1833 ff., I (1833), p. 189

51 *Ibid.*, pp. 186–87

52 *Ibid.*, p. 187

53 *Notice sur les ruines d'Agrigente*

54 Quatremère de Quincy, *op. cit.*, II (1801), 'coupole'

55 Lepère's design was circulated as a printed broadsheet upon the laying of the cornerstone. See Hammer, *op. cit.*, ch. VII; Van Zanten, *Architectural polychromy*, pl. 29

56 This project survives among the Hittorff papers in Cologne. See Van Zanten, *Architectural polychromy*, pls 30 and 31

57 See two analyses of the building upon its completion: A. de Colonne, 'Eglise de St Vincent-de-Paul: coup d'oeil général', *Journal des artistes*, 27 October 1844, pp. 257–60; E. Bareste, 'Eglise de St Vincent-de-Paul', *Moniteur des arts* I, no. 1 (2 February 1845), pp. 3–4; no. 2 (16 February 1845), pp. 17–18. The idea seems to have long been current at the Ecole des Beaux-Arts and I discuss it in 'Architectural Composition from Charles Percier to Charles Garnier', in Drexler, *op. cit.*, pp. 134–35. But it was never clearly articulated, Quatremère's more abstract (and impractical) ideas being accepted as the academic doctrine until his retirement in 1839. The idea was already being formulated during the second half of the 18th century (R. D. Middleton, 'The Abbé de Cordemoy and the Greco-Gothic Ideal: a Prelude to Romantic Classicism', *Journal of the Warburg and Courtauld Institutes*, XXV, 1962, pp. 278–320; XXVI, 1963, pp. 90–123) and found clear expression in J.-N.-L. Durand's *Précis des leçons données à l'Ecole polytechnique* ... (3 vols, Paris 1802, 1805, 1821). This idea of an architectural vocabulary of parts fitted together was probably communicated orally in the *ateliers* at the Ecole des Beaux-Arts, Quatremère's philosophical embroideries being deemed appropriate for formal circumstances but not given much practical application, while it was codified and written down by Durand who was teaching a one-year architecture course for engineers without the paraphernalia of *ateliers* and philosophizing at the Académie

58 H. Bramsen, *Gottlieb Bindesbøll: liv og arbejder*, Copenhagen 1959, pp. 17–19; C. Lipsius, *Gottfried Semper in seiner Bedeutung als Architekt*, Berlin, 1880, p. 2 (Semper's stay seems to have been divided into two parts, from 1826 to the end of 1827 and from July 1829 into 1830). Dr Karl Hammer has been studying Gau and I am indebted to him for the information that Gau conducted an actual school, not just an *atelier*

59 *Plans, Elevations, Sections and Details of the Alhambra*, London 1836–45

60 While a student in Rome, Gau met the luminaries of the German community there, particularly the historian B. G. Niebuhr, who later contributed to Gau's *Antiquités de la Nubie*, Paris 1821–27 (F. Noack, *Deutsches Leben in Rom, 1700 bis 1900*, Berlin 1907, pp. 186, 434). In the 1820s he participated in the Salon of Gérard and became a correspond-

ent of Sulpiz Boisserée (P. Moisy, *Les Séjours en France de Sulpice Boisserée*, Paris 1956, pp. 118, 247, 252, 274, 310, 331). He also corresponded with Ludwig I's trusted art agent, Johann Martin von Wagner, and with the Stuttgart *literatus* Ludwig Schorn

61 *Antiquités de la Nubie* and *Les Ruines de Pompéi*, 4 vols (first two volumes edited by François Mazois), Paris 1812–38. From 1839 until his death in 1853 he designed and erected the Gothic church of Ste-Clotilde in Paris

62 G. Semper, *Die vier Elemente der Baukunst*, Brunswick, 1851, p. 3

63 See C. Brunn and L. P. Fenger, *Thorwaldsens Museum Historie*, Copenhagen 1892; V. Wanscher, *Architekten G. Bindesbøll*, Copenhagen 1903; H. Bramsen, *op. cit.*; and B. Jørgensen, 'Thorwaldsen's Museum: A National Monument', *Apollo*, n.s. XCVI (1972), pp. 198–205. It should be compared to the more conventionally polychrome Neue Pinakothek in Munich erected by August von Voigt in 1843–54 (W. Mittlmeier, *Die Neue Pinakothek in München, 1843–1854: Plannung, Baugeschichte und Fresken*, Munich 1977)

64 See Wanscher and Bramsen cited above. Also V. Wanscher, 'Gottlieb Bindesbøll, 1800–1856, der Erbauer von Thorwaldsens Museum', *Artes*, I (1932), pp. 57–185

65 L. Ettlinger, *Gottfried Semper und die Antike*, Halle 1937. Semper's travel sketches are in the Semperarchiv at the Eidgenössische Technische Hochschule, Zurich

66 Not all the drawings executed for *Anwendung der Farben* were published, owing to its swift discontinuation

67 G. Semper had attended the lectures of Ottfried Müller while a student at Göttingen in 1823–25; his standards were not those of a dilettante

68 *Vorläufige Bemerkungen* (republished in G. Semper, *Kleine Schriften*, Berlin 1884, pp. 242–43)

69 *Vier Elemente*, pp. 52 ff.

70 *Der Stil in den technischen und tektonischen Künsten*, 2 vols, Frankfurt 1860, and Munich 1863, I, p. 209ff

71 See M. Darby, *Owen Jones and the Oriental Influence in Nineteenth Century Design*, Reading University doctoral dissertation, 1974

72 As well as the archaeologist Penrose, the chemist Michael Faraday (who had tested the traces of

polychromy scientifically), the theorist James Fergusson and the architects C. R. Cockerell and Hector Horeau (the last in London because he placed first in the design competition for the Crystal Palace). It was a remarkable gathering

73 1851, pp. 5–7, 42–50

74 *Vorläufige Bemerkungen*, 1884 ed., pp. 236–37

75 *Civil Engineer and Architect's Journal*, 1851, p. 49

76 *Ibid.*, p. 50

77 These begin with the text of his *Alhambra* and include: 'Gleanings from the Great Exhibition of 1851', *Journal of Design and Manufactures* V, (1851), pp. 89–93; *On the True and False in the Decorative Arts*, (London 1852); *An Apology for the Colouring of the Greek Court at the Crystal Palace*, (London 1854); *The Grammar of Ornament*, (London 1856); and *Lectures on Architecture and the Decorative Arts*, (London 1864)

78 *Alhambra*, text to pl. 36

79 *Grammar of Ornament*, introduction, 'proposition 22'

80 See M. Darby and D. Van Zanten, 'Owen Jones's Iron Buildings of the 1850s', *Architectura*, 1974, pp. 53–75

81 Jones explained this in a lecture before the Royal Institute of British Architects on 5 December 1850, now preserved in the Institute's library (MS SP. 10), which was published in full in the *The Times*, London, 16 December. Chevreul's theory was laid out in his *De la Loi du contraste simultané des couleurs*, 3 vols, Paris 1839; Field's in his *Chromatics, or an Essay on the Analogy and Harmony of Colours*, London 1817, and his *Chromotography*, London 1835

82 G. Semper, 'On the Study of Polychromy', *Museum of Classical Antiquities* I, (1851), pp. 228–55, especially p. 245

83 In Semper's original text a small 'e' is used, but this makes no sense; Semper must mean Oriental, not eastward

84 Semper says as much: *Vorläufige Bemerkungen*, 1884 ed., p. 221

85 *Civil Engineer and Architect's Journal, loc. cit.*, p. 49

86 Jones was by no means the first to believe that there was some sort of harmony between Greek architecture and the Greek environment. Among others, the archaeologist Otto Magnus von Stackelberg devoted his career to exploring such analogies (G. Rodenwalt, *O.-M. von Stackelberg: der Entdecker der*

griechischen Landschaft, Berlin, n.d.)
87 *Alhambra*, text to pl. 38
88 W. W. Hudson, *A Crystal Age*, London 1887 (American edition, 1917, p. 208)
89 For a description of the exterior colouring and its effect, see: (anonymous) *The Palace: an Artist's Sketch of the 10th of June, 1854*, London 1854
90 *Revue générale de l'architecture* VI, (1846), col. 12
91 Jones believed firmly in the Industrial Revolution's having ushered in a new age of society and art. See his lecture of 1835 in *Lectures on Architecture and the Decorative Arts*, lecture I
92 Published by Denis Sharp in his introduction to the translation of Paul Scheerbart's *Glasarchitektur*, London, 1972, pp. 8–9. Ruskin continues: 'And still, I ask you, what after this? Do you suppose those imaginations of yours will ever lie down there to sleep beneath the shade of your iron leafage, or within the coloured light of your enchanted dome?' *The Two Paths: Art and the Imagination*, 1840

XI 'The synthesis of all I have seen' the architecture of Edmond Duthoit

1 E. Viollet-le-Duc, *Entretiens sur l'architecture*, vol. 2, Paris 1872, p. 445
2 I am indebted to M. Robert Duthoit for his assistance and permission to examine his family's collection of papers and designs. Appreciation is also due to Robin Middleton for assistance and advice in the preparation of my BA thesis for the University of Cambridge (1979) on which this account is based. The biography of Duthoit is treated only in an anonymous pamphlet, *Edmond Duthoit, Architecte*, Amiens 1890, and the entries in Thieme-Becker and Bellier-Auvray and *L'Encyclopédie nouvelle*. In recent literature his career is mentioned in D. Watkin and R. D. Middleton, *Architettura Moderna*, Milan 1977 (English ed. 1980), and in the excellent catalogue of the Philadelphia Museum of Art, *The Second Empire*, Philadelphia 1978
3 The critical catalyst in the rejection of revivalism was the 1846 controversy over Ste-Clotilde in

Paris. See D. Watkin and R. D. Middleton, *op. cit.*, pp. 356–57
4 See R. D. Middleton, 'Viollet-le-Duc's academic ventures and the Entretiens sur l'Architecture' in *Gottfried Semper und die Mitte des Neunzehnten Jahrhunderts*, Basel 1976, pp. 239–54
5 N. Levine, *Architectural Reasoning in the Age of Positivism: The Néo-Grec Idea of Henri Labrouste's Bibliothèque Ste Geneviève*, Ph.D. thesis, Yale University, 1975
6 Viollet-le-Duc, *Entretiens* I, p. 7
7 See F. Boudon, 'Recherche sur la pensée et l'oeuvre d'Anatole de Baudot' in *Architecture, Mouvement, Continuité* XXVIII (1973), pp. 1–67, and J.-B. Ache, 'De Baudot, Précurseur', in *Les Monuments historiques de France* III (1965), pp. 113–21
8 P. Foucart traces the family to a Pierre Duthoit who was active in Lille *c.* 1668, see P. Foucart, *L'Hôtel Bouctot-Vagniez et son architecte Louis Duthoit*, Amiens 1978, pp. 54–56
9 'Deux Grands Artistes Chrétiens', *Revue de l'art chrétien*, 1875, p. 52. Family tradition ascribes the MS version of this notice in the collection of M. Robert Duthoit to Edmond Duthoit
10 *Ibid.*, p. 53
11 *Ibid.*, p. 52
12 *Ibid.*, p. 54
13 See G. Durand, *Monographie de l'Eglise Notre-Dame, Cathédrale d'Amiens*, 3 vols, Paris 1901–03
14 P. Ansant, 'Il était une fois', *Discours à la réception de l'Académie d'Amiens, 15 mai 1931*, Amiens 1933, p. 13
15 P. Gout, *Viollet-le-Duc. Sa vie, son oeuvre, sa doctrine*, Paris 1914, p. 159
16 *Congrès archéologique* LX (1893), Paris 1895, p. 132
17 Letter of 27 February 1862 from Nicosia: 'Comment va mon ciborium? Les mesures que j'ai demandées à Papa ne sont pas arrivées plus que tout le reste.' I am grateful to M. Duthoit for permission to quote from the letters in his possession. Future citations will be included by the date in the text
18 Alexandre Chertier specialized in neo-medieval design and worked extensively for Viollet-le-Duc and his circle. See the entry in the Philadelphia Museum of Art catalogue, *op. cit.*, pp. 140–41
19 Ruprich-Robert published an article on his course in the *Revue générale de l'architecture*: XI (1853), cols 241 *ff.* In 1857 the same journal

published a translation of the principles from Owen Jones's *Grammar of Ornament*. Later Ruprich-Robert published the method in *Flore ornementale, essai sur la composition de l'ornement, elements tirés de la nature et principes de leur application*, Paris 1876
20 *Ecclesiologist* XVI, (1855), p. 275
21 A. de Baudot, 'Ciborium situé dans la Chapelle du Petit Séminaire de Saint Riquier', *Gazette des architects et du bâtiment (GAB)*, 1865, p. 342
22 A. Blouet, *Expedition scientifique de la Morée*, Paris 1831–38, vol. 3, n.p.
23 E. Renan, *Une Mission de Phénicie*, 2 vols, Paris 1864. On Renan's relationship to positivist historical interpretations, see O. Chadwick, *The secularisation of the European mind in the nineteenth century*, Cambridge 1975, pp. 191 *ff.* For the French military expedition of 1860 see Abbé Jobin, *La Syrie en 1860 et 1861*, Lille 1862, p. 209 *ff.*
24 W. H. Waddington (b. 1828) is known principally as an epigraphist and Hellenist. Born in Paris of English parents he attended the University of Cambridge but later was naturalized in France. In addition to his writings, he served as representative of the Aisne dept. in the National Assembly and was elected to the Académie des Inscriptions et Belles-Lettres in 1865
25 H. Butler, *Early Churches in Syria*, Princeton, 1929. For a summary of architectural expeditions see R. Dussand, P. Deschamps, H. Seyrig, *La Syrie antique et moderne*, Paris 1931, pp. 15–20
26 de Vogüé, *Syrie centrale* I, pp. 16–17
27 E. Duthoit, 'Lettre de M. Duthoit à propos de son travail sur le couvent de St-Siméon-Stylite (Syrie)', *Encyclopédie d'Architecture* 1864, pp. 78–79
28 L. Vitet, 'Des Monuments de Paris', *La Revue française* V, (February–March 1838), p. 227
29 Viollet-le-Duc, *Entretiens* I, p. 229
30 *Lettres inédites de Viollet-le-Duc recueillies et annotées par son fils*, Paris 1902, p. 15
31 Viollet-le-Duc, *Entretiens* I, p. 232
32 *Ibid.*, p. 240
33 *Ibid.*, p. 214
34 A. de Baudot, 'Eglise construite en Syrie', *GAB* 1866, pp. 49–50
35 L. Hautecoeur, *L'Histoire de l'architecture classique en France*, vol. 7,

p. 294. R. D. Middleton, 'Viollet-le-Duc's Academic Ventures', *op. cit.*, p. 248, relates a similar incident concerning Viollet's own *atelier*: 'he lost all patience with a student who hoped to please him by using Gothic arcading on a building intended for Algiers'. Moreover, de Baudot elaborates the story into a whole town for Algeria in *L'Architecture*, Paris 1916, p. 198

36 A. de Baudot, 'Eglises cypriotes du moyen-âge', *GAB*, 1864, p. 253

37 Quoted in E. Duthoit, 'Un Amienois en Orient, Edmond Duthoit, architecte 1837–1889', *Conférence faite à la séance des Rosati Picards du 21 Juin 1924*, Fontenay-le-Comte 1936, p. 39

38 *Ibid.*, p. 41

39 G. Viollet-le-Duc, ed., *Viollet-le-Duc: lettres d'Italie, 1836–1837*, Paris 1971, p. 47

40 *Ibid.*, p. 58

41 Quoted in E. Duthoit, *op. cit.*, p. 41

42 See A. Darcel, 'Salon de 1863', *Gazette des Beaux-Arts* XV, (1863), p. 144, and A. de Baudot, 'Salon', EA, 1864, p. 74

43 H.-R. Hitchcock, *Architecture Nineteenth and Twentieth Centuries*, Fourth edition, Harmondsworth, Mx. 1977, p. 605, n. 17, and D. Watkin and R. D. Middleton, *op. cit.*, p. 356

44 See C. Handley-Read, 'Notes on William Burges's Painted Furniture', *Burlington Magazine* CV (1963), pp. 496–509

45 See S. Jervis, 'Ludwig II of Bavaria: His Architecture, Design and Decoration in context', *Designs for the Dream King*, London 1978, p. 11

46 The best sources for the history of the château are J. Gardelles, *Les Châteaux du moyen-âge dans la France du sud-ouest, la Gascogne anglaise de 1216 à 1327*, Geneva 1972, pp. 208, and L. Drouyn, *La Guienne militaire*, Bordeaux 1865

47 P. Julian, 'Les Conquettes de Roquetaillade', *Connaissance des arts*, May 1971, pp. 84–95 ascribed the work solely to Viollet-le-Duc although he acknowledged the assistance of a pupil named 'Duthuit'. This inaccuracy was corrected in a note in *Connaissance des arts*, May 1972, p. 25

48 The document in the château archive is undated but as reference is made to work on the staircase, 1866 seems a most likely date. I am grateful to Mme Anne de Brem and

M. Alain de Baritault for their assistance with the Roquetaillade archives

49 Viollet-le-Duc, *Dictionnaire raisonné de l'architecture* VIII, p. 14

50 See P. Mérimée, 'De la Peinture murale et de son emploi dans l'architecture moderne', in *Revue générale de l'architecture (RGA)* 9 (1851) cols 258–73 and 327–37. See also M. Ouradou, *Chapelles de Notre-Dame de Paris*, Paris 1868

51 E. Boeswillwald, 'Menuiserie Arabe: Plafond', *GAB*, 1863, pp. 49–50

52 A. de Baudot, 'Mobilier', *GAB*, 1869–70, p. 247

53 E. Duthoit, 'Mobilier et Orfèvrerie', *GAB*, 1867 ('Etudes sur l'Exposition Universelle de 1867', special supplement), p. 234

54 *Ibid.*, p. 237

55 For illustrations see *Mémoires de l'Académie des Sciences de l'Institut de France*, second series, vol. 50

56 On Abbadie see *Dictionnaire de biographie française*, vol. 1, Paris 1938, cols 37–41

57 J. de Fouille et A. le Sourd, *Les châteaux de France*, Paris, n.d., p. 326

58 See A. de Baudot, *Compositions et Dessins de Viollet-le-Duc*, Paris 1885, pl. LXXIX

59 H. Kreisel, *Kunst des deutschen Möbels*, vol. 3, Munich 1973, p. 180. For Oppler see Peter Eilitz, *Leben und Werk des Königl. Hannoverischen Baurats Edwin Oppler*, Hannoversche Geschichtsblätter, n.f. vol. 45, Hannover 1971. Duthoit may well have known Oppler, who had worked under Viollet-le-Duc on the restoration of Amiens Cathedral

60 Edmond Duthoit, *op. cit.*, p. 25

61 A.-H.-A. Delamare, *Exploration scientifique de l'Algérie pendant les années 1840, 1841, 1842 par ordre du gouvernement*, 2 vols, plates, Paris 1856, and S. Gsell, text, Paris 1912

62 E. Boeswillwald, 'Monuments de la Tunisie', RGA 43 (1886), cols 131–47, 209–10

63 A. Milvoy, *Ville Romaine de Thamugas*, Amiens 1890, and E. Boeswillwald, Gagnat, and A. Ballu, *Timgad, une cité africaine sous l'empire romain*, Paris 1891–1905

64 E. Duthoit, 'Rapport sur une mission scientifique en Algérie', *Archives des missions scientifiques*, Third series, 1873, p. 312

65 See D. Van Zanten, *The Architectural Polychromy of the 1830s*, New York 1970

66 Viollet-le-Duc, 'Revue', GAB, 1868, p. 20, and J. Bourgoin and E.-E.

Viollet-le-Duc, *Les Arts arabes*, A. Morel, Paris 1873 (1868–73)

67 E. Viollet-le-Duc, *De la décoration appliquée aux édifices*, Paris 1879, p. 46

68 M.-P. Morey, *La Charpente de la Cathédrale de Messine*, Paris 1841

69 E. Boeswillwald, 'Menuiserie', *op. cit.*, p. 49

70 E. Duthoit, 'Mobilier', *op. cit.*

71 Viollet-le-Duc, *Dictionnaire* III, pp. 300 *ff.* This idea has been elaborated by Neil Levine in a lecture delivered at the Symposium on the Ecole des Beaux-Arts and French 19th-century Architecture at the Architectural Association, London, on 26 May 1978

72 P. Hamerton, 'The Present State of the Fine Arts in France', *The Portfolio* XXII, (1891), pp. 223–24

73 On Godin see E. Carnoy, *Dictionnaire des hommes du Nord*, Paris 1894, pp. 213–16. On a comparable pilgrimage church see F. Loyer, 'La Basilique Ste-Anne d'Auray, monument de l'éclectisme', *Bulletin de la Société de l'Histoire de l'Art Français*, 1977, p. 237–64

74 Quoted in Yves-Saint-Marie, *Notre-Dame-de-Brébières*, Boulogne-sur-Seine 1908, p. 407

75 Edmond Duthoit, *op. cit.*, pp. 39–42

76 *Ibid.*, p. 42

77 F. de Dartein, *Etude sur l'architecture lombarde et les origines du style romano-byzantin*, Paris 1865–82. See also G. Rohault de Fleury, *Les Monuments de Pise au moyen-âge*, 2 vols, Paris 1866

78 Saint-Marie-Perrin, 'Pierre Bossan', *L'Architecture* II, (1889), p. 322

79 E. Viollet-le-Duc, *Entretiens* I, p. 458

80 L. Vitet, 'De l'architecture lombarde' reprinted in *Etudes sur les Beaux-Arts*, Paris 1864, vol. 2, pp. 1–25

81 L. Vitet, 'Des monumens de Paris', *op. cit.*, p. 230

82 *Ibid.*, p. 230

83 A. Couchaud, *Choix d'églises byzantines de la Grèce*, Paris 1842

84 L. Vaudoyer and A. Lenoir, 'Etudes de l'architecture en France', *Magasin Pittoresque* VII, (1840), p. 398

85 *Ibid.* This view would later be emphatically stated by Heinrich Hübsch, *Die Altchristliche Kirchen*, Karlsruhe 1862–63 (French translation, *Monuments de l'architecture chrétienne*, Paris 1866)

86 *Ibid.*

87 *Ibid.*

88 D. Van Zanten, 'Architectural composition from the era of Percier to the era of Garnier', in A. Drexler (ed.), *The Architecture of the Ecole des Beaux-Arts*, New York and London 1977, p. 230

89 Vitet, *op. cit.*, p. 229

90 Henry Gally Knight, *Saracenic and Norman Remains to Illustrate the Normans in Sicily*, John Murray, London (1840?)

91 M.-P. Morey, *op. cit.*, p. 6

92 L. Vaudoyer, *op. cit.*, 1839, p. 262

93 Edmond Duthoit, *op. cit.*, p. 42

94 E. Viollet-le-Duc, *De la décoration*, *op. cit.*, p. 48

95 E. Viollet-le-Duc, *Entretiens* I, p. 450

96 A. de Baudot, *L'Architecture*, *op. cit.*, p. 71

97 *Ibid.*, p. 53

Acknowledgments for photographs

The authors are grateful to individuals and institutions mentioned in the captions, and, in addition, to the following for photographs:

Archives Photographiques, Paris 118, 119, 166; James Austin 124, 149, 157; Bibliothèque Nationale, Paris 4–6, 8, 9, 11, 12, 14, 18, 21, 23–33, 36, 37, 52–54, 122, 140, 143; Bulloz, Paris 55–59, 123; Courtauld Institute of Art, University of London 152; CVP 1; Larrey-Photo 177, 178; J. Musy, Caisse Nationale des Monuments Historiques et des Sites II; Hans Petersen, for the Thorvaldsen Museum VI; Réunion des Musées Nationaux 22; Roger-Viollet 130, 133; Secrétariat général de la Commission nationale de l'Inventaire, Ministère des Affaires Culturelles 7, 10; Werner Szambien 13, 15–17, 19, 30, 34, 35.

Index

Page numbers in *italics* indicate illustrations. Roman numerals refer to colour plates. **Bold** figures in brackets refer to note numbers.

EBA = Ecole des Beaux-Arts